EXPOSITORY THOUGHTS ON THE GOSPELS

VOL. 4: JOHN

By

J.C. Ryle

www.gideonhousebooks.com

Expository Thoughts on the Gospels: John

J.C. Ryle

© 2016 Gideon House Books

Published by:
Gideon House Books
2137 Ash Grove Way
Dallas, TX 75228
www.gideonhousebooks.com

Typesetting & Cover Design: Josh Pritchard

ISBN-13: 978-1-943133-30-7

Contents

PREFACE

I send forth the volume now in the reader's hands, with much reticence, and a very deep sense of responsibility. It is no light matter to publish an exposition of any book in the Bible. It is a peculiarly serious undertaking to attempt a Commentary on the Gospel of John.

I do not forget that we are all apt to exaggerate the difficulties of our own particular department of literary labor. But I think every intelligent student of Scripture will bear me out when I say, that John's Gospel is pre-eminently full of things "hard to be understood." (2 Pet. 3:16.) It contains a large portion of our Lord Jesus Christ's doctrinal teaching. It abounds in "deep things of God," and "sayings of the King," which we instinctively feel we have no line to fully fathom, no mind to fully comprehend, no words to fully explain. It must needs be that such a book of Scripture should be difficult. I can truly say that I have commented on many a verse in this Gospel with fear and trembling. I have often said to myself, "Who is sufficient for these things?"—"The place whereon you stands is holy ground." (2 Cor. 2:16; Exod. 3:5.)

The nature of the work now published, requires a few words of explanation. It is a continuation of the "Expository Thoughts on the Gospels," of which the first three Gospels, have been already sent forth. Like the previous volumes, the composition of this book is a continuous series of short expositions, intended for family or private reading, or for the use of those who visit the sick and the poor.

We live in a day of abounding vagueness and indistinctness on doctrinal subjects in religion. Now, if ever, it is the duty of all advocates of clear, well-defined, sharply-cut theology, to supply proof that their views are thoroughly borne out by Scripture. I have endeavored to do so in this Commentary. I hold that the Gospel of John, rightly interpreted, is the best and simplest answer to those who profess to admire a vague and indistinct Christianity.

The theological stand-point which the writer of this Commentary occupies will be obvious to any intelligent reader. Such an one will see at a glance that I belong to that school in the Church of England which, rightly or wrongly, is called "Evangelical." He will see that I have no sympathy whatever with either Romish or Neologian tendencies. He will see that I hold firmly the distinctive theological views of the Reformers and doctrinal Puritans, and that I totally disapprove the loose and broad theology of some modern schools of divines-But while I say all this, I must be allowed to add, that in interpreting Scripture, I "call no man master or father." I abhor the idea of twisting and warping God's Word in order to made it support party views. Throughout this Commentary I have endeavored honestly and conscientiously to find out the real meaning of every sentence on which I have commented. I have evaded no difficulty, and shrunk from no inference. I have simply followed Scripture wherever its words seemed to point, and accepted whatever they seemed to mean. I have never hesitated to express my disagreement from the views of other commentators if occasion required; but when I have done so I have tried to do it with courtesy and respect.

I now conclude this preface with an earnest prayer, that it may please God to pardon the many deficiencies of this volume, and to use it for His own glory and the good of souls. It has cost me a large amount of time and thought and labor. But if the Holy Spirit shall make it useful to the Church of Christ, I shall feel abundantly repaid.

Ignorance of Scripture is the root of every error in religion, and the source of every heresy. To be allowed to remove a few grains of ignorance, and to throw a few rays of light on God's precious word, is, in my opinion, the greatest honor that can be put on a Christian.

Chapter 1

1:1-5

The Prologue to the Gospel

In the beginning was the Word, and the Word was with God, and the Word was fully God. The Word was with God in the beginning. All things were created by him, and apart from him not one thing was created that has been created. In him was life, and the life was the light of mankind. And the light shines on in the darkness, but the darkness has not mastered it.

The Gospel of John, which begins with these verses, is in many respects very unlike the other three Gospels. It contains many things which they omit. It omits many things which they contain. Good reason might easily be shown for this unlikeness. But it is enough to remember that Matthew, Mark, Luke, and John wrote under the direct inspiration of God. In the general plan of their respective Gospels, and in the particular details—in everything that they record, and in everything that they do not record—they were all four equally and entirely guided by the Holy Spirit.

About the matters which John was specially inspired to relate in his Gospel, one general remark will suffice. The things which are peculiar to his Gospel are among the most precious possessions of the Church of Christ. No one of the four Gospel-writers has given us such full statements about the divinity of Christ—about justification by faith—about the offices of Christ—about the work of the Holy Spirit—and about the privileges of believers, as we read in the pages of John. On none of these great subjects, undoubtedly, have

Matthew, Mark, and Luke been silent. But in John's Gospel, they stand out prominently on the surface, so that he who runs may read.

The five verses now before us contain a statement of matchless sublimity concerning the divine nature of our Lord Jesus Christ. He it is, beyond all question, whom John means, when he speaks of "the Word." No doubt there are heights and depths in that statement which are far beyond man's understanding. And yet there are plain lessons in it, which every Christian would do well to treasure up in his mind.

We learn, firstly, that our Lord Jesus Christ is eternal. John tells us that "in the beginning was the Word." He did not begin to exist when the heavens and the earth were made. Much less did He begin to exist when the Gospel was brought into the world. He had glory with the Father "before the world was." (John 17:5.) He was existing when matter was first created, and before time began. He was "before all things." (Col. 1:17.) He was from all eternity.

We learn, secondly, that our Lord Jesus Christ is a Person distinct from God the Father, and yet one with Him. John tells us that "the Word was with God." The Father and the Word, though two persons, are joined by an ineffable union. Where God the Father was from all eternity, there also was the Word, even God the Son—their glory equal, their majesty co-eternal, and yet their Godhead one. This is a great mystery! Happy is he who can receive it as a little child, without attempting to explain it.

We learn, thirdly, that the Lord Jesus Christ is very God. John tells us that "the Word was God." He is not merely a created angel, or a being inferior to God the Father, and invested by Him with power to redeem sinners. He is nothing less than perfect God—equal to the Father as touching His Godhead—God of the substance of the Father, begotten before the worlds.

We learn, fourthly, that the Lord Jesus Christ is the Creator of all things. John tells us that "by Him were all things made, and without Him was not anything made that was made." So far from being a creature of God, as some heretics have falsely asserted, He is the Being who made the worlds and all that they contain. "He commanded and they were created." (Psalm 148:5.)

We learn, lastly, that the Lord Jesus Christ is the source of all spiritual life and light. John tells us, that "in Him was life, and the life was the light of men." He is the eternal fountain, from which alone the sons of men have ever derived life. Whatever spiritual life and light Adam and Eve possessed before the fall, was from Christ. Whatever deliverance from sin and spiritual death any child of Adam has ever enjoyed since the fall, whatever light of conscience or understanding any one has obtained, all has flowed from

Christ. The vast majority of mankind in every age have refused to know Him, have forgotten the fall, and their own need of a Savior. The light has been constantly shining "in darkness." The most have "not comprehended the light." But if any men and women out of the countless millions of mankind have ever had spiritual life and light, they have owed all to Christ.

Such is a brief summary of the leading lessons which these wonderful verses appear to contain. There is much in them, without controversy, which is above our reason but there is nothing contrary to it. There is much that we cannot explain, and must be content humbly to believe. Let us however never forget that there are plain PRACTICAL CONSEQUENCES flowing from the passage, which we can never grasp too firmly, or know too well.

Would we know, for one thing, the exceeding sinfulness of sin? Let us often read these first five verses of John's Gospel. Let us mark what kind of Being the Redeemer of mankind must needs be, in order to provide eternal redemption for sinners. If no one less than the Eternal God, the Creator and Preserver of all things, could take away the sin of the world, sin must be a far more abominable thing in the sight of God than most men suppose. The right measure of sin's sinfulness is the dignity of Him who came into the world to save sinners. If Christ is so great, then sin must indeed be sinful!

Would we know, for another thing, the strength of a true Christian's foundation for hope? Let us often read these first five verses of John's Gospel. Let us mark that the Savior in whom the believer is bid to trust is nothing less than the Eternal God, One able to save to the uttermost all that come to the Father by Him. He that was "with God," and "was God," is also "Emmanuel, God with us." Let us thank God that our help is laid on One that is mighty. (Psalm 89:19.) In ourselves we are great sinners. But in Jesus Christ we have a great Savior. He is a strong foundation-stone, able to bear the weight of a world's sin. He that believes on Him shall not be confounded. (1 Peter 2:6.)

1:6-13

A man came, sent from God, whose name was John. He came as a witness to testify about the light so that everyone may believe through him. He himself was not the light, but he came to testify about the light. The true light, who gives light to everyone, was coming into the world. He was in the world, and the world was created by him, but the world did not recognize him. He came to what was his own, but his own people did not receive him. But to all who have received him—those who believe in his name—he has given the right to become God's children—children not born by human parents or by human desire or a husband's decision, but by God.

John, after beginning his gospel with a statement of our Lord's nature as God, proceeds to speak of His forerunner, John the Baptist. The contrast between the language used about the Savior, and that used about His forerunner, ought not to be overlooked. Of Christ we are told that He was the eternal God-the Creator of all things—the source of life and light. Of John the Baptist we are told simply, that "there was a man sent from God, whose name was John."

We see, firstly, in these verses, the true nature of a Christian minister's office. We have it in the description of John the Baptist—"He came for a witness, to bear witness of the light, that all men through him might believe."

Christian ministers are not priests, nor mediators between God and man. They are not agents into whose hands men may commit their souls, and carry on their religion by deputy. They are witnesses. They are intended to bear testimony to God's truth, and specially to the great truth that Christ is the only Savior and light of the world. This was Peter's ministry on the day of Pentecost. "With many other words did he testify." (Acts 2:40.) This was the whole tenor of Paul's ministry. "He testified both to the Jews and Greeks repentance towards God, and faith towards our Lord Jesus Christ." (Acts 20:21.) Unless a Christian minister bears a full testimony to Christ, he is not faithful to his office. So long as he does testify of Christ, he has done his part, and will receive his reward, although his hearers may not believe his testimony. Until a minister's hearers believe on that Christ of whom they are told, they receive no benefit from the ministry. They may be pleased and interested; but they are not profited until they believe. The great end of a minister's testimony is "that through him, men may believe."

We see, secondly, in these verses, one principal position which our Lord Jesus Christ occupies towards mankind. We have it in the words, "He was the true light which lights every man that comes into the world."

Christ is to the souls of men what the sun is to the world. He is the center and source of all spiritual light, warmth, life, health, growth, beauty, and fertility. Like the sun, He shines for the common benefit of all mankind—for high and for low, for rich and for poor, for Jew and for Greek. Like the sun, He is free to all. All may look at Him, and drink health out of His light. If millions of mankind were mad enough to dwell in caves underground, or to bandage their eyes, their darkness would be their own fault, and not the fault of the sun. So, likewise, if millions of men and women love spiritual "darkness rather than light," the blame must be laid on their blind hearts, and not on Christ. "Their foolish hearts are darkened." (John 3:19; Rom. 1:21.) But whether men will see or not, Christ is the true sun, and the light of the world. There is no light for sinners except in the Lord Jesus.

We see, thirdly, in these verses, the desperate wickedness of man's natural heart. We have it in the words, Christ "was in the world, and the world was made by Him, and the world knew Him not. He came unto His own, and His own received Him not."

Christ was in the world invisibly, long before He was born of the Virgin Mary. He was there from the very beginning, ruling, ordering, and governing the whole creation. By Him all things are held together. (Coloss. 1:17.) He gave to all life and breath, rain from heaven, and fruitful seasons. By Him kings reigned, and nations were increased or diminished. Yet men knew Him not, and honored Him not. They "worshiped and served the creature more than the Creator." (Rom. 1:25.) Well may the natural heart be called "wicked!"

But Christ came visibly into the world, when He was born at Bethlehem, and fared no better. He came to the very people whom He had brought out from Egypt, and purchased for His own. He came to the Jews, whom He had separated from other nations, and to whom He had revealed Himself by the prophets. He came to those very Jews who had read of Him in the Old Testament Scriptures—seen Him under types and figures in their temple services—and professed to be waiting for His coming. And yet, when He came, those very Jews received Him not. They even—rejected Him, despised Him, and slew Him. Well may the natural heart be called "desperately wicked!"

We see, lastly, in these verses, the vast privileges of all who receive Christ, and believe on Him. We are told that "as many as received Him, to them gave He power to become you sons of God, even to those who believe on His name."

Christ will never be without some servants. If the vast majority of the Jews did not receive Him as the Messiah, there were, at any rate, a few who did. To them He gave the privilege of being God's children. He adopted them as members of His Father's family. He reckoned them His own brethren and sisters, bone of His bone, and flesh of His flesh. He conferred on them a dignity which was ample recompense for the cross which they had to carry for His sake. He made them sons and daughters of the Lord Almighty.

Privileges like these, be it remembered, are the possession of all, in every age, who receive Christ by faith, and follow Him as their Savior. They are "children of God by faith in Christ Jesus." (Gal. 3:26.) They are born again by a new and heavenly birth, and adopted into the family of the King of kings.

Few in number, and despised by the world as they are, they are cared for with infinite love by a Father in heaven, who, for His Son's sake, is well pleased with them. In time He provides them with everything that is for their good. In eternity He will give them a crown of glory that fades not away. These are great things! But faith in Christ gives men an ample title to them. Good masters care for their servants, and Christ cares for His.

Are we ourselves sons of God? Have we been born again? Have we the MARKS which always accompany the new birth—sense of sin, faith in Jesus, love of others, righteous living, separation from the world? Let us never be content until we can give a satisfactory answer to these questions.

Do we desire to be sons of God? Then let us "receive Christ" as our Savior, and believe on Him with the heart. To everyone that so receives Him, He will give the privilege of becoming a son of God.

1:14

Now the Word became flesh and took up residence among us. We saw his glory— the glory of the one and only, full of grace and truth, who came from the Father.

The passage of Scripture now before us is very short, if we measure it by words. But it is very long, if we measure it by the nature of its contents. The substance of it is so immensely important that we shall do well to give it separate and distinct consideration. This single verse contains more than enough matter for a whole exposition.

The main truth which this verse teaches is the reality of our Lord Jesus Christ's incarnation, or being made man. John tells us that "the Word was made flesh, and dwelt among us."

The plain meaning of these words is, that our divine Savior really took human nature upon Him, in order to save sinners. He really became a man like ourselves in all things, sin only excepted. Like ourselves, he was born of a woman, though born in a miraculous manner. Like ourselves, He grew from infancy to boyhood, and from boyhood to man's estate, both in wisdom and in stature. (Luke 2:52.) Like ourselves, he hungered, thirsted, ate, drank, slept, was wearied, felt pain, wept, rejoiced, marveled, was moved to anger and compassion. Having become flesh, and taken a body, He prayed, read the Scriptures, suffered being tempted, and submitted His human will to the will of God the Father. And finally, in the same body, He really suffered and shed His blood, really died, was really buried, really rose again, and really ascended up into heaven. And yet all this time He was God as well as man!

This union of two natures in Christ's one Person is doubtless one of the greatest mysteries of the Christian religion. It needs to be carefully stated. It is just one of those great truths which are not meant to be curiously pried into, but to be reverently believed. Nowhere, perhaps, shall we find a more wise and judicious statement than in the second article of the Church of England. "The Son, who is the Word of the Father, begotten from everlasting of the Father, the very and eternal God, and of one substance with the Father, took man's nature in the womb of the blessed Virgin of her substance—so that two whole and perfect natures, that is to say, the Godhead and the manhood, were joined together in one Person, never to be divided, whereof is one Christ, truly God and truly man." This is a most valuable declaration. This is "sound speech, which cannot be condemned."

But while we do not pretend to explain the union of two natures in our Lord Jesus Christ's Person, we must not hesitate to fence the subject with well-defined cautions. While we state most carefully what we do believe, we must not shrink from declaring boldly what we do not believe. We must never forget, that though our Lord was God and man at the same time, the divine and human natures in Him were never confounded. One nature did not swallow up the other. The two natures remained perfect and distinct. The divinity of Christ was never for a moment laid aside, although veiled. The manhood of Christ, during His life-time, was never for a moment unlike our own, though by union with the Godhead, greatly dignified. Though perfect God, Christ has always been perfect man from the first moment of His incarnation. He who is gone into heaven, and is sitting at the Father's right hand to intercede for sinners, is man as well as God. Though perfect man, Christ never ceased to be perfect God. He that suffered for sin on the cross, and was made sin for us, was "God manifest in the flesh." The blood with which the Church was purchased, is called the blood "of God." (Acts 20:28.) Though He became "flesh" in the fullest sense, when He was born of the Virgin Mary, He never at any period ceased to be the Eternal Word. To say that He constantly manifested His divine nature during His earthly ministry, would, of course, be contrary to plain facts. To attempt to explain why His Godhead was sometimes veiled and at other times unveiled, while He was on earth, would be venturing on ground which we had better leave alone. But to say that at any instant of His earthly ministry He was not fully and entirely God, is nothing less than heresy.

The cautions just given may seem at first sight needless, wearisome, and hair-splitting. It is precisely the neglect of such cautions which ruins many souls. This constant undivided union of two perfect natures in Christ's Person is exactly that which gives infinite value to His mediation, and qualifies Him to be the very Mediator that sinners need. Our Mediator is One who can sympathize with us, because He is very MAN. And yet, at the same time, He is One who can deal with the Father for us on equal terms, because He is very GOD. It is the same union which gives infinite value to His righteousness, when imputed to believers. It is the righteousness of One who was God as well as man. It is the same union which gives infinite value to the atoning blood which He shed for sinners on the cross. It is the blood of One who was God as well as man. It is the same union which gives infinite value to His resurrection. When He rose again, as the Head of the body of believers, He rose not as a mere man, but as God. Let these things sink deeply into our hearts. The second Adam is far greater than the first Adam was. The first Adam was only man, and so he fell. The second Adam was God as well as man, and so He completely conquered.

Let us leave the subject with feelings of deep gratitude and thankfulness. It is full of abounding consolation for all who know Christ by faith, and believe on Him.

Did the Word become flesh? Then He is One who can be touched with the feeling of His people's infirmities, because He has suffered Himself, being tempted. He is almighty because He is God, and yet He can sympathize with us, because He is man.

Did the Word become flesh? Then He can supply us with a perfect pattern and example for our daily life. Had he walked among us as an angel or a spirit, we could never have copied Him. But having dwelt among us as a man, we know that the true standard of holiness is to "walk even as He walked." (1 John 2:6.) He is a perfect pattern, because He is God. But He is also a pattern exactly suited to our needs, because He is man.

Finally, did the Word become flesh? Then let us see in our mortal bodies a real, true dignity, and not defile them by sin. Vile and weak as our body may seem, it is a body which the Eternal Son of God was not ashamed to take upon Himself, and to take up to heaven. That simple fact is a pledge that He will raise our bodies at the last day, and glorify them together with His own.

1:15-18

John testified about him and cried out, "This one was the one about whom I said, 'He who comes after me is greater than I am, because he existed before me.'" For we have all received from his fullness one gracious gift after another. For the law was given through Moses, but grace and truth came about through Jesus Christ. No one has ever seen God. The only one, himself God, who is in the presence of the Father, has made God known.

The passage before us contains three great declarations about our Lord Jesus Christ. Each of the three is among the foundation-principles of Christianity.

We are taught, firstly, that it is Christ alone who supplies all the spiritual needs of all believers. It is written that "of his fullness have we all received, and grace for grace."

There is an infinite fullness in Jesus Christ. As Paul says, "It pleased the Father that in him should all fullness dwell." "In Him are hidden all the treasures of wisdom and knowledge." (Coloss. 1:19; 2:3.) There is laid up in Him, as in a treasury, a boundless supply of all that any sinner can need, either in time or eternity. The Spirit of Life is His special gift to the Church, and conveys from Him, as from a great root, sap and vigor to all the believing branches. He is rich in mercy, grace, wisdom, righteousness, sanctification, and redemption. Out of Christ's fullness, all believers in every age of the world, have been supplied. They did not clearly understand the fountain from which their supplies flowed, in Old Testament times. The Old Testament saints only saw Christ afar off, and not face to face. But from Abel downwards, all saved souls have received all they have had from Jesus Christ alone. Every saint in glory will at last acknowledge that he is Christ's debtor for all he is. Jesus will prove to have been all in all.

We are taught, secondly, the vast superiority of Christ to Moses, and of the Gospel to the Law. It is written that "the law was given by Moses, but grace and truth came by Jesus Christ."

Moses was employed by God "as a servant," to convey to Israel the moral and ceremonial law. (Heb. 3:5.) As a servant, he was faithful to Him who appointed him, but he was only a servant. The moral law, which he brought down from Mount Sinai, was holy, and just, and good. But it could not justify. It had no healing power. It could wound, but it could not bind up. It "worked wrath." (Rom. 4:15.) It pronounced a curse against any imperfect obedience. The ceremonial law, which he was commanded to impose on Israel, was full of deep meaning and typical instruction. Its ordinances and ceremonies made it an excellent schoolmaster to guide men toward Christ. (Gal. 3:24.) But the ceremonial law was only a schoolmaster. It could not make him that kept it perfect, as pertaining to the conscience. (Heb. 9:9.) It laid a grievous yoke on men's hearts, which they were not able to bear. It was a ministration of death and condemnation. (2 Cor. 3:7-9.) The light which men got from Moses and the law was at best only starlight compared to noon-day.

Christ, on the other hand, came into the world "as a Son," with the keys of God's treasury of grace and truth entirely in His hands, (Heb. 3:6.) Grace came by Him, when He made fully known God's gracious plan of salvation, by faith in His own blood, and opened the fountain of mercy to all the world. Truth came by Him, when He fulfilled in His own Person the types of the Old Testament, and revealed Himself as the true Sacrifice, the true mercy-seat, and the true Priest. No doubt there was much of "grace and truth" under the law of Moses. But the whole of God's grace, and the whole truth about redemption, were never known until Jesus came into the world, and died for sinners.

We are taught, thirdly, that it is Christ alone who has revealed God the Father to man. It is written that "no man has seen God at any time—the only begotten Son, who is in the bosom of the Father, he has declared him."

The eye of mortal man has never beheld God the Father. No man could bear the sight. Even to Moses it was said, "You cannot see my face—for there shall no man see me, and live." (Exod. 33:20.) Yet all that mortal man is capable of knowing about God the Father is fully revealed to us by God the Son. He, who was in the bosom of the Father from all eternity, has been pleased to take our nature upon Him, and to exhibit to us in the form of man, all that our minds can comprehend of the Father's perfections. In Christ's words, and deeds, and life, and death, we learn as much concerning God the Father as our feeble minds can at present bear. His perfect wisdom—His almighty power-His unspeakable love to sinners—His incomparable holiness—His hatred of sin, could never be represented to our eyes more clearly than we see them in Christ's life and death. In truth, "God was manifest in the flesh," when the Word took on Him a body. "He was the brightness of the Father's glory, and the express image of His person." He says Himself, "I and my Father are one." "He that has seen me has seen the Father." "In Him dwells all the fullness of the Godhead bodily." (Coloss. 2:9.) These are deep and mysterious things. But they are true. (1 Tim. 3:16; Heb. 1:3; John 10:30; 14:9.)

And now, after reading this passage, can we ever give too much honor to Christ? Can we ever think too highly of Him? Let us banish the unworthy thought from our minds forever. Let us learn to exalt Him more in our hearts, and to rest more confidingly the whole weight of our souls in His hands. Men may easily fall into error about the three Persons in the holy Trinity if they do not carefully adhere to the teaching of Scripture. But no man ever errs on the side of giving too much honor to God the Son. Christ is the meeting-point between the Trinity and the sinner's soul. "He that honors not the Son, honors not the Father which sent Him." (John 5:23.)

1:19-28

The Testimony of John the Baptist

Now this was John's testimony when the Jewish leaders sent to him priests and Levites from Jerusalem to ask him, "Who are you?" He confessed—he did not deny but confessed—"I am not the Christ." So they asked him, "Then who are you? Are you Elijah?" He said, "I am not." "Are you the Prophet?" He answered, "No." Then they said to him, "Who are you? Tell us so that we can give an answer to those who sent us. What do you say about yourself?"

John said, "I am the voice of one crying out in the wilderness, 'Make straight the way for the Lord,' as Isaiah the prophet said." (Now they had been sent from the Pharisees. So they asked John, "Why then are you baptizing if you are not the Christ, nor Elijah, nor the Prophet?"

John answered them, "I baptize with water. Among you stands one whom you do not recognize, who is coming after me. I am not worthy to untie the strap of his sandal!" These things happened in Bethany across the Jordan River where John was baptizing.

The verses we have now read begin the properly historical part of John's Gospel. Hitherto we have been reading deep and weighty statements about Christ's divine nature, incarnation, and dignity. Now we come to the plain narrative of the days of Christ's earthly ministry, and the plain story of Christ's doings and sayings among men. And here, like the other Gospel-writers, John begins at once with "the record" or testimony of John the Baptist. (Matt. 3:1; Mark 1:2; Luke 3:2.)

We have, for one thing, in these verses, an instructive example of true humility. That example is supplied by John the Baptist himself.

John the Baptist was an eminent saint of God. There are few names which stand higher than his in the Bible calendar of great and good men. The Lord Jesus Himself declared that "Among those who are born of woman there has not risen a greater than John the Baptist." (Matt. 11:11.) The Lord Jesus Himself declared that he was "a burning and a shining light." (John 5:35.) Yet here in this passage we see this eminent saint lowly, self-abased, and full of humility. He puts away from himself the honor which the Jews from Jerusalem were ready to pay him. He declines all flattering titles. He speaks of himself as nothing more than the "voice of one crying in the wilderness," and as one who "baptized with water." He proclaims loudly that there is One standing among the Jews far greater than himself, One whose shoe-latchet he is not worthy to unloose. He claims honor not for himself but for Christ. To exalt Christ was his mission, and to that mission he steadfastly adheres.

The greatest saints of God in every age of the Church have always been men of John the Baptist's spirit. In gifts, and knowledge, and general character they have often differed widely. But in one respect they have always been alike-they have been "clothed with humility." (1 Pet. 5:5.) They have not sought their own honor. They have thought little of themselves. They have been ever willing to decrease if Christ might only increase, to be nothing if Christ might be all. And here has been the secret of the honor God has put upon them. "He that humbles himself shall be exalted." (Luke 14:11.)

If we profess to have any real Christianity, let us strive to be of John the Baptist's spirit. Let us study HUMILITY. This is the grace with which all must begin, who would be saved. We have no true religion about us, until we cast away our high thoughts, and feel ourselves sinners. This is the grace which all saints may follow after, and which none have any excuse for neglecting. All God's children have not gifts, or money, or time to work, or a wide sphere of usefulness; but all may be humble. This is the grace, above all, which will appear most beautiful in our latter end. Never shall we feel the need of humility so deeply, as when we lie on our deathbeds, and stand before the judgment-seat of Christ. Our whole lives will then appear a long catalogue of imperfections, ourselves nothing, and Christ all.

We have, for another thing, in these verses, a mournful example of the blindness of unconverted men. That example is supplied by the state of the Jews who came to question John the Baptist.

These Jews professed to be waiting for the appearance of Messiah. Like all the Pharisees they prided themselves on being children of Abraham, and possessors of the covenants. They rested in the law, and made their boast of God. They professed to know God's will, and to believe God's promises. They were confident that they themselves were guides of the blind, and lights of those who sat in darkness. (Rom. 2:17-19.) And yet at this very moment their souls were utterly in the dark. "There was standing among them," as John the Baptist told them, "One whom they knew not." Christ Himself, the promised Messiah, was in the midst of them, and yet they neither knew Him, nor saw Him, nor received Him, nor acknowledged Him, nor believed Him. And worse than this, the vast majority of them never would know Him! The words of John the Baptist are a prophetic description of a state of things which lasted during the whole of our Lord's earthly ministry. Christ "stood among the Jews," and yet the Jews knew Him not, and the greater part of them died in their sins.

It is a solemn thought that John the Baptist's words in this place apply strictly to thousands in the present day. Christ is still standing among many who neither see, nor know, nor believe. Christ is passing by in many a parish and many a congregation, and the vast majority have neither an eye to see Him, nor an ear to hear Him. The spirit of slumber seems poured out upon them. Money, and pleasure, and the world they know; but they know not Christ. The kingdom of God is close to them; but they sleep. Salvation is within their reach; but they sleep. Mercy, grace, peace, heaven, eternal life, are so near that they might touch them; and yet they sleep. "Christ stands among them and they know him not." These are sorrowful things to write down. But every faithful minister of Christ can testify, like John the Baptist, that they are true.

What are we doing ourselves? This, after all, is the great question that concerns us. Do we know the extent of our religious privileges in this country, and in these times? Are we aware that Christ is going to and fro in our land, inviting souls to join Him and to be His disciples? Do we know that the time is short and that the door of mercy will soon be closed for evermore? Do we know that Christ rejected will soon be Christ withdrawn? Happy are they who can give a good account of these inquiries and who "know the day of their visitation!" (Luke 19:44.) It will be better at the last day never to have been born, than to have had Christ "standing among us" and not to have known Him.

1:29-34

Jesus the Lamb of God

On the next day John saw Jesus coming toward him and said, "Look, the Lamb of God who takes away the sin of the world! This is the one about whom I said, 'After me comes a man who is greater than I am, because he existed before me.' I did not recognize him, but I came baptizing with water so that he could be revealed to Israel."

Then John testified, "I saw the Spirit descending like a dove from heaven, and it remained on him. And I did not recognize him, but the one who sent me to baptize with water said to me, 'The one on whom you see the Spirit descending and remaining, this is the one who baptizes with the Holy Spirit.' I have both seen and testified that this man is the Chosen One of God."

This passage contains a verse which ought to be printed in great letters in the memory of every reader of the Bible. All the stars in heaven are bright and beautiful, and yet one star exceeds another star in glory. So also all texts of Scripture are inspired and profitable, and yet some texts are richer than others. Of such texts the first verse before us is preeminently one. Never was there a fuller testimony borne to Christ upon earth, than that which is here borne by John the Baptist.

Let us notice, firstly, in this passage, the peculiar name which John the Baptist gives to Christ. He calls Him "The Lamb of God."

This name did not merely mean, as some have supposed, that Christ was meek and gentle as a lamb. This would be truth no doubt, but only a very small portion of the truth. There are greater things here than this! It meant that Christ was the great sacrifice for sin, who was come to make atonement for transgression by His own death upon the cross. He was the true Lamb which Abraham told Isaac at Moriah God would provide. (Gen. 22:8.) He was the true Lamb to which every morning and evening sacrifice in the temple had daily pointed. He was the Lamb of which Isaiah had prophesied, that He would be "brought to the slaughter." (Isaiah 53:7.) He was the true Lamb of which the passover lamb in Egypt had been a vivid type. In short, He was the great propitiation for sin which God had covenanted from all eternity to send into the world. He was God's Lamb.

Let us take heed that in all our thoughts of Christ, we first think of Him as John the Baptist here represents Him. Let us serve him faithfully as our Master. Let us obey Him loyally as our King. Let us study His teaching as our Prophet. Let us walk diligently after Him as our Example. Let us look anxiously for Him as our coming Redeemer of body as well as soul. But above all, let us prize Him as our Sacrifice, and rest our whole weight on His death as an atonement for sin. Let His blood be more precious in our eyes every year we live. Whatever else we glory in about Christ, let us glory above all things in His cross. This is the corner-stone, this is the citadel, this is the rule of true Christian theology. We know nothing rightly about Christ, until we see him with John the Baptist's eyes, and can rejoice in Him as "the Lamb that was slain."

Let us notice, secondly, in this passage, the peculiar WORK which John the Baptist describes Christ as doing. He says that "he takes away the sin of the world."

Christ is a SAVIOR. He did not come on earth to be a conqueror, or a philosopher, or a mere teacher of morality. He came to save sinners. He came to do that which man could never do for himself—to do that which money and learning can never obtain—to do that which is essential to man's real happiness, He came to "take away sin."

Christ is a COMPLETE savior. He "takes away sin." He did not merely make vague proclamations of pardon, mercy, and forgiveness. He "took" our sins upon Himself, and carried them away. He allowed them to be laid upon Himself, and "bore them in His own body on the tree." (1 Pet. 2:24.) The sins of every one that believes on Jesus are made as though they had never been sinned at all. The Lamb of God has taken them clean away.

Christ is an ALMIGHTY Savior, and a Savior for all mankind. He "takes away the sin of the world." He did not die for the Jews only, but for the Gentile as well as the Jew. He did not suffer for a few people only, but for all mankind. The payment that He made on the cross was more than enough to make satisfaction for the debts of all. The blood that He shed was precious enough to wash away the sins of all. His atonement on the cross was sufficient for all mankind, though efficient only to those who believe. The sin that He took up and bore on the cross was the sin of the whole world.

Last, but not least, Christ is a PERPETUAL and UNWEARIED Savior. He "takes away" sin. He is daily taking it away from every one that believes on Him—daily purging, daily cleansing, daily washing the souls of His people, daily granting and applying fresh supplies of mercy. He did not cease to work for His saints, when He died for them on the cross. He lives in heaven as a Priest, to present His sacrifice continually before God. In grace as well as is providence, Christ works still. He is ever taking away sin.

These are golden truths indeed. Well would it be for the Church of Christ, if they were used by all who know them! Our very familiarity with texts like these is one of our greatest dangers. Blessed are they who not only keep this text in their memories, but feed upon it in their hearts!

Let us notice, lastly, in this passage, the peculiar office which John the Baptist attributes to Christ. He speaks of Him as Him "who baptizes with the Holy Spirit."

The baptism here spoken of is not the baptism of water. It does not consist either of dipping or sprinkling. It does not belong exclusively either to infants or to grown up people. It is not a baptism which any man can give, Episcopalian or Presbyterian, Independent or Methodist, layman or minister. It is a baptism which the great Head of the Church keeps exclusively in His own hands. It consists of the implanting of grace into the inward man. It is the same thing with the new birth. It is a baptism, not of the body, but of the heart. It is a baptism which the penitent thief received, though neither dipped nor sprinkled by the hand of man. It is a baptism which Ananias and Sapphira did not receive, though admitted into church-communion by apostolic men.

Let it be a settled principle in our religion that the baptism of which John the Baptist speaks here, is the baptism which is absolutely necessary to salvation. It is well to be baptized into the visible Church; but it is far better to be baptized into that Church which is made up of true believers. The baptism of water is a most blessed and profitable ordinance, and cannot be neglected without great sin. But the baptism of the Holy Spirit is of far greater importance. The man who dies with his heart not baptized by Christ can never be saved.

Let us ask ourselves, as we leave this passage, Whether we are baptized with the Holy Spirit, and whether we have any real interest in the Lamb of God? Thousands, unhappily, are wasting their time in controversy about water baptism, and neglecting the baptism of the heart. Thousands more are content with a head-knowledge of the Lamb of God, or have never sought Him by faith, that their own sins may be actually taken away. Let us take heed that we ourselves have new hearts, and believe to the saving of our souls.

1:35-42

Again the next day John was standing there with two of his disciples. Gazing at Jesus as he walked by, he said, "Look, the Lamb of God!" When his two disciples heard him say this, they followed Jesus. Jesus turned around and saw them following and said to them, "What do you want?" So they said to him, "Rabbi" (which is translated Teacher), "where are you staying?" Jesus answered, "Come and you will see." So they came and saw where he was staying, and they stayed with him that day. Now it was about four o'clock in the afternoon.

Andrew, the brother of Simon Peter, was one of the two disciples who heard what John said and followed Jesus. He found first his own brother Simon and told him, "We have found the Messiah!" (which is translated Christ). Andrew brought Simon to Jesus. Jesus looked at him and said, "You are Simon, the son of John. You will be called Cephas" (which is translated Peter).

These verses ought always to be interesting to every true Christian. They describe the first beginnings of the Christian Church. Vast as that church is now, there was a time when it consisted of only two weak members. The calling of those two members is described in the passage which is now before our eyes.

We see, for one thing, in these verses, what good is done by continually testifying of Christ.

The first time that John the Baptist cried, "Behold the Lamb of God," no result appears to have followed. We are not told of any who heard, inquired, and believed. But when he repeated the same words the next day, we read that two of his disciples "heard him speak and followed Jesus." They were received most graciously by Him whom they followed. "They came and saw where he dwelt, and abode with him that day." Truly it was a day in their lives most eventful, and most blessed! From that day they became fast and firm disciples of the new-found Messiah. They took up the cross. They continued with Him in His temptations. They followed Him wherever He went. One of them at least, if not both, became a chosen apostle, and a master builder in the Christian temple. And all was owing to John the Baptist's testimony, "Behold the lamb of God." That testimony was a little seed. But it bore mighty fruits.

This simple story is a pattern of the way in which good has been done to souls in every age of the Christian Church. By such testimony as that before us, and by none else, men and women are converted and saved. It is by EX-ALTING CHRIST, not the church—Christ, not the sacraments—Christ, not the ministry-it is by this means that hearts are moved, and sinners are turned to God. To the world such testimony may seem weakness and foolishness. Yet, like the ram's horns, before whose blast the walls of Jericho fell down, this testimony is mighty to the pulling down of strongholds. The story of the crucified Lamb of God has proved in every age, the power of God unto salvation. Those who have done most for Christ's cause in every part of the world, have been men like John the Baptist. They have not cried, Behold me, or Behold the church, or Behold the ordinances, but "Behold the Lamb." If souls are to be saved, men must be pointed directly to Christ.

One thing, however, must never be forgotten. There must be patient continuance in preaching and teaching the truth, if we want good to be done. Christ must be set forth again and again, as the "Lamb of God who takes away the sin of the world." The story of grace must be told repeatedly—line upon line, and precept upon precept. It is the constant dropping which wears away the stone. The promise shall never be broken, that "God's word shall not return unto him void." (Isaiah. 55:11.) But it is nowhere said that it shall do good the very first time that it is preached. It was not the first proclamation of John the Baptist, but the second, which made Andrew and his companion follow Jesus.

We see, for another thing, what good a believer may do to others, by speaking to them about Christ.

No sooner does Andrew become a disciple, than he tells his brother Simon what a discovery he has made. Like one who has unexpectedly heard good tidings, he hastens to impart it to the one nearest and dearest to him. He says to his brother, "We have found the Messiah," and he "brings him to Jesus." Who can tell what might have happened if Andrew had been of a silent, reserved, and uncommunicative spirit, like many a Christian in the present day? Who can tell but his brother might have lived and died a fisherman on the Galilean lake? But happily for Simon, Andrew was not a man of this sort. He was one whose heart was so full that he must speak.

And to Andrew's out-spoken testimony, under God, the great apostle Peter owed the first beginning of light in his soul.

The fact before us is most striking and instructive. Out of the three first members of the Christian Church, one at least was brought to Jesus, by the private, quiet word of a relative. He seems to have heard no public preaching. He saw no mighty miracle wrought. He was not convinced by any powerful reasoning. He only heard his brother telling him that he had found a Savior himself, and at once the work began in his soul. The simple testimony of a warm-hearted brother was the first link in the chain by which Peter was drawn out of the world, and joined to Christ. The first blow in that mighty work by which Peter was made a pillar of the Church, was struck by Andrew's words, "We have found the Christ."

Well would it be for the Church of Christ, if all believers were more like Andrew! Well would it be for souls if all men and women who have been converted themselves, would speak to their friends and relatives on spiritual subjects, and tell them what they have found! How much good might be done! How many might be led to Jesus, who now live and die in unbelief! The work of testifying the Gospel of the grace of God ought not to be left to ministers alone. All who have received mercy ought to find a tongue, and to declare what God has done for their souls. All who have been delivered from the power of the devil, ought to "go home and tell their friends what great things God has done for them." (Mark 5:19.) Thousands, humanly speaking, would listen to a word from a friend, who will not listen to a sermon. Every believer ought to be a home-missionary, a missionary to his family, children, servants, neighbors, and friends. Surely, if we can find nothing to say to others about Jesus, we may well doubt whether we are savingly acquainted with Him ourselves.

Let us take heed that we are among those who really follow Christ, and abide with Him. It is not enough to hear Him preached from the pulpit, and to read of Him as described in books. We must actually follow Him, pour out our hearts before Him, and hold personal communion with Him. Then, and not until then, we shall feel constrained to speak of Him to others. The man who only knows Christ by the hearing of the ear, will never do much for the spread of Christ's cause in the earth.

1:43-51

The Calling of More Disciples

On the next day Jesus wanted to set out for Galilee. He found Philip and said to him, "Follow me." (Now Philip was from Bethsaida, the town of Andrew and Peter.) Philip found Nathanael and told him, "We have found the one Moses wrote about in the law, and the prophets also wrote about—Jesus of Nazareth, the son of Joseph." Nathanael replied, "Can anything good come out of Nazareth?" Philip replied, "Come and see."

Jesus saw Nathanael coming toward him and exclaimed, "Look, a true Israelite in whom there is no deceit!" Nathanael asked him, "How do you know me?" Jesus replied, "Before Philip called you, when you were under the fig tree, I saw you." Nathanael answered him, "Rabbi, you are the Son of God; you are the king of Israel!" Jesus said to him, "Because I told you that I saw you under the fig tree, do you believe? You will see greater things than these." He continued, "I tell all of you the solemn truth—you will see heaven opened and the angels of God ascending and descending on the Son of Man."

Let us observe, as we read these verses, how various are the paths by which souls are led into the narrow way of life.

We are told of a man, named Philip, being added to the little company of Christ's disciples. He does not appear to have been moved, like Andrew and his companions, by the testimony of John the Baptist. He was not drawn, like Simon Peter, by the out-spoken declaration of a brother. He seems to have been called directly by Christ Himself, and the agency of man seems not to have been used in his calling. Yet in faith and life he became one with those who were disciples before him. Though led by different paths, they all entered the same road, embraced the same truths, served the same Master, and at length reached the same home.

The fact before us is a deeply important one. It throws light on the history of all God's people in every age, and of every tongue. There are diversities of operations in the saving of souls. All true Christians are led by one Spirit, washed in one blood, serve one Lord, lean on one Savior, believe one truth, and walk by one general rule. But all are not converted in one and the same manner. All do not pass through the same experience. In conversion, the Holy Spirit acts as a sovereign. He calls every one severally as He will.

A careful recollection of this point may save us much trouble. We must beware of making the experience of other believers the measure of our own. We must beware of denying another's grace, because he has not been led by the same way as ourselves. Has a man got the real grace of God? This is the only question that concerns us. Is he a penitent man? Is he a believer? Does he live a holy life? Provided these inquiries can be answered satisfactorily, we may well be content. It matters nothing by what path a man has been led, if he has only been led at last into the right way.

Let us observe, secondly, in these verses, how much of Christ there is in the Old Testament Scriptures. We read that when Philip described Christ to Nathanael, he says, "We have found Him of whom Moses in the law and the prophets did write."

Christ is the sum and substance of the Old Testament. To Him the earliest promises pointed in the days of Adam, and Enoch, and Noah, and Abraham, and Isaac, and Jacob. To Him every sacrifice pointed in the ceremonial worship appointed at Mount Sinai. Of Him every high priest was a type, and every part of the tabernacle was a shadow, and every judge and deliverer of Israel was a figure. He was the prophet like unto Moses, whom the Lord God promised to send, and the King of the house of David, who came to be David's Lord as well as son. He was the Son of the virgin, and the Lamb, foretold by Isaiah—the righteous Branch mentioned by Jeremiah—the true Shepherd, foreseen by Ezekiel—the Messenger of the Covenant, promised by Malachi—and the Messiah, who, according to Daniel, was to be cut off, though not for Himself. The further we read in the volume of the Old Testament, the clearer do we find the testimony about Christ. The light which the inspired writers enjoyed in ancient days was, at best, but dim, compared to that of the Gospel. But the coming Person they all saw afar off, and on whom they all fixed their eyes, was one and the same. The Spirit, which was in them, testified of Christ. (1 Pet. 1:11.)

Do we stumble at this saying? Do we find it hard to see Christ in the Old Testament, because we do not see His name? Let us be sure that the fault is all our own. It is our spiritual vision which is to blame, and not the book. The eyes of our understanding need to be enlightened. The veil has yet to be taken away. Let us pray for a more humble, childlike, and teachable spirit, and let us take up "Moses and the prophets" again. Christ is there, though our eyes may not yet have seen Him. May we never rest until we can subscribe to our Lord's words about the Old Testament Scriptures, "They are they which testify of me." (John 5:39.)

Let us observe, thirdly, in these verses, the good advice which Philip gave to Nathanael. The mind of Nathanael was full of doubts about the Savior, of whom Philip told Him. "Can there any good thing," he said, "come out of Nazareth?" And what did Philip reply? He said, "Come and see."

Wiser counsel than this it would be impossible to conceive! If Philip had reproved Nathanael's unbelief, he might have driven him back for many a day, and given offence. If he had reasoned with him, he might have failed to convince him, or might have confirmed him in his doubts. But by inviting him to prove the matter for himself, he showed his entire confidence in the truth of his own assertion, and his willingness to have it tested and proved. And the result shows the wisdom of Philip's words. Nathanael owed his early acquaintance with Christ to that frank invitation, "Come and see."

If we call ourselves true Christians, let us never be afraid to deal with people about their souls as Philip dealt with Nathanael. Let us invite them boldly to make proof of our religion. Let us tell them confidently that they cannot know its real value until they have tried it. Let us assure them that vital Christianity courts every possible inquiry. It has no secrets. It has nothing to conceal. Its faith and practice are spoken against, just because they are not known. Its enemies speak evil of things with which they are not acquainted. They understand neither what they say nor whereof they affirm. Philip's mode of dealing, we may be sure, is one principal way to do good. Few are ever moved by reasoning and argument. Still fewer are frightened into repentance. The man who does most good to souls, is often the simple believer who says to his friends, "I have found a Savior; come and see Him."

Let us observe, lastly, in these verses, the high character which Jesus gives of Nathanael. He calls him "an Israelite indeed, in whom is no guile."

Nathanael, there can be no doubt, was a true child of God, and a child of God in difficult times. He was one of a very little flock. Like Simeon and Anna, and other pious Jews, he was living by faith and waiting prayerfully for the promised Redeemer, when our Lord's ministry began. He had that which grace alone can give, an honest heart, a heart without guile. His knowledge was probably small. His spiritual eyesight was dim. But he was one who had lived carefully up to his light. He had diligently used such knowledge as he possessed. His eye had been single, though his vision had not been strong. His spiritual judgment had been honest, though it had not been powerful. What he saw in Scripture, he had held firmly, in spite of Pharisees and Sadducees, and all the fashionable religion of the day. He was an honest Old Testament believer, who had stood alone. And here was the secret of our Lord peculiar commendation! He declared Nathanael to be a true son of Abraham—a Jew inwardly, possessing circumcision in the spirit as well as in the letter—an Israelite in heart, as well as a son of Jacob in the flesh.

Let us pray that we may be of the same spirit as Nathanael. An honest, unprejudiced mind—a child-like willingness to follow the truth, wherever the truth may lead us—a simple, hearty desire to be guided, taught, and led by the Spirit—a thorough determination to use every spark of light which we have-are a possession of priceless value. A man of this spirit may live in the midst of much darkness, and be surrounded by every possible disadvantage to his soul. But the Lord Jesus will take care that such a man does not miss the way to heaven. "The meek will he guide in judgment—and the meek will he teach his way." (Psalm 25:9.)

Chapter 2

2:1-11

Turning Water into Wine

Now on the third day there was a wedding at Cana in Galilee. Jesus' mother was there, and both Jesus and his disciples were also invited to the wedding. When the wine ran out, Jesus' mother said to him, "They have no wine left." Jesus replied, "Woman, why are you saying this to me? My time has not yet come." His mother told the servants, "Whatever he tells you, do it."

Now there were six stone water jars there for Jewish ceremonial washing, each holding twenty or thirty gallons. Jesus told the servants, "Fill the water jars with water." So they filled them up to the very top. Then he told them, "Now draw some out and take it to the head steward," and they did. When the head steward tasted the water that had been turned to wine, not knowing where it came from (though the servants who had drawn the water knew), he called the bridegroom and said to him, "Everyone serves the good wine first, and then the cheaper wine when the guests are drunk. You have kept the good wine until now!" Jesus did this as the first of his miraculous signs, in Cana of Galilee. In this way he revealed his glory, and his disciples believed in him.

These verses describe a miracle which should always possess a special interest in the eyes of a true Christian. It is the first, in order of time, of the many mighty works which Jesus did, when He was upon earth. We are distinctly told, "This beginning of miracles did Jesus in Cana of Galilee." Like every other miracle which John was inspired to record, it is related with great minuteness and particularity. And, like every other miracle in John's Gospel, it is rich in spiritual lessons.

We learn, firstly, from these verses, how honorable in the sight of Christ is the estate of matrimony. To be present at a "marriage" was almost the first public act of our Lord's earthly ministry.

Marriage is not a sacrament, as the Church of Rome asserts. It is simply a state of life ordained by God for man's benefit. But it is a state which ought never to be spoken of with levity, or regarded with disrespect. The Prayerbook service has well described it, as "an honorable estate, instituted of God in the time of man's innocency, and signifying unto us the mystical union that is between Christ and his Church." Society is never in a healthy condition, and true religion never flourishes in that land where the marriage tie is lightly esteemed. They who lightly esteem it have not the mind of Christ. He who "beautified and adorned the estate of matrimony by His presence and first miracle that He wrought in Cana of Galilee," is One who is always of one mind. "Marriage," says the Holy Spirit by Paul, "is honorable in all." (Heb. 13:4.)

One thing, however, ought not to be forgotten. Marriage is a step which so seriously affects the temporal happiness and spiritual welfare of two immortal souls, that it ought never to be taken in hand "unadvisedly, lightly, wantonly, and without due consideration." To be truly happy, it should be undertaken "reverently, discreetly, soberly, and in the fear of God." Christ's blessing and presence are essential to a happy wedding. The marriage at which there is no place for Christ and His disciples, is not one that can justly be expected to prosper.

We learn, secondly, from these verses, that there are times when it is lawful to be merry and rejoice. Our Lord Himself sanctioned a wedding-feast by His own presence. He did not refuse to be a guest at "a marriage in Cana of Galilee." "A feast," it is written, "is made for laughter, and wine makes merry." (Eccles. 10:19.) Our Lord, in the passage before us, approves both the feast and the use of wine.

True religion was never meant to make men melancholy. On the contrary, it was intended to increase real joy and happiness among men. The servant of Christ unquestionably ought to have nothing to do with races, balls, theaters, and such-like amusements, which tend to frivolity and indulgence, if not to sin. But he has no right to hand over innocent recreations and family gatherings to the devil and the world. The Christian who withdraws entirely from the society of his fellow-men, and walks the earth with a face as melancholy as if he was always attending a funeral, does injury to the cause of the Gospel. A cheerful, kindly spirit is a great recommendation to a believer. It is a real misfortune to Christianity when a Christian cannot smile. A merry heart, and a readiness to take part in all innocent mirth, are gifts of inestimable value. They go far to soften prejudices, to take up stumbling-blocks out of the way, and to make way for Christ and the Gospel.

The subject no doubt is a difficult and delicate one. On no point of Christian practice is it so hard to hit the balance between that which is lawful and that which is unlawful, between that which is right and that which is wrong. It is very hard indeed to be both merry and wise. High spirits soon degenerate into levity. Acceptance of many invitations to feasts soon leads to waste of time, and begets leanness of soul. Frequent eating and drinking at other men's tables, soon lowers a Christian's tone of religion. Going often into company is a heavy strain on spirituality of heart. Here, if anywhere, God's children have need to be on their guard. Each must know his own strength and natural temperament, and act accordingly. One believer can go without risk where another cannot. Happy is he who can use his Christian liberty without abusing it! It is possible to be sorely wounded in soul at marriage feasts and the tables of friends.

One golden rule on the subject may be laid down, the use of which will save us much trouble. Let us take care that we always go to feasts in the spirit of our divine Master, and that we never go where He would not have gone. Like Him, let us endeavor to be always "about our Father's business." (Luke 2:49.) Like Him, let us willingly promote joy and gladness, but let us strive that it may be sinless joy, if not joy in the Lord. Let us endeavor to bring the salt of grace into every company, and to drop the word in season in every ear we address. Much good may be done in society by giving a healthy tone to conversation. Let us never be ashamed to show our colors, and to make men see whose we are and whom we serve. We may well say, "Who is sufficient for these things?" But if Christ went to a marriage feast in Cana there is surely something that Christians can do on similar occasions. Let them only remember that if they go when their Master went, they must go in their Master's spirit.

We learn lastly, from these verses, the Almighty power of our Lord Jesus Christ. We are told of a miracle which He wrought at the marriage feast, when the wine failed. By a mere act of will He changed water into wine, and so supplied the need of all the guests.

The manner in which the miracle was worked deserves especial notice. We are not told of any outward visible action which preceded or accompanied it. It is not said that He touched the waterpots containing the water that was made wine. It is not said that He commanded the water to change its qualities, or that He prayed to His Father in Heaven. He simply willed the change, and it took place. We read of no prophet or apostle in the Bible who ever worked a miracle after this fashion. He who could do such a mighty work, in such a manner, was nothing less than very God.

It is a comfortable thought that the same almighty power of will which our Lord here displayed is still exercised on behalf of His believing people. They have no need of His bodily presence to maintain their cause. They have no reason to be cast down because they cannot see Him with their eyes interceding for them, or touch Him with their hands, that they may cling to Him for safety. If He "wills" their salvation and the daily supply of all their spiritual need, they are as safe and well provided for as if they saw Him standing by them. Christ's will is as mighty and effectual as Christ's deed. The will of Him who could say to the Father, "I will that they whom you have given me be with me where I am," is a will that has all power in heaven and earth, and must prevail. (John 17:24.)

Happy are those who, like the disciples, believe on Him by whom this miracle was wrought. A greater marriage feast than that of Cana will one day be held, when Christ Himself will be the bridegroom and believers will be the bride. A greater glory will one day be manifested, when Jesus shall take to Himself His great power and reign. Blessed will they be in that day who are called to the marriage supper of the Lamb! (Rev. 19:9)

2:12-25

Cleansing the Temple, Jesus at the Passover Feast

After this he went down to Capernaum with his mother and brothers and his disciples, and they stayed there a few days. Now the Jewish feast of Passover was near, so Jesus went up to Jerusalem.

He found in the temple courts those who were selling oxen and sheep and doves, and the money changers sitting at tables. So he made a whip of cords and drove them all out of the temple courts, with the sheep and the oxen. He scattered the coins of the money changers and overturned their tables. To those who sold the doves he said, "Take these things away from here! Do not make my Father's house a marketplace!" His disciples remembered that it was written, "Zeal for your house will devour me."

So then the Jewish leaders responded, "What sign can you show us, since you are doing these things?" Jesus replied, "Destroy this temple and in three days I will raise it up again." Then the Jewish leaders said to him, "This temple has been under construction for forty-six years, and are you going to raise it up in three days?" But Jesus was speaking about the temple of his body. So after he was raised from the dead, his disciples remembered that he had said this, and they believed the scripture and the saying that Jesus had spoken.

Now while Jesus was in Jerusalem at the feast of the Passover, many people believed in his name because they saw the miraculous signs he was doing. But Jesus would not entrust himself to them, because he knew all people. He did not need anyone to testify about man, for he knew what was in man.

The second miracle which our Lord is recorded to have wrought demands our attention in these verses. Like the first miracle at Cana, it is eminently typical and significant of things yet to come. To attend a marriage feast, and cleanse the temple from profanation were among the first acts of our Lord's ministry at His first coming. To purify the whole visible Church, and hold a marriage supper, will be among His first acts, when He comes again.

We see, for one thing, in this passage, how much Christ disapproves all irreverent behavior in the house of God.

We are told that He drove out of the temple those whom He found selling oxen and sheep and doves within its walls—that He poured out the changers' money and overthrew their tables—and that He said to those who sold doves, "Take these things away from here! Do not make my Father's house a marketplace!" On no occasion in our Lord's earthly ministry do we find Him acting so energetically, and exhibiting such righteous indignation, as on the occasion now before us. Nothing seems to have called from Him such a marked display of holy wrath as the gross irreverence which the priests permitted in the temple, notwithstanding all their boasted zeal for God's law. Twice, it will be remembered, He discovered the same profanation of His Father's house going on, within three years, once at the beginning of His ministry and once at the end. Twice we see Him expressing his displeasure in the strongest terms. "The thing is doubled" in order to impress a lesson more strongly on our minds.

The passage is one that ought to raise deep searchings of heart in many quarters. Are there none who profess and call themselves Christians, behaving every Sunday just as badly as these Jews? Are there none who secretly bring into the house of God their money, their lands, their houses, their cattle, and a whole train of worldly affairs? Are there none who bring their bodies only into the place of worship, and allow their hearts to wander into the ends of the earth? Are there none who are "almost in all evil, in the midst of the congregation?" (Prov. 5:14.) These are serious questions! Multitudes, it may be feared, could not give them a satisfactory answer. Christian churches and chapels, no doubt, are very unlike the Jewish temple. They are not built after a divine pattern. They have no altars or holy places. Their furniture has no typical meaning. But they are places where God's word is read, and where Christ is specially present. The man who professes to worship in them should surely behave with reverence and respect. The man who brings his worldly matters with him when he professes to worship, is doing that which is evidently most offensive to Christ. The words which Solomon wrote by the Holy Spirit are applicable to all times, "Keep your foot when you go to the house of God." (Eccles. 5:1.)

We see, for another thing, in this passage, how men may remember words of religious truth long after they are spoken, and may one day see a meaning in those who at first they did not see.

We are told that our Lord said to the Jews, "Destroy this temple and in three days I will raise it up." John informs us distinctly that "He spoke of the temple of His body," that he referred to His own resurrection. Yet the meaning of the sentence was not understood by our Lord's disciples at the time that it was spoken. It was not until "He was risen from the dead," three years after the events here described, that the full significance of the sentence flashed on their hearts. For three years it was a dark and useless saying to them. For three years it lay sleeping in their minds, like a seed in a tomb, and bore no fruit. But at the end of that time the darkness passed away. They saw the application of their Master's words, and as they saw it were confirmed in their faith. "They remembered that He had said this," and as they remembered "they believed."

It is a comfortable and cheering thought, that the same kind of thing that happened to the disciples is often going on at the present day. The sermons that are preached to apparently heedless ears in churches, are not all lost and thrown away. The instruction that is given in schools and pastoral visits, is not all wasted and forgotten. The texts that are taught by parents to children are not all taught in vain. There is often a resurrection of sermons, and texts, and instruction, after an interval of many years. The good seed sometimes springs up after he that sowed it has been long dead and gone.

Let preachers go on preaching, and teachers go on teaching, and parents go on training up children in the way they should go. Let them sow the good seed of Bible truth in faith and patience. Their labor is not in vain in the Lord. Their words are remembered far more than they think, and will yet spring up "after many days." (1 Cor. 15:58; Eccles. 11:1.)

We see, lastly, in this passage, how perfect is our Lord Jesus Christ's knowledge of the human heart.

We are told that when our Lord was at Jerusalem, the first time, He "did not commit Himself" to those who professed belief in Him. He knew that they were not to be depended on. They were astonished at the miracles which they saw Him work. They were even intellectually convinced that He was the Messiah, whom they had long expected. But they were not "disciples indeed." (John 8:31.) They were not converted, and true believers. Their hearts were not right in the sight of God, though their feelings were excited. Their inward man was not renewed, whatever they might profess with their lips. Our Lord knew that nearly all of them were stony-ground hearers. (Luke 8:13.) As soon as tribulation or persecution arose because of the word, their so-called faith would probably wither away and come to an end. All this our Lord saw clearly, if others around Him did not. Andrew, and Peter, and John, and Philip, and Nathanael, perhaps wondered that their Master did not receive these seeming believers with open arms. But they could only judge things by the outward appearance. Their Master could read hearts. "He knew what was in man."

The truth now before us, is one which ought to make hypocrites and false professors tremble. They may deceive men, but they cannot deceive Christ. They may wear a cloak of religion, and appear, like whited sepulchers, beautiful in the eyes of men. But the eyes of Christ see their inward rottenness, and the judgment of Christ will surely overtake them, except they repent. Christ is already reading their hearts, and as He reads He is displeased. They are known in heaven, if they are not known on earth, and they will be known at length to their shame, before assembled worlds, if they die unchanged. It is written, "I know your works, that you have a name that you live, and are dead." (Rev. 3:1.)

But the truth before us has two sides, like the pillar of cloud and fire at the Red sea. (Exod. 14:20.) If it looks darkly on hypocrites, it looks brightly on true believers. If it threatens wrath to false professors, it speaks peace to all who love the Lord Jesus Christ in sincerity. A real Christian may be weak, but he is true. One thing, at any rate, the servant of Christ can say, when cast down by a sense of his own infirmity, or pained by the slander of a lying world. He can say, "Lord, I am a poor sinner, but I am in earnest, I am true. You know all things—you know that I love you. You know all hearts, and you know that, weak as my heart is, it is a heart that cleaves to you." The false Christian shrinks from the eye of an all-seeing Savior. The true Christian desires his Lord's eye to be on him morning, noon, and night. He has nothing to hide.

Chapter 3

Conversation with Nicodemus

Now a certain man, a Pharisee named Nicodemus who was a member of the Jewish ruling council, came to Jesus at night and said to him, "Rabbi, we know that you are a teacher who has come from God. For no one could perform the miraculous signs that you do unless God is with him." Jesus replied, "I tell you the solemn truth, unless a person is born from above, he cannot see the kingdom of God." Nicodemus said to him, "How can a man be born when he is old? He cannot enter his mother's womb and be born a second time, can he?"

Jesus answered, "I tell you the solemn truth, unless a person is born of water and spirit, he cannot enter the kingdom of God. What is born of the flesh is flesh, and what is born of the Spirit is spirit. Do not be amazed that I said to you, 'You must all be born from above.' The wind blows wherever it will, and you hear the sound it makes, but do not know where it comes from and where it is going. So it is with everyone who is born of the Spirit."

The conversation between Christ and Nicodemus, which begins with these verses, is one of the most important passages in the whole Bible. Nowhere else do we find stronger statements about those two mighty subjects, the new birth, and salvation by faith in the Son of God. The servant of Christ will do well to make himself thoroughly acquainted with this chapter. A man may be ignorant of many things in religion, and yet be saved. But to be ignorant of the matters handled in this chapter, is to be in the broad way which leads to destruction.

We should notice, firstly, in these verses, what a weak and feeble beginning a man may make in religion, and yet finally prove a strong Christian. We are told of a certain Pharisee, named Nicodemus, who feeling concerned about his soul, "came to Jesus by night."

There can be little doubt that Nicodemus acted as he did on this occasion from the fear of man. He was afraid of what man would think, or say, or do, if his visit to Jesus was known. He came "by night," because he had not faith and courage enough to come by day. And yet there was a time afterwards when this very Nicodemus took our Lord's part in open day in the council of the Jews. "Does our law judge any man," he said, "before it hear him, and know what he does." (John 7:51.). Nor was this all. There came a time when this very Nicodemus was one of the only two men who did honor to our Lord's dead body. He helped Joseph of Arimathea to bury Jesus, when even the apostles had forsaken their Master and fled. His last things were more than his first. Though he began badly, he ended well.

The history of Nicodemus is meant to teach us that we should never "despise the day of small things" in religion. (Zec. 4:10.) We must not set down a man as having no grace, because his first steps towards God are timid and wavering, and the first movements of his soul are uncertain, hesitating, and stamped with much imperfection. We must remember our Lord's reception of Nicodemus. He did not "break the bruised reed, or quench the smoking flax," which He saw before Him. (Matt. 12:20.) Like Him, let us take inquirers by the hand, and deal with them gently and lovingly. In everything there must be a beginning. It is not those who make the most flaming profession of religion at first, who endure the longest and prove the most steadfast. Judas Iscariot was an apostle when Nicodemus was just groping his way slowly into full light, Yet afterwards, when Nicodemus was boldly helping to bury his crucified Savior, Judas Iscariot had betrayed Him, and hanged himself! This is a fact which ought not to be forgotten.

We should notice, secondly, in these verses, what a mighty change our Lord declares to be needful to salvation, and what a remarkable expression He uses in describing it. He speaks of a new birth. He says to Nicodemus, "Except a man be born again, he cannot see the kingdom of God." He announces the same truth in other words, in order to make it more plain to his hearer's mind—"Except a man be born of water and of the Spirit, he cannot enter into the kingdom of God." By this expression He meant Nicodemus to understand that "no one could become His disciple, unless his inward man was as thoroughly cleansed and renewed by the Spirit, as the outward man is cleansed by water." To possess the privileges of Judaism a man only needed to be born of the seed of Abraham after the flesh. To possess the privileges of Christ's kingdom, a man must be born again of the Holy Spirit.

The change which our Lord here declares needful to salvation is evidently no slight or superficial one. It is not merely reformation, or amendment, or moral change, or outward alteration of life. It is a thorough change of heart, will, and character. It is a resurrection. It is a new creation. It is a passing from death to life. It is the implanting in our dead hearts of a new principle from above. It is the calling into existence of a new creature, with a new nature, new habits of life, new tastes, new desires, new appetites, new judgments, new opinions, new hopes, and new fears. All this, and nothing less than this is implied, when our Lord declares that we all need a "new birth."

This change of heart is rendered absolutely necessary to salvation by the corrupt condition in which we are all, without exception, born. "That which is born of the flesh is flesh." Our nature is thoroughly fallen. The carnal mind is enmity against God. (Rom. 8:7.) We come into the world without faith, or love, or fear toward God. We have no natural inclination to serve Him or obey Him, and no natural pleasure in doing His will. Left to himself, no child of Adam would ever turn to God. The truest description of the change which we all need in order to make us real Christians, is the expression, "new birth."

This mighty change, it must never be forgotten, we cannot give to ourselves. The very name which our Lord gives to it is a convincing proof of this. He calls it "a birth." No man is the author of his own existence, and no man can quicken his own soul. We might as well expect a dead man to give himself life, as expect a natural man to make himself spiritual. A power from above must be put in exercise, even that same power which created the world. (2 Cor. 4:6.) Man can do many things; but he cannot give life either to himself or to others. To give life is the peculiar prerogative of God. Well may our Lord declare that we need to be "born again!"

This mighty change, we must, above all, remember, is a thing without which we cannot go to heaven, and could not enjoy heaven if we went there. Our Lord's words on this point are distinct and express. "Except a man be born again, he can neither see nor enter the kingdom of God." Heaven may be reached without money, or rank, or learning. But it is clear as daylight, if words have any meaning, that nobody can enter heaven without a "new birth."

We should notice, lastly, in these verses, the instructive comparison which our Lord uses in explaining the new birth. He saw Nicodemus perplexed and astonished by the things he had just heard. He graciously helped his wondering mind by an illustration drawn from "the wind." A more beautiful and fitting illustration of the work of the Spirit it is impossible to conceive.

There is much about the wind that is mysterious and inexplicable. "You can not tell," says our Lord, "whence it comes and where it goes." We cannot handle it with our hands, or see it with our eyes. When the wind blows, we cannot point out the exact spot where its breath first began to be felt, and the exact distance to which its influence shall extend. But we do not on that account deny its presence. It is just the same with the operations of the Spirit, in the new birth of man. They may be mysterious, sovereign, and incomprehensible to us in many ways. But it is foolish to stumble at them because there is much about those who we cannot explain.

But whatever mystery there may be about the wind, its presence may always be known by its sound and effects. "You hear the sound thereof," says our Lord. When our ears hear it whistling in the windows, and our eyes see the clouds driving before it, we do not hesitate to say, "There is wind." It is just the same with the operations of the Holy Spirit in the new birth of man. Marvelous and incomprehensible as His work may be, it is work that can always be seen and known. The new birth is a thing that "cannot be hidden." There will always be visible "fruits of the Spirit" in every one that is born of the Spirit.

Would we know what the marks of the new birth are? We shall find them already written for our learning in the First Epistle of John. The man born of God "believes that Jesus is the Christ,"—"does not commit sin,"—"does righteousness,"—"loves the brethren,"—"overcomes the world,"—"keeps himself from the wicked one." This is the man born of the Spirit! Where these fruits are to be seen, there is the new birth of which our Lord is speaking. He that lacks these marks, is yet dead in trespasses and sins. (1 John 5:1; 3:9; 2:29; 3:14; 5:4; 5:18.)

And now let us solemnly ask ourselves whether we know anything of the mighty change of which we have been reading? Have we been born again? Can any marks of the new birth be seen in us? Can the sound of the Spirit be heard in our daily conversation? Is the image and superscription of the Spirit to be discerned in our lives? Happy is the man who can give satisfactory answers to these questions! A day will come when those who are not born again will wish that they had never been born at all.

3:9-21

Nicodemus replied, "How can these things be?" Jesus answered, "Are you the teacher of Israel and yet you don't understand these things? I tell you the solemn truth, we speak about what we know and testify about what we have seen, but you people do not accept our testimony. If I have told you people about earthly things and you don't believe, how will you believe if I tell you about heavenly things? No one has ascended into heaven except the one who descended from heaven—the Son of Man. Just as Moses lifted up the serpent in the wilderness, so must the Son of Man be lifted up, so that everyone who believes in him may have eternal life."

For this is the way God loved the world—he gave his one and only Son that everyone who believes in him should not perish but have eternal life. For God did not send his Son into the world to condemn the world, but that the world should be saved through him. The one who believes in him is not condemned. The one who does not believe has been condemned already, because he has not believed in the name of the one and only Son of God. Now this is the basis for judging that the light has come into the world and people loved the darkness rather than the light, because their deeds were evil. For everyone who does evil deeds hates the light and does not come to the light, so that their deeds will not be exposed. But the one who practices the truth comes to the light, so that it may be plainly evident that his deeds have been done in God.

We have in these verses the second part of the conversation between our Lord Jesus Christ and Nicodemus. A lesson about regeneration is closely followed by a lesson about justification! The whole passage ought always to be read with affectionate reverence. It contains words which have brought eternal life to myriads of souls.

These verses show us, firstly, what gross spiritual ignorance there may be in the mind of a great and learned man. We see a "master of Israel" unacquainted with the first elements of saving religion. Nicodemus is told about the new birth, and at once exclaims, "How can these things be?" When such was the darkness of a Jewish teacher, what must have been the state of the Jewish people? It was indeed due time for Christ to appear! The pastors of Israel had ceased to feed the people with knowledge. The blind were leading · the blind, and both were falling into the ditch. (Matt. 15:14.)

Ignorance like that of Nicodemus is unhappily far too common in the Church of Christ. We must never be surprised if we find it in quarters where we might reasonably expect knowledge. Learning, and rank, and high ecclesiastical office are no proof that a minister is taught by the Spirit.

The successors of Nicodemus, in every age, are far more numerous than the successors of Peter. On no point is religious ignorance so common as on the work of the Holy Spirit. That old stumbling-block, at which Nicodemus stumbled, is as much an offence to thousands in the present day as it was in the days of Christ. "The natural man receives not the things of the Spirit of God." (1 Cor. 2:14.) Happy is he who has been taught to prove all things by Scripture, and to call no man master upon earth. (1 Thess. 5:21; Matt. 23:9.)

These verses show us, secondly, the original source from which man's salvation springs. That source is the love of God the Father. Our Lord says to Nicodemus, "God so loved the world that He gave His only begotten Son, that whoever believes in Him should not perish, but have everlasting life."

This wonderful verse has been justly called by Luther, "The Bible in miniature." No part of it, perhaps, is so deeply important as the first five words, "God so loved the world." The love here spoken of is not that special love with which the Father regards His own elect, but that mighty pity and compassion with which He regards the whole race of mankind. Its object is not merely the little flock which He has given to Christ from all eternity, but the whole "world" of sinners, without any exception. There is a deep sense in which God loves that world. All whom He has created He regards with pity and compassion. Their sins He cannot love—but He loves their souls. "His tender mercies are over all His works." (Psalm. 145:9.) Christ is God's gracious gift to the whole world.

Let us take heed that our views of the love of God are Scriptural and well-defined. The subject is one on which error abounds on either side. On the one hand we must beware of vague and exaggerated opinions. We must maintain firmly that God hates wickedness, and that the end of all who persist in wickedness will be destruction. It is not true that God's love is "lower than hell." It is not true that God so loved the world that all mankind will be finally saved, but that He so loved the world that He gave His Son to be the Savior of all who believe. His love is offered to all men freely, fully, honestly, and unreservedly, but it is only through the one channel of Christ's redemption. He that rejects Christ cuts himself off from God's love, and will perish everlastingly.

On the other hand, we must beware of narrow and contracted opinions. We must not hesitate to tell any sinner that God loves him. It is not true that God cares for none but His own elect, or that Christ is not offered to any but those who are ordained to eternal life. There is a "kindness and love" in God towards all mankind. It was in consequence of that love that Christ came into the world, and died upon the cross. Let us not be wise above that which is written, or more systematic in our statements than Scripture itself. God has no pleasure in the death of the wicked. God is not willing that any should perish. God would have all men to be saved. God loves the world. (John 6:32; Titus 3:4; 1 John4:10; 2 Pet. 3:9; 1 Tim. 2:4; Ezek. 33:11.)

These verses show us, thirdly, the peculiar plan by which the love of God has provided salvation for sinners. That plan is the atoning death of Christ on the cross. Our Lord says to Nicodemus, "As Moses lifted up the serpent in the wilderness, even so must the Son of man be lifted up, that whoever believes in Him should not perish, but have eternal life."

By being "lifted up," our Lord meant nothing less than His own death upon the cross. That death, He would have us know, was appointed by God to be "the life of the world." (John 6:51.) It was ordained from all eternity to be the great propitiation and satisfaction for man's sin. It was the payment, by an Almighty Substitute and Representative, of man's enormous debt to God. When Christ died upon the cross, our many sins were laid upon Him. He was made "sin" for us. He was made "a curse" for us. (2 Cor. 5:21; Gal. 3:13.) By His death He purchased pardon and complete redemption for sinners.

The bronze serpent, lifted up in the camp of Israel, brought health and cure within the reach of all who were bitten by the snakes. Christ crucified, in like manner, brought eternal life within reach of lost mankind. Christ has been lifted up on the cross, and man looking to Him by faith may be saved.

The truth before us is the very foundation-stone of the Christian religion. Christ's death is the Christian's life. Christ's cross is the Christian's title to heaven. Christ "lifted up" and put to shame on Calvary is the ladder by which Christians "enter into the holiest," and are at length landed in glory. It is true that we are sinners—but Christ has suffered for us. It is true that we deserve death—but Christ has died for us. It is true that we are guilty debtors—but Christ has paid our debts with His own blood. This is the real Gospel! This is the good news! On this let us lean while we live. To this let us cling when we die. Christ has been "lifted up" on the cross, and has thrown open the gates of heaven to all believers.

These verses show us, fourthly, the way in which the benefits of Christ's death are made our own. That way is simply to put faith and trust in Christ. Faith is the same thing as believing. Three times our Lord repeats this glorious truth to Nicodemus. Twice He proclaims that "whoever believes shall not perish." Once He says, "He that believes on the Son of God is not condemned."

Faith in the Lord Jesus is the very key of salvation. He that has it has life, and he that has it not has not life. Nothing whatever beside this faith is necessary to our complete justification; but nothing whatever, except this faith, will give us an interest in Christ. We may fast and mourn for sin, and do many things that are right, and use religious ordinances, and give all our goods to feed the poor, and yet remain unpardoned, and lose our souls. But if we will only come to Christ as guilty sinners, and believe on Him, our sins shall at once be forgiven, and our iniquities shall be entirely put away. Without faith there is no salvation; but through faith in Jesus, the vilest sinner may be saved.

If we would have a peaceful conscience in our religion, let us see that our views of saving faith are distinct and clear. Let us beware of supposing that justifying faith is anything more than a sinner's simple trust in a Savior, the grasp of a drowning man on the hand held out for his relief. Let us beware of mingling anything else with faith in the matter of justification. Here we must always remember faith stands entirely alone. A justified man, no doubt, will always be a holy man. True believing will always be accompanied by godly living. But that which gives a man a saving interest in Christ, is not his living, but his faith. If we would know whether our faith is genuine, we do well to ask ourselves how we are living. But if we would know whether we are justified by Christ, there is but one question to be asked. That question is, "Do we believe?"

These verses show us, lastly, the true cause of the loss of man's soul. Our Lord says to Nicodemus, "This is the condemnation, that light is come into the world, and men loved darkness rather than light, because their deeds were evil."

The words before us form a suitable conclusion to the glorious tidings which we have just been considering. They completely clear God of injustice in the condemnation of sinners. They show in simple and unmistakable terms, that although man's salvation is entirely of God, his ruin, if he is lost, will be entirely from himself. He will reap the fruit of his own sowing.

The doctrine here laid down ought to be carefully remembered. It supplies an answer to a common cavil of the enemies of God's truth. There is no decreed reprobation, excluding any one from heaven. "God sent not His Son into the world to condemn the world, but that the world through Him might be saved." There is no unwillingness on God's part to receive any sinner, however great his sins. God has sent "light" into the world, and if man will not come to the light, the fault is entirely on man's side. His blood will be on his own head, if he makes shipwreck of his soul. The blame will be at his own door, if he misses heaven. His eternal misery will be the result of his own choice. His destruction will be the work of his own hand. God loved him, and was willing to save him; out he "loved darkness," and therefore darkness must be his everlasting portion. He would not come to Christ, and therefore he could not have life. (John 5:40.)

The truths we have been considering are peculiarly weighty and solemn. Do we live as if we believed them?. Salvation by Christ's death is close to us today. Have we embraced it by faith, and made it our own? Let us never rest until we know Christ as our own Savior. Let us look to Him without delay for pardon and peace, if we have never looked before. Let us go on believing on Him, if we have already believed. "Whoever," is His own gracious word-"whoever believes on Him, shall not perish, but have eternal life."

3:22-36

Further Testimony About Jesus by John the Baptist

After this, Jesus and his disciples came into Judean territory, and there he spent time with them and was baptizing. John was also baptizing at Aenon near Salim, because water was plentiful there, and people were coming and being baptized. (For John had not yet been thrown into prison.)

Now a dispute came about between some of John's disciples and a Jew concerning ceremonial washing. So they came to John and said to him, "Rabbi, the one who was with you on the other side of the Jordan River, about whom you testified—see, he is baptizing, and everyone is flocking to him!"

John replied, "No one can receive anything unless it has been given to him from heaven. You yourselves can testify that I said, 'I am not the Christ,' but rather, 'I have been sent before him.' The one who has the bride is the bridegroom. The friend of the bridegroom, who stands by and listens for him, rejoices greatly when he hears the bridegroom's voice. This then is my joy, and it is complete. He must become more important while I become less important."

The one who comes from above is superior to all. The one who is from the earth belongs to the earth and speaks about earthly things. The one who comes from heaven is superior to all. He testifies about what he has seen and heard, but no one accepts his testimony. The one who has accepted his testimony has confirmed clearly that God is truthful. For the one whom God has sent speaks the words of God, for he does not give the Spirit sparingly. The Father loves the Son and has placed all things under his authority. The one who believes in the Son has eternal life. The one who rejects the Son will not see life, but God's wrath remains on him.

On one account, this passage deserves the special attention of all devout readers of the Bible. It contains the last testimony of John the Baptist concerning our Lord Jesus Christ. That faithful man of God was the same at the end of his ministry that he was at the beginning. the same in his views of self—the same in his views of Christ. Happy is that church whose ministers are as steady, bold, and constant to one thing, as John the Baptist!

We have, firstly, in these verses, a humbling example of the petty jealousies and party-spirit which may exist among professors of religion. We are told, that the disciples of John the Baptist were offended, because the ministry of Jesus began to attract more attention than that of their master. "They came unto John, and said unto him, Rabbi, he that was with you beyond Jordan, to whom you barest witness, behold the same baptizes, and all men come to him."

The spirit exhibited in this complaint, is unhappily too common in the Churches of Christ. The succession of these complainers has never failed. There are never lacking religions professors who care far more for the increase of their own party, than for the increase of true Christianity; and who cannot rejoice in the spread of religion, if it spreads anywhere except within their own denomination. There is a generation which can see no good being done, except in the ranks of its own congregations; and which seems ready to shut men out of heaven, if they will not enter therein under their banner.

The true Christian must watch and pray against the spirit here manifested by John's disciples. It is very insidious, very contagious, and very injurious to the cause of religion. Nothing so defiles Christianity and gives the enemies of truth such occasion to blaspheme, as jealousy and party-spirit among Christians. Wherever there is real grace, we should be ready and willing to acknowledge it, even though it may be outside our own pale. We should strive to say with the apostle, "If Christ be preached, I rejoice, yes! and will rejoice." (Phil. 1:18.) If good is done, we ought to be thankful, though it even may not be done in what we think the best way. If souls are saved, we ought to be glad, whatever be the means that God may think fit to employ.

We have, secondly, in these verses, a splendid pattern of true and godly humility. We see in John the Baptist a very different spirit from that displayed by his disciples. He begins by laying down the great principle, that acceptance with man is a special gift of God; and that we must therefore not presume to find fault, when others have more acceptance than ourselves. "A man can receive nothing except it be given him from heaven." He goes on to remind his followers of his repeated declaration, that one greater than himself was coming—"I said, I am not the Christ." He tells those who his office compared to that of Christ, is that of the bridegroom's friend, compared to the bridegroom. And finally, he solemnly affirms, that Christ must and will become greater and greater, and that he himself must become less and less important, until, like a star eclipsed by the rising sun, he has completely disappeared.

A frame of mind like this, is the highest degree of grace to which mortal man can attain. The greatest saint in the sight of God, is the man who is most thoroughly "clothed with humility." (1 Peter 5:5.) Would we know the prime secret of being men of the stamp of Abraham, and Moses, and Job, and David, and Daniel, and Paul, and John the Baptist? They were all eminently humble men. Living at different ages, and enjoying very different degrees of light, in this matter at least they were all agreed. In themselves they saw nothing but sin and weakness. To God they gave all the praise of what they were. Let us walk in their steps. Let us covet earnestly the best gifts; but above all, let us covet humility. The way to true honor is to be humble. No man ever was so praised by Christ, as the very man who says here, "I must decrease," the humble John the Baptist.

We have, thirdly, in these verses, an instructive declaration of Christ's honor and dignity. John the Baptist teaches his disciples once more, the true greatness of the Person whose growing popularity offended them. Once more, and perhaps for the last time, he proclaims Him as one worthy of all honor and praise. He uses one striking expression after another, to convey a correct idea of the majesty of Christ. He speaks of Him as "the bridegroom" of the Church—as "him that comes from above,"—as "him whom God has sent,"-as "him to whom the Spirit is given without measure,"—as Him "whom the Father loves," and into "whose hands all things are given,"—to believe in whom is life everlasting, and to reject whom is eternal ruin. Each of these phrases is full of deep meaning, and would supply matter for a long sermon. All show the depth and height of John's spiritual attainments. More honorable things are nowhere written concerning Jesus, than these verses recorded as spoken by John the Baptist.

Let us endeavor in life and death, to hold the same views of the Lord Jesus, to which John here gives expression. We can never make too much of Christ. Our thoughts about the Church, the ministry, and the sacraments, may easily become too high and extravagant. We can never have too high thoughts about Christ, can never love Him too much, trust Him too implicitly, lay too much weight upon Him, and speak too highly in His praise. He is worthy of all the honor that we can give Him. He will be all in heaven. Let us see to it, that He is all in our hearts on earth.

We have, lastly, in these verses, a broad assertion of the nearness and presentness of the salvation of true Christians. John the Baptist declares, "He that believes on the Son has everlasting life." He is not intended to look forward with a sick heart to a far distant privilege. He "has" everlasting life as soon as he believes. Pardon, peace, and a complete title to Heaven, are an immediate possession. They become a believer's own, from the very moment he puts faith in Christ. They will not be more completely his own, if he lives to the age of Methuselah.

The truth before us, is one of the most glorious privileges of the Gospel. There are no works to be done, no conditions to be fulfilled, no price to be paid, no wearing years of probation to be passed, before a sinner can be accepted with God. Let him only believe on Christ, and he is at once forgiven. Salvation is close to the chief of sinners. Let him only repent and believe, and this day it is his own. By Christ all that believe are at once justified from all things.

Let us leave the whole passage with one grave and heart-searching thought. If faith in Christ brings with it present and immediate privileges, to remain unbelieving is to be in a state of tremendous peril. If heaven is very near to the believer, hell must be very near to the unbeliever. The greater the mercy that the Lord Jesus offers, the greater will be the guilt of those who neglect and reject it. "He that believes not the Son shall not see life; but the wrath of God abides on him."

Chapter 4

4:1-6

Conversation With a Samaritan Woman

Now when Jesus knew that the Pharisees had heard that he was winning and baptizing more disciples than John (although Jesus himself was not baptizing, but his disciples were), he left Judea and set out once more for Galilee.

But he had to pass through Samaria. Now he came to a Samaritan town called Sychar, near the plot of land that Jacob had given to his son Joseph. Jacob's well was there, so Jesus, since he was tired from the journey, sat right down beside the well. It was about noon.

There are two sayings in these verses which deserve particular notice. They throw light on two subjects in religion, on which clear and well defined opinions are of great importance.

We should observe, for one thing, what is said about baptism. We read that "Jesus himself baptized not, but his disciples."

The expression here used is a very remarkable one. In reading it we seem irresistibly led to one instructive conclusion. That conclusion is, that baptism is not the principal part of Christianity, and that to baptize is not the principal work for which Christian ministers are ordained. Frequently we read of our Lord preaching and praying. Once we read of His administering the Lord's supper. But we have not a single instance recorded of His ever baptizing any one. And here we are distinctly told, that it was a subordinate work, which He left to others. Jesus "himself baptized not, but his disciples."

The lesson is one of peculiar importance in the present day. Baptism, as a sacrament ordained by Christ Himself, is an honorable ordinance, and ought never to be lightly esteemed in the churches. It cannot be neglected or despised without great sin. When rightly used, with faith and prayer, it is calculated to convey the highest blessings. But baptism was never meant to be exalted to the position which many now-a-days assign to it in religion. It does not act as a charm. It does not necessarily convey the grace of the Holy Spirit. The benefit of it depends greatly on the manner in which it is used. The doctrine taught, and the language employed about it, in some quarters, are utterly inconsistent with the fact announced in the text. If baptism was all that some say it is, we would never have been told, that "Jesus himself baptized not."

Let it be a settled principle in our minds that the first and chief business of the Church of Christ is to preach the Gospel. The words of Paul ought to be constantly remembered—"Christ sent me not to baptize, but to preach the Gospel." (1 Cor. 1:17.) When the Gospel of Christ is faithfully and fully preached we need not fear that the sacraments will be undervalued. Baptism and the Lord's supper will always be most truly reverenced in those churches where the truth as it is in Jesus is most fully taught and known.

We should observe, for another thing, in this passage, what is said about our Lord's human nature. We read that Jesus was "wearied with his journey."

We learn from this, as well as many other expressions in the Gospels, that our Lord had a body exactly like our own. When "the Word became flesh," He took on Him a nature like our own in all things, sin only excepted. Like ourselves, He grew from infancy to youth, and from youth to man's estate. Like ourselves, He hungered, thirsted, felt pain, and needed sleep. He was liable to every sinless infirmity to which we are liable. In all things His body was framed like our own.

The truth before us is full of comfort for all who are true Christians. He to whom sinners are bid to come for pardon and peace, is one who is man as well as God. He had a real human nature when He was upon earth. He took a real human nature with Him, when He ascended up into heaven. We have at the right hand of God a High Priest who can be touched with the feeling of our infirmities, because He has suffered Himself being tempted. When we cry to Him in the hour of bodily pain and weakness, He knows well what we mean. When our prayers and praises are feeble through bodily weariness, He can understand our condition. He knows our frame. He has learned by experience what it is to be a man. To say that the Virgin Mary, or anyone else, can feel more sympathy for us than Christ, is ignorance no less than blasphemy. The man Christ Jesus can enter fully into everything that belongs to man's condition. The poor, the sick, and the suffering, have in heaven One who is not only an almighty Savior, but a most sympathetic Friend.

The servant of Christ should grasp firmly this great truth, that there are two perfect and complete natures in the one Person whom he serves. The Lord Jesus, in whom the Gospel bids us believe, is, without doubt, almighty God-equal to the Father in all things, and able to save to the uttermost all those that come unto God by Him. But that same Jesus is no less certainly perfect man—able to sympathize with man in all his bodily sufferings, and acquainted by experience with all that man's body has to endure. Power and sympathy are marvelously combined in Him who died for us on the cross. Because He is God, we may repose the weight of our souls upon Him with unhesitating confidence. He is mighty to save. Because He is man, we may speak to Him with freedom, about the many trials to which flesh is heir. He knows the heart of a man. Here is rest for the weary! Here is good news! Our Redeemer is man as well as God, and God as well as man. He that believes on Him, has everything that a child of Adam can possibly require, either for safety or for peace.

4:7-26

Conversation With a Samaritan Woman

But he had to pass through Samaria. Now he came to a Samaritan town called Sychar, near the plot of land that Jacob had given to his son Joseph. Jacob's well was there, so Jesus, since he was tired from the journey, sat right down beside the well. It was about noon.

A Samaritan woman came to draw water. Jesus said to her, "Give me some water to drink." (For his disciples had gone off into the town to buy supplies.) So the Samaritan woman said to him, "How can you—a Jew—ask me, a Samaritan woman, for water to drink?" (For Jews use nothing in common with Samaritans.)

Jesus answered her, "If you had known the gift of God and who it is who said to you, 'Give me some water to drink,' you would have asked him, and he would have given you living water." "Sir," the woman said to him, "you have no bucket and the well is deep; where then do you get this living water? Surely you're not greater than our ancestor Jacob, are you? For he gave us this well and drank from it himself, along with his sons and his livestock."

Jesus replied, "Everyone who drinks some of this water will be thirsty again. But whoever drinks some of the water that I will give him will never be thirsty again, but the water that I will give him will become in him a fountain of water springing up to eternal life." The woman said to him, "Sir, give me this water, so that I will not be thirsty or have to come here to draw water." He said to her, "Go call your husband and come back here." The woman replied, "I have no husband." Jesus said to her, "Right you are when you said, 'I have no husband,' for you have had five husbands and the man you are living with now is not your husband. This you said truthfully!"

The woman said to him, "Sir, I see that you are a prophet. Our fathers worshiped on this mountain, and you people say that the place where people must worship is in Jerusalem." Jesus said to her, "Believe me, woman, a time is coming when you will worship the Father neither on this mountain nor in Jerusalem. You people worship what you do not know. We worship what we know, because salvation is from the Jews. But a time is coming—and now is here—when the true worshipers will worship the Father in spirit and truth, for the Father seeks such people to be his worshipers. God is spirit, and the people who worship him must worship in spirit and truth." The woman said to him, "I know that Messiah is coming" (the one called Christ); "whenever he comes, he will tell us everything." Jesus said to her, "I, the one speaking to you, am he."

The history of the Samaritan woman, contained in these verses, is one of the most interesting and instructive passages in John's Gospel. John has shown us, in the case of Nicodemus, how our Lord dealt with a self-righteous formalist. He now shows us how our Lord dealt with an ignorant, carnal-minded woman, whose moral character was more than ordinarily bad. There are lessons in the passage for ministers and teachers, which they would do well to ponder.

We should mark, firstly, the mingled tact and humility of Christ in dealing with a careless sinner.

Our Lord was sitting by Jacob's well when a woman of Samaria came there to draw water. At once He says to her, "Give me to drink." He does not wait for her to speak to Him. He does not begin by reproving her sins, though He doubtless knew them. He opens communication by asking a favor. He approaches the woman's mind by the subject of "water," which was naturally uppermost in her thoughts. Simple as this request may seem, it opened a door to spiritual conversation. It threw a bridge across the gulf which lay between her and Him. It led to the conversion of her soul.

Our Lord's conduct in this place should be carefully remembered by all who want to do good to the thoughtless and spiritually ignorant. It is vain to expect that such people will voluntarily come to us, and begin to seek knowledge. We must begin with them, and go down to them in the spirit of courteous and friendly offensive. It is vain to expect that such people will be prepared for our instruction, and will at once see and acknowledge the wisdom of all we are doing. We must go to work WISELY. We must study the best avenues to their hearts, and the most likely way of arresting their attention. There is a handle to every mind, and our chief aim must be to get hold of it. Above all, we must be KIND in manner, and beware of showing that we feel conscious of our own superiority. If we let ignorant people fancy that we think we are doing them a great favor in talking to them about religion, there is little hope of doing good to their souls.

We should mark, secondly, Christ's readiness to give mercies to careless sinners. He tells the Samaritan woman that if she had asked, "He would have given her living water." He knew the character of the person before Him perfectly well. Yet He says, "If she had asked, He would have given,"—He would have given the living water of grace, mercy, and peace.

The infinite willingness of Christ to receive sinners is a golden truth, which ought to be treasured up in our hearts, and diligently impressed on others. The Lord Jesus is far more ready to hear than we are to pray, and far more ready to give favors than we are to ask them. All day long He stretches out His hands to the disobedient and gainsaying. He has thoughts of pity and compassion towards the vilest of sinners, even when they have no thoughts of Him. He stands waiting to bestow mercy and grace on the worst and most unworthy, if they will only cry to Him. He will never draw back from that well known promise, "Ask and you shall receive—seek and you shall find." The lost will discover at the last day, that they had not, because they asked not.

We should mark, thirdly, the priceless excellence of Christ's gifts when compared with the things of this world. Our Lord tells the Samaritan woman, "He that drinks of this water shall thirst again, but he that drinks of the water that I shall give him shall never thirst."

The truth of the principle here laid down may be seen on every side by all who are not blinded by prejudice or love of the world. Thousands of men have every temporal good thing that heart could wish, and are yet weary and dissatisfied. It is now as it was in David's time—"There be many that say, Who will show us any good." (Psalm 4:6.) Riches, and rank, and place, and power, and learning, and amusements, are utterly unable to fill the soul. He that only drinks of these waters is sure to thirst again. Every Ahab finds a Naboth's vineyard nearby his palace, and every Haman sees a Mordecai at the gate. There is no heart satisfaction in this world, until we believe on Christ. Jesus alone can fill up the empty places of our inward man. Jesus alone can give solid, lasting, enduring happiness. The peace that He imparts is a fountain, which, once set flowing within the soul, flows on to all eternity. Its waters may have their ebbing seasons; but they are living waters, and they shall never be completely dried.

We should mark, fourthly, the absolute necessity of conviction of sin before a soul can be converted to God. The Samaritan woman seems to have been comparatively unmoved until our Lord exposed her breach of the seventh commandment. Those heart-searching words, "Go, call your husband," appear to have pierced her conscience like an arrow. From that moment, however ignorant, she speaks like an earnest, sincere inquirer after truth. And the reason is evident. She felt that her spiritual disease was discovered. For the first time in her life she saw herself.

To bring thoughtless people to this state of mind should be the principal aim of all teachers and ministers of the Gospel. They should carefully copy their Master's example in this place. Until men and women are brought to feel their sinfulness and need, no real good is ever done to their souls. Until a sinner sees himself as God sees him, he will continue careless, trifling, and unmoved. By all means we must labor to convince the unconverted man of sin, to pierce his conscience, to open his eyes, to show him himself. To this end we must expound the length and breadth of God's holy law. To this end we must denounce every practice contrary to that law, however fashionable and customary. This is the only way to do good. Never does a soul value the Gospel medicine until it feels its disease. Never does a man see any beauty in Christ as a Savior, until he discovers that he is himself a lost and ruined sinner. Ignorance of sin is invariably attended by neglect of Christ.

We should mark, fifthly, the utter uselessness of any religion which only consists of formality. The Samaritan woman, when awakened to spiritual concern, started questions about the comparative merits of the Samaritan and Jewish modes of worshiping God. Our Lord tells her that true and acceptable worship depends not on the place in which it is offered, but on the state of the worshiper's heart. He declares, "The hour comes when you shall neither in this place nor at Jerusalem worship the Father." He adds that "the true worshipers shall worship in spirit and in truth."

The principle contained in these sentences can never be too strongly impressed on professing Christians. We are all naturally inclined to make religion a mere matter of outward forms and ceremonies, and to attach an excessive importance to our own particular manner of worshiping God. We must beware of this spirit, and especially when we first begin to think seriously about our souls. The heart is the principal thing in all our approaches to God. "The Lord looks on the heart." (1 Sam. 16:7.) The most gorgeous cathedral service is offensive in God's sight, if all is gone through coldly, heartlessly, and without grace. The feeblest gathering of three or four poor believers in a lowly cottage to read the Bible and pray, is a more acceptable sight to Him who searches the heart than the fullest congregation which is ever gathered in St. Peter's at Rome.

We should mark, lastly, Christ's gracious willingness to reveal Himself to the chief of sinners. He concludes His conversation with the Samaritan woman by telling her openly and unreservedly that He is the Savior of the world. "I that speak to you," He says, "am the Messiah." Nowhere in all the Gospels do we find our Lord making such a full avowal of His nature and office as He does in this place. And this avowal, be it remembered, was made not to learned Scribes, or moral Pharisees, but to one who up to that day had been an ignorant, thoughtless, and immoral person!

Dealings with sinners, such as these, form one of the grand peculiarities of the Gospel. Whatever a man's past life may have been, there is hope and a remedy for him in Christ. If he is only willing to hear Christ's voice and follow Him, Christ is willing to receive him at once as a friend, and to bestow on him the fullest measure of mercy and grace. The Samaritan woman, the penitent thief, the Philippian jailor, the tax-collector Zaccheus, are all patterns of Christ's readiness to show mercy, and to confer full and immediate pardons. It is His glory that, like a great physician, He will undertake to cure those who are apparently incurable, and that none are too bad for Him to love and heal. Let these things sink down into our hearts. Whatever else we doubt, let us never doubt that Christ's love to sinners passes knowledge, and that Christ is as willing to receive as He is almighty to save.

What are we ourselves? This is the question, after all, which demands our attention. We may have been up to this day careless, thoughtless, sinful as the woman whose story we have been reading. But yet there is hope—He who talked with the Samaritan woman at the well is yet living at God's right hand, and never changes. Let us only ask, and He will "give us living water."

4:27-30

The Disciples Return

Now at that very moment his disciples came back. They were shocked because he was speaking with a woman; however, no one said, "What do you want?" or "Why are you speaking with her?" Then the woman left her water jar, went off into the town and said to the people, "Come, see a man who told me everything I ever did. Surely he can't be the Messiah, can he?" So they left the town and began coming to him.

These verses continue the well-known story of the Samaritan woman's conversion. Short as the passage may appear, it contains points of deep interest and importance. The mere worldling, who cares, nothing about experimental religion, may see nothing particular in these verses. To all who desire to know something of the experience of a converted person, they will be found full of food for thought.

We see, firstly, in this passage, how marvelous in the eyes of man are Christ's dealings with souls. We are told that the disciples "marveled that he talked with the woman." That their Master should take the trouble to talk to a woman at all, and to a Samaritan woman, and to an adulterous woman at a well, when He was wearied with His journey—all this was amazing to the eleven disciples. It was a sort of thing which they did not expect. It was contrary to their idea of what a religious teacher should do. It startled them and filled them with surprise.

The feeling displayed by the disciples on this occasion, does not stand alone in the Bible. When our Lord allowed publicans and sinners to draw near to Him and be in His company, the Pharisees marveled. They exclaimed, "This man receives sinners and eats with them." (Luke 15:2.). When Saul came back from Damascus, a converted man and a new creature, the Christians at Jerusalem were astonished. "They did not believe that he was a disciple." (Acts 9:26.). When Peter was delivered from Herod's prison by an angel, and brought to the door of the house where disciples were praying for his deliverance, they were so taken by surprise that they could not believe it was Peter. "When they saw him they were astonished." (Acts 12:16.)

But why should we stop short in Bible instances? The true Christian has only to look around him in this world in order to see abundant illustrations of the truth before us. How much astonishment every fresh conversion occasions. What surprise is expressed at the change in the heart, life, tastes, and habits of the converted person! What wonder is felt at the power, the mercy, the patience, the compassion of Christ! It is now as it was eighteen hundred years ago. The dealings of Christ are still a marvel both to the Church and to the world.

If there was more real faith on the earth, there would be less surprise felt at the conversion of souls. If Christians believed more, they would expect more, and if they understood Christ better, they would be less startled and astonished when He calls and saves the chief of sinners. We should consider nothing impossible, and regard no sinner as beyond the reach of the grace of God. The astonishment expressed at conversions is a proof of the weak faith and ignorance of these latter days. The thing that ought to fill us with surprise is the obstinate unbelief of the ungodly, and their determined perseverance in the way to ruin. This was the mind of Christ. It is written that He thanked the Father for conversions. But He marveled at unbelief. (Matt. 11:25; Mark 6:6.)

We see, secondly, in this passage, how absorbing is the influence of grace, when it first comes into a believer's heart. We are told that after our Lord had told the woman He was the Messiah, "She left her water-pot and went her way into the city, and said to the men, Come, see a man which told me all things that ever I did." She had left her home for the express purpose of drawing water. She had carried a large vessel to the well, intending to bring it back filled. But she found at the well a new heart, and new objects of interest. She became a new creature. Old things passed away. All things became new. At once everything else was forgotten for the time. She could think of nothing but the truths she had heard, and the Savior she had found. In the fullness of her heart she "left her water-pot," and hastened away to tell others.

We see here the expulsive power of the grace of the Holy Spirit. Grace once introduced into the heart drives out old tastes and interests. A converted person no longs cares for what he once cared for. A new tenant is in the house. A new pilot is at the helm. The whole world looks different. All things have become new. It was so with Matthew the tax-collector. The moment that grace came into his heart he left the receipt of custom. (Matt. 9:9.). It was so with Peter, James, and John, and Andrew. As soon as they were converted they forsook their nets and fishing-boats. (Mark 1:19.). It was so with Saul the Pharisee. As soon as he became a Christian he gave up all his brilliant prospects as a Jew, in order to preach the faith he had once despised. (Acts 9:20.). The conduct of the Samaritan woman was precisely of the same kind. For the time present the salvation she had found completely filled her mind. That she never returned for her water-pot would be more than we have a right to say. But under the first impressions of new spiritual life, she went away and "left her water-pot" behind.

Conduct like that here described is doubtless uncommon in the present day. Rarely do we see a person so entirely taken up with spiritual matters, that attention to this world's affairs is made a secondary matter, or postponed. And why is it so? Simply because true conversions to God are uncommon. Few really feel their sins, and flee to Christ by faith. Few really pass from death to life, and become new creatures. Yet these few are the real Christians of the world. These are the people whose religion, like the Samaritan woman's, tells on others. Happy are they who know something by experience of this woman's feelings, and can say with Paul, "I count all things but loss for the excellency of the knowledge of Christ!" Happy are they who have given up everything for Christ's sake, or at any rate have altered the relative importance of all things in their minds! "If your eye be single your whole body shall be full of light." (Philip. 3:8; Matt. 6:22.)

We see, lastly, in this passage, how zealous a truly converted person is to do good to others. We are told that the Samaritan woman "went into the city, and said to the men, Come, see a man who told me all things that ever I did—is not this the Christ?" In the day of her conversion she became a missionary! She felt so deeply the amazing benefit she had received from Christ, that she could not hold her peace about Him. Just as Andrew told his brother Peter about Jesus, and Philip told Nathanael that he had found Messiah, and Saul, when converted, immediately preached Christ, so, in the same way, the Samaritan woman said, "Come and see Christ." She used no abstruse arguments. She attempted no deep reasoning about our Lord's claim to be the Messiah. She only said, "Come and see." Out of the abundance of her heart her mouth spoke.

That which the Samaritan woman here did, all true Christians ought to do likewise. The Church needs it. The state of the world demands it. Common sense points out that it is right. Every one who has received the grace of God, and tasted that Christ is gracious, ought to find words to testify of Christ to others. Where is our faith, if we believe that souls around us are perishing, and that Christ alone can save them, and yet remain silent? Where is our charity if we can see others going down to hell, and yet say nothing to them about Christ and salvation? We may well doubt our own love to Christ, if our hearts are never moved to speak of Him. We may well doubt the safety of our own souls, if we feel no concern about the souls of others.

What are WE ourselves? This is the question, after all, which demands our notice. Do we feel the supreme importance of spiritual things, and the comparative nothingness of the things of the world? Do we ever talk to others about God, and Christ, and eternity, and the soul, and heaven, and hell? If not, what is the value of our faith? Where is the reality of our Christianity? Let us take heed lest we awake too late, and find that we are lost forever, a wonder to angels and devils, and, above all, a wonder to ourselves, because of our own obstinate blindness and folly.

4:31-42

Workers for the Harvest

Meanwhile the disciples were urging him, "Rabbi, eat something." But he said to them, "I have food to eat that you know nothing about." So the disciples began to say to one another, "No one brought him anything to eat, did they?" Jesus said to them, "My food is to do the will of the one who sent me and to complete his work. Don't you say, 'There are four more months and then comes the harvest?' I tell you, look up and see that the fields are already white for harvest! The one who reaps receives pay and gathers fruit for eternal life, so that the one who sows and the one who reaps can rejoice together. For in this instance the saying is true, 'One sows and another reaps.' I sent you to reap what you did not work for; others have labored and you have entered into their labor."

Now many Samaritans from that town believed in him because of the report of the woman who testified, "He told me everything I ever did." So when the Samaritans came to him, they started asking him to stay with them. He stayed there two days, and because of his word many more believed. They said to the woman, "No longer do we believe because of your words, for we have heard for ourselves, and we know that this one really is the Savior of the world."

We have, for one thing, in these verses, an instructive pattern of zeal for the good of others. We read, that our Lord Jesus Christ declares, "My food is to do the will of him who sent me, and to finish his work." To do good was not merely duty and pleasure to Him. He counted it as His food and drink. Job, one of the holiest Old Testament saints, could say, that he esteemed

God's word "more than his necessary food." (Job 23:12.) The Great Head of the New Testament Church went even further. He could say the same of God's work.

Do we do any work for God? Do we try, however feebly, to set forward His cause on earth—to check that which is evil, to promote that which is good? If we do, let us never be ashamed of doing it with all our heart, and soul, and mind, and strength. Whatever our hand finds to do for the souls of others, let us do it with our might. (Eccles. 9:10.) The world may mock and sneer, and call us enthusiasts. The world can admire zeal in any service but that of God, and can praise enthusiasm on any subject but that of religion. Let us work on unmoved. Whatever men may say and think, we are walking in the steps of our Lord Jesus Christ.

Let us, beside this, take comfort in the thought that Jesus Christ never changes. He that sat by the well of Samaria, and found it "food and drink" to do good to an ignorant soul, is always in one mind. High in heaven at God's right hand, He still delights to save sinners, and still approves zeal and labor in the cause of God. The work of the missionary and the evangelist may be despised and ridiculed in many quarters. But while man is mocking, Christ is well pleased! Thanks be to God, Jesus is the, same yesterday, and today, and forever.

We have, for another thing, in these verses, strong encouragement held out to those who labor to do good to souls. We read, that our Lord described the world as a "field white for the harvest;" and then said to His disciples, "He that reaps, receives wages, and gathers fruit unto life eternal."

Work for the souls of men, is undoubtedly attended by great discouragements. The heart of natural man is very hard and unbelieving. The blindness of unsaved men to their own lost condition and peril of ruin, is something past description. "The carnal mind is enmity against God." (Rom. 8:7.) No one can have any just idea of the desperate hardness of men and women, until he has tried to do good. No one can have any conception of the small number of those who repent and believe, until he has personally endeavored to "save some." (1 Cor. 9:22.) To suppose that everybody will become a true Christian, who is told about Christ, and entreated to believe, is mere childish ignorance. "Few there be that find the narrow way!" The laborer for Christ will find the vast majority of those among whom he labors, unbelieving and impenitent, in spite of all that he can do. "The many" will not turn to Christ. These are discouraging facts. But they are facts, and facts that ought to be known.

The true antidote against despondency in God's work, is an abiding recollection of such promises as that before us. There are "wages" laid up for faithful reapers. They shall receive a reward at the last day, far exceeding anything they have done for Christ—a reward proportioned not to their success, but to the quantity of their work. They are gathering "fruit," which shall endure when this world has passed away—fruit, in some souls saved, if many will not believe, and fruit in evidences of their own faithfulness, to be brought out before assembled worlds. Do our hands ever hang down, and our knees wax faint? Do we feel disposed to say, "my labor is in vain and my words without profit." Let us lean back at such seasons on this glorious promise. There are "wages" yet to be paid. There is "fruit" yet to be exhibited. "We are a sweet savor of Christ, both in those who are saved and in those who perish." (2 Cor. 2:15.) Let us work on. "He that goes forth and weeps, bearing precious seed, shall doubtless come again with rejoicing, bringing his sheaves with him." (Psalm. 126:6.) One single soul saved, shall outlive and outweigh all the kingdoms of the world.

We have, lastly, in these verses, a most teaching instance of the variety of ways by which men are led to believe Christ. We read that "many of the Samaritans believed on Christ for the saying of the woman." But this is not all. We read again, "Many more believed because of Christ's own word." In short, some were converted trough the means of the woman's testimony, and some were converted by hearing Christ Himself.

The words of Paul should never be forgotten, "There are diversities of operations, but it is the same God which works all in all." (1 Cor. 12:6.) The way in which the Spirit leads all God's people is always one and the same. But the paths by which they are severally brought into that road are often widely different. There are some in whom the work of conversion is sudden and instantaneous. There are others in whom it goes on slowly, quietly, and by imperceptible degrees. Some have their hearts gently opened, like Lydia. Others are aroused by violent alarm, like the jailor at Philippi. All are finally brought to repentance toward God, faith toward our Lord Jesus Christ, and holiness of conversation. But all do not begin with the same experience. The weapon which carries conviction to one believer's soul, is not the one which first pierces another. The arrows of the Holy Spirit are all drawn from the same quiver. But He uses sometimes one and sometimes another, according to His own sovereign will.

Are we converted ourselves? This is the one point to which our attention ought to be directed. Our experience may not tally with that of other believers. But that is not the question. Do we feel sin, hate it, and flee from it? Do we love Christ, and rest solely on Him for salvation? Are we bringing forth fruits of the Spirit in righteousness and true holiness? If these things are so we may thank God, and take courage.

4:43-54

Healing the Royal Official's Son

After the two days he departed from there to Galilee. (For Jesus himself had testified that a prophet has no honor in his own country.) So when he came to Galilee, the Galileans welcomed him because they had seen all the things he had done in Jerusalem at the feast (for they themselves had gone to the feast).

Now he came again to Cana in Galilee where he had made the water wine. In Capernaum there was a certain royal official whose son was sick. When he heard that Jesus had come back from Judea to Galilee, he went to him and begged him to come down and heal his son, who was about to die. So Jesus said to him, "Unless you people see signs and wonders you will never believe." "Sir," the official said to him, "come down before my child dies." Jesus told him, "Go home; your son will live." The man believed the word that Jesus spoke to him, and set off for home.

While he was on his way down, his slaves met him and told him that his son was going to live. So he asked them the time when his condition began to improve, and they told him, "Yesterday at one o'clock in the afternoon the fever left him." Then the father realized that it was the very time Jesus had said to him, "Your son will live," and he himself believed along with his entire household. Jesus did this as his second miraculous sign when he returned from Judea to Galilee.

Four great lessons stand out boldly on the face of this passage. Let us fix them in our memories, and use them continually as we journey through life.

We learn, firstly, that the rich have afflictions as well as the poor. We read of a nobleman in deep anxiety because his son was sick. We need not doubt that every means of restoration was used that money could procure. But money is not almighty. The sickness increased, and the nobleman's son lay at the point of death.

The lesson is one which needs to be constantly impressed on the minds of men. There is no more common, or more mischievous error, than to suppose that the rich have no cares. The rich are as liable to sickness as the poor; and have a hundred anxieties beside, of which the poor know nothing at all. Silks and satins often cover very heavy hearts. The dwellers in palaces often sleep more uneasily than the dwellers in poor cottages. Gold and silver can lift no man beyond the reach of trouble. They may shut out debt and rags, but they cannot shut out care, disease, and death. The higher the tree, the more it is shaken by storms. The broader its branches, the greater is the mark which it exposes to the tempest. David was a happier man when he kept his father's sheep at Bethlehem, than when he dwelt as a king at Jerusalem, and governed the twelve tribes of Israel.

Let the servant of Christ beware of desiring riches. They are certain cares, and uncertain comforts. Let him pray for the rich, and not envy them. How hardly shall a rich man enter the kingdom of God! Above all, let him learn to be content with such things as he has. He only is truly rich, who has treasure in heaven.

We learn, secondly, in this passage, that sickness and death come to the young as well as to the old. We read of a son sick unto death, and a father in trouble about him. We see the natural order of things inverted. The elder is obliged to minister to the younger, and not the younger to the elder. The child draws near to the grave before the parent, and not the parent before the child.

The lesson is one which we are all slow to learn. We are apt to shut our eyes to plain facts, and to speak and act, as if young people, as a matter of course, never died when young. And yet the grave-stones in every churchyard would tell us, that few people out of a hundred ever live to be fifty years old, while many never grow up to man's estate at all. The first grave that ever was dug on this earth, was that of a young man. The first person who ever died, was not a father but a son. Aaron lost two sons at a stroke. David, the man after God's own heart, lived long enough to see three children buried. Job was deprived of all his children in one day. These things were carefully recorded for our learning.

He that is wise, will never consider long life as a certainty. We never know what a day may bring forth. The strongest and fairest are often cut down and hurried away in a few hours, while the old and feeble linger on for many years. The only true wisdom is to be always prepared to meet God, to put nothing off which concerns eternity, and to live like men ready to depart at any moment. So living, it matters little whether we die young or old. Joined to the Lord Jesus, we are safe in any event.

We learn, thirdly, from this passage, what benefits affliction can confer on the soul. We read, that anxiety about a son led the nobleman to Christ, in order to obtain help in time of need. Once brought into Christ's company, he learned a lesson of priceless value. In the end, "he believed, and his whole house." All this, be it remembered, hinged upon the son's sickness. If the nobleman's son had never been ill, his father might have lived and died in his sins!

Affliction is one of God's medicines. By it He often teaches lessons which would be learned in no other way. By it He often draws souls away from sin and the world, which would otherwise have perished everlastingly. Health is a great blessing, but sanctified disease is a greater. Prosperity and worldly comfort, are what all naturally desire; but losses and crosses are far better for us, if they lead us to Christ. Thousands at the last day, will testify with David, and the nobleman before us, "It is good for me that I have been afflicted." (Psalm. 119:71.)

Let us beware of murmuring in the time of trouble. Let us settle it firmly in our minds, that there is a meaning, a needs-be, and a message from God, in every sorrow that falls upon us. There are no lessons so useful as those learned in the school of affliction. There is no commentary that opens up the Bible so much as sickness and sorrow. "No chastening for the present seems to be joyous, but grievous—nevertheless afterward it yields peaceable fruit." (Heb. 12:11.) The resurrection morning will prove, that many of the losses of God's people were in reality eternal gains.

We learn, lastly, from this passage, that Christ's word is as good as Christ's presence. We read, that Jesus did not come down to Capernaum to see the sick young man, but only spoke the word, "Your son lives." Almighty power went with that little sentence. That very hour the patient began to amend. Christ only spoke, and the cure was done. Christ only commanded, and the deadly disease stood fast.

The fact before us is singularly full of comfort. It gives enormous value to every promise of mercy, grace, and peace, which ever fell from Christ's lips. He that by faith has laid bold on some word of Christ, has placed his feet upon a ROCK. What Christ has said, He is able to do; and what He has undertaken, He will never fail to make good. The sinner who has really reposed his soul on the word of the Lord Jesus, is safe to all eternity. He could not be safer, if he saw the book of life, and his own name written in it. If Christ has said, "Him that comes to me, I will in no wise cast out," and our hearts can testify, "I have come," we need not doubt that we are saved. In the things of this world, we say that seeing is believing. But in the things of the Gospel, believing is as good as seeing. Christ's word is as good as man's deed. He of whom Jesus says in the Gospel, "He lives," is alive for evermore, and shall never die.

And now let us remember that afflictions, like that of the nobleman, are very common. They will probably come to our door one day. Have we known anything of bearing affliction? Would we know where to turn for help and comfort when our time comes? Let us fill our minds and memories betimes with Christ's words. They are not the words of man only, but of God. The words that he speaks are spirit and life. (John 6:63.)

Chapter 5

5:1-15

Healing a Paralytic at the Pool of Bethesda

*A*fter this there was a Jewish feast, and Jesus went up to Jerusalem. Now there is in Jerusalem by the Sheep Gate a pool called Bethesda in Aramaic, which has five covered walkways. A great number of sick, blind, lame, and paralyzed people were lying in these walkways. Now a man was there who had been disabled for thirty-eight years. When Jesus saw him lying there and when he realized that the man had been disabled a long time already, he said to him, "Do you want to become well?" The sick man answered him, "Sir, I have no one to put me into the pool when the water is stirred up. While I am trying to go into the water, someone else goes down before me." Jesus said to him, "Stand up! Pick up your mat and walk." Immediately the man was healed, and he picked up his mat and started walking. (Now that day was a Sabbath.)

So the Jewish authorities said to the man who had been healed, "It is the Sabbath, and you are not permitted to carry your mat." But he answered them, "The man who made me well said to me, 'Pick up your mat and walk.'" They asked him, "Who is the man who said to you, 'Pick up your mat and walk'?" But the man who had been healed did not know who it was, for Jesus had slipped out since there was a crowd in that place.

After this Jesus found him at the temple and said to him, "Look, you have become well. Don't sin any more, lest anything worse happen to you." The man went away and informed the Jewish authorities that Jesus was the one who had made him well.

We have in this passage one of the few miracles of Christ, which John records. Like every other miracle in this Gospel, it is described with great minuteness and particularity. And like more than one other miracle it leads on to a discourse full of singularly deep instruction.

We are taught, for one thing, in this passage, what misery sin has brought into the world. We read of a man who had been ill for no less than thirty-eight years! For thirty-eight weary summers and winters he had endured pain and infirmity. He had seen others healed at the waters of Bethesda, and going to their homes rejoicing. But for him there had been no healing. Friendless, helpless, and hopeless, he lay near the wonder-working waters, but derived no benefit from them. Year after year passed away, and left him still uncured. No relief or change for the better seemed likely to come, except from the grave.

When we read of cases of sickness like this, we should remember how deeply we ought to hate sin! Sin was the original root, and cause, and fountain of every disease in the world. God did not create man to be full of aches, and pains, and infirmities. These things are the fruits of the Fall. There would have been no sickness, if there had been no sin.

No greater proof can be shown of man's inbred unbelief, than his carelessness about sin. "Fools," says the wise man, "make a mock at sin." (Pro. 14:9.) Thousands delight in things which are explicitly evil, and run greedily after that which is downright poison. They love that which God abhors, and dislike that which God loves. They are like the madman, who loves his enemies and hates his friends. Their eyes are blinded. Surely if men would only look at hospitals and infirmaries, and think what havoc sin has made on this earth, they would never take pleasure in sin as they do.

Well may we be told to pray for the coming of God's kingdom! Well may we be told to long for the second advent of Jesus Christ! Then, and not until then, shall there be no more curse on the earth, no more suffering, no more sorrow, and no more sin. Tears shall be wiped from the faces of all who love Christ's appearing, when their Master returns. Weakness and infirmity shall all pass away. Hope deferred shall no longer make hearts sick. There will be no chronic invalids and incurable cases, when Christ has renewed this earth.

We are taught, for another thing, in this passage, how great is the mercy and compassion of Christ. He "saw" the poor sufferer lying in the crowd. Neglected, overlooked, and forgotten in the great multitude, he was observed by the all-seeing eye of Christ. "He knew" full well, by His Divine knowledge, how long he had been "in that case," and pitied him. He spoke to him unexpectedly, with words of gracious sympathy. He healed him by miraculous power, at once and without tedious delay, and sent him home rejoicing.

This is just one among many examples of our Lord Jesus Christ's kindness and compassion. He is full of undeserved, unexpected, abounding love towards man. "He delights in mercy." (Micah 7:18.) He is far more ready to save than man is to be saved, far more willing to do good than man is to receive it.

No one ever need be afraid of beginning the life of a true Christian, if he feels disposed to begin. Let him not hang back and delay, under the vain idea that Christ is not willing to receive him. Let him come boldly, and trust confidently. He who healed the cripple at Bethesda is still the same.

We are taught, lastly, the lesson that recovery from sickness ought to impress upon us. That lesson is contained in the solemn words which our Savior addressed to the man He had cured—"Sin no more, lest a worse thing come unto you."

Every sickness and sorrow is the voice of God speaking to us. Each has its peculiar message. Happy are they who have an eye to see God's hand, and an ear to hear His voice, in all that happens to them. Nothing in this world happens by chance.

And as it is with sickness, so it is with recovery. Renewed health should send us back to our post in the world with a deeper hatred of sin, a more thorough watchfulness over our own ways, and a more constant purpose of mind to live for God. Far too often the excitement and novelty of returning health tempt us to forget the vows and intentions of the sick-room. There are spiritual dangers attending a recovery! Well would it be for us all after illness to grave these words on our hearts, "Let me sin no more, lest a worse thing come unto me."

Let us leave the passage with grateful hearts, and bless God that we have such a Gospel and such a Savior as the Bible reveals. Are we ever sick and ill? Let us remember that Christ sees, and knows, and can heal as He thinks fit. Are we ever in trouble? Let us hear in our trouble the voice of God, and learn to hate sin more.

5:16-23

Responding to Jewish Authorities

Now because Jesus was doing these things on the Sabbath, the Jewish authorities began persecuting him. So Jesus told them, "My Father is working until now, and I too am working." For this reason the Jewish authorities were trying even harder to kill him, because not only was he breaking the Sabbath, but he was also calling God his own Father, thus making himself equal with God.

So Jesus answered them, "I tell you the solemn truth, the Son can do nothing on his own initiative, but only what he sees the Father doing. For whatever the Father does, the Son does likewise. For the Father loves the Son and shows him everything he does, and greater deeds than these he will show him, so that you may be amazed. For just as the Father raises the dead and gives them life, so also the Son gives life to whomever he wishes. Furthermore, the Father does not judge anyone, but has assigned all judgment to the Son, so that all people may honor the Son just as they honor the Father. The one who does not honor the Son does not honor the Father who sent him.

These verses begin one of the most deep and solemn passages in the four Gospels. They show us the Lord Jesus asserting His own Divine nature, His unity with God the Father, and the high dignity of His office. Nowhere does our Lord dwell so fully on these subjects as in the chapter before us. And nowhere, we must confess, do we find out so thoroughly the weakness of man's understanding! There is much, we must all feel, that is far beyond our comprehension in our Lord's account of Himself. Such knowledge, in short, is too astonishing for us. "It is high—we cannot attain unto it." (Psalm 139:6.) How often men say that they want clear explanations of such doctrines as the Trinity. Yet here we have our Lord handling the subject of His own Person, and, behold! we cannot follow Him. We seem only to touch His meaning with the tip of our fingers.

We learn, for one thing, from the verses before us, that there are some works which it is lawful to do on the Sabbath day.

The Jews, as on many other occasions, found fault because Jesus healed a man who had been ill for thirty-eight years, on the Sabbath. They charged our Lord with a breach of the fourth commandment.

Our Lord's reply to the Jews is very remarkable. "My Father," he says, "works hitherto, and I also work." It is as though He said—"Though my Father rested on the seventh day from His work of creation, He has never rested for a moment from His providential government of the world, and from His merciful work of supplying the daily needs of all His creatures. Were He to rest from such work, the whole frame of nature would stand still. And I also work works of mercy on the Sabbath day. I do not break the fourth commandment when I heal the sick, any more than my Father breaks it when He causes the sun to rise and the grass to grow on the Sabbath."

We must distinctly understand, that neither here nor elsewhere does the Lord Jesus overthrow the obligation of the fourth commandment. Neither here nor elsewhere is there a word to justify the vague assertions of some modern teachers, that "Christians ought not to keep a Sabbath," and that it is "a Jewish institution which has passed away." The utmost that our Lord does, is to place the claims of the Sabbath on the right foundation. He clears the day of rest from the false and superstitious teaching of the Jews, about the right way of observing it. He shows us clearly that works of necessity and works of mercy are no breach of the fourth commandment.

After all, the errors of Christians on this subject, in these latter days, are of a very different kind from those of the Jews. There is little danger of men keeping the Sabbath too strictly. The thing to be feared is the disposition to keep it loosely and partially, or not to keep it at all. The tendency of the age is not to exaggerate the fourth commandment, but to cut it out of the Decalogue, and throw it aside altogether. Against this tendency it becomes us all to be on our guard. The experience of eighteen centuries supplies abundant proofs that vital religion never flourishes when the Sabbath is not well kept.

We learn, for another thing, from these verses, the dignity and greatness of our Lord Jesus Christ.

The Jews, we are told, sought to kill Jesus because He said "that God was his Father, making himself equal with God." Our Lord, in reply, on this special occasion, enters very fully into the question of His own Divine nature. In reading His words, we must all feel that we are reading mysterious things, and treading on very holy ground. But we must feel a deep conviction, however little we may understand, that the things He says could never have been said by one who was only man. The Speaker is nothing less than "God manifest in the flesh. (1 Tim. 3:16.)

He asserts His own unity with God the Father. No other reasonable meaning can be put on the expressions—"The Son can do nothing of himself, but what he sees the Father do—for what things soever he does, these also does the Son likewise. The Father loves the Son, and shows him all things that himself does." Such language, however deep and high, appears to mean that in operation, and knowledge, and heart, and will, the Father and the Son are One—two Persons, but one God. Truths such as these are of course beyond man's power to explain particularly. Enough for us to believe and rest upon them.

He asserts, in the next place, His own Divine power to give life. He tells us, "The Son gives life to whom he will." Life is the highest and greatest gift that can be bestowed. It is precisely that thing that man, with all his cleverness, can neither give to the work of his hands, nor restore when taken away. But life, we are told, is in the hands of the Lord Jesus, to bestow and give at His discretion. Dead bodies and dead souls are both alike under His dominion. He has the keys of death and hell. In Him is life. He is the life. (John 1:4. Rev. 1:18.)

He asserts, in the last place, His own authority to judge the world. "The Father," we are told, "has committed all judgment unto the Son." All power and authority over the world is committed to Christ's hands. He is the King and the Judge of mankind. Before Him every knee shall bow, and every tongue shall confess that he is Lord. He that was once despised and rejected of man, condemned and crucified as a malefactor, shall one day hold a great judgment, and judge all the world. "God shall judge the secrets of man by Jesus Christ." (Rom. 2:16.)

And now let us think whether it is possible to make too much of Christ in our religion. If we have ever thought so, let us cast aside the thought forever. Both in His Own nature as God, and in His office as commissioned Mediator, He is worthy of all honor. He that is one with the Father—the Giver of life—the King of kings—the coming Judge, can never be too much exalted. "The one who does not honor the Son, does not honor the Father who sent him."

If we desire salvation, let us lean our whole weight on this mighty Savior. So leaning, we never need be afraid. Christ is the rock of ages, and he that builds on Him shall never be confounded—neither in sickness, nor in death, nor in the judgment-day. The hand that was nailed to the cross is almighty! The Savior of sinners is "mighty to save." (Isaiah 63:1)

5:24-29

"I tell you the solemn truth, the one who hears my message and believes the one who sent me, has eternal life and will not be condemned, but has crossed over

from death to life. I tell you the solemn truth, a time is coming and is now here when the dead will hear the voice of the Son of God, and those who hear will live. For just as the Father has life in himself, thus he has granted the Son to have life in himself, and he granted the Son authority to execute judgment because he is the Son of Man.

"Do not be amazed at this, because a time is coming when all who are in the tombs will hear his voice and will come out—the ones who have done what is good to the resurrection resulting in life, and the ones who have done what is evil to the resurrection resulting in damnation.

The passage before us is singularly rich in weighty truths. To the minds of Jews, who were familiar with the writings of Moses and Daniel, it would come home with peculiar power. In the words of our Lord they would not fail to see fresh assertions of His claim to be received as the promised Messiah.

We see in these verses that the salvation of our soul depends on hearing Christ. It is the man, we are told, who "hears Christ's word," and believes that God the Father sent Him to save sinners, who "has everlasting life." Such "hearing" of course is something more than mere listening. It is hearing as a humble learner—hearing as an obedient disciple—hearing with faith and love-hearing with a heart ready to do Christ's will—this is the hearing that saves. It is the very hearing of which God spoke in the famous prediction of a "prophet like unto Moses"—"Unto him shall you hearken."—"Whoever will not hearken unto my words which he shall speak in my name, I will require it of him." (Deut. 18:15-19.)

To "hear" Christ in this way, we must never forget, is just as needful now as it was eighteen hundred years ago. It is not enough to hear sermons, and run after preachers, though some people seem to think this makes up the whole of religion. We must go much further than this—we must "hear Christ." To submit our hearts to Christ's teaching—to sit humbly at His feet by faith, and learn of Him—to enter His school as penitents, and become His believing scholars—to hear His voice and follow Him—this is the way to heaven. Until we know something experimentally of these things, there is no life in us.

We see, secondly, in these verses, how rich and full are the privileges of the true hearer and believer. Such a man enjoys a present salvation. Even now, at this present time, he "has everlasting life." Such a man is completely justified and forgiven. There remains no more condemnation for him. His sins are put away. "He shall not come into condemnation." Such a man is in an entirely new position before God. He is like one who has moved from one side of a gulf to another; "He has passed from death unto life."

The privileges of a true Christian are greatly underrated by many. Chiefly from deplorable ignorance of Scripture, they have little idea of the spiritual treasures of every believer in Jesus. These treasures are brought together here in beautiful order, if we will only look at them. One of a true Christian's treasures is the "presentness" of his salvation. It is not a far distant thing which he is to have at last, if he does his duty and is good. It is his own in title the moment he believes. He is already pardoned, forgiven, and saved, though not in heaven. Another of a true Christian's treasures is the "completeness" of his justification. His sins are entirely removed, taken away, and blotted out of God's book, by Christ's blood. He may look forward to judgment without fear, and say, "who is he that condemns?" (Rom. 8:34.) He shall stand without fault before the throne of God. The last, but not the least, of a true Christian's treasures, is the entire change in his relation and position toward God. He is no longer as one dead before Him—dead, legally, like a man sentenced to die, and dead in heart. He is "alive unto God." (Rom. 6:11.) "He is a new creature. Old things are passed away, and all things are become new." (2 Cor. 5:17.) Well would it be for Christians if these things were better known! It is lack of knowledge, in many cases, that is the secret of lack of peace.

We see, thirdly, in these verses, a striking declaration of Christ's power to give life to dead souls. Our Lord tells us that "the hour is coming and now is, when the dead shall hear the voice of the Son of God; and those who hear shall live." It seems most unlikely that these words were meant to be confined to the rising of men's bodies, and were fulfilled by such miracles as that of raising Lazarus from the grave. It appears far more probable that what our Lord had in view was the quickening of souls, the resurrection of conversion. (Ephes. 2:1; Colos. 2:13.)

The words were fulfilled in not a few cases, during our Lord's own ministry. They were fulfilled far more completely after the day of Pentecost, through the ministry of the Apostles. The myriads of converts at Jerusalem, at Antioch, at Ephesus, at Corinth, and elsewhere, were all examples of their fulfillment. In all these cases, "the voice of the Son of God" awakened dead hearts to spiritual life, and made them feel their need of salvation, repent, and believe. They are fulfilled at this very day, in every instance of true conversion. Whenever any men or women among ourselves awaken to a sense of their soul's value, and become alive to God, the words are made good before our eyes. It is Christ who has spoken to their hearts by His Spirit. It is "the dead hearing Christ's voice, and living."

We see, lastly, in these verses, a most solemn prophecy of the final resurrection of all the dead. Our Lord tells us that "the hour is coming when all that are in the grave shall hear his voice, and shall come forth; those who have done good to the resurrection of life, and those who have done evil to the resurrection of damnation."

The passage is one of those that ought to sink down very deeply into our hearts, and never be forgotten. All is not over when men die. Whether they like it or not, they will have to come forth from their graves at the last day, and to stand at Christ's judgment bar. None can escape His summons. When His voice calls them before Him, all must obey. When men rise again, they will not all rise in the same condition. There will be two classes—two parties—two groups of people. Not all will go to heaven. Not all will be saved. Some will rise again to inherit eternal life, but some will rise again only to be condemned. These are alarming things! But the words of Christ are plain and unmistakable. Thus it is written, and thus it must be.

Let us make sure that we hear Christ's quickening voice now, and are numbered among His true disciples. Let us know the privileges of true believers, while we have life and health. Then, when His voice shakes heaven and earth, and is calling the dead from their graves, we shall feel confidence, and not be "ashamed before Him at his coming." (1 John 2:28.)

5:30-39

I can do nothing on my own initiative. Just as I hear, I judge, and my judgment is just, because I do not seek my own will, but the will of the one who sent me.

"If I testify about myself, my testimony is not true. There is another who testifies about me, and I know the testimony he testifies about me is true. You have sent to John, and he has testified to the truth. (I do not accept human testimony, but I say this so that you may be saved.) He was a lamp that was burning and shining, and you wanted to rejoice greatly for a short time in his light.

"But I have a testimony greater than that from John. For the deeds that the Father has assigned me to complete—the deeds I am now doing—testify about me that the Father has sent me. And the Father who sent me has himself testified about me. You people have never heard his voice nor seen his form at any time, nor do you have his word residing in you, because you do not believe the one whom he

sent. You study the scriptures thoroughly because you think in them you possess eternal life, and it is these same scriptures that testify about me.

In these verses we see the proof of our Lord Jesus Christ being the promised Messiah, set forth before the Jews in one view. Four different witnesses are brought forward. Four kinds of evidence are offered. His Father in heaven–His forerunner, John the Baptist—the miraculous works He had done—the Scriptures, which the Jews professed to honor—each and all are named by our Lord, as testifying that He was the Christ, the Son of God. Hard must those hearts have been which could hear such testimony; and yet remain unmoved! But it only proves the truth of the old saying—that unbelief does not arise so much from lack of evidence, as from lack of will to believe.

Let us observe for one thing in this passage, the honor Christ puts on His faithful SERVANTS. See how He speaks of John the Baptist. "He bore witness of the truth"—"He was a burning and a shining light." John had probably passed away from his earthly labors when these words were spoken. He had been persecuted, imprisoned, and put to death by Herod–none interfering, none trying to prevent his murder. But this murdered disciple was not forgotten by his Divine Master. If no one else remembered him, Jesus did. He had honored Christ, and Christ honored him.

These things ought not to be overlooked. They are written to teach us that Christ cares for all His believing people, and never forgets them. Forgotten and despised by the world, perhaps, they are never forgotten by their Savior. He knows where they dwell, and what their trials are. A book of remembrance is written for them. "Their tears are all in His bottle." (Psalm 56:8.) Their names are engraved on the palms of His hands. He notices all they do for Him in this evil world, though they think it not worth notice, and He will confess it one day publicly, before His Father and the holy angels. He that bore witness to John the Baptist never changes. Let believers remember this. In their worst estate they may boldly say with David—"I am poor and needy; yet the Lord thinks upon me." (Psalm 40:17.)

Let us observe, for another thing, the honor Christ puts upon MIRACLES, as an evidence of His being the Messiah. He says—"The works which the Father has given me to finish, the same works that I do, bear witness of me that the Father has sent me."

The miracles of the Lord receive far less attention, in the present day, as proofs of His Divine mission, than they ought to do. Too many regard them with a silent incredulity, as things which, not having seen, they cannot be expected to care for. Not a few openly avow that they do not believe in the possibility of such things as miracles, and would like to strike them out of the Bible as weak stories, which, like burdensome lumber, should be cast overboard, to lighten the ship.

But, after all, there is no getting over the fact, that in the days when our Lord was upon earth, His miracles produced an immense effect on the minds of men. They aroused attention to Him who worked them. They excited inquiry, if they did not convert. They were so many, so public, and so incapable of being explained away, that our Lord's enemies could only say that they were done by satanic agency. That they were done, they could not deny. "This man," they said, "does many miracles." (John 11:47.) The facts which wise men pretend to deny now, no one pretended to deny eighteen hundred years ago.

Let the enemies of the Bible take our Lord's last and greatest miracle. His own resurrection from the dead and disprove it if they can. When they have done that, it will be time to consider what they say about miracles in general. They have never answered the evidence of it yet, and they never will. Let the friends of the Bible not be moved by objections against miracles, until that one miracle has been fairly disposed of. If that is proved unassailable, they need not care much for quibbling arguments against other miracles. If Christ did really rise from the dead by His own power, there is none of His mighty works which man need hesitate to believe.

Let us observe, lastly, in these verses, the honor that Christ puts upon the SCRIPTURE. He refers to them in concluding His list of evidences, as the great witnesses to Him. "Search the Scriptures," He says—"these are they which testify of me."

The "Scriptures" of which our Lord speaks are of course the Old Testament. And His words show the important truth which too many are apt to overlook, that every part of our Bibles is meant to teach us about Christ. Christ is not merely in the Gospels and Epistles. Christ is to be found directly and indirectly in the Law, the Psalms, and the Prophets. In the promises to Adam, Abraham, Moses, and David—in the types and emblems of the ceremonial law—in the predictions of Isaiah and the other prophets—Jesus, the Messiah, is everywhere to be found in the Old Testament.

How is it that men see these things so little? The answer is plain. They do not "search the Scriptures." They do not dig into that wondrous mine of wisdom and knowledge, and seek to become acquainted with its contents. Simple, regular reading of our Bibles is the grand secret of establishment in the faith. Ignorance of the Scriptures is the root of all error.

And now what will men believe, if they do not believe the Divine mission of Christ? Great indeed is the obstinacy of infidelity. A cloud of witnesses testify that Jesus was the Son of God. To talk of lacking evidence is childish folly. The plain truth is, that the chief seat of unbelief is the heart. Many do not wish to believe, and therefore remain unbelievers.

5:40-47

"But you are not willing to come to me so that you may have life.

I do not accept praise from people, but I know you, that you do not have the love of God within you. I have come in my Father's name, and you do not accept me. If someone else comes in his own name, you will accept him. How can you believe, if you accept praise from one another and don't seek the praise that comes from the only God?

"Do not suppose that I will accuse you before the Father. The one who accuses you is Moses, in whom you have placed your hope. If you believed Moses, you would believe me, because he wrote about me. But if you do not believe what Moses wrote, how will you believe my words?"

This passage concludes our Lord Jesus Christ's wondrous defense of His own divine mission. It is a conclusion worthy of the defense, full of heart-searching appeals to the consciences of His enemies, and rich in deep truths. A mighty sermon is followed by a mighty application.

Let us mark, in this passage, the reason why many souls are lost. The Lord Jesus says to the unbelieving Jews—"You will not come to me that you might have life."

These words are a golden sentence, which ought to be engraved in our memories, and treasured up in our minds. It is lack of will to come to Christ for salvation that will be found, at last, to have shut the many out of heaven. It is not men's sins. All manner of sin may be forgiven. It is not any decree of God. We are not told in the Bible of any whom God has only created to be destroyed. It is not any limit in Christ's work of redemption. He has paid a price sufficient for all mankind. It is something far more than this. It is man's own innate unwillingness to come to Christ, repent, and believe. Either from pride, or laziness, or love of sin, or love of the world, the many have no mind, or wish, or heart, or desire to seek life in Christ. "God has given to us eternal life, and this life is in his Son." (1 John 5:11.) But men stand still, and will not stir hand or foot to get life. And this is the whole reason why many of the lost are not saved.

This is a painful and solemn truth, but one that we can never know too well. It contains a first principle in Christian theology. Thousands, in every age, are constantly laboring to shift the blame of their condition from off themselves. They talk of their inability to change. They tell you complacently, that they cannot help being what they are! They know, undeniably, that they are wrong, but they cannot be different! It will not do. Such talk will not stand the test of the Word of Christ before us. The unconverted are what they are because they have no will to be better. "Light has come into the world, and men love darkness rather than light." (John 3:19.) The words of the Lord Jesus will silence many—"I would have gathered you, and you would not be gathered." (Matt. 23:37.)

Let us mark, secondly, in this passage, one principal cause of unbelief. The Lord Jesus says to the Jews, "How can you believe which receive honor one of another, and seek not the honor that comes of God only?" He meant by that saying, that they were not honest in their religion. With all their apparent desire to hear and learn, they cared more in reality for pleasing man than God. In this state of mind they were never likely to believe.

A deep principle is contained in this saying of our Lord's, and one that deserves special attention. True faith does not depend merely on the state of man's head and understanding, but on the state of his heart. His mind may be convinced. His conscience may be pierced. But so long as there is anything the man is secretly loving more than God, there will be no true faith. The man himself may be puzzled, and wonder why he does not believe. He does not see that he is like a child sitting on the lid of his box, and wishing to open it, but not considering that his own weight keeps it shut. Let a man make sure that he honestly and really desires first the praise of God. It is the lack of an honest heart which makes many stick fast in their false religion all their days, and die at length without peace. Those who complain that they hear, and approve, and assent, but make no progress, and cannot get any hold on Christ, should ask themselves this simple question—"Am I honest? Am I sincere? Do I really desire first the praise of God?"

Let us mark, lastly, in this passage, the manner in which Christ speaks of MOSES. He says to the Jews, "Had you believed Moses you would have believed me—for he wrote of me."

These words demand our special attention in these latter days. That there really was such a person as Moses—that he really was the author of the writings commonly ascribed to him—on both these points our Lord's testimony is distinct. "He wrote of me." Can we suppose for a moment that our Lord was only accommodating Himself to the prejudices and traditions of His hearers, and that He spoke of Moses as a writer, though He knew in His heart that Moses never wrote at all? Such an idea is profane. It would make out our Lord to have been dishonest. Can we suppose for a moment that our Lord was ignorant about Moses, and did not know the wonderful discoveries which learned men, falsely so called, have made in the nineteenth century? Such an idea is ridiculous blasphemy. To imagine the Lord Jesus speaking ignorantly in such a chapter as the one before us, is to strike at the root of all Christianity. There is but one conclusion about the matter. There was such a person as Moses. The writings commonly ascribed to him were written by him. The facts recorded in them are worthy of all credit. Our Lord's testimony is an unanswerable argument. The skeptical writers against Moses and the Pentateuch have greatly erred.

Let us beware of handling the Old Testament irreverently, and allowing our minds to doubt the truth of any part of it, because of alleged difficulties. The simple fact that the writers of the New Testament continually refer to the Old Testament, and speak even of the most miraculous events recorded in it as undoubtedly true, should silence our doubts. Is it at all likely, probable, or credible, that we of the nineteenth century are better informed about Moses than Jesus and His Apostles? God forbid that we should think so! Then let us stand fast, and not doubt that every word in the Old Testament, as well as in the New, was given by inspiration of God.

Chapter 6

*A*fter this Jesus went away to the other side of the Sea of Galilee (also called the Sea of Tiberias). A large crowd was following him because they were observing the miraculous signs he was performing on the sick. So Jesus went on up the mountainside and sat down there with his disciples. (Now the Jewish feast of the Passover was near.) Then Jesus, when he looked up and saw that a large crowd was coming to him, said to Philip, "Where can we buy bread so that these people may eat?" (Now Jesus said this to test him, for he knew what he was going to do.) Philip replied, "Two hundred silver coins worth of bread would not be enough for them, for each one to get a little." One of Jesus' disciples, Andrew, Simon Peter's brother, said to him, "Here is a boy who has five barley loaves and two fish, but what good are these for so many people?"

Jesus said, "Have the people sit down." (Now there was a lot of grass in that place.) So the men sat down, about five thousand in number. Then Jesus took the loaves, and when he had given thanks, he distributed the bread to those who were seated. He then did the same with the fish, as much as they wanted. When they were all satisfied, Jesus said to his disciples, "Gather up the broken pieces that are left over, so that nothing is wasted." So they gathered them up and filled twelve baskets with broken pieces from the five barley loaves left over by the people who had eaten.

So when the people saw the miraculous sign that Jesus performed, they began to say to one another, "This is certainly the Prophet who is to come into the world."

These verses describe one of our Lord's most remarkable miracles. Of all the great works that He did, none was done so publicly as this, and before so many witnesses. Of all the miracles related in the Gospels, this is the only one which all the four Gospel-writers alike record. This fact alone (like the four times repeated account of the crucifixion and resurrection) is enough to show that it is a miracle demanding special attention.

We have, for one thing, in this miracle, a lesson about Christ's almighty power. We see our Lord feeding five thousand men with "five barley loaves and two small fish." We see clear proof that a miraculous event took place in the "twelve baskets of fragments" that remained after all had eaten. Creative power was manifestly exercised. Food was called into existence that did not exist before. In healing the sick, and raising the dead, something was amended or restored that had already existed. In feeding five thousand men with five loaves, something must have been created which before had no existence.

Such a history as this ought to be specially instructive and encouraging to all who endeavor to do good to souls. It shows us the Lord Jesus "able to save to the uttermost." He is One who has all power over dead hearts. Not only can He mend that which is broken—build up that which is ruined—heal that which is sick—strengthen that which is weak. He can do even greater things than these. He can call into being that which was not before, and call it out of nothing. We must never despair of any one being saved. So long as there is life there is hope. Reason and sense may say that some poor sinner is too hardened, or too old to be converted. Faith will reply—"Our Master can create as well as renew. With a Savior who, by His Spirit, can create a new heart, nothing is impossible."

We have, for another thing, in this miracle, a lesson about the office of ministers. We see the apostles receiving the bread from our Lord's hands, after He had blessed it, and distributing it to the multitude. It was not their hands that made it increase and multiply, but their Master's. It was His almighty power that provided an unfailing supply. It was their work to receive humbly, and distribute faithfully.

Now here is a lively emblem of the work which a true minister of the New Testament is meant to do. He is not a mediator between God and man. He has no power to put away sin, or impart grace. His whole business is to receive the bread of life which his Master provides, and to distribute it among the souls among whom he labors. He cannot make men value the bread, or receive it. He cannot make it soul-saving, or life-giving, to anyone. This is not his work. For this he is not responsible. His whole business is to be a faithful distributor of the food which his Divine Master has provided; and that done, his office is discharged.

We have, lastly, in this miracle, a lesson about the sufficiency of the Gospel for the needs of all mankind. We see the Lord Jesus supplying the hunger of a huge multitude of five thousand men. The provision seemed, at first sight, utterly inadequate for the occasion. To satisfy so many craving mouths with such scanty fare, in such a wilderness, seemed impossible. But the event showed that there was enough and to spare. There was not one who could complain that he was not filled.

There can be no doubt that this was meant to teach the adequacy of Christ's Gospel to supply the necessities of the whole world. Weak, and feeble, and foolish as it may seem to man, the simple story of the Cross is enough for all the children of Adam in every part of the globe. The tidings of Christ's death for sinners, and the atonement made by that death, is able to meet the hearts and satisfy the consciences of all nations, and peoples, and kindreds, and tongues. Carried by faithful messengers, it feeds and supplies all ranks and classes. "The preaching of the cross is to those who perish foolishness, but to us who are saved it is the power of God." (1 Cor. 1:18.) Five barley loaves and two small fishes seemed scanty provision for a hungry crowd. But blessed by Christ, and distributed by His disciples, they were more than sufficient.

Let us never doubt for a moment, that the preaching of Christ crucified—the old story of His blood, and righteousness, and substitution—is enough for all the spiritual necessities of all mankind. It is not worn out. It is not obsolete. It has not lost its power. We need nothing new—nothing more broad and kind-nothing more intellectual—nothing more effectual. We need nothing but the true bread of life, distributed faithfully among starving souls. Let men sneer or ridicule as they will. Nothing else can do good in this sinful world. No other teaching can fill hungry consciences, and give them peace. We are all in a wilderness. We must feed on Christ crucified, and the atonement made by His death, or we shall die in our sins.

6:15-21

Walking on Water

Then Jesus, because he knew they were going to come and seize him by force to make him king, withdrew again up the mountainside alone.

Now when evening came, his disciples went down to the lake, got into a boat, and started to cross the lake to Capernaum. (It had already become dark, and Jesus had not yet come to them.) By now a strong wind was blowing and the sea was getting rough. Then when they had rowed about three or four miles, they caught sight of Jesus walking on the lake, approaching the boat, and they were frightened. But he said to them, "It is I. Do not be afraid." Then they wanted to take him into the boat, and immediately the boat came to the land where they had been heading.

We should notice, in these verses, our Lord Jesus Christ's humility. We are told that, after feeding the multitude, He "perceived that they would come and take him by force to make him a king." At once He departed, and left them. He wanted no such honors as these. He had come, "not to be ministered unto, but, to minister and to give his life a ransom for many." (Matt. 20:28.)

We see the same spirit and frame of mind all through our Lord's earthly ministry. From His cradle to His grave He was "clothed with humility." (1 Pet. 5:5.) He was born of a poor woman, and spent the first thirty years of His life in a carpenter's house at Nazareth. He was followed by poor companions-many of them no better than fishermen. He was poor in his manner of living-"The foxes had holes, and the birds of the air their nests—but the Son of man had not where to lay his head" (Matt. 8:20.) When He went on the Sea of Galilee, it was in a borrowed boat. When He rode into Jerusalem, it was on a borrowed donkey. When He was buried, it was in a borrowed tomb. "Though he was rich, yet for our sakes he became poor." (2 Cor. 8:9.)

The example is one which ought to be far more remembered than it is. How common are pride, and ambition, and high-mindedness! How rare are humility and lowly-mindedness! How few ever refuse greatness when offered to them! How many are continually seeking great things for themselves, and forgetting the injunction—"Seek them not!" (Jer. 45:5.) Surely it was not for nothing that our Lord, after washing the disciples' feet, said—"I have given you an example that you should do as I have done." (John 13:15.) There is little, it may be feared, of that feet-washing spirit among Christians. But whether men will hear or forbear, humility is the queen of the graces. "Tell me," it has been said, "how much humility a man has, and I will tell you how much religion he has." Humility is the first step toward heaven, and the true way to honor. "He that humbles himself shall be exalted." (Luke 18:14.)

We should notice, secondly, in these verses, the trials through which Christ's disciples had to pass. We are told that they were sent over the lake by themselves, while their Master tarried behind. And then we see them alone in a dark night, tossed about by a great wind on stormy waters, and, worst of all, Christ not with them. It was a strange transition. From witnessing a mighty miracle, and helping it instrumentally, amid an admiring crowd, to solitude, darkness, winds, waves, storm, anxiety, and danger, the change was very great! But Christ knew it, and Christ appointed it, and it was working for their good.

Trial, we must distinctly understand, is part of the diet which all true Christians must expect. It is one of the means by which their grace is proved, and by which they find out what there is in themselves. Winter as well as summer-cold as well as heat—clouds as well as sunshine—are all necessary to bring the fruit of the Spirit to ripeness and maturity. We do not naturally like this. We would rather cross the lake with calm weather and favorable winds, with Christ always by our side, and the sun shining down on our faces. But it may not be. It is not in this way that God's children are made "partakers of His holiness." (Heb. 12:10.) Abraham, and Jacob, and Moses, and David, and Job were all men of many trials. Let us be content to walk in their footsteps, and to drink of their cup. In our darkest hours we may seem to be left—but we are never really alone.

Let us notice, in the last place, our Lord Jesus Christ's power over the waves of the sea. He came to His disciples as they were rowing on the stormy lake, "walking on" the waters. He walked on them as easily as we walk on dry land. They bore Him as firmly as the pavement of the Temple, or the hills around Nazareth. That which is contrary to all natural reason was perfectly possible to Christ.

The Lord Jesus, we must remember, is not only the Lord, but the Maker of all creation. "All things were made by him; and without him was not anything made that was made." (John 1:3.) It was just as easy for Him to walk on the sea as to form the sea at the beginning—just as easy to suspend the common laws of nature, as they are called, as to impose those laws at the first. Learned men talk solemn nonsense sometimes about the eternal fixity of the "laws of nature," as if they were above God Himself, and could never be suspended. It is well to be reminded sometimes by such miracles as that before us, that these so-called "laws of nature" are neither immutable nor eternal. They had a beginning, and will one day have an end.

Let all true Christians take comfort in the thought that their Savior is Lord of waves and winds, of storms and tempests, and can come to them in the darkest hour, "walking upon the sea." There are waves of trouble far heavier than any on the Lake of Galilee. There are days of darkness which test the faith of the holiest Christian. But let us never despair if Christ is our Friend. He can come to our aid in an hour when we do not think, and in ways that we did not expect. And when He comes, all will be calm.

6:22-27

Jesus' Discourse About the Bread of Life

The next day the crowd that remained on the other side of the lake realized that only one small boat had been there, and that Jesus had not boarded it with his disciples, but that his disciples had gone away alone. But some boats from Tiberias came to shore near the place where they had eaten the bread after the Lord had given thanks. So when the crowd realized that neither Jesus nor his disciples were there, they got into the boats and came to Capernaum looking for Jesus.

When they found him on the other side of the lake, they said to him, "Rabbi, when did you get here?" Jesus replied, "I tell you the solemn truth, you are looking for me not because you saw miraculous signs, but because you ate all the loaves of bread you wanted. Do not work for the food that disappears, but for the food that remains to eternal life—the food that the Son of Man will give to you. For God the Father has put his seal of approval on him."

We should mark first, in this passage, what knowledge of man's heart our Lord Jesus Christ possesses. We see Him exposing the false motives of those who followed Him for the sake of the loaves and fishes. They had followed Him across the Lake of Galilee. They seemed at first sight ready to believe in Him, and do Him honor. But He knew the inward springs of their conduct, and was not deceived. "You seek me," He said, "not because you saw the miracles, but because you ate the loaves, and were filled."

The Lord Jesus, we should never forget, is still the same. He never changes. He reads the secret motives of all who profess and call themselves Christians. He knows exactly why they do all they do in their religion. The reasons why they go to Church, and why they receive the sacrament—why they attend family prayers, and why they keep Sunday holy—all are naked and opened to the eyes of the great Head of the Church. By Him actions are weighed as well as seen. "Man looks on the outward appearance, but the Lord looks at the heart." (1 Sam. 16:7.)

Let us be real, true, and sincere in our religion, whatever else we are. The sinfulness of hypocrisy is very great, but its folly is greater still. It is not hard to deceive ministers, relatives, and friends. A little decent outward profession will often go a long way. But it is impossible to deceive Christ.

"His eyes are as a flame of fire." (Rev. 1:14.) He sees us through and through. Happy are those who can say—"You, Lord, who know all things, know that we love you." (John 21:17.)

We should mark, secondly, in this passage, what Christ forbids. He told the crowds who followed Him so diligently for the loaves and fishes, "not to labor for the food that perishes." It was a remarkable saying, and demands explanation.

Our Lord, we may be sure, did not mean to encourage idleness. It would be a great mistake to suppose this hard labor was the appointed lot of Adam in Paradise. Labor was ordained to be man's occupation after the fall. Labor is honorable in all men. No one need be ashamed of belonging to "the working classes." Our Lord himself worked in the carpenter's shop at Nazareth. Paul wrought as a tent-maker with his own hands.

What our Lord did mean to rebuke was, that excessive attention to labor for the body, while the soul is neglected, which prevails everywhere in the world. What He reproved was, the common habit of laboring only for the things of time, and letting alone the things of eternity—of minding only the life that now is, and disregarding the life to come. Against this habit He delivers a solemn warning.

Surely, we must all feel our Lord did not say the words before us without good cause. They are a startling caution which should ring in the ears of many in these latter days. How many in every rank of life are doing the very thing against which Jesus warns us! They are laboring night and day for "the food that perishes," and doing nothing for their immortal souls. Happy are those who early learn the respective value of soul and body, and give the first and best place in their thoughts to salvation. One thing is needful. He that seeks first the kingdom of God, will never fail to find "all other things added to him." (Matt. 6:33.)

We should mark, thirdly, in this passage, what Christ advises. He tells us to "labor for the food that endures to everlasting life." He would have us take pains to find food and satisfaction for our souls. That food is provided in rich abundance in Him. But he that would have it must diligently seek it.

How are we to labor? There is but one answer. We must labor in the use of all appointed means. We must read our Bibles, like men digging for hidden treasure. We must wrestle earnestly in prayer, like men contending with a deadly enemy for life. We must take our whole heart to the house of God, and worship and hear like those who listen to the reading of a benefactor's will. We must fight daily against sin, the world, and the devil, like those who fight for liberty, and must conquer, or be slaves. These are the ways we must walk in if we would find Christ, and be found of Him. This is "laboring." This is the secret of getting on about our souls.

Labor like this no doubt is very uncommon. In carrying it on we shall have little encouragement from man, and shall often be told that we are "extreme," and go too far. Strange and absurd as it is, the natural man is always fancying that we may take too much thought about religion, and refusing to see that we are far more likely to take too much thought about the world. But whatever man may say, the soul will never get spiritual food without labor. We must "strive," we must "run," we must "fight," we must throw our whole heart into our soul's affairs. It is "the violent" who take the kingdom. (Matt. 11:12.)

We should mark, lastly, in this passage, what a promise Christ holds out. He tells us that He himself will give eternal food to all who seek it—"The Son of man shall give you the food that endures unto everlasting life."

How gracious and encouraging these words are! Whatever we need for the relief of our hungering souls, Christ is ready and willing to bestow. Whatever mercy, grace, peace, strength we require, the Son of man will give freely, immediately, abundantly, and eternally. He is "sealed," and appointed, and commissioned by God the Father for this very purpose. Like Joseph in the Egyptian famine, it is His office to be the Friend, and Benefactor, and Reliever of a sinful world. He is far more willing to give than man is to receive. The more sinners apply to Him, the better He is pleased.

And now, as we leave this rich passage, let us ask ourselves, what use we make of it? For what are we laboring ourselves? What do we know of lasting food and satisfaction for our inward man? Never let us rest until we have eaten of the food which Christ alone can give. Those who are content with any other spiritual food will sooner or later "lie down in sorrow." (Isa. 50:11.)

6:28-34

So then they said to him, "What must we do to accomplish the deeds God requires?" Jesus replied, "This is the deed God requires—to believe in the one whom he sent." So they said to him, "Then what miraculous sign will you perform, so that we may see it and believe you? What will you do? Our ancestors ate the manna in the wilderness, just as it is written, 'He gave them bread from heaven to eat.'"

Then Jesus told them, "I tell you the solemn truth, it is not Moses who has given you the bread from heaven, but my Father is giving you the true bread from heaven. For the bread of God is the one who comes down from heaven and gives life to the world." So they said to him, "Sir, give us this bread all the time!"

These verses form the beginning of one of the most remarkable passages in the Gospels. None, perhaps, of our Lord's discourses has occasioned more controversy, and been more misunderstood, than that which we find in the Sixth Chapter of John.

We should observe, for one thing, in these verses, the spiritual ignorance and unbelief of the natural man. Twice over we see this brought out and exemplified. When our Lord instructed his hearers to "labor for the food which endures to eternal life," they immediately began to think of 'works to be done', and a goodness of their own to be established. "What shall we do that we might work the works of God?" Doing, doing, doing, was their only idea of the way to heaven. Again, when our Lord spoke of Himself as One sent of God, and the need of believing on Him at once, they turn round with the question,"What sign show you? what do you work?" Fresh from the mighty miracle of the loaves and fishes, one might have thought they had had a sign sufficient to convince them. Taught by our Lord Jesus Christ himself, one might have expected a greater readiness to believe. But alas! there are no limits to man's dulness, prejudice, and unbelief in spiritual matters. It is a striking fact that the only thing which our Lord is said to have "marveled" at during His earthly ministry, was man's "unbelief." (Mark 6:6.)

We shall do well to remember this, if we ever try to do good to others in the matter of religion. We must not be cast down because our words are not believed, and our efforts seem thrown away. We must not complain of it as a strange thing, and suppose that the people we have to deal with are peculiarly stubborn and hard. We must recollect that this is the very cup of which our Lord had to drink, and like Him we must patiently work on. If even He, so perfect and so plain a Teacher, was not believed, what right have we to wonder if men do not believe us? Happy are the ministers, and missionaries, and teachers who keep these things in mind! It will save them much bitter disappointment. In working for God, it is of first importance to understand what we must expect in man. Few things are so little realized as the extent of human unbelief.

We should observe, for another thing, in these verses, the high honor Christ puts on faith in Himself. The Jews had asked Him—"What shall we do, that we might work the works of God?" In reply He says—"This is the work of God, that you believe on him whom he has sent." A truly striking and remarkable expression! If any two things are put in strong contrast, in the New Testament, they are faith and works. Not working, but believing, not of works, but through faith—are words familiar to all careful Bible-readers. Yet here the great Head of the Church declares that believing on Him is the highest and greatest of all "works!" It is "the work of God."

Doubtless our Lord did not mean that there is anything meritorious in believing. Man's faith, at the very best, is feeble and defective. Regarded as a "work," it cannot stand the severity of God's judgment, deserve pardon, or purchase heaven. But our Lord did mean that faith in Himself, as the only Savior, is the first act of the soul which God requires at a sinner's hands. Until a man believes on Jesus, and rests on Jesus as a lost sinner, he is nothing. Our Lord did mean that faith in Himself is that act of the soul which specially pleases God. When the Father sees a sinner casting aside his own righteousness, and simply trusting in His dear Son, He is well pleased. Without such faith it is impossible to please God. Our Lord did mean that faith in Himself is the root of all saving religion. There is no life in a man until he believes. Above all, our Lord did mean that faith in Himself is the hardest of all spiritual acts to the natural man. Did the Jews want something to do in religion? Let them know that the greatest thing they had to do was, to cast aside their pride, confess their guilt and need, and humbly believe.

Let all who know anything of true faith thank God and rejoice. Blessed are those who believe! It is an attainment which many of the wise of this world have never yet reached. We may feel ourselves to be poor, weak sinners. But do we believe? We may fail and come short in many things. But do we believe? He that has learned to feel his sins, and to trust Christ as a Savior, has learned the two hardest and greatest lessons in Christianity. He has been in the best of schools. He has been taught by the Holy Spirit.

We shall observe, lastly, in these verses, the far greater privileges of Christ's hearers than of those who lived in the times of Moses. Wonderful and miraculous as the manna was which fell from heaven, it was nothing in comparison to the true bread which Christ had to bestow on His disciples. He himself was the bread of God, who had come down from heaven to give life to the world. The bread which fell in the days of Moses could only feed and satisfy the body. The Son of man had come to feed the soul. The bread which fell in the days of Moses was only for the benefit of Israel. The Son of man had come to offer eternal life to the world. Those who ate the manna died and were buried, and many of them were lost forever. But those who ate the bread which the Son of man provided, would be eternally saved.

And now let us take heed to ourselves, and make sure that we are among those who eat the bread of God and live. Let us not be content with lazy waiting, but let us actually come to Christ, and eat the bread of life, and believe to the saving of our souls. The Jews could say—"Evermore give us this bread." But it may be feared they went no further. Let us never rest until, by faith, we have eaten this bread, and can say, "Christ is mine. I have tasted that the Lord is gracious. I know and feel that I am His."

6:35-40

Jesus said to them, "I am the bread of life. The one who comes to me will never go hungry, and the one who believes in me will never be thirsty. But I told you that you have seen me and still do not believe. Everyone whom the Father gives me will come to me, and the one who comes to me I will never send away. For I have come down from heaven not to do my own will but the will of the one who sent me. Now this is the will of the one who sent me—that I should not lose one person of every one he has given me, but raise them all up at the last day. For this is the will of my Father—for everyone who looks on the Son and believes in him to have eternal life, and I will raise him up at the last day."

Three of our Lord Jesus Christ's great sayings are strung together, like pearls, in this passage. Each of them ought to be precious to every true Christian. All taken together, they form a mine of truth, into which he that searches need never search in vain.

We have, first, in these verses, a saying of Christ about Himself. We read that Jesus said—"I am the bread of life—he that comes to me shall never hunger, and he that believes on me shall never thirst."

Our Lord would have us know that He himself is the appointed food of man's soul. The soul of every man is naturally starving and famishing through sin. Christ is given by God the Father, to be the Satisfier, the Reliever, and the Physician of man's spiritual need. In Him and His mediatorial office—in Him and His atoning death—in Him and His priesthood—in Him and His grace, love, and power—in Him alone will empty souls find their needs supplied. In Him there is life. He is "the bread of life."

With what divine and perfect wisdom this name is chosen! Bread is necessary food. We can manage tolerably well without many things on our table, but not without bread. So is it with Christ. We must have Christ, or die in our own sins. Bread is food that suits all. Some cannot eat meat, and some cannot eat vegetables. But all like bread. It is food both for the Queen and the pauper. So is it with Christ. He is just the Savior that meets the needs of every class. Bread is food that we need daily. Other kinds of food we take, perhaps, only occasionally. But we need bread every morning and evening in our lives. So is it with Christ. There is no day in our lives but we need His blood, His righteousness, His intercession, and His grace. Well may He be called, "The bread of life!"

Do we know anything of spiritual hunger? Do we feel anything of craving and emptiness in conscience, heart, and affections? Let us distinctly understand that Christ alone can relieve and supply us, and that it is His office to relieve. We must come to Him by faith. We must believe on Him, and commit our souls into His hands. So coming, He pledges His royal word we shall find lasting satisfaction both for time and eternity. It is written—"He that comes unto me shall never hunger, and he that believes on me shall never thirst."

We have, secondly, in these verses, a saying of Christ about those who come to Him. We read that Jesus said—"Him that comes to me I will never cast out."

What does "coming to Christ" mean? It means that movement of the soul which takes place when a man, feeling his sins, and finding out that he cannot save himself, hears of Christ, applies to Christ, trusts in Christ, lays hold on Christ, and leans all his weight on Christ for salvation. When this happens, a man is said, in Scripture language, to "come" to Christ.

What did our Lord mean by saying—"I will never cast him out"? He meant that He will not refuse to save any one who comes to Him, no matter what he may have been. His past sins may have been very great. His present weakness and infirmity may be very great. But does he come to Christ by faith? Then Christ will receive him graciously, pardon him freely, place him in the number of His dear children, and give him everlasting life.

These are golden words indeed! They have smoothed down many a dying pillow, and calmed many a troubled conscience. Let them sink down deeply into our memories, and abide there continually. A day will come when flesh and heart shall fail, and the world can help us no more. Happy shall we be in that day, if the Spirit witnesses with our spirit that we have really come to Christ!

We have, lastly, in these verses, a saying of Christ about the will of His Father. Twice overcome the solemn words—"This is the will of him that sent me." Once we are told it is His will, "that every one that sees the Son may have everlasting life." Once we are told it is His will that, "of all which he has given to Christ he shall lose nothing."

We are taught by these words that Christ has brought into the world a salvation open and free to everyone. Our Lord draws a picture of it, from the story of the bronze serpent, by which bitten Israelites in the wilderness were healed. Every one that chose to "look" at the bronze serpent might live. Just in the same way, everyone who desires eternal life may "look" at Christ by faith, and have it freely. There is no barrier, no limit, no restriction. The terms of the Gospel are wide and simple. Every one may "look and live."

We are taught, furthermore, that Christ will never allow any soul that is committed to Him to be lost and cast away. He will keep it safe, from grace to glory, in spite of the world, the flesh, and the devil. Not one bone of His mystical body shall ever be broken. Not one lamb of His flock shall ever be left behind in the wilderness. He will raise to glory, in the last day, the whole flock entrusted to His charge, and not one shall be found missing.

Let the true Christian feed on the truths contained in this passage, and thank God for them. Christ the Bread of life—Christ the Receiver of all who come to Him—Christ the Preserver of all believers—Christ is for every man who is willing to believe on Him, and Christ is the eternal possession of all who so believe. Surely this is glad tidings and good news!

6:41-51

Then the Jews who were hostile to Jesus began complaining about him because he said, "I am the bread that came down from heaven," and they said, "Isn't this Jesus the son of Joseph, whose father and mother we know? How can he now say, 'I have come down from heaven'?"

Jesus replied, "Do not complain about me to one another. No one can come to me unless the Father who sent me draws him, and I will raise him up at the last day. It is written in the prophets, 'And they shall all be taught by God.' Everyone who hears and learns from the Father comes to me. (Not that anyone has seen the Father except the one who is from God—he has seen the Father.) I tell you the solemn truth, the one who believes has eternal life. I am the bread of life. Your ancestors ate the manna in the wilderness, and they died. This is the bread that

*has come down from heaven, so that a person may eat from it and not die. I am
the living bread that came down from heaven. If anyone eats from this bread he
will live forever. The bread that I will give for the life of the world is my flesh.*

Truths of the weightiest importance follow each other in rapid succession in the chapter we are now reading. There are probably very few parts
of the Bible which contain so many "deep things" as the Sixth Chapter of
John. Of this the passage before as is a signal example.

We learn, for one thing, from this passage, that Christ's lowly condition, when He was upon earth, is a stumbling-block to the natural man. We
read that "the Jews murmured, because Jesus said, I am the bread that came
down from heaven. And they said, Is not this Jesus, the son of Joseph, whose
father and mother we know? How is it then that he says, I came down from
heaven?" Had our Lord come as a conquering king, with wealth and honors
to bestow on His followers, and mighty armies in His train, they would have
been willing enough to receive Him. But a poor, and lowly, and suffering
Messiah was an offence to them. Their pride refused to believe that such
an one was sent from God.

There is nothing that need surprise us in this. It is human nature showing
itself in its true colors. We see the same thing in the days of the Apostles.
Christ crucified was "to the Jews a stumbling-block, and to the Greeks
foolishness." (1 Cor. 1:23.) The cross was an offence to many wherever the
Gospel was preached. We may see the same thing in our own times. There
are thousands around us who loathe the distinctive doctrines of the Gospel
on account of their humbling character. They cannot tolerate the atonement, and the sacrifice, and the substitution of Christ. His moral teaching
they approve. His example and self-denial they admire. But speak to them
of Christ's blood—of Christ being made sin for us—of Christ's death being
the corner-stone of our hope—of Christ's poverty being our riches—and
you will find they hate these things with a deadly hatred. Truly the offence
of the cross is not yet ceased!

We learn, for another thing, from this passage, man's natural helplessness and inability to repent or believe. We find our Lord saying—"No man
can come unto me, except the Father who has sent me draws him." Until the
Father draws the heart of man by His grace, man will not believe.

The solemn truth contained in these words is one that needs careful
weighing. It is vain to deny that without the grace of God no one ever can
become a true Christian. We are spiritually dead, and have no power to give
ourselves life. We need a new principle put in us from above. Facts prove it.

Preachers see it. The Tenth Article of our own Church expressly declares it—"The condition of man after the fall of Adam is such that he cannot turn and prepare himself, by his own natural strength and good works, to faith and calling upon God." This witness is true.

But after all, of what does this inability of man consist? In what part of our inward nature does this impotence reside? Here is a point on which many mistakes arise. Forever let us remember that the will of man is the part of him which is in fault. His inability is not physical, but moral. It would not be true to say that a man has a real wish and desire to come to Christ, but no power to come. It would be far more true to say that a man has no power to come because he has no desire or wish. It is not true that he would come if he could. It is true that he could come if he would. The corrupt will—the secret disinclination—the lack of heart, are the real causes of unbelief. It is here the mischief lies. The power that we lack is a new will. It is precisely at this point that we need the "drawing" of the Father.

These things, no doubt, are deep and mysterious. By truths like these God proves the faith and patience of His people. Can they believe Him? Can they wait for a fuller explanation at the last day? What they see not now they shall see hereafter. One thing at any rate is abundantly clear, and that is—man's responsibility for his own soul. His inability to come to Christ does not make an end of his accountableness. Both things are equally true. If lost at last, it will prove to have been his own fault. His blood will be on his own head. Christ would have saved him, but he would not be saved. He would not come to Christ, that he might have life.

We learn, lastly, in this passage, that the salvation of a believer is a present thing. Our Lord Jesus Christ says—"Verily, verily, I say unto you, he that believes on me HAS everlasting life." Life, we should observe, is a present possession. It is not said that he shall have it at last, in the judgment day. It is now, even now, in this world, his property. He has it the very day that he believes.

The subject is one which it much concerns our peace to understand, and one about which errors abound. How many seem to think that forgiveness and acceptance with God are things which we cannot attain in this life—that they are things which are to be earned by a long course of repentance and faith and holiness—things which we may receive at the bar of God at last, but must never pretend to touch while we are in this world! It is a complete mistake to think so. The very moment a sinner believes on Christ he is justified and accepted. There is no condemnation for him. He has peace with

God, and that immediately and without delay. His name is in the book of life, however little he may be aware of it. He has a title to heaven, which death and hell and Satan cannot overthrow. Happy are those who know this truth! It is an essential part of the good news of the Gospel.

After all, the great point we have to consider is whether we believe. What shall it profit us that Christ has died for sinners, if we do not believe on Him? "He that believes on the Son has everlasting life—and he that believes not the Son shall not see life; but the wrath of God abides on him." (John 3:36.)

6:52-59

Then the Jews who were hostile to Jesus began to argue with one another, "How can this man give us his flesh to eat?"

Jesus said to them, "I tell you the solemn truth, unless you eat the flesh of the Son of Man and drink his blood, you have no life in yourselves. The one who eats my flesh and drinks my blood has eternal life, and I will raise him up on the last day. For my flesh is true food, and my blood is true drink. The one who eats my flesh and drinks my blood resides in me, and I in him. Just as the living Father sent me, and I live because of the Father, so the one who consumes me will live because of me. This is the bread that came down from heaven; it is not like the bread your ancestors ate, but then later died. The one who eats this bread will live forever." Jesus said these things while he was teaching in the synagogue in Capernaum.

Few passages of Scripture have been so painfully twisted and perverted as that which we have now read. The Jews are not the only people who have striven about its meaning. A sense has been put upon it, which it was never intended to bear. Fallen man, in interpreting the Bible, has an unhappy aptitude for turning food into poison. The things that were written for his benefit, he often makes an occasion for falling.

Let us first consider carefully, what these verses do NOT mean. The "eating and drinking" of which Christ speaks do not mean any literal eating and drinking. Above all, the words were not spoken with any reference to the Sacrament of the Lord's Supper. We may eat the Lord's Supper, and yet not eat and drink Christ's body and blood. We may eat and drink Christ's body and blood, and yet not eat the Lord's Supper. Let this never be forgotten.

The opinion here expressed may startle some who have not looked closely into the subject. But it is an opinion which is supported by three weighty reasons. For one thing, a literal "eating and drinking" of Christ's body and blood would have been an idea utterly revolting to all Jews, and flatly contradictory to an often-repeated precept of their law. For another thing, to take a literal view of "eating and drinking," is to interpose a bodily act between the soul of man and salvation. This is a thing for which there is no precedent in Scripture. The only things without which we cannot be saved are repentance and faith. Last, but not least, to take a literal view of "eating and drinking," would involve most blasphemous and profane consequences. It would shut out of heaven the penitent thief. He died long after these words were spoken, without any literal eating and drinking. Will any dare to say he had "no life" in Him? It would admit to heaven thousands of ignorant, godless communicants in the present day. They literally eat and drink, no doubt! But they have no eternal life, and will not be raised to glory at the last day. Let these reasons be carefully pondered.

The plain truth is, there is a melancholic anxiety in fallen man to put a carnal sense on Scriptural expressions, wherever he possibly can. He struggles hard to make religion a matter of forms and ceremonies—of doing and performing-of sacraments and ordinances—of sense and of sight. He secretly dislikes that system of Christianity which makes the state of the heart the principal thing, and labors to keep sacraments and ordinances in the second place. Happy is that Christian who remembers these things, and stands on his guard! Baptism and the Lord's supper, no doubt, are holy sacraments, and mighty blessings, when rightly used. But it is worse than useless to drag them in everywhere, and to see them everywhere in God's Word.

Let us next consider carefully, what these verses do mean. The expressions they contain are, no doubt, very remarkable. Let us try to get some clear notion of their meaning.

The "flesh and blood of the Son of man" mean that sacrifice of His own body, which Christ offered up on the cross, when He died for sinners. The atonement made by His death, the satisfaction made by his sufferings, as our Substitute, the redemption effected by His enduring the penalty of our sins in His own body on the tree—this seems to be the true idea that we should set before our minds.

The "eating and drinking," without which there is no life in us, means that reception of Christ's sacrifice which takes place when a man believes on Christ crucified for salvation. It is an inward and spiritual act of the heart, and has nothing to do with the body. Whenever a man, feeling his own guilt and sinfulness, lays hold on Christ, and trusts in the atonement made for him by Christ's death, at once he "eats the flesh of the Son of man, and drinks His blood." His soul feeds on Christ's sacrifice, by faith, just as his body would feed on bread. Believing, he is said to "eat." Believing, he is said to "drink." And the special thing that he eats, and drinks, and gets benefit from, is the atonement made for his sins by Christ's death for him on Calvary.

The practical lessons which may be gathered from the whole passage are weighty and important. The point being once settled, that "the flesh and blood" in these verses means Christ's atonement, and the "eating and drinking" mean faith, we may find in these verses great principles of truth, which lie at the very root of Christianity.

We may learn, that faith in Christ's atonement is a thing of absolute necessity to salvation. Just as there was no safety for the Israelite in Egypt who did not eat the passover-lamb, in the night when the first-born were slain, so there is no life for the sinner who does not eat the flesh of Christ and drink His blood.

We may learn that faith in Christ's atonement unites us by the closest possible bonds to our Savior, and entitles us to the highest privileges. Our souls shall find full satisfaction for all their needs—"His flesh is food indeed, and His blood is drink indeed." All things are secured to us that we can need for time and eternity—"Whoever eats my flesh and drinks my blood has eternal life, and I will raise him up at the last day."

Last, but not least, we may learn that faith in Christ's atonement is a personal act, a daily act, and an act that can be felt. No one can eat and drink for us, and no one, in like manner, can believe for us. We need food every day, and not once a week or once a month—and, in like manner, we need to employ faith every day. We feel benefit when we have eaten and drunk, we feel strengthened, nourished, and refreshed; and, in like manner, if we believe truly, we shall feel the better for it, by sensible hope and peace in our inward man.

Let us take heed that we use these truths, as well as know them. The food of this world, for which so many take thought, will perish in the using, and not feed our souls. He only that eats of "the bread that came down from heaven" shall live forever.

6:60-65

Many Followers Depart

Then many of his disciples, when they heard these things, said, "This is a difficult saying! Who can understand it?" When Jesus was aware that his disciples were complaining about this, he said to them, "Does this cause you to be offended? Then what if you see the Son of Man ascending where he was before? The Spirit is the one who gives life; human nature is of no help! The words that I have spoken to you are spirit and are life. But there are some of you who do not believe." (For Jesus had already known from the beginning who those were who did not believe, and who it was who would betray him.) So Jesus added, "Because of this I told you that no one can come to me unless the Father has enabled him to come."

We learn from these verses that some of Christ's sayings seem hard to flesh and blood. We are told that "many" who had followed our Lord for a season, were offended when He spoke of "eating his flesh and drinking his blood." They murmured and said, "This is an hard saying; who can accept it?"

Murmurs and complaints of this kind are very common. It must never surprise us to hear them. They have been, they are, they will be as long as the world stands. To some Christ's sayings appear hard to understand. To others, as in the present case, they appear hard to believe, and harder still to obey. It is just one of the many ways in which the natural corruption of man shows itself. So long as the heart is naturally proud, worldly, unbelieving, and fond of self-indulgence, if not of sin, so long there will never be lacking people who will say of Christian doctrines and precepts, "These are hard sayings; who can hear them?"

Humility is the frame of mind which we should labor and pray for, if we would not be offended by scriptural teaching. If we find any of Christ's sayings hard to understand, we should humbly remember our present ignorance, and believe that we shall know more by and bye. If we find any of His sayings difficult to obey, we should humbly recollect that He will never require of us impossibilities, and that what He bids us do, He will give us grace to perform.

We learn, secondly, from these verses, that we must beware of putting a carnal meaning on spiritual words. We read that our Lord said to the murmuring Jews who stumbled at the idea of eating His flesh and drinking His blood, "It is the Spirit who gives life; the flesh profits nothing—the words that I speak unto you, they are spirit and they are life."

It is useless to deny that this verse is full of difficulties. It contains expressions "hard to be understood." It is far more easy to have a general impression of the meaning of the whole sentence, than to explain it word by word. Some things nevertheless we can see clearly and grasp firmly. Let us consider what they are.

Our Lord says, "It is the Spirit who gives life." By this He means that it is the Holy Spirit who is the special author of spiritual life in man's soul. By His agency it is first imparted, and afterwards sustained and kept up. If the Jews thought He meant that man could have spiritual life by bodily eating or drinking, they were greatly mistaken.

Our Lord says, "The flesh profits nothing." By this He means that neither His flesh nor any other flesh, literally eaten, can do good to the soul. Spiritual benefit is not to be had through the mouth, but through the heart. The soul is not a material thing, and cannot therefore be nourished by material food.

Our Lord says, "the words that I speak unto you, they are spirit and they are life." By this He signifies that His words and teachings, applied to the heart by the Holy Spirit, are the true means of producing spiritual influence and conveying spiritual life. By words thoughts are begotten and aroused. By words mind and conscience are stirred. And Christ's words especially are spirit-stirring and life-giving.

The principle contained in this verse, however faintly we may grasp its full meaning, deserves peculiar attention in these times. There is a tendency in many minds to attach an excessive importance to the outward and visible or "doing" part of religion. They seem to think that the sum and substance of Christianity consists in Baptism and the Supper of the Lord, in public ceremonies and forms, in appeals to the eye and ear and bodily excitement. Surely they forget that it is "the Spirit who gives live," and that the "flesh profits nothing." It is not so much by noisy public demonstrations, as by the still quiet work of the Holy Spirit on hearts that God's cause prospers. It is Christ's words entering into consciences, which "are spirit and life."

We learn, lastly, from these verses, that Christ has a perfect knowledge of the hearts of men. We read that "He know from the beginning who they were that believed not, and who should betray him."

Sentences like this are found so frequently in the Gospels that we are apt to underrate their importance. Yet there are few truths which we shall find it so good for our souls to remember as that which is contained in the sentence before us. The Savior with whom we have to do is one who knows all things!

What light this throws on the marvelous patience of the Lord Jesus in the days of His earthly ministry! He knew the sorrow and humiliation before Him, and the manner of His death. He knew the unbelief and treachery of some who professed to be His familiar friends. But "for the joy that was set before Him" he endured it all. (Heb. 12:2.)

What light this throws on the folly of hypocrisy and false profession in religion! Let those who are guilty of it recollect that they cannot deceive Christ. He sees them, knows them, and will expose them at the last day, except they repent. Whatever we are as Christians, and however weak, let us be real, true, and sincere.

Finally, what light this throws on the daily pilgrimage of all true Christians! Let them take comfort in the thought that their Master knows them. However much unknown and misunderstood by the world, their Master knows their hearts, and will comfort them at the last day. Happy is he who, in spite of many infirmities, can say with Peter—"Lord, you know all things; you know that I love you." (John 21:17.)

6:66-71

Peter's Confession

After this many of his disciples quit following him and did not accompany him any longer. So Jesus said to the twelve, "You don't want to go away too, do you?" Simon Peter answered him, "Lord, to whom will we go? You have the words of eternal life. We have come to believe and to know that you are the Holy One of God!"

Jesus replied, "Didn't I choose you, the twelve, and yet one of you is the devil?" (Now he said this about Judas son of Simon Iscariot, for Judas, one of the twelve, was going to betray him.)

These verses form a sorrowful conclusion to the famous discourse of Christ which occupies the greater part of the sixth chapter. They supply a melancholy proof of the hardness and corruption of man's heart. Even when the Son of God was the preacher, many seem to have heard in vain.

Let us mark in this passage what an old sin apostasy is. We read that when our Lord had explained what He meant by "eating and drinking his flesh and blood,"—"After this, many of his disciples quit following him and did not accompany him any longer."

The true grace of God no doubt is an everlasting possession. From this men never fall away entirely, when they have once received it. "The foundation of God stands sure." "My sheep shall never perish." (2 Tim. 2:19; John 10:28.) But there is counterfeit grace and unreal religion in the Church, wherever there is true; and from counterfeit grace thousands may, and do, fall away. Like the stony ground hearers, in the parable of the sower, many "have no root in themselves, and so in time of trial fall away." All is not gold that glitters. All blossoms do not come to fruit. All are not Israel which are called Israel. Men may have feelings, desires, convictions, resolutions, hopes, joys, sorrows in religion, and yet never have the grace of God. They may run well for a season, and bid fair to reach heaven, and yet break down entirely after a time, go back to the world, and end like Demas, Judas Iscariot, and Lot's wife.

It must never surprise us to see and hear of such cases in our own days. If it happened in our Lord's time and under our Lord's teaching, much more may we expect it to happen now. Above all, it must never shake our faith and discourage us in our course. On the contrary, we must make up our minds that there will be apostasy in the Church as long as the world stands. The sneering infidel, who defends his unbelief by pointing at them, must find some better argument than their example. He forgets that there will always be counterfeit coin where there is true money.

Let us mark, secondly, in this passage, the noble declaration of faith which the Apostle Peter made. Our Lord had said to the twelve, when many went back, "Will you also go away?" At once Peter replied, with characteristic zeal and fervor, "Lord, to whom shall we go? you have the words of eternal life. And we believe and are sure that you are that Christ, the Son of the living God."

The confession contained in these words is a very remarkable one. Living in a professedly Christian land, and surrounded by Christian privileges; we can hardly form an adequate idea of its real value. For a humble Jew to say of one whom Scribes, and Pharisees, and Sadducees agreed in rejecting, "You have the words of eternal life; you are the Christ," was an act of mighty faith. No wonder that our Lord said, in another place, "Blessed are you, Simon son of Jonah—for flesh and blood has not revealed it unto you, but my Father who is heaven." (Matt. 16:17.)

But the question with which Peter begins, is just as remarkable as his confession. "To whom shall we go?" said the noble-hearted Apostle. "Whom shall we follow? To what teacher shall we betake ourselves? Where shall we find any guide to heaven to compare with you? What shall we gain by forsaking you? What Scribe, what Pharisee, what Sadducee, what Priest, what Rabbi can show us such words of eternal life as you show?"

The question is one which every true Christian may boldly ask, when urged and tempted to give up his religion, and go back to the world. It is easy for those who hate religion to pick holes in our conduct, to make objections to our doctrines, to find fault with our practices. It may be hard sometimes to give them any answer. But after all, "To whom shall we go," if we give up our religion? Where shall we find such peace, and hope, and solid comfort as in serving Christ, however poorly we serve Him? Can we better ourselves by turning our back on Christ, and going back to our old ways? We cannot. Then let us hold on our way and persevere.

Let us mark, lastly, in this passage, what little benefit some men get from religious privileges. We read that our Lord said, "Have not I chosen you twelve, and one of you is a devil." And it goes on, "He spoke of Judas Iscariot, the son of Simon."

If ever there was a man who had great privileges and opportunities, that man was Judas Iscariot. A chosen disciple, a constant companion of Christ, a witness of His miracles, a hearer of His sermons, a commissioned preacher of His kingdom, a fellow and friend of Peter, James, and John—it would be impossible to imagine a more favorable position for a man's soul. Yet if anyone ever fell hopelessly into hell, and made shipwreck at last for eternity, that man was Judas Iscariot. The character of that man must have been black indeed, of whom our Lord could say he is "a devil."

Let us settle it firmly in our minds, that the possession of religious privileges alone is not enough to save our souls. It is neither place, nor light, nor company, nor opportunities, but grace that man needs to make him a Christian. With grace we may serve God in the most difficult position—like Daniel in Babylon, Obadiah in Ahab's court, and the saints in Nero's household. Without grace we may live in the full sunshine of Christ's countenance, and yet, like Judas, be miserably cast away. Then let us never rest until we have grace reigning in our souls. Grace is to be had for the asking. There is One sitting at the right hand of God who has said—"Ask, and it shall be given you." (Matt. 7:7.) The Lord Jesus is more willing to give grace than man is to seek it. If men have it not, it is because they do not ask it.

Chapter 7

*A*fter this Jesus traveled throughout Galilee. He stayed out of Judea because the Jewish authorities wanted to kill him. Now the Jewish feast of Tabernacles was near. So Jesus' brothers advised him, "Leave here and go to Judea so your disciples may see your miracles that you are performing. For no one who seeks to make a reputation for himself does anything in secret. If you are doing these things, show yourself to the world." (For not even his own brothers believed in him.)

So Jesus replied, "My time has not yet arrived, but you are ready at any opportunity. The world cannot hate you, but it hates me, because I am testifying about it that its deeds are evil. You go up to the feast yourselves. I am not going up to this feast yet, because my time has not yet fully arrived." When he had said this, he remained in Galilee.

But when his brothers had gone up to the feast, then Jesus himself also went up, not openly but in secret. So the Jewish authorities were looking for him at the feast, asking, "Where is he?" There was a lot of grumbling about him among the crowds. Some were saying, "He is a good man," but others, "He deceives the common people." However, no one spoke openly about him for fear of the Jewish authorities.

The chapter we now begin is divided from the preceding one by a wide interval of time. The many miracles which our Lord wrought, while He "walked in Galilee," are passed over by John in comparative silence. The events which he was specially inspired to record are those which took place in or near Jerusalem.

We should observe in this passage the desperate hardness and unbelief of human nature. We are told that even our Lord's "brethren did not believe in Him." Holy and harmless and blameless as He was in life, some of his nearest relatives, according to the flesh, did not receive Him as the Messiah. It was bad enough that His own people, "the Jews sought to kill Him." But it was even worse that "His brethren did not believe."

That great Scriptural doctrine, man's need of preventing and converting grace, stands out here, as if written with a sunbeam. It becomes all who question that doctrine to look at this passage and consider. Let them observe that seeing Christ's miracles, hearing Christ's teaching, living in Christ's own company, were not enough to make men believers. The mere possession of spiritual privileges never yet made any one a Christian. All is useless without the effectual and applying work of God the Holy Spirit. No wonder that our Lord said in another place, "No man can come to me, except the Father who has sent me draw him." (John 6:44.)

The true servants of Christ in every age will do well to remember this. They are often surprised and troubled to find that in religion they stand alone. They are apt to fancy that it must be their own fault that all around them are not converted like themselves. They are ready to blame themselves because their families remain worldly and unbelieving. But let them look at the verse before us. In our Lord Jesus Christ there was no fault either in temper, word, or deed. Yet even Christ's own "brethren did not believe in Him."

Our blessed Master has truly learned by experience how to sympathize with all his people who stand alone. This is a thought "full of sweet, pleasant, and unspeakable comfort." He knows the heart of every isolated believer, and can be touched with the feeling of his trials. He has drunk this bitter cup. He has passed through this fire. Let all who are fainting and cast down, because brothers and sisters despise their religion, turn to Christ for comfort, and pour out their hearts before Him. He "has suffered Himself being tempted" in this way, and He can help as well as feel. (Heb. 2:18.)

We should observe, for another thing, in this passage, one principal reason why many hate Christ. We are told that our Lord said to His unbelieving brethren, "The world cannot hate you; but me it hates, because I testify of it, that the works thereof are evil."

These words reveal one of those secret principles which influence men in their treatment of Christ. They help to explain that deadly enmity with which many during our Lord's earthly ministry regarded Him and His Gospel. It was not so much the high doctrines which He preached, as the high standard of practice which He proclaimed, which gave offence. It was not even His claim to be received the Messiah which men disliked so much, as His witness against the wickedness of their lives. In short, they could have tolerated His opinions if He would only have spared their sins.

The principle, we may be sure, is one of universal application. It is at work now just as much as it was eighteen hundred years ago. The real cause of many people's dislike to the Gospel is the holiness of living which it demands. Teach abstract doctrines only, and few will find any fault. Denounce the fashionable sins of the day, and call on men to repent and walk consistently with God, and thousands at once will be offended. The true reason why many profess to be infidels, and abuse Christianity, is the witness that Christianity bears against their own bad lives. Like Ahab, they hate it, "because it does not prophesy good concerning them, but evil." (1 Kings 22:8.)

We should observe, lastly, in this passage, the strange variety of opinions about Christ, which were current from the beginning. We are told that "there was much murmuring among the people concerning him—for some said, He is a good man others said, No, but he deceives the people." The words which old Simeon had spoken thirty years before were here accomplished in a striking manner. He had said to our Lord's mother, "This child is set for the fall and rising again of many in Israel—and for a sign which shall be spoken against—that the thoughts of many hearts may be revealed." (Luke 2:34, 35.) In the diversities of opinion about our Lord which arose among the Jews, we see the good old man's saying fulfilled.

In the face of such a passage as this, the endless differences and divisions about religion, which we see on all sides, in the present day, ought never to surprise us. The open hatred of some toward Christ—the carping, fault-finding, prejudiced spirit of others—the bold confession of the few faithful ones—the timid, man-fearing temperament of the many faithless ones—the unceasing war of words and strife of tongues with which the Churches of Christ are so sadly familiar—are only modern symptoms of an old disease. Such is the corruption of human nature, that Christ is the cause of division among men, wherever He is preached. So long as the world stands, some, when they hear of Him, will love, and some will hate—some will believe, and some will believe not. That deep, prophetical saying of His will be continually verified—"Do not think that I am come to send peace on earth; I came not to send peace, but a sword." (Matt. 10:34.)

What do we think of Christ ourselves? This is the one question with which we have to do. Let us never be ashamed to be of that little number who believe on Him, hear His voice, follow Him, and confess Him before men. While others waste their time in vain jangling and unprofitable controversy, let us take up the cross and give all diligence to make our calling and election sure. The children of this world may hate us, as it hated our Master, because our religion is a standing witness against them. But the last day will show that we chose wisely, lost nothing, and gained a crown of glory that fades not away.

7:14-24

Teaching in the Temple

When the feast was half over, Jesus went up to the temple and began to teach. Then the Jewish authorities were astonished and said, "How does this man know so much when he has never had formal instruction?" So Jesus replied, "My teaching is not from me, but from the one who sent me. If anyone wants to do God's will, he will know about my teaching, whether it is from God or whether I speak from my own authority. The person who speaks on his own authority desires to receive honor for himself; the one who desires the honor of the one who sent him is a man of integrity, and there is no unrighteousness in him. Hasn't Moses given you the law? Yet not one of you keeps the law! Why do you want to kill me?"

The crowd answered, "You're possessed by a demon! Who is trying to kill you?" Jesus replied, "I performed one miracle and you are all amazed. However, because Moses gave you the practice of circumcision (not that it came from Moses, but from the forefathers), you circumcise a male child on the Sabbath. But if a male child is circumcised on the Sabbath so that the law of Moses is not broken, why are you angry with me because I made a man completely well on the Sabbath? Do not judge according to external appearance, but judge with proper judgment."

We learn first in this passage, that honest obedience to God's will is one way to obtain clear spiritual knowledge. Our Lord says, "If anyone wants to do God's will, he will know about my teaching, whether it is from God or whether I speak from my own authority."

The difficulty of finding out "what is truth" in religion is a common subject of complaint among men. They point to the many differences which prevail among Christians on matters of doctrine, and profess to be unable to decide who is right. In thousands of cases this professed inability to find out truth becomes an excuse for living without any religion at all.

The saying of our Lord before us is one that demands the serious attention of people in this state of mind. It supplies an argument whose edge and point they will find it hard to evade. It teaches that one secret of getting the key of knowledge is to practice honestly what we know, and that if we conscientiously use the light that we now have, we shall soon find more light coming down into our minds. In short, there is a sense in which it is true, that by doing we shall come to knowing.

There is a mine of truth in this principle. Well would it be for men if they would act upon it. Instead of saying, as some do—"I must first know everything clearly, and then I will act,"—we should say—"I will diligently use such knowledge as I possess, and believe that in the using fresh knowledge will be given to me." How many mysteries this simple plan would solve! How many hard thing would soon become plain if men would honestly live up to their light, and "follow on to know the Lord!" (Hosea 6:3.)

It should never be forgotten that God deals with us as moral beings, and not as beasts or stones. He loves to encourage us to self-exertion and diligent use of such means as we have in our hands. The plain things in religion are undeniably very many. Let a man honestly attend to them, and he shall be taught the deep things of God.

Whatever some may say about their inability to find out truth, you will rarely find one of them who does not know better than he practices. Then if he is sincere, let him begin here at once. Let him humbly use what little knowledge he has got, and God will soon give him more. "If your eye be single, your whole body shall be full of light." (Matt. 6:22.)

We learn, secondly, in this passage, that a self-exalting spirit in ministers of religion is entirely opposed to the mind of Christ. Our Lord says, "He that speaks of himself seeks his own glory; but he that seeks His glory that sent him, the same is true, and no unrighteousness is in him."

The wisdom and truth of this sentence will be evident at once to any reflecting mind. The minister truly called of God will be deeply sensible of his Master's majesty and his own infirmity, and will see in himself nothing but unworthiness. He, on the other hand, who knows that he is not "inwardly moved by the Holy Spirit," will try to cover over his defects by magnifying himself and his office. The very desire to exalt ourselves is a bad symptom. It is a sure sign of something wrong within.

Does anyone ask illustrations of the truth before us? He will find them, on the one side, in the Scribes and Pharisees of our Lord's times. If one thing more than another distinguished these unhappy men, it was their desire to get praise for themselves. He will find them, on the other side, in the character of the Apostle Paul. The keynote that runs through all his Epistles is personal humility and zeal for Christ's glory—"I am less than the least of all saints—I am not fit to be called an Apostle—I am chief of sinners—we preach not ourselves but Christ Jesus the Lord, and ourselves your servants for Jesus' sake." (Ephes. 3:8; 1 Cor. 15:9; 1 Tim. 1:15; 2 Cor 4:5.)

Does anyone ask for a test by which he may discern the real man of God from the false shepherd in the present day? Let him remember our Lord's weighty words, and notice carefully what is the main object that a minister loves to exalt. Not he who is ever crying—"Behold the Church! behold the Sacraments! behold the ministry!" but he who says—"Behold the Lamb!"—is the pastor after God's own heart. Happy indeed is that minister who forgets SELF in his pulpit, and desires to be hid behind the cross. This man shall be blessed in his work, and be a blessing.

We learn, lastly, in this passage, the danger of forming a hasty judgment. The Jews at Jerusalem were ready to condemn our Lord as a sinner against the law of Moses, because He had done a miracle of healing on the Sabbath day. They forgot in their blind enmity that the fourth commandment was not meant to prevent works of necessity or works of mercy. A work on the Sabbath our Lord had done, no doubt, but not a work forbidden by the law. And hence they drew down on themselves the rebuke, "Judge not according to the appearance, but judge righteous judgment."

The practical value of the lesson before us is very great. We shall do well to remember it as we travel through life, and to correct our estimate of people and things by the light which it supplies.

We are often too ready to be deceived by an appearance of GOOD. We are in danger of rating some men as very good Christians, because of a little outward profession of religion, and a decent Sunday formality—because, in short, they talk the language of Canaan, and wear the garb of pilgrims. We forget that all is not good that appears good, even as all is not gold that glitters, and that daily practice, choice, tastes, habits, conduct, private character, are the true evidence of what a man is. In a word, we forget our Lord's saying—"Judge not according to the appearance."

We are too ready, on the other hand, to be deceived by the appearance of EVIL. We are in danger of setting down some men as not true Christians, because of a few faults or inconsistencies, and "making them offenders because of a word." (Isa. 29:21.) We must remember that the best of men are but men at their very best, and that the most eminent saints may be overtaken by temptation, and yet be saints at heart after all. We must not hastily suppose that all is evil, where there is an occasional appearance of evil. The holiest man may fall sadly for a time, and yet the grace within him may finally get a victory. Is a man's general character godly? Then let us suspend our judgment when he falls, and hope on. Let us "judge righteous judgment."

In any case let us take care that we pass fair judgment on OURSELVES. Whatever we think of others, let us beware of making mistakes about our own character. There, at any rate, let us be just, honest, and fair. Let us not flatter ourselves that all is right, because all is apparently right before men. "The Lord," we must remember, "looks on the heart." (1 Sam. 16:7.) Then let us judge ourselves with righteous judgment, and condemn ourselves while we live, lest we be judged of the Lord and condemned forever at the last day. (1 Cor. 11:31.)

7:25-36

Questions about Jesus' Identity

Then some of the residents of Jerusalem began to say, "Isn't this the man they are trying to kill? Yet here he is, speaking publicly, and they are saying nothing to him. Do the rulers really know that this man is the Christ? But we know where this man comes from. Whenever the Christ comes, no one will know where he comes from."

Then Jesus, while teaching in the temple courts, cried out, "You both know me and know where I come from! And I have not come on my own initiative, but the one who sent me is true. You do not know him, but I know him, because I have come from him and he sent me."

So then they tried to seize Jesus, but no one laid a hand on him, because his time had not yet come. Yet many of the crowd believed in him and said,

"Whenever the Christ comes, he won't perform more miraculous signs than this man did, will he?"

The Pharisees heard the crowd murmuring these things about Jesus, so the chief priests and the Pharisees sent officers to arrest him. Then Jesus said, "I will be with you for only a little while longer, and then I am going to the one who sent me. You will look for me but will not find me, and where I am you cannot come."

Then the Jews who were hostile to Jesus said to one another, "Where is he going to go that we cannot find him? He is not going to go to the Jewish people dispersed among the Greeks and teach the Greeks, is he? What did he mean by saying, 'You will look for me but will not find me, and where I am you cannot come'?"

We see in these verses, the obstinate blindness of the unbelieving Jews. We find them defending their denial of our Lord's Messiahship, by saying, "But we know where this man comes from. Whenever the Christ comes, no one will know where he comes from." And yet in both these assertions they were wrong!

They were wrong in saying that they "knew where our Lord came from." They meant no doubt to say that He was born at Nazareth, and belonged to Nazareth, and was therefore a Galilean. Yet the fact was, that our Lord was born at Bethlehem, that He belonged legally to the tribe of Judah, and that His mother and Joseph were of the house and lineage of David. It is incredible to suppose that the Jews could not have found this out, if they had honestly searched and inquired. It is notorious that pedigrees, genealogies, and family histories were most carefully kept by the Jewish nation. Their ignorance was without excuse.

They were wrong again in saying, "Whenever the Christ comes, no one will know where he comes from." There was a well-known prophecy, with which their whole nation was familiar, that Christ was to come out of the town of Bethlehem. (Micah 5:2; Matt. 2:5; John 7:42.) It is absurd to suppose that they had forgotten this prophecy. But apparently they found it inconvenient to remember it on this occasion. Men's memories are often sadly dependent on their wills.

The Apostle Peter, in a certain place, speaks of some as "willingly ignorant." (2 Pet. 3:5.) He had good reason to use the expression. It is a sore spiritual disease, and one most painfully common among men. There are thousands in the present day just as blind in their way as the Jews. They shut their eyes against the plainest facts and doctrines of Christianity. They pretend to say that they do not understand, and cannot therefore believe the things that we press on their attention, as needful to salvation. But, alas! in nineteen cases out of twenty it is a willful ignorance. They do not believe what they do not like to believe. They will neither read, nor listen, nor search, nor think, nor inquire, honestly after truth. Can any one wonder if such people are ignorant? Faithful and true is that old proverb—"There are none so blind as those who will not see."

We see, for another thing, in these verses, the overruling hand of God over all His enemies. We find that the unbelieving Jews "Sought to take our Lord—but no man laid hands on Him, because his hour was not yet come." They had the will to hurt him, but by an invisible restraint from above, they had not the power.

There is a mine of deep truth in the words before us, which deserves close attention. They show us plainly that all our Lord's sufferings were undergone voluntarily, and of His own free will. He did not go to the cross because He could not help it. He did not die because He could not prevent His death. Neither Jew nor Gentile, Pharisee nor Sadducee, Annas nor Caiaphas, Herod nor Pontius Pilate, could have injured our Lord, except power had been given them from above. All that they did was done under control, and by permission. The crucifixion was part of the eternal counsels of the Trinity. The sufferings and death of our Lord could not begin until the very hour which God had appointed. This is a great mystery. But it is a truth.

The servants of Christ in every age should treasure up the doctrine before us, and remember it in time of need. It is "full of sweet, pleasant, and unspeakable comfort to godly people." Let such never forget that they live in a world where God overrules all times and events, and where nothing can happen but by God's permission. The very hairs of their heads are all numbered. Sorrow and sickness, and poverty, and persecution, can never touch them, unless God sees fit. They may boldly say to every cross—"You could have no power against me, except it were given you from above." Then let them work on confidently. They are immortal, until their work is done. Let them suffer patiently, if needs be that they suffer. Their "times are in God's hand." (Psalm. 31:15.) That hand guides and governs all things here below, and makes no mistakes.

We see lastly, in these verses, the miserable end to which unbelievers may one day come. We find our Lord saying to His enemies—"You shall seek me, and shall not find me; and where I am there you cannot come."

We can hardly doubt that these words were meant to have a prophetical sense. Whether our Lord had in view individual cases of unbelief among His hearers, or whether He looked forward to the national remorse which many would feel too late in the final siege of Jerusalem, are points which we cannot perhaps decide. But that many Jews did remember Christ's sayings long after He had ascended into heaven, and did in a way seek Him and wish for Him when it was too late, we may be very sure.

It is far too much forgotten that there is such a thing as finding out truth too late. There may be convictions of sin, discoveries of our own folly, desires after peace, anxieties about heaven, fears of hell, but all too late. The teaching of Scripture on this point is clear and express. It is written in Proverbs—"Then shall they call upon me, but I will not answer; they shall seek me early, but they shall not find me." (Prov. 1:28.) It is written of the foolish virgins in the parable, that when they found the door shut, they knocked in vain, saying, "Lord, Lord, open to us." (Matt. 25:11.) Dreadful as it may seem, it is possible, by continually resisting light and warnings, to sin away our own souls. It sounds frightening, but it is true.

Let us take heed to ourselves lest we sin after the example of the unbelieving Jews, and never seek the Lord Jesus as a Savior until it is too late. The door of mercy is still open. The throne of grace is still waiting for us. Let us give diligence to make sure our interest in Christ, while it is called today. Better never have been born than hear the Son of God say at last, "Where I am, there you cannot come."

7:37-39

Teaching about the Spirit

On the last day of the feast, the greatest day, Jesus stood up and shouted out, "If anyone is thirsty, let him come to me, and let the one who believes in me drink. Just as the scripture says, 'From within him will flow rivers of living water.'" (Now he said this about the Spirit, whom those who believed in him were going to receive, for the Spirit had not yet been given, because Jesus was not yet glorified.)

It has been said that there are some passages in Scripture which deserve to be printed in letters of gold. Of such passages the verses before us form one. They contain one of those wide, full, free invitations to mankind, which make the Gospel of Christ so eminently the "good news of God." Let us see of what it consists.

We have, first, in these verses, a case supposed. The Lord Jesus says, "If any man thirst." These words no doubt were meant to have a spiritual meaning. The thirst before us is of a purely spiritual kind. It means anxiety of soul—conviction of sin—desire of pardon—longing after peace of conscience. When a man feels his sins, and wants forgiveness—is deeply sensible of his soul's need, and earnestly desires help and relief—then he is in that state of mind which our Lord had in view, when he said, "If any man thirst." The Jews who heard Peter preach on the day of Pentecost, and were "pierced in their hearts,"—the Philippian jailer who cried to Paul and Silas, "What must I do to be saved?" are both examples of what the expression means. In both cases there was "thirst."

Such thirst as this, unhappily, is known by few. All ought to feel it, and all would feel it if they were wise. Sinful, mortal, dying creatures as we all are, with souls that will one day be judged and spend eternity in heaven or hell, there lives not the man or woman on earth who ought not to "thirst" after salvation. And yet the many thirst after everything almost except salvation. Money, pleasure, honor, rank, self-indulgence—these are the things which they desire. There is no clearer proof of the fall of man, and the utter corruption of human nature, than the careless indifference of most people about their souls. No wonder the Bible calls the natural man "blind," and "asleep," and "dead," when so few can be found who are awake, alive, and athirst about salvation.

Happy are those who know something by experience of spiritual "thirst." The beginning of all true Christianity is to discover that we are guilty, empty, needy sinners. Until we know that we are lost, we are not in the way to be saved. The very first step toward heaven is to be thoroughly convinced that we deserve hell. That sense of sin which sometimes alarms a man and makes him think his own case desperate, is a good sign. It is in fact a symptom of spiritual life—"Blessed indeed are they which hunger and thirst after righteousness, for they shall be filled." (Matt. 5:6.)

We have, secondly, in these verses, a remedy proposed. The Lord Jesus says, "If any man thirst, let him come unto me and drink." He declares that He is the true fountain of life, the supplier of all spiritual necessities, the reliever of all spiritual needs. He invites all who feel the burden of sin heavy, to apply to Him, and proclaims Himself their helper.

Those words "let him come unto me," are few and very simple. But they settle a mighty question which all the wisdom of Greek and Roman philosophers could never settle; they show how man can have peace with God. They show that peace is to be had in Christ by trusting in Him as our mediator and substitute, in one word, by believing. To "come" to Christ is to believe on Him, and to "believe" on Him is to come. The remedy may seem a very simple one, too simple to be true. But there is no other remedy than this; and all the wisdom of the world can never find a flaw in it, or devise a better one.

To use this grand prescription of Christ is the secret of all saving Christianity. The saints of God in every age have been men and women who drank of this fountain by faith, and were relieved. They felt their guilt and emptiness, and thirsted for deliverance. They heard of a full supply of pardon, mercy, and grace in Christ crucified for all penitent believers. They believed the good news and acted upon it. They cast aside all confidence in their own goodness and worthiness, and came to Christ by faith as sinners. So coming they found relief. So coming daily they lived. So coming they died. Really to feel the sinfulness of sin and to thirst, and really to come to Christ and believe, are the two steps which lead to heaven. But they are mighty steps. Thousands are too proud and careless to take them. Few, alas! think, and still fewer believe.

We have, lastly, in these verses, a promise held out. The Lord Jesus says, "He that believes on me, from within him will flow rivers of living water." These words of course were meant to have a figurative sense. They have a double application. They teach, for one thing, that all who come to Christ by faith shall find in Him abundant satisfaction. They teach, for another thing, that believers shall not only have enough for the needs of their own souls, but shall also become fountains of blessings to others.

The fulfillment of the first part of the promise could be testified by thousands of living Christians in the present day. They would say, if their evidence could be collected, that when they came to Christ by faith, they found in Him more than they expected. They have tasted peace, and hope, and comfort, since they first believed, which, with all their doubts and fears, they would not exchange for anything in this world. They have found grace according to their need, and strength according to their days. In themselves and their own hearts they have often been disappointed; but they have never been disappointed in Christ.

The fulfillment of the other half of the promise will never be fully known until the judgment-day. That day alone shall reveal the amount of good that every believer is made the instrument of doing to others, from the very day of his conversion. Some do good while they live, by their tongues; like the Apostles and first preachers of the Gospel. Some do good when they are dying; like Stephen and the penitent thief, and our own martyred Reformers at the stake. Some do good long after they are dead, by their writings; like Baxter and Bunyan and M'Cheyne. But in one way or another, probably, almost all believers will be found to have been fountains of blessings. By word or by deed, by precept or by example, directly or indirectly, they are always leaving their marks on others. They know it not now; but they will find at last that it is true. Christ's saying shall be fulfilled.

Do we ourselves know anything of "coming to Christ?" This is the question that should arise in our hearts as we leave this passage. The worst of all states of soul is to be without feeling or concern about eternity—to be without "thirst." The greatest of all mistakes is to try to find relief in any other way than the one before us—the way of simply "coming to Christ." It is one thing to come to Christ's Church, Christ's ministers, and Christ's ordinances. It is quite another thing to come to Christ Himself. Happy is he who not only knows these things, but acts upon them!

7:40-53

Differing Opinions About Jesus

When they heard these words, some of the crowd began to say, "This really is the Prophet!" Others said, "This is the Christ!" But still others said, "No, for the Christ doesn't come from Galilee, does he? Don't the scriptures say that the Christ is a descendant of David and comes from Bethlehem, the village where David lived?" So there was a division in the crowd because of Jesus. Some of them were wanting to seize him, but no one laid a hand on him.

Then the officers returned to the chief priests and Pharisees, who said to them, "Why didn't you bring him back with you?" The officers replied, "No one ever spoke like this man!" Then the Pharisees answered, "You haven't been deceived too, have you? None of the rulers or the Pharisees have believed in him, have they? But this rabble who do not know the law are accursed!"

Nicodemus, who had gone to Jesus before and who was one of the rulers, said, "Our law doesn't condemn a man unless it first hears from him and learns what he is doing, does it?" They replied, "You aren't from Galilee too, are you? Investigate carefully and you will see that no prophet comes from Galilee!" And every man went unto his own house.

These verses show us, for one thing, how useless is knowledge in religion, if it is not accompanied by grace in the heart. We are told that some of our Lord's hearers knew clearly where Christ was to be born. They referred to Scripture, like men familiar with its contents. "Has not the Scripture said that Christ comes of the seed of David, and out of the town of Bethlehem, where David was?" And yet the eyes of their understanding were not enlightened. Their own Messiah stood before them, and they neither received, nor believed, nor obeyed Him.

A certain degree of religious knowledge, beyond doubt, is of vast importance. Ignorance is certainly not the mother of true devotion, and helps nobody toward heaven. An "unknown God" can never be the object of a reasonable worship. Happy indeed would it be for Christians if they all knew the Scriptures as well as the Jews seem to have done, when our Lord was on earth!

But while we value religious knowledge, we must take care that we do not overvalue it. We must not think it enough to know the facts and doctrines of our faith, unless our hearts and lives are thoroughly influenced by what we know. The very devils know the creed intellectually, and "believe and tremble," but remain devils still. (James 2:19.) It is quite possible to be familiar with the letter of Scripture, and to be able to quote texts appropriately, and reason about the theory of Christianity, and yet to remain dead in trespasses and sins. Like many of the generation to which our Lord preached, we may know the Bible well, and yet remain faithless and unconverted.

Heart-knowledge, we must always remember, is the one thing needful. It is something which schools and universities cannot confer. It is the gift of God. To find out the plague of our own hearts and hate sin—to become familiar with the throne of grace and the fountain of Christ's blood—to sit daily at the feet of Jesus, and humbly learn of Him—this is the highest degree of knowledge to which mortal man can attain. Let anyone thank God who knows anything of these things. He may be ignorant of Greek, Latin, Hebrew, and mathematics, but he shall be saved.

These verses show us, for another thing, how eminent must have been our Lord's gifts, as a public Teacher of religion. We are told that even the officers of the chief priests, who were sent to take Him, were struck and amazed. They were, of course, not likely to be prejudiced in His favor. Yet even they reported—"Never man spoke like this Man."

Of the MANNER of our Lord's public speaking, we can of necessity form little idea. Action, and voice, and delivery are things that must be seen and heard to be appreciated. That our Lord's manner was peculiarly solemn, arresting, and impressive, we need not doubt. It was probably something very unlike what the Jewish officers were accustomed to hear. There is much in what is said in another place—"He taught them as One having authority, and not as the Scribes." (Matt. 7:29.)

Of the matter of our Lord's public speaking, we may form some conception from the discourses which are recorded in the four Gospels. The leading features of these discourses are plain and unmistakable. The world has never seen anything like them, since the gift of speech was given to man. They often contain deep truths, which we have no line to fathom. But they often contain simple things, which even a child can understand. They are bold and outspoken in denouncing national and ecclesiastical sins, and yet they are wise and discreet in never giving needless offence. They are faithful and direct in their warnings, and yet loving and tender, in their invitations. For a combination of power and simplicity, of courage and prudence, of faithfulness and tenderness, we may well say, "Never man spoke like this Man!"

It would be well for the Church of Christ if ministers and teachers of religion would strive more to speak after their Lord's pattern. Let them remember that elegant bombastic language, and a sensational, theatrical style of address, are utterly unlike their Master. Let them realize, that an eloquent simplicity is the highest attainment of public speaking. Of this their Master left them a glorious example. Surely they need never be ashamed of walking in His steps.

These verses show us, lastly, how slowly and gradually the work of grace goes on in some hearts. We are told that Nicodemus stood up in the council of our Lord's enemies, and mildly pleaded that He deserved fair dealing. "Does our law judge any man," he asked, "before it hear him, and know what he does?"

This very Nicodemus, we must remember, is the man who, eighteen months before, had come to our Lord by night as an ignorant inquirer. He evidently knew little then, and dared not come to Christ in open day. But now, after eighteen months, he has got on so far that he dares to say something on our Lord's side. It was but little that he said, no doubt, but it was better than nothing at all. And a day was yet to come, when he would go further still. He was to help Joseph of Arimathaea in doing honor to our Lord's dead body, when even His chosen Apostles had forsaken Him and fled.

The case of Nicodemus is full of useful instruction. It teaches us, that there are diversities in the operation of the Holy Spirit. All are undoubtedly led to the same Savior, but all are not led precisely in the same way. It teaches us, that the work of the Spirit does not always go forward with the same speed in the hearts of men. In some cases it may go forward very slowly indeed, and yet may be real and true.

We shall do well to remember these things, in forming our opinion of other Christians. We are often ready to condemn some as graceless, because their experience does not exactly tally with our own, or to set them down as not in the narrow way at all, because they cannot run as fast as ourselves. We must beware of hasty judgments. It is not always the fastest runner that wins the race. It is not always those who begin suddenly in religion, and. profess themselves rejoicing Christians, who continue steadfast to the end. Slow work is sometimes the surest and most enduring. Nicodemus stood firm, when Judas Iscariot fell away and went to his own place. No doubt it would be a pleasant thing, if everybody who was converted came out boldly, took up the cross, and confessed Christ in the day of his conversion. But it is not always given to God's children to do so.

Have we any grace in our hearts at all? This, after all, is the grand question that concerns us. It may be small—but have we any? It may grow slowly, as in the case of Nicodemus—but does it grow at all? Better a little grace than none! Better move slowly than stand still in sin and the world!

Chapter 8

A Woman Caught in Adultery

*B*ut Jesus went to the Mount of Olives. Early in the morning he came to the temple courts again. All the people came to him, and he sat down and began to teach them. The experts in the law and the Pharisees brought a woman who had been caught committing adultery. They made her stand in front of them and said to Jesus, "Teacher, this woman was caught in the very act of adultery. In the law Moses commanded us to stone to death such women. What then do you say?" (Now they were asking this in an attempt to trap him, so that they could bring charges against him.) Jesus bent down and wrote on the ground with his finger. When they persisted in asking him, he stood up straight and replied, "Whoever among you is guiltless may be the first to throw a stone at her." Then he bent over again and wrote on the ground.

Now when they heard this, they began to drift away one at a time, starting with the older ones, until Jesus was left alone with the woman standing before him. Jesus straightened up and said to her, "Woman, where are they? Did no one condemn you?" She replied, "No one, Lord." And Jesus said, "I do not condemn you either. Go, and from now on do not sin anymore."

The narrative which begins the eighth chapter of John's Gospel is of a rather peculiar character. In some respects it stands alone. There is nothing quite like it in the whole range of the four Gospels. In every age some scrupulous minds have stumbled at the passage, and have doubted whether it was ever written by John at all. But the justice of such scruples is a point that cannot easily be proved.

To suppose, as some have thought, that the narrative before us palliates the sin of adultery, and exhibits our Lord as making light of the seventh commandment, is surely a great mistake. There is nothing in the passage to justify such an assertion. There is not a sentence in it to warrant our saying anything of the kind. Let us calmly weigh the matter, and examine the contents of the passage.

Our Lord's enemies brought before Him a woman guilty of adultery, and asked him to say what punishment she deserved. We are distinctly told that they asked the question, "to trap Him." They hoped to entrap Him into saying something for which they might accuse Him. They fancied perhaps that He who preached pardon and salvation to "publicans and harlots" might be induced to say something which would either contradict the law of Moses, or His own words.

Our Lord knew the hearts of the malicious questioners before Him, and dealt with them with perfect wisdom, as He had done in the case of the "tribute-money." (Matt. 22:17.) He refused to be a "judge" and lawgiver among them, and specially in a case which their own law had already decided. He gave them at first no answer at all.

But "when they continued asking," our Lord silenced them with a withering and heart-searching reply. "He that is without sin among you," he said, "let him first cast a stone at her." He did not say that the woman had not sinned, or that her sin was a trifling and excusable one. But He reminded her accusers that they at any rate were not the people to bring a charge against her. Their own motives and lives were far from pure. They themselves did not come into the case with clean hands. What they really desired was not to vindicate the purity of God's law, and punish a sinner, but to wreak their malice on Himself.

Last of all, when those who had brought the unhappy woman to our Lord had gone out from His presence, "convicted by their own conscience," He dismissed the guilty sinner with the solemn words, "Neither do I condemn you-go and sin no more." That she did not deserve punishment He did not say. But He had not come to be a judge. Moreover, in the absence of all witnesses or accusers, there was no case before Him. Let her then depart as one whose guilt was "not proven," even though she was really guilty, and let her "sin no more."

To say in the face of these simple facts that our Lord made light of the sin of adultery is not fair. There is nothing in the passage before us to prove it. Of all whose words are recorded in the Bible there is none who has spoken so strongly about the breach of the seventh commandment as our divine Master. It is He who has taught that it may be broken by a look or a thought, as well as by an open act. (Matt. 5:28.) It is He who has spoken more strongly than any about the sanctity of the marriage relation. (Matt. 19:5.) In all that is recorded here, we see nothing inconsistent with the rest of His teaching. He simply refused to usurp the office of the judge and to pronounce condemnation on a guilty woman, for the gratification of His deadly enemies.

In leaving this passage, we must not forget that it contains two lessons of great importance. Whatever difficulties the verses before us may present, these two lessons at any rate are clear, plain, and unmistakable.

We learn, for one thing, the power of conscience. We read of the woman's accusers, that when they heard our Lord's appeal, "being convicted by their own conscience, they went out one by one, beginning at the eldest, even into the last." Wicked and hardened as they were, they felt something within which made them cowards. Fallen as human nature is, God has taken care to leave within every man a witness that will be heard.

Conscience is a most important part of our inward man, and plays a most prominent part in our spiritual history. It cannot save us. It never yet led any one to Christ. It is blind, and liable to be misled. It is lame and powerless, and cannot guide us to heaven. Yet conscience is not to be despised. It is the minister's best friend, when he stands up to rebuke sin from the pulpit. It is the mother's best friend, when she tries to restrain her children from evil and quicken them to good. It is the teacher's best friend, when he presses home on boys and girls their moral duties. Happy is he who never stifles his conscience, but strives to keep it tender! Still happier is he who prays to have it enlightened by the Holy Spirit, and sprinkled with Christ's blood.

We learn, for another thing, the nature of true repentance. When our Lord had said to the sinful woman, "Neither do I condemn you," He dismissed her with the solemn words, "go and sin no more." He did not merely say, "go home and repent." He pointed out the chief thing which her case required—the necessity of immediate breaking off from her sin.

Let us never forget this lesson. It is the very essence of genuine repentance, as the Church catechism well teaches, to "forsake sin." That repentance which consists in nothing more than feeling, talking, professing, wishing, meaning, hoping, and resolving, is worthless in God's sight. Action is the very life of "repentance unto salvation not to be repented of." Until a man ceases to do evil and turns from his sins, he does not really repent. Would we know whether we are truly converted to God, and know anything of godly sorrow for sin, and repentance such as causes "joy in heaven"? Let us search and see whether we forsake sin. Let us not rest until we can say as in God's sight, "I hate all sin, and desire to sin no more."

8:12-20

Jesus as the Light of the World

Then Jesus spoke out again, "I am the light of the world. The one who follows me will never walk in darkness, but will have the light of life." So the Pharisees objected, "You testify about yourself; your testimony is not true!" Jesus answered, "Even if I testify about myself, my testimony is true, because I know where I came from and where I am going. But you people do not know where I came from or where I am going. You people judge by outward appearances; I do not judge anyone. But if I judge, my evaluation is accurate, because I am not alone when I judge, but I and the Father who sent me do so together. It is written in your law that the testimony of two men is true. I testify about myself and the Father who sent me testifies about me."

Then they began asking him, "Who is your father?" Jesus answered, "You do not know either me or my Father. If you knew me you would know my Father too." (Jesus spoke these words near the offering box while he was teaching in the temple courts. No one seized him because his time had not yet come.)

The conversation between our Lord and the Jews, which begins with these verses, is full of difficulties. The connection between one part and another, and the precise meaning of some of the expressions which fell from our Lord's lips, are "things hard to be understood." In passages like this it is true wisdom to acknowledge the great imperfection of our spiritual vision, and to be thankful if we can glean a few handfuls of truth.

Let us notice, for one thing, in these verses, what the Lord Jesus says of Himself. He proclaims, "I am the light of the world."

These words imply that the world needs light, and is naturally in a dark condition. It is so in a moral and spiritual point of view—and it has been so for nearly 6,000 years. In ancient Egypt, Greece, and Rome, in modern England, France, and Germany, the same report is true. The vast majority of men neither see nor understand the value of their souls, the true nature of

God, nor the reality of a world to come! Notwithstanding all the discoveries of art and science, "darkness still covers the earth, and gross darkness the people." (Isaiah. 60:2.)

For this state of things, the Lord Jesus Christ declares Himself to be the only remedy. He has risen, like the sun, to diffuse light, and life, and peace, and salvation, in the midst of a dark world. He invites all who want spiritual help and guidance to turn to Him, and take Him for their leader. What the sun is to the whole solar system—the center of light, and heat, and life, and fertility—that He has come into the world to be to sinners.

Let this saying sink down into our hearts. It is weighty and full of meaning. False lights on every side invite man's attention in the present day. Reason, philosophy, earnestness, liberalism, conscience, and the voice of the Church, are all, in their various ways, crying loudly that they have got "the light" to show us. Their advocates know not what they say. Wretched are those who believe their high professions! He only is the true light who came into the world to save sinners, who died as our substitute on the cross, and sits at God's right hand to be our Friend. "In His light we shall see light." (Psalm 36:9.)

Let us notice, secondly, in these verses, what the Lord Jesus says of those who follow Him. He promises, "He who follows Me shall not walk in darkness, but shall have the light of life."

To follow Christ is to commit ourselves wholly and entirely to Him as our only leader and Savior, and to submit ourselves to Him in every matter, both of doctrine and practice. "Following" is only another word for "believing." It is the same act of soul, only seen from a different point of view. As Israel followed the pillar of cloud and fire in all their journeyings—moving whenever it moved, stopping whenever it tarried, asking no questions, marching on in faith—so must a man deal with Christ. He must "follow the Lamb wherever He goes." (Rev. 14:4.)

He that so follows Christ shall "not walk in darkness." He shall not be left in ignorance, like the many around him. He shall not grope in doubt and uncertainty, but shall see the way to heaven, and know where he is going. He "shall have the light of life." He shall feel within him the light of God's countenance shining on him. He shall find in his conscience and understanding a living light, which nothing can altogether quench. The lights with which many please themselves shall go out in the valley of the shadow of death, and prove worse than useless. But the light that Christ gives to every one that follows Him shall never fail.

Let us notice, lastly, in these verses, what the Lord Jesus says of His enemies. He tells the Pharisees that, with all their pretended wisdom, they were ignorant of God. "You neither know Me nor my Father—if you had known Me, you would have known my Father also."

Ignorance like this is only too common. There are thousands who are conversant with many branches of human learning, and can even argue and reason about religion, and yet know nothing really about God. That there is such a Being as God they fully admit. But His character and attributes revealed in Scripture, His holiness, His purity, His justice, His perfect knowledge, His unchangeableness, are things with which they are little acquainted. In fact, the subject of God's nature and character makes them uncomfortable, and they do not like to dwell upon it.

The grand secret of knowing God is to draw near to Him through Jesus Christ. Approached from this side, there is nothing that need make us afraid. Viewed from this standpoint, God is the sinner's friend. God, out of Christ, may well fill us with alarm. How shall we dare to look at so high and holy a Being? God in Christ is full of mercy, grace, and peace. His law's demands are satisfied. His holiness need not make us afraid. Christ in one word is the way and door, by which we must ever draw near to the Father. If we know Christ, we shall know the Father. It is His own word—"No man comes unto the Father but by Me." (John 14:6.) Ignorance of Christ is the root of ignorance of God. Wrong at the starting-point, the whole sum of a man's religion is full of error.

And now, where are we ourselves? Do we know? Many are living and dying in a kind of fog. Where are we going? Can we give a satisfactory answer? Hundreds go out of existence in utter uncertainty. Let us leave nothing uncertain that concerns our everlasting salvation. Christ, the light of the world, is for us as well as for others, if we humbly follow Him, cast our souls on Him, and become His disciples. Let us not, like thousands, waste our lives in doubting, and arguing, and reasoning, but simply follow. The child that says. "I will not learn anything until I know something," will never learn at all. The man that says. "I must first understand everything before I become a Christian," will die in his sins. Let us begin by "following," and then we shall find light.

8:21-30

Then Jesus said to them again, "I am going away, and you will look for me but will die in your sin. Where I am going you cannot come." So the Jewish leaders began to say, "Perhaps he is going to kill himself, because he says, 'Where I am going you cannot come.'" Jesus replied, "You people are from below; I am from above. You people are from this world; I am not from this world. Thus I told you that you will die in your sins. For unless you believe that I am the Christ, you will die in your sins."

So they said to him, "Who are you?" Jesus replied, "What I have told you from the beginning. I have many things to say and to judge about you, but the Father who sent me is truthful, and the things I have heard from him I speak to the world." (They did not understand that he was telling them about his Father.)

Then Jesus said, "When you lift up the Son of Man, then you will know that I am he, and I do nothing on my own initiative, but I speak just what the Father taught me. And the one who sent me is with me. He has not left me alone, because I always do those things that please him." While he was saying these things, many people believed in him.

This passage contains deep things, so deep that we have no line to fathom them. As we read it we should call to mind the Psalmist's words—"Your thoughts are very deep." (Psalm 92:5.) But it also contains, in the opening verses, some things which are clear, plain, and unmistakable. To these let us give our attention and root them firmly in our hearts.

We learn, for one thing, that it is possible to seek Christ in vain. Our Lord says to the unbelieving Jews, "You shall seek Me, and shall die in your sins." He meant, by these words, that the Jews would one day seek Him in vain.

The lesson before us is a very painful one. That such a Savior as the Lord Jesus, so full of love, so willing to save, should ever be sought "in vain," is a sorrowful thought. Yet so it is! A man may have many religious feelings about Christ, without any saving religion. Sickness, sudden affliction, the fear of death, the failure of usual sources of comfort—all these causes may draw out of a man a good deal of "religiousness." Under the immediate pressure of these he may say his prayers fervently, exhibit a strong spiritual feelings, and profess for a season to "seek Christ," and be a different man. And yet all this time his heart may never be touched at all! Take away the peculiar circumstances that affected him, and he may possibly return at once to his old ways. He sought Christ "in vain," because he sought Him from false motives, and not with his whole heart.

Unhappily this is not all. There is such a thing as a settled habit of resisting light and knowledge, until we seek Christ "in vain." Scripture and experience alike prove that men may reject God until God rejects them, and will not hear their prayer. They may go on stifling their convictions, quenching the light of conscience, fighting against their own better knowledge, until God is provoked to give them over and let them alone. It is not for nothing that these words are written—"Then shall they call upon Me, but I will not answer; they shall seek Me early, but they shall not find Me—for they hated knowledge, and did not choose the fear of the Lord." (Prov. 1:28, 29.) Such cases may not be common; but they are possible, and they are sometimes seen. Some ministers can testify that they have visited people on their deathbeds who seem to seek Christ, and yet to seek in vain.

There is no safety but in seeking Christ while He may be found, and calling on Him while He is near—seeking Him with a true heart, and calling on Him with an honest spirit. Such seeking, we may be very sure, is never in vain. It will never be recorded of such seekers, that they "died in their sins." He that really comes to Christ shall never be "cast out." The Lord has solemnly declared that "He has no pleasure in the death of him that dies,"—and that "He delights in mercy." (Ezekiel 18:32; Micah 7:18.)

We learn for another thing, how wide is the difference between Christ and the ungodly. Our Lord says to the unbelieving Jews—"You are from beneath, I am from above—you are of this world, I am not of this world."

These words, no doubt, have a special application to our Lord Jesus Christ Himself. In the highest and most literal sense, there never was but One who could truly say, "I am from above—I am not of this world." That One is He who came forth from the Father, and was before the world—even the Son of God.

But there is a lower sense, in which these words are applicable to all Christ's living members. Compared to the thoughtless multitude around them, they are "from above," and "not of this world," like their Master. The thoughts of the ungodly are about things beneath; the true Christian's affections are set on things above. The ungodly man is full of this world; its cares, and pleasures, and profits, absorb his whole attention. The true Christian, though in the world, is not of it; his citizenship is in heaven, and his best things are yet to come.

The true Christian will do well never to forget this line of demarcation. If he loves his soul, and desires to serve God, he must be content to find himself separated from many around him by a gulf that cannot be passed. He may not like to seem peculiar and unlike others; but it is the certain consequence of grace reigning within him. He may find it brings on him hatred, ridicule, and hard speeches; but it is the cup which his Master drank, and of which his Master forewarned all His disciples. "If you were of the world the world would love His own, but because you are not of the world, but I have chosen you out of the world, therefore the world hates you." (John 15:19.). Then let the Christian never be ashamed to stand alone and show his colors. He must carry the cross if he would wear the crown. If he has within him a new principle "from above," it must be seen.

We learn, lastly, how dreadful is the end to which unbelief can bring man. Our Lord says to his enemies, "If you believe not that I am He, you shall die in your sins."

These solemn words are invested with peculiar solemnity when we consider from whose lips they came. Who is this that speaks of men dying "in their sins," unpardoned, unforgiven, unfit to meet God—of men going into another world with all their sins upon them? He that says this is no other than the Savior of mankind, who laid down His life for His sheep—the loving, gracious, merciful, compassionate Friend of sinners. It is Christ Himself! Let this simple fact not be overlooked.

They are greatly mistaken who suppose that it is harsh and unkind to speak of hell and future punishment. How can such people get over such language as that which is before us? How can they account for many a like expression which our Lord used, and specially for such passages as those in which He speaks of the "worm that dies not, and the fire that is not quenched"? (Mark 9:46.) They cannot answer these questions. Misled by a false charity and a morbid amiability, they are condemning the plain teaching of the Scripture, and are wise above that which is written.

Let us settle it in our minds, as one of the great foundation truths of our faith, that there is a hell. Just as we believe firmly that there is an eternal heaven for the godly, so let us believe firmly that there is an eternal hell for the wicked. Let us never suppose that there is any lack of charity in speaking of hell. Let us rather maintain that it is the highest love to warn men plainly of danger, and to beseech them to "flee from the wrath to come." It was Satan, the deceiver, murderer, and liar, who said to Eve in the beginning, "You shall not surely die." (Gen. 3:4.) To shrink from telling men, that except they believe they will "die in their sins," may please the devil, but surely it cannot please God.

Finally, let us never forget that unbelief is the special sin that ruins men's souls. Had the Jews believed on our Lord, all manner of sin and blasphemy might have been forgiven them. But unbelief bars the door in mercy's face, and cuts off hope. Let us watch and pray hard against it. Immorality slays its thousands, but unbelief its tens of thousands. One of the strongest sayings ever used by our Lord was this—"He that believes not shall be damned." (Mark 16:16.)

8:31-36

Abraham's Children and the Devil's Children

Then Jesus said to those Jewish people who had believed him, "If you continue to follow my teaching, you are really my disciples and you will know the truth, and the truth will set you free." "We are descendants of Abraham," they replied, "and have never been anyone's slaves! How can you say, 'You will become free'?" Jesus answered them, "I tell you the solemn truth, everyone who practices sin is a slave of sin. The slave does not remain in the family forever, but the son remains forever. So if the son sets you free, you will be really free."

These verses show us, for one thing, the importance of steady perseverance in Christ's service. There were many, it seems, at this particular period, who professed to believe on our Lord, and expressed a desire to become His disciples. There is nothing to show that they had true faith. They appear to have acted under the influence of temporary excitement, without considering what they were doing. And to them our Lord addresses this instructive warning—"If you continue in My word, then are you My disciples indeed."

This sentence contains a mine of wisdom. To make a beginning in religious life is comparatively easy. Not a few mixed motives assist us. The love of novelty, the praise of well-meaning but imprudent professors, the secret self-satisfaction of feeling "how good I am," the universal excitement attending a new position—all these things combine to aid the young beginner. Aided by them he begins to run the race that leads to heaven, lays aside many bad habits, takes up many good ones, has many comfortable frames and feelings, and gets on splendidly for a time. But when the newness of his position is past and gone, when the freshness of his feelings is rubbed off and lost, when the world and the devil begin to pull hard at him, when the weakness of his own heart begins to appear, then it is that he finds out the real difficulties of vital Christianity. Then it is that he discovers the deep wisdom of our Lord's saying now before us. It is not beginning, but "continuing" a religious profession, that is the test of true grace.

We should remember these things in forming our estimate of other people's religion. No doubt we ought to be thankful when we see any one ceasing to do evil and learning to do well. We must not "despise the day of small things." (Zech. 4:10.) But we must not forget that to begin is one thing, and to go on is quite another. Patient continuance in well-doing is the only sure evidence of grace. Not he that runs fast and furiously at first, but he that keeps up his speed, is he that "runs so as to obtain." By all means let us be hopeful when we see anything like conversion. But let us not make too sure that it is real conversion, until time has set its seal upon it. Time and wear test metals, and prove whether they are solid or plated. Time and wear, in like manner, are the surest tests of a man's religion. Where there is spiritual life there will be continuance and steady perseverance. It is the man who goes on as well as begins, that is "the disciple indeed."

These verses show us, for another thing, the nature of true slavery. The Jews were fond of boasting, though without any just cause, that they were politically free, and were not in bondage to any foreign power. Our Lord reminds those who there was another bondage to which they were giving no heed, although enslaved by it. "He that commits sin is the slave of sin."

How true that is! How many on every side are total slaves, although they do not acknowledge it! They are led captive by their besetting corruptions and infirmities, and seem to have no power to get free. Ambition, the love of money, the passion for drink, the craving for pleasure and excitement, gambling, gluttony, illicit relationships—all these are so many tyrants among men. Each and all have crowds of unhappy prisoners bound hand and foot in their chains. The wretched prisoners will not admit their bondage. They will even boast sometimes that they are eminently free. But many of them know better. There are times when the iron enters into their souls, and they feel bitterly that they are slaves.

There is no slavery like this. Sin is indeed the hardest of all taskmasters. Misery and disappointment in the way, despair and hell in the end—these are the only wages that sin pays to its servants. To deliver men from this bondage, is the grand object of the Gospel. To awaken people to a sense of their degradation, to show them their chains, to make them arise and struggle to be free—this is the great end for which Christ sent forth His ministers. Happy is he who has opened his eyes and found out his danger. To know that we are being led captive, is the very first step toward deliverance.

These verses, show us, lastly, the nature of true liberty. Our Lord declares this to the Jews in one comprehensive sentence. He says, "If the Son shall make you free, you shall be free indeed."

Liberty, most Englishmen know, is rightly esteemed one of the highest temporal blessings. Freedom from foreign dominion, a free constitution, free trade, a free press, civil and religious liberty—what a world of meaning lies beneath these phrases! How many would sacrifice life and fortune to maintain the things which they represent! Yet, after all our boasting, there are many so-called freemen who are nothing better than slaves. There are many who are totally ignorant of the highest, purest form of liberty. The noblest liberty is that which is the property of the true Christian. Those only are perfectly free people whom the Son of God "makes free." All else will sooner or later be found slaves.

Wherein does the liberty of true Christians consist? Of what is their freedom made up? They are freed from the guilt and consequences of sin by the blood of Christ. Justified, pardoned, forgiven, they can look forward boldly to the day of judgment, and cry "Who shall lay anything to our charge? Who is he that condemns?" They are freed from the power of sin by the grace of Christ's Spirit. Sin has no longer dominion over them. Renewed, converted, sanctified, they mortify and tread down sin, and are no longer led captive by it. Liberty, like this, is the portion of all true Christians in the day that they flee to Christ by faith, and commit their souls to Him. That day they become free men. Liberty, like this, is their portion forevermore. Death cannot stop it. The grave cannot even hold their bodies for more than a little season. Those whom Christ makes free are free to all eternity.

Let us never rest until we have some personal experience of this freedom ourselves. Without it all other freedom is a worthless privilege. Free speech, free laws, political freedom, commercial freedom, national freedom—all these cannot smooth down a dying pillow, or disarm death of his sting, or fill our consciences with peace. Nothing can do that but the freedom which Christ alone bestows. He gives it freely to all who seek it humbly. Then let us never rest until it is our own.

8:37-47

"I know that you are Abraham's descendants. But you want to kill me, because my teaching makes no progress among you. I am telling you the things I have

seen while with my Father, but you are practicing the things you have heard from your father."

They answered him, "Abraham is our father!" Jesus replied, "If you were Abraham's children, you would be doing the deeds of Abraham. But now you are trying to kill me, a man who has told you the truth I heard from God. Abraham did not do this! You people are doing the deeds of your father."

Then they said to Jesus, "We were not born as a result of immorality! We have only one Father, God himself." Jesus replied, "If God were your Father, you would love me, for I have come from God and am now here. I have not come on my own initiative, but he sent me. Why don't you understand what I am saying? It is because you cannot accept my teaching. You people are from your father the devil, and you want to do what your father desires. He was a murderer from the beginning, and does not uphold the truth, because there is no truth in him. Whenever he lies, he speaks according to his own nature, because he is a liar and the father of lies. But because I am telling you the truth, you do not believe me. Who among you can prove me guilty of any sin? If I am telling you the truth, why don't you believe me? The one who belongs to God listens and responds to God's words. You don't listen and respond, because you don't belong to God."

There are things taught in this passage of Scripture which are peculiarly truth for the times. Well would it be for the Churches if all Christians would ponder carefully the matter which it contains.

We are taught for one thing the ignorant self-righteousness of the natural man. We find the Jews pluming themselves on their natural descent from Abraham, as if that must of necessity, cover all deficiencies—"Abraham is our father." We find them going even further than this, and claiming to be God's special favorites and God's own family—"We have one Father, even God." They forgot that fleshly relationship to Abraham was useless, unless they shared Abraham's grace. They forgot that God's choice of their father to be head of a favored nation was never meant to carry salvation to the children, unless they walked in their father's footsteps. All this in their blind self-conceit they refused to see. "We are Jews. We are God's children. We are the true Church. We are in the covenant. We must be all right." This was their whole argument!

Strange as it may seem, there are multitudes of so-called Christians who are exactly like these Jews. Their whole religion consist of a few notions neither wiser nor better than those propounded by the enemies of our Lord. They will tell you "that they are regular Church people; they have been baptized; they go to the Lord's table"—but they can tell you no more. Of all the essential doctrines of the Gospel they are totally ignorant. Of faith, and grace, and repentance, and holiness, and spiritual mindedness they know nothing at all. Unquestionably they are Churchmen, and so they hope to go to heaven! There are myriads in this condition. It sounds sad, but unhappily it is only too true.

Let us settle firmly in our minds that connection with a good Church and good ancestors is no proof whatever that we ourselves are in a way to be saved. We need something more than this. We must be joined to Christ himself by a living faith. We must know something experimentally of the work of the Spirit in our hearts. "Church principles," and "sound Churchmanship," are fine words and excellent party cries. But they will not deliver our souls from the wrath to come, or give us boldness in the day of judgment.

We are taught for another thing the true marks of spiritual sonship. Our Lord makes this point most plain by two mighty sayings. Did the Jews say, "We have Abraham to our father"? He replies, "If you were Abraham's children you would do the work of Abraham." Did the Jews say, "We have one Father, even God"? He replies, "If God were your Father you would love Me."

Let these two sayings of Christ sink down into our hearts. They supply an answer to two of the most mischievous, yet most common, errors of the present day. What more common, on one side, than vague talk about the universal Fatherhood of God? "All men," we are told, "are God's children, whatever be their creed or religion; all are finally to have a place in the Father's house, "where there are many mansions." What more common, on another side, than high-sounding statements about the effect of baptism and the privileges of Church-membership?

"By baptism," we are confidently told, "all baptized people are made children of God; all members of the Church, without distinction, have a right to be addressed as sons and daughters of the Lord Almighty."

Statements like these can never be reconciled with the plain language of our Lord in the passage before us. If words mean anything, no man is really a child of God, who does not love Jesus Christ. The charitable judgment of a baptismal service, or the hopeful estimate of a catechism, may call him by the name of a son, and reckon him among God's children. But the reality of sonship to God, and all its blessings, no one possesses who does not love the Lord Jesus Christ in sincerity. (Ephes. 6:24.) In matters like these we need not be shaken by mere assertions. We may well afford to despise the charge of undervaluing the sacraments. We have only to ask one question—"What is written? What says the Lord?" And with this saying before us, we can only come to one conclusion—"Where there is no love to Christ, there is no sonship to God."

We are taught, lastly, in these verses, the reality and character of the devil. Our Lord speaks of him as one whose personality and existence are beyond dispute. In solemn words of stern rebuke He says to His unbelieving enemies, "You are of your father the devil"—led by him, doing his will, and showing unhappily that you are like him. And then He paints his picture in dark colors, describing him as a "murderer" from the beginning, as a "liar" and the father of lies.

There is a devil! We have a mighty invisible enemy always near us—one who never slumbers and never sleeps—one who is about our path and about our bed, and spies out all our ways, and will never leave us until we die. He is a murderer! His great aim and object is, to ruin us forever and kill our souls. To destroy, to rob us of eternal life, to bring us down to the second death in hell, are the things for which he is unceasingly working. He is ever going about, seeking whom he may devour. He is a liar! He is continually trying to deceive us by false representations, just as he deceived Eve at the beginning. He is always telling us that good is evil and evil good—truth is falsehood and falsehood truth—the broad way good and the narrow way bad. Millions are led captive by his deceit, and follow him, both rich and poor, both high and low, both learned and unlearned. Lies are his chosen weapons. By lies he slays many.

These are dreadful things; but they are true. Let us live as if we believed them. Let us not be like many who mock, and sneer, and scoff, and deny the existence of the very being who is invisibly leading them to hell. Let us believe there is a devil, and watch, and pray, and fight hard against his temptations. Strong as he is, there is One stronger than him, who said to Peter, "I have prayed for you, that your faith fail not," and who still intercedes at God's right hand. Let us commit our souls to Him. (Luke 22:32.) With such a being as the devil going to and fro in the world, we never need wonder to see evil abounding. But with Christ on our side, we need not be afraid. Greater is He that is for us than he that is against us. It is written, "Resist the devil, and he shall flee from you." "The God of peace shall bruise Satan under your feet shortly." (James 4:7; Rom. 16:20.)

8:48-59

The Jewish people who had been listening to him replied, "Aren't we correct in saying that you are a Samaritan and are possessed by a demon?" Jesus answered, "I am not possessed by a demon, but I honor my Father and yet you dishonor me. I am not trying to get praise for myself. There is one who demands it, and he also judges. I tell you the solemn truth, if anyone obeys my teaching, he will never see death."

Then the Jewish people who had been listening to him responded, "Now we know you're possessed by a demon! Both Abraham and the prophets died, and yet you say, 'If anyone obeys my teaching, he will never taste of death.' You aren't greater than our father Abraham who died, are you? And the prophets died too! Who do you claim to be?" Jesus replied, "If I glorify myself, my glory is worthless. The one who glorifies me is my Father, about whom you people say, 'He is our God.' Yet you do not know him, but I know him. If I say that I do not know him, I will be a liar like you. But I do know him, and I obey his teaching. Your father Abraham was overjoyed to see my day, and he saw it and was glad."

Then the Jewish people who had been listening to him replied, "You are not yet fifty years old! Have you seen Abraham?" Jesus said to them, "I tell you the solemn truth, before Abraham came into existence, I am!" Then they picked up stones to throw at him, but Jesus hid himself and went out from the temple area.

We should observe, first, in this passage, what blasphemous and slander-ous language was addressed to our Lord by His enemies. We read that the Jews "Aren't we correct in saying that you are a Samaritan and are possessed by a demon?" Silenced in argument, these wicked men resorted to personal abuse. To lose temper, and call names, is a common sign of a defeated cause.

Nicknames, insulting epithets, and violent language, are favorite weapons with the devil. When other means of carrying on his warfare fail, he stirs up his servants to smite with the tongue. Grievous indeed are the sufferings which the saints of God have had to endure from the tongue in every age. Their characters have been slandered. Evil reports have been circulated about them. Lying stories have been diligently invented, and greedily swallowed, about their conduct. No wonder that David said, "Deliver my soul, O Lord, from lying lips, and from a deceitful tongue." (Psalm 120:2.)

The true Christian in the present day must never be surprised to find that he has constant trials to endure from this quarter. Sinful human nature never changes. So long as he serves the world, and walks in the broad way, little perhaps will be said against him. Once let him take up the cross and follow Christ, and there is no lie too monstrous, and no story too absurd, for some to tell against him, and for others to believe. But let him take comfort in the thought that he is only drinking the cup which his blessed Master drank before him. The lies of his enemies do him no injury in heaven, whatever they may on earth. Let him bear them patiently, and not fret, or lose his temper. When Christ was reviled, "He reviled not again." (1 Peter 2:23.) Let the Christian do likewise.

We should observe, secondly, what glorious encouragement our Lord holds out to His believing people. We read that He said, "I tell you the solemn truth, if anyone obeys my teaching, he will never see death."

Of course these words do not mean that true Christians shall never die. On the contrary, we all know that they must go down to the grave, and cross the river just like others. But the words do mean, that they shall not be hurt by the second death—that final ruin of the whole man in hell, of which the first death is only a faint type or figure. (Rev. 21:8.) And they do mean that the sting of the first death shall be removed from the true Christian. His flesh may fail, and his bones may be racked with strong pain; but the bitter sense of unpardoned sins shall not crush him down. This is the worst part of death—and in this he shall have the "victory through our Lord Jesus Christ." (1 Cor. 15:57.)

This blessed promise, we must not forget to notice, is the peculiar property of the man who "obeys Christ's teachings." That expression, it is clear, can never be applicable to the mere outward professing Christian, who neither knows nor cares anything about the Gospel. It belongs to him who receives into his heart, and obeys in his life, the message which the Lord Jesus brought from heaven. It belongs, in short, to those who are Christians, not in name and form only, but in deed and in truth. It is written—"He that overcomes shall not be hurt of the second death." (Rev. 2:11.)

We should observe, thirdly, in this passage, what clear knowledge of Christ Abraham possessed. We read that our Lord said to the Jews, "Your father Abraham rejoiced to see My day—and he saw it and was glad."

When our Lord used these remarkable words, Abraham had been dead and buried at least 1850 years! And yet he is said to have seen our Lord's day! How astonishing that sounds! Yet it was quite true. Not only did Abraham "see" our Lord and talk to Him when He "appeared unto him in the plains of Mamre," the night before Sodom was destroyed, (Gen. 18:1,) but by faith he looked forward to the day of our Lord's incarnation yet to come, and as he looked he "was glad." That he saw many things, through a glass darkly, we need not doubt. That he could have explained fully the whole manner and circumstances of our Lord's sacrifice on Calvary, we are not obliged to suppose. But we need not shrink from believing that he saw in the far distance a Redeemer, whose advent would finally make all the earth rejoice. And as he saw it, he "was glad."

The plain truth is, that we are too apt to forget that there never was but one way of salvation, one Savior, and one hope for sinners, and that Abraham and all the Old Testaments saints looked to the same Christ that we look to ourselves. We shall do well to call to mind the Seventh Article of the Church of England—"The Old Testament is not contrary to the New—for both in the Old and New Testament everlasting life is offered through Christ, who is the only Mediator between God and man, being both God and man. Wherefore they are not to be heard, who assume that the old Fathers did look only for transitory promises." This is truth that we must never forget in reading the Old Testament. This is sound speech that cannot be condemned.

We should observe, lastly, in this prophecy, how distinctly our Lord declares His own pre-existence. We read that He said to the Jews, "Before Abraham was, I am."

Without a controversy, these remarkable words are a great deep. They contain things which we have no eyes to see through, or mind to fathom. But if language means anything, they teach us that our Lord Jesus Christ existed long before He came into the world. Before the days of Abraham He was. Before man was created He was. In short, they teach us that the Lord Jesus was no mere man like Moses or David. He was One whose goings forth were from everlasting, the same yesterday, today, and forever, very and eternal God.

Deep as these words are, they are full of practical comfort. They show us the length, and breadth, and depth, and height of that great foundation, on which sinners are invited to rest their souls. He to whom the Gospel bids us come with our sins, and believe for pardon and peace, is no mere man. He is nothing less than very God, and therefore "able to save to the uttermost" all who come to Him. Then let us begin coming to Him with confidence. Let us continue leaning on Him without fear. The Lord Jesus Christ is the true God, and our eternal life is secure.

Chapter 9

9:1-12

Healing a Man Born Blind

*Now as Jesus was passing by, he saw a man who had been blind from birth.
His disciples asked him, "Rabbi, who committed the sin that caused him to
be born blind, this man or his parents?" Jesus answered, "Neither this man nor
his parents sinned, but he was born blind so that the acts of God may be revealed
through what happens to him. We must perform the deeds of the one who sent me
as long as it is daytime. Night is coming when no one can work. As long as I am
in the world, I am the light of the world." Having said this, he spit on the ground
and made some mud with the saliva. He smeared the mud on the blind man's eyes
and said to him, "Go wash in the pool of Siloam" (which is translated "sent"). So
the blind man went away and washed, and came back seeing.*

*Then the neighbors and the people who had seen him previously as a beggar
began saying, "Is this not the man who used to sit and beg?" Some people said, "This
is the man!" while others said, "No, but he looks like him." The man himself kept
insisting, "I am the one." So they asked him, "How then were you made to see?"
He replied, "The man called Jesus made mud, smeared it on my eyes and told me,
'Go to Siloam and wash.' So I went and washed, and was able to see." They said to
him, "Where is that man?" He replied, "I don't know."*

The chapter we now begin records one of the few great works of Christ
which John has reported. It tell us how our Lord gave sight to a man who
had been "blind from his birth." Here, as elsewhere in this Gospel, we find
the circumstances of the miracle narrated with peculiar fullness, minute-

ness, and particularity. Here too, as elsewhere, we find the narrative rich in spiritual lessons.

We should observe, first, in this passage, how much sorrow sin has brought into the world. A sorrowful case is brought before us. We are told of a man "who was blind from his birth." A more serious affliction can hardly be conceived. Of all the bodily crosses that can be laid on man, without taking away life, none perhaps is greater than the loss of sight. It cuts us off from some of the greatest enjoyments of life. It shuts us up within a narrow world of our own. It makes us painfully helpless and dependent on others. In fact, until men lose their eyesight, they never fully realize its value.

Now blindness, like every other bodily infirmity, is one of the fruits of sin. If Adam had never fallen, we cannot doubt that people would never have been blind, or deaf, or mute. The many ills that flesh is heir to, the countless pains, and diseases, and physical defects to which we are all liable, came in when the curse came upon the earth. "By one man sin entered into the world, and death by sin." (Rom. 5:12.)

Let us learn to hate sin with a godly hatred, as the root of more than half of our cares and sorrows. Let us fight against it, mortify it, crucify it, and abhor it both in ourselves and others. There cannot be a clearer proof that man is a fallen creature than the fact that he can love sin and take pleasure in it.

We should observe, secondly, in this passage, what a solemn lesson Christ gives us about the use of opportunities. He says to the disciples who asked Him about the blind man, "I must work while it is called today—the night comes, when no man can work."

That saying was eminently true when applied to our Lord Himself. He knew well that his own earthly ministry would only last three years altogether, and knowing this He diligently redeemed the time. He let slip no opportunity of doing works of mercy, and attending to His Father's business. Morning, noon, and night He was always carrying on the work which the Father gave Him to do. It was His food and drink to do His Father's will, and to finish His work. His whole life breathed one sentiment—"I must work—the night comes, when no man can work."

The saying is one which should be remembered by all professing Christians. The life that we now live in the flesh is our day. Let us take care that we use it well, for the glory of God and the good of our souls. Let us work out our salvation with fear and trembling, while it is called today. There is no work nor labor in the grave, toward which we are all fast hastening. Let us pray, and read, and keep our Sabbaths holy, and hear God's Word, and do good in our generation, like men who never forget that "the night is at hand." Our time is very short. Our daylight will soon be gone. Opportunities once lost can never be retrieved. A second lease of life is granted to no man. Then let us resist procrastination as we would resist the devil. Whatever our hand finds to do, let us do it with our might. "The night comes, when no man can work."

We should observe, thirdly, in this passage, what different means Christ used in working miracles on different occasions. In healing the blind man He might, if He had thought fit, have merely touched Him with his finger, or given command with His tongue. But He did not rest content with doing so. We are told that "He spit on the ground, and made clay of the spittle, and He anointed the eyes of the blind man with the clay." In all these means of course there was no inherent healing virtue. But for wise reasons the Lord was pleased to use them.

We need not doubt that in this, as in every other action of our Lord, there is an instructive lesson. It teaches us, we may well believe, that the Lord of heaven and earth will not be tied down to the use of any one means or instrumentality. In conferring blessings on man, He will work in His own way, and will allow no one to prescribe to Him. Above all, it should teach those who have received anything at Christ's hands, to be careful how they measure other men's experience by their own. Have we been healed by Christ, and made to see and live? Let us thank God for it, and be humbled. But let us beware of saying that no other man has been healed, except he has been brought to spiritual life in precisely the same manner. The great question is—"Are the eyes of our understanding opened? Do we see? Have we spiritual life?"—Enough for us if the cure is effected and health restored. If it is, we must leave it to the great Physician to choose the instrument, the means, and the manner—the clay, the touch, or the command.

We should observe, lastly, in this passage, the almighty power that Christ holds in His hands. We see Him doing that which in itself was impossible. Without medicines He cures an incurable case. He actually gives eyesight to one who was born blind.

Such a miracle as this is meant to teach an old truth, which we can never know too well. It shows us that Jesus the Savior of sinners "has all power in heaven—and earth." Such mighty works could never have been done by one that was merely man. In the cure of this blind man we see nothing less than the finger of God.

Such a miracle, above all, is meant to make us hopeful about our own souls and the souls of others. Why should we despair of salvation while we have such a Savior? Where is the spiritual disease that He cannot take away? He can open the eyes of the most sinful and ignorant, and make them see things they never saw before. He can send light into the darkest heart, and cause blindness and prejudice to pass away.

Surely, if we are not saved, the fault will be all our own. There lives at God's right hand One who can heal us if we apply to Him. Let us take heed lest those solemn words are found true of us—"Light has come into the world but men loved darkness rather than light, because their deeds were evil." "You will not come to Me that you might have life." (John 3:19; 5:40)

9:13-25

The Pharisees' Reaction to the Healing

They brought the man who used to be blind to the Pharisees. (Now the day on which Jesus made the mud and caused him to see was a Sabbath.) So the Pharisees asked him again how he had gained his sight. He replied, "He put mud on my eyes and I washed, and now I am able to see."

Then some of the Pharisees began to say, "This man is not from God, because he does not observe the Sabbath." But others said, "How can a man who is a sinner perform such miraculous signs?" Thus there was a division among them. So again they asked the man who used to be blind, "What do you say about him, since he caused you to see?" "He is a prophet," the man replied.

Now the Jewish authorities refused to believe that he had really been blind and had gained his sight until at last they summoned the parents of the man who had become able to see. They asked the parents, "Is this your son, whom you say was born blind? Then how does he now see?" So his parents replied, "We know that this is our son and that he was born blind. But we do not know how he is now able to see, nor do we know who caused him to see. Ask him, he is a mature adult. He will speak for himself." (His parents said these things because they were afraid of the Jewish authorities. For the Jewish authorities had already agreed that anyone who confessed Jesus to be the Christ would be put out of the synagogue. For this reason his parents said, "He is a mature adult, ask him.")

Then they summoned the man who used to be blind a second time and said to him, "Promise before God to tell the truth. We know that this man is a sinner." He replied, "I do not know whether he is a sinner. I do know one thing—that although I was blind, now I can see."

These verses show us how little the Jews of our Lord's time understood the right use of the Sabbath day. We read that some of the Pharisees found fault because a blind man was miraculously healed on the Sabbath. They said, "This man is not of God, because He keeps not the Sabbath day." A good work had manifestly been done to a helpless fellow-creature. A heavy bodily infirmity had been removed. A mighty act of mercy had been performed. But the blind-hearted enemies of Christ could see no beauty in the act. They called it a breach of the Fourth Commandment!

These would-be wise men completely mistook the intention of the Sabbath. They did not see that it was "made for man," and meant for the good of man's body, mind, and soul. It was a day to be set apart from others, no doubt, and to be carefully sanctified and kept holy. But its sanctification was never intended to prevent works of necessity and acts of mercy. To heal a sick man was no breach of the Sabbath day. In finding fault with our Lord for so doing, the Jews only exposed their ignorance of their own law. They had forgotten that it is as great a sin to add to a commandment, as to take it away.

Here, as in other places, we must take care that we do not put a wrong meaning on our Lord's conduct. We must not for a moment suppose that the Sabbath is no longer binding on Christians, and that they have nothing to do with the Fourth Commandment. This is a great mistake, and the root of great evil. Not one of the Ten Commandments has ever been repealed or put aside. Our Lord never meant the Sabbath to become a day of pleasure, or a day of business, or a day of traveling and idle dissipation. He meant it to be "kept holy" as long as the world stands. It is one thing to employ the Sabbath in works of mercy, in ministering to the sick, and doing good to the distressed. It is quite another thing to spend the day in visiting, feasting, and self-indulgence. Whatever men may please to say, the way in which we use the Sabbath a sure test of the state of our religion. By the Sabbath may be found out whether we love communion with God. By the Sabbath may be found out whether we are in tune for heaven. By the Sabbath, in short, the secrets of many hearts are revealed. There are only too many of whom we may say with sorrow, "These men are not of God, because they keep not the Sabbath day."

These verses show us, secondly, the desperate lengths to which prejudice will sometimes carry wicked men. We read that the "Jews agreed that if any man did confess that Jesus was Christ, he should be put out of the synagogue." They were determined not to believe. They were resolved that no evidence should change their minds, and no proofs influence their will. They were like men who shut their eyes and tie a bandage over them, and refuse to have it untied. Just as in after times they stopped their ears when Stephen preached, and refused to listen when Paul made his defense, so they behaved at this period of our Lord's ministry.

Of all states of mind into which unconverted men can fall, this is by far the most dangerous to the soul. So long as a person is open, fair, and honest minded, there is hope for him, however ignorant he may be. He may be much in the dark at present. But is he willing to follow the light, if set before him? He may be walking in the broad road with all his might. But is he ready to listen to any one who will show him a more excellent way? In a word, is he teachable, childlike, and unfettered by prejudice? If these questions can be answered satisfactorily, we never need despair about the man's soul.

The state of mind we should always desire to possess is that of the noble-minded Bereans. When they first heard the Apostle Paul preach, they listened with attention. They received the Word "with all readiness of mind." They "searched the Scriptures," and compared what they heard with God's Word. "And therefore," we are told, "many of them believed." Happy are those who go and do likewise! (Acts 17:11, 12.)

These verses show us, lastly, that nothing convinces a man so thoroughly as his own senses and feelings. We read that the unbelieving Jews tried in vain to persuade the blind man whom Jesus healed, that nothing had been done for him. They only got from him one plain answer—"One thing I know, that whereas I was blind, now I see." How the miracle had been worked, he did not pretend to explain. Whether the person who had healed him was a sinner, he did not profess to know. But that something had been done for him he stoutly maintained. He was not to be reasoned out of his senses. Whatever the Jews might think, there were two distinct facts of which he was conscious—"I was blind—now I see."

There is no kind of evidence so satisfactory as this to the heart of a real Christian. His knowledge may be small. His faith may be feeble. His doctrinal views may be at present confused and indistinct. But if Christ has really wrought a work of grace in his heart by His Spirit, he feels within him something that you cannot overthrow. "I was dark, and now I have light. I was afraid of God, and now I love Him. I was fond of sin, and now I hate it. I was blind, and now I see." Let us never rest until we know and feel within us some real work of the Holy Spirit. Let us not be content with the name and form of Christianity. Let us desire to have true experimental acquaintance with it. Feelings no doubt, are deceitful, and are not everything in religion. But if we have no inward feelings about spiritual matters, it is a very bad sign. The hungry man eats, and feels strengthened; the thirsty man drinks, and feels refreshed. Surely the man who has within him the grace of God, ought to be able to say, "I feel its power."

9:26-41

Then they said to him, "What did he do to you? How did he cause you to see?"
He answered, "I told you already and you didn't listen. Why do you want to hear it again? You people don't want to become his disciples too, do you?"
They heaped insults on him, saying, "You are his disciple! We are disciples of Moses! We know that God has spoken to Moses! We do not know where this man comes from!" The man replied, "This is a remarkable thing, that you don't know where he comes from, and yet he caused me to see! We know that God doesn't listen to sinners, but if anyone is devout and does his will, God listens to him. Never before has anyone heard of someone causing a man born blind to see. If this man were not from God, he could do nothing." They replied, "You were born completely in sinfulness, and yet you presume to teach us?" So they threw him out.
Jesus heard that they had thrown him out, so he found the man and said to him, "Do you believe in the Son of Man?" The man replied, "And who is he, sir, that I may believe in him?" Jesus told him, "You have seen him; he is the one speaking with you." He said, "Lord, I believe," and he worshiped him. Jesus said, "For judgment I have come into this world, so that those who do not see may gain their sight, and the ones who see may become blind."
Some of the Pharisees who were with him heard this and asked him, "We are not blind too, are we?" Jesus replied, "If you were blind, you would not be guilty of sin, but now because you claim that you can see, your guilt remains."

We see in these verses how much wiser the poor sometimes are than the rich. The man whom our Lord healed of his blindness was evidently a person of very humble condition. It is written that he was one who "sat and begged." (See v. 8.) Yet he saw things which the proud rulers of the Jews could not see, and would not receive. He saw in our Lord's miracle an unanswerable proof of our Lord's divine commission. "If this Man were not of God," he cries, "He could do nothing." In fact, from the day of his cure his position was completely altered. He had eyes, and the Pharisees were blind.

The same thing may be seen in other places of Scripture. The servants of Pharaoh saw "the finger of God" in the plagues of Egypt, when their master's heart was hardened. The servants of Naaman saw the wisdom of Elisha's advice, when their master was turning away in a rage. The high, the great, and the noble are often the last to learn spiritual lessons. Their possessions and their position often blind the eyes of their understanding, and keep them back from the kingdom of God. It is written that "not many wise men after the flesh, not many mighty, not many noble, are called." (1 Cor. 1:26.)

The Christian poor man never need be ashamed of his poverty. It is a sin to be proud, and worldly-minded, and unbelieving; but it is no sin to be poor. The very riches which many long to possess are often veils over the eyes of men's souls, and prevent their seeing Christ. The teaching of the Holy Spirit is more frequently to be seen among men of low degree than among men of rank and education. The words of our Lord are continually proved most true, "How hard it is for rich people to get into the Kingdom of God!" "You have hid these things from the wise and prudent, and have revealed them unto babes." (Mark 10:23; Matt. 11:25.)

We see, secondly, in these verses, how cruelly and unjustly unconverted men will sometimes treat those who disagree with them. When the Pharisees could not frighten the blind man who had been cured, they expelled him from the Jewish Church. Because he manfully refused to deny the evidence of his own senses, they excommunicated him, and put him to an open shame. They cast him out "as a heathen man and a tax-collector."

The temporal injury that such treatment did to a poor Jew was very great indeed. It cut him off from the outward privileges of the Jewish Church. It made him an object of scorn and suspicion among all true Israelites. But it could do no harm to his soul. That which wicked men bind on earth is not bound in heaven. "The curse causeless shall not come." (Prov. 26:2.)

The children of God in every age have only too frequently met with like treatment. Excommunication, persecution, and imprisonment have generally been favorite weapons with ecclesiastical tyrants. Unable, like the Pharisees, to answer arguments, they have resorted to violence and injustice. Let the child of God console himself with the thought that there is a true Church out of which no man can cast him, and a Church-membership which no earthly power can take away. He only is blessed whom Christ calls blessed; and he only is accursed whom Christ shall pronounce accursed at the last day.

We see, thirdly, in these verses, how great is the kindness and condescension of Christ. No sooner was this poor blind man cast out of the Jewish

Church than Jesus finds him and speaks words of comfort. He knew full well how heavy an affliction excommunication was to an Israelite, and at once cheered him with kind words. He now revealed Himself more fully to this man than He did to anyone except the Samaritan woman. In reply to the question, "Who is the Son of God?" He says plainly, "You have both seen Him, and it is He that talks with you."

We have here one among many beautiful illustrations of the mind of Christ. He sees all that His people go through for His sake, and feels for all, from the highest to the lowest. He keeps account of all their losses, crosses, and persecutions. "Are they not all written in His book?" (Psalm. 56:8.) He knows how to come to their hearts with consolation in their time of need, and to speak peace to them when all men seem to hate them. The time when men forsake us is often the very time when Christ draws near, saying, "Fear not, for I am with you—be not dismayed, for I am your God—I will strengthen you-yes, I will help you; yes, I will uphold you with the right hand of my righteousness." (Isaiah. 41:10.)

We see, lastly, in these verses, how dangerous it is to possess knowledge, if we do not make a good use of it. The rulers of the Jews were fully persuaded that they knew all religious truth. They were indignant at the very idea of being ignorant and devoid of spiritual eyesight. "Are we blind also?" they cried. And then came the mighty sentence, "If you were blind, you should have no sin-but now you say, 'We see'; therefore your sin remains."

Knowledge undoubtedly is a very great blessing. The man who cannot read, and is utterly ignorant of Scripture, is in a pitiable condition. He is at the mercy of any false teacher who comes across him, and may be taught to take up any absurd creed, or to follow any vicious practice. Almost any education is better than no education at all.

But when knowledge only sticks in a man's head, and has no influence over his heart and life, it becomes a most perilous possession. And when, in addition to this, its possessor is self-conceited and self-satisfied, and imagines he knows everything, the result is one of the worst states of soul into which man can fall. There is far more hope about him who says, "I am a poor blind sinner and want God to teach me," than about him who is ever saying, "I know it, I know it, I am not ignorant," and yet cleaves to his sins. The sin of that man "remains."

Let us use diligently whatever religious knowledge we possess, and ask continually that God would give us more. Let us never forget that the devil himself is a creature of vast head-knowledge, and yet none the better for it, because it is not rightly used. Let our constant prayer be that which David so often sent up in the hundred and nineteenth Psalm. "Lord, teach me your statutes give me understanding—unite my heart to fear Your name."

Chapter 10

"*I tell you the solemn truth, the one who does not enter the sheepfold by the door, but climbs in some other way, is a thief and a robber. The one who enters by the door is the shepherd of the sheep. The doorkeeper opens the door for him, and the sheep hear his voice. He calls his own sheep by name and leads them out. When he has brought all his own sheep out, he goes ahead of them, and the sheep follow him because they recognize his voice. They will never follow a stranger, but will run away from him, because they do not recognize the stranger's voice." Jesus told them this parable, but they did not understand what he was saying to them.*

So Jesus said to them again, "I tell you the solemn truth, I am the door for the sheep. All who came before me were thieves and robbers, but the sheep did not listen to them. I am the door. If anyone enters through me, he will be saved, and will come in and go out, and find pasture.

The chapter we have now begun is closely connected with the preceding one. The parable before us was spoken with direct reference to the blind teachers of the Jewish Church. The Scribes and Pharisees were the people our Lord had in view, when He described the false shepherd. The very men who had just said "We see," were denounced with holy boldness, as "thieves and robbers."

We have, for one thing, in these verses, a vivid picture of a false teacher of religion. Our Lord says that he is one who "enters not by the door into the sheepfold, but climbs up some other way."

The "door," in this sentence, must evidently mean something far more than outward calling and commission. The Jewish teachers, at any rate, were not deficient in this point—they could probably trace up their orders in direct succession to Aaron himself. Ordination is no proof whatever that a man is fit to show others the way to heaven. He may have been regularly set apart by those who have authority to call ministers, and yet all his life may never come near the door, and at last may die nothing better than "a thief and a robber."

The true sense of the "door" must be sought in our Lord's own interpretation. It is Christ Himself who is "the door." The true shepherd of souls is he who enters the ministry with a single eye to Christ, desiring to glorify Christ, doing all in the strength of Christ, preaching Christ's doctrine, walking in Christ's steps, and laboring to bring men and women to Christ. The false shepherd of souls is he who enters the ministerial office with little or no thought about Christ, from worldly and self-exalting motives, but from no desire to exalt Jesus, and the great salvation that is in Him. Christ, in one word, is the grand touchstone of the minister of religion. The man who makes much of Christ is a pastor after God's own heart, whom God delights to honor. The minister who makes little of Christ is one whom God regards as an impostor—as one who has climbed up to his holy office not by the door, but by "some other way."

The sentence before us is a sorrowful and humbling one. That it condemns the Jewish teachers of our Lord's time all men can see. There was no "door" in their ministry. They taught nothing rightly about Messiah. They rejected Christ Himself when He appeared—but all men do not see that the sentence condemns thousands of so-called Christian teachers, quite as much as the leaders and teachers of the Jews. Thousands of ordained men in the present day know nothing whatever about Christ, except His name. They have not entered "the door" themselves, and they are unable to show it to others. Well would it be for Christendom if this were more widely known, and more seriously considered! Unconverted ministers are the dry-rot of the Church. "When the blind lead the blind" both must fall into the ditch. If we would know the value of a man's ministry, we must never fail to ask, Where is the Lamb? Where is the Door? Does he bring forward Christ, and give Him his rightful place?

We have, for another thing, in these verses, a peculiar picture of true Christians. Our Lord describes them as sheep who "hear the voice of a true

Shepherd, and know His voice;" and as "sheep who will not follow a stranger, but will flee from him, for they know not the voice of strangers."

The thing taught in these words is a very curious one, and may seem "foolishness" to the world. There is a spiritual instinct in most true believers, which generally enables them to distinguish between true and false teaching. When they hear unsound religious instruction, there is something within them that says, "This is wrong." When they hear the real truth as it is in Jesus, there is something in their hearts which responds, "This is right." The careless man of the world may see no difference whatever between minister and minister, sermon and sermon. The poorest sheep of Christ, as a general rule, will "distinguish things that differ," though he may sometimes be unable to explain why.

Let us beware of despising this spiritual instinct. Whatever a sneering world may please to say, it is one of the peculiar marks of the indwelling of the Holy Spirit. As such, it is specially mentioned by John, when he says, "You have an anointing from the Holy One, and you know all things." (1 John 2:20.) Let us rather pray for it daily, in order that we may be kept from the influence of false shepherds. To lose all power of distinguishing between bitter and sweet is one of the worst symptoms of bodily disease. To be unable to see any difference between law and gospel, truth and error, Protestantism and Popery, the doctrine of Christ and the doctrine of man, is a sure proof that we are yet dead in heart, and need conversion.

We have, lastly, in these verses, a most instructive picture of Christ Himself. He utters one of those golden sayings which ought to be dear to all true Christians. They apply to people as well as to ministers. "I am the door—by me if any man enter in, he shall be saved, and shall go in and out, and find pasture." We are all by nature separate and far off from God. Sin, like a great barrier-wall, rises between us and our Maker. The sense of guilt makes us afraid of Him. The sense of His holiness keeps us at a distance from Him.

Born with a heart at enmity with God, we become more and more alienated from Him, by practice, the longer we live. The very first questions in religion that must be answered, are these—"How can I draw near to God? How can I be justified? How can a sinner like me be reconciled to my Maker?"

The Lord Jesus Christ has provided an answer to these mighty questions. By His sacrifice for us on the cross, He has opened a way through the great barrier, and provided pardon and peace for sinners. He has "suffered for sin, the just for the unjust, to bring us to God." He has opened a way into the holiest, through His blood, by which we may draw near to God with boldness, and approach God without fear. And now He is able to save to the uttermost all who come unto God by Him. In the highest sense He is "the door." No one "can come to the Father" but by Him.

Let us take heed that we use this door, and do not merely stand outside looking at it. It is a door free and open to the chief of sinners—"If any man enter in by it, he shall be saved." It is a door within which we shall find a full and constant supply for every need of our souls. We shall find that we can "go in and out," and enjoy liberty and peace. The day comes when this door will be shut forever, and men shall strive to enter in, but not be able. Then let us make sure work of our own salvation. Let us not stand tarrying outside, and halting between two opinions. Let us enter in and be saved.

1:10-18

"The thief comes only to steal and kill and destroy; I have come so that they may have life, and may have it abundantly.

"I am the good shepherd. The good shepherd lays down his life for the sheep. The hired hand who is not a shepherd and does not own sheep, sees the wolf coming and abandons the sheep and runs away. So the wolf attacks the sheep and scatters them. Because he is a hired hand and is not concerned about the sheep, he runs away.

"I am the good shepherd. I know my own and my own know me—just as the Father knows me and I know the Father—and I lay down my life for the sheep. I have other sheep that do not come from this sheepfold. I must bring them too, and they will listen to my voice, so that there will be one flock and one shepherd. This is why the Father loves me—because I lay down my life, so that I may take it back again. No one takes it away from me, but I lay it down of my own free will. I have the authority to lay it down, and I have the authority to take it back again. This commandment I received from my Father."

These verses show us, for one thing, the great object for which Christ came into the world. He says, I have come that men "might have life, and that they might have it more abundantly."

The truth contained in these words is of vast importance. They supply an antidote to many crude and unsound notions which are abroad in the world. Christ did not come to be only a teacher of new morality, or an example of holiness and self-denial, or a founder of new ceremonies, as some have vainly asserted. He left heaven, and dwelt for thirty-three years on earth for far higher ends than these. He came to procure eternal life for man, by the price of His own vicarious death. He came to be a mighty fountain of spiritual life for all mankind, to which sinners coming by faith might drink; and, drinking, might live for evermore. By Moses came laws, rules, ordinances, ceremonies. By Christ came grace, truth, and eternal life.

Important as this doctrine is, it requires to be fenced with one word of caution. We must not overstrain the meaning of our Lord Jesus Christ's words. We must not suppose that eternal life was a thing entirely unknown until Christ came, or that the Old Testament saints were in utter darkness about the world to come. The way of life by faith in a Savior was a way well known to Abraham and Moses and David. A Redeemer and a Sacrifice was the hope of all God's children from Abel down to John the Baptist; but their vision of these things was necessarily imperfect. They saw them afar off, and not distinctly. They saw them in outline only, and not completely. It was the coming of Christ which made all things plain, and caused the shadows to pass away. Life and immortality were brought into full light by the Gospel. In short, to use our Lord's own words, even those who had life had it "more abundantly," when Christ came into the world.

These verses show us, for another thing, one of the principal offices which Jesus Christ fills for true Christians. Twice over our Lord uses an expression which, to an Eastern hearer, would be singularly full of meaning. Twice over he says emphatically, "I am the Good Shepherd." It is a saying rich in consolation and instruction.

Like a good shepherd, Christ KNOWS all His believing people. Their names, their families, their dwelling-places, their circumstances, their private history, their experience, their trials—with all these things Jesus is perfectly acquainted. There is not a thing about the least and lowest of them with which He is not familiar. The children of this world may not know Christians, and may count their lives folly; but the Good Shepherd knows them thoroughly, and, wonderful to say, though He knows them, does not despise them.

Like a Good Shepherd, Christ CARES tenderly for all His believing people. He provides for all their needs in the wilderness of this world, and leads them by the right way to a city of habitation. He bears patiently with their many weaknesses and infirmities, and does not cast them off because they are wayward, erring, sick, footsore, or lame. He guards and protects them against all their enemies, as Jacob did the flock of Laban; and of those that the Father has given Him He will be found at last to have lost none.

Like a Good Shepherd, Christ LAYS DOWN HIS LIFE for the sheep. He did it once for all, when He was crucified for them. When He saw that nothing could deliver them from hell and the devil, but His blood, He willingly made His soul an offering for their sins. The merit of that death He is now presenting before the Father's throne. The sheep are saved for evermore, because the Good Shepherd died for them. This is indeed a love that passes knowledge! "Greater love has no man than this, that a man lay down his life for his friends." (John 15:13.)

Let us only take heed that this office of Christ is not set before us in vain. It will profit us nothing at the last day that Jesus was a Shepherd, if during our lifetime, we never heard His voice and followed Him. If we love life, let us join His flock without delay. Except we do this, we shall be found at the left hand in the day of judgment, and lost for evermore.

These verses show us, lastly, that when Christ died, He died of His own voluntary free will. He uses a remarkable expression to teach this—"I lay down my life that I might take it again. No man takes it from Me, but I lay it down of myself. I have power to lay it down, and I have power to take it again."

The point before us is of no small importance. We must never suppose for a moment that our Lord had no power to prevent His sufferings, and that He was delivered up to His enemies and crucified because He could not help it. Nothing could be further from the truth than such an idea. The treachery of Judas, the armed band of priests' servants, the enmity of Scribes and Pharisees, the injustice of Pontius Pilate, the crude hands of Roman soldiers, the scourge, the nails, and the spear—all these could not have harmed a hair of our Lord's head, unless He had allowed them. Well might He say those remarkable words, "Do you think that I cannot now pray to my Father, and He shall presently give Me more than twelve legions of angels? But how, then, shall the Scripture be fulfilled?" (Matt. 26:53.)

The plain truth is, that our Lord submitted to death of His own free will, because He knew that His death was the only way of making atonement for man's sins. He poured out His soul unto death with all the desire of His heart, because He had determined to pay our debt to God, and redeem us from hell. For the joy set before Him He willingly endured the cross, and laid down His life, in order that we, through His death, might have eternal life. His death was not the death of a martyr, who sinks at last overwhelmed by enemies, but the death of a triumphant conqueror, who knows that even in dying he wins for himself and his people a kingdom and a crown of glory.

Let us lean back our souls on these mighty truths, and be thankful. A willing Savior, a loving Savior, a Savior who came specially into the world to bring life to man, is just the Savior that we need. If we hear His voice, repent and believe, He is our own.

10:19-30

Another sharp division took place among the Jewish authorities because of these words. Many of them were saying, "He is possessed by a demon and has lost his mind. Why do you listen to him?" Others said, "These are not the words of someone possessed by a demon. A demon cannot cause the blind to see, can it?"

Then came the feast of the Dedication in Jerusalem. It was winter, and Jesus was walking in the temple area in Solomon's Portico. The Jewish religious leaders surrounded him and said, "How long will you keep us in suspense? If you are the Christ, tell us plainly." Jesus replied, "I told you and you do not believe. The deeds I do in my Father's name testify about me. But you refuse to believe because you are not my sheep. My sheep listen to my voice, and I know them, and they follow me. I give them eternal life, and they will never perish; no one will snatch them from my hand. My Father who has given them to me is greater than all, and no one can snatch them from my Father's hand. The Father and I are one."

We should notice, first, in this passage, what strifes and controversies our Lord occasioned when He was on earth. We read that "there was a division among the Jews for His sayings"—and that "many of them said He has a devil, and is mad," while others took an opposite view. It may seem strange, at first sight, that He who came to preach peace between God and man should be the cause of contention. But herein were His own words literally fulfilled—"I came not to send peace, but a sword." (Matt. 10:34.) The fault was not in Christ or His doctrine, but in the carnal mind of His Jewish hearers.

Let us never be surprised if we see the same thing in our own day. Human nature never changes. So long as the heart of man is without grace, so long we must expect to see it dislike the Gospel of Christ. Just as oil and water, acids and alkalies, cannot combine, so in the same way unconverted people cannot really like the people of God. "The carnal mind is enmity against God." "The natural man receives not the things of the Spirit of God." (Rom. 8:7; 1 Cor. 2:14)

The servant of Christ must think it no strange thing if he goes through the same experience as his Master. He will often find his ways and opinions in religion the cause of strife in his own family. He will have to endure ridicule, harsh words, and petty persecution, from the children of this world.

He may even discover that he is thought a fool or a madman on account of his Christianity. Let none of these things move him. The thought that he is a partaker of the afflictions of Christ ought to steel him against every trial. "If they have called the Master of the house Beelzebub, how much more shall they call them of his household." (Matt. 10:25)

One thing, at any rate, should never be forgotten. We must not allow ourselves to think the worse of religion because of the strifes and dissensions to which it gives rise. Whatever men may please to say, it is human nature, and not religion, which is to blame. We do not blame the glorious sun because its rays draw forth noxious vapors from the marsh. We must not find fault with the glorious Gospel, if it stirs up men's corruptions, and causes the "thoughts of many hearts to be revealed." (Luke 2:35.)

We should notice, secondly, the name which Christ gives to true Christians. He uses a figurative expression which, like all His language, is full of deep meaning. He calls them, "My sheep."

The word "sheep," no doubt, points to something in the character and ways of true Christians. It would be easy to show that weakness, helplessness, harmlessness, usefulness, are all points of resemblance between the sheep and the believer. But the leading idea in our Lord's mind was the entire dependence of the sheep upon its Shepherd. Just as sheep hear the voice of their own shepherd, and follow him, so do believers follow Christ. By faith they listen to His call. By faith they submit themselves to His guidance. By faith they lean on Him, and commit their souls implicitly to His direction. The ways of a shepherd and his sheep are a most useful illustration of the relation between Christ and the true Christian.

The expression, "My sheep," points to the close connection that exists between Christ and believers. They are His by gift from the Father, His by purchase, His by calling and choice, and His by their own consent and heart submission. In the highest sense they are Christ's property; and just as a man feels a special interest in that which he has bought at a great price and made his own, so does the Lord Jesus feel a peculiar interest in His people.

Expressions like these should be carefully treasured up in the memories of true Christians. They will be found cheering and heart-strengthening in days of trial. The world may see no beauty in the ways of a godly man, and may often pour contempt on him. But he who knows that he is one of Christ's sheep has no cause to be ashamed. He has within him a "well of water springing up into everlasting life." (John 4:14.)

We should notice, lastly, in this passage, the vast privileges which the Lord Jesus Christ bestows on true Christians. He uses words about them of singular richness and strength. "I know them. I give unto them eternal life. They shall never perish—neither shall any man pluck them out of my hand." This sentence is like the cluster of grapes which came from Eshcol. A stronger form of speech perhaps can hardly be found in the whole range of the Bible.

Christ "knows" his people with a special knowledge of approbation, interest, and affection. By the world around them they are comparatively unknown, uncared for, or despised. But they are never forgotten or over-looked by Christ.

Christ "gives" his people "eternal life." He bestows on them freely a right and title to heaven, pardoning their many sins, and clothing them with a perfect righteousness. Money, and health, and worldly prosperity He often wisely withholds from them. But He never fails to give them grace, peace, and glory.

Christ declares that His people "shall never perish." Weak as they are they shall all be saved. Not one of them shall be lost and cast away—not one of them shall miss heaven. If they err, they shall be brought back; if they fall, they shall be raised. The enemies of their souls may be strong and mighty, but their Savior is mightier; and none shall pluck them out of their Savior's hands.

A promise like this deserves the closest attention. If words mean any-thing, it contains that great doctrine, the perseverance, or continuance in grace, of true believers. That doctrine is literally hated by worldly people. No doubt, like every other truth of Scripture, it is liable to be abused. But the words of Christ are too plain to be evaded. He has said it, and He will make it good—"My sheep shall never perish."

Whatever men may please to say against this doctrine, it is one which God's children ought to hold fast, and defend with all their might. To all who feel within them the workings of the Holy Spirit, it is a doctrine full of encouragement and consolation. Once inside the ark, they shall never be cast out. Once converted and joined to Christ, they shall never be cut off from His mystical body. Hypocrites and false professors shall doubtless make shipwreck forever, unless they repent. But true "sheep" shall never be con-founded. Christ has said it, and Christ cannot lie—"they shall never perish."

Would we get the benefit of this glorious promise? Let us take care that we belong to Christ's flock. Let us hear His voice and follow Him. The man who, under a real sense of sin, flees to Christ and trusts in Him, is one of those who shall never be plucked out of Christ's hand.

10:31-42

The Jewish authorities picked up rocks again to stone him to death. Jesus said to them, "I have shown you many good deeds from the Father. For which one of them are you going to stone me?" The Jewish authorities replied, "We are not going to stone you for a good deed but for blasphemy, because you, a man, are claiming to be God."

Jesus answered, "Is it not written in your law, 'I said, you are gods'? If those people to whom the word of God came were called 'gods' (and the scripture cannot be broken), do you say about the one whom the Father set apart and sent into the world, 'You are blaspheming,' because I said, 'I am the Son of God'? If I do not perform the deeds of my Father, do not believe me. But if I do them, even if you do not believe me, believe the deeds, so that you may come to know and understand that I am in the Father and the Father is in me." Then they attempted again to seize him, but he escaped their clutches.

Jesus went back across the Jordan River again to the place where John had been baptizing at an earlier time, and he stayed there. Many came to him and began to say, "John performed no miraculous sign, but everything John said about this man was true!" And many believed in Jesus there.

We should observe, in these verses, the extreme wickedness of human nature. The unbelieving Jews at Jerusalem was neither moved by our Lord's miracles, nor by His preaching. They were determined not to receive Him as their Messiah. Once more it is written that "they took up stones to stone Him."

Our Lord had done the Jews no injury. He was no robber, murderer, or rebel against the law of the land. He was one whose whole life was love, and who "went about doing good." (Acts 10:38.) There was no fault or inconsistency in His character. There was no crime that could be laid to His charge. So perfect and spotless a man had never walked on the face of this earth. But yet the Jews hated Him, and thirsted for His blood. How true are the words of Scripture—"They hated Him without a cause." (John 15:25.) How just the remark of an old divine—"Unconverted men would kill God Himself if they could only get at Him."

The true Christian has surely no right to wonder if he meets with the same kind of treatment as our blessed Lord. In fact, the more like he is to his Master, and the more holy and spiritual his life, the more probable is it that he will have to endure hatred and persecution. Let him not suppose that any degree of consistency will deliver him from this cross. It is not his faults, but his graces, which call forth the enmity of men. The world hates to see anything of God's image. The children of the world are vexed and pierced in conscience when they see others better than themselves. Why did Cain hate his brother Abel, and slay him? "Because," says John, "his own works were evil, and his brother's righteous." (1 John 3:12.) Why did the Jews hate Christ? Because He exposed their sins and false doctrines; and they knew in their own hearts that he was right and they were wrong. "The world," said our Lord, "hates Me, because I testify of it, that the works thereof are evil." (John 7:7.) Let Christians make up their minds to drink the same cup, and let them drink it patiently and without surprise. There is One in heaven who said, "If the world hate you, you know that it hated Me before it hated you." (John 15:18.) Let them remember this and take courage. The time is short. We are traveling on towards a day when all shall be set right, and every man shall receive according to his works. "There is an end—and our expectation shall not be cut off." (Prov. 23:18.)

We should observe, secondly, in these verses, the high honor that Jesus Christ puts on the Holy Scriptures. We find Him using a text out of the Psalms as an argument against His enemies, in which the whole point lies in the single word "gods." And then having quoted the text, He lays down the great principle, "the Scripture cannot be broken." It is as though He said, "Wherever the Scripture speaks plainly on any subject, there can be no more question about it. The cause is settled and decided. Every jot and tittle of Scripture is true, and must be received as conclusive."

The principle here laid down by our Lord is one of vast importance. Let us grasp it firmly, and never let it go. Let us maintain boldly the complete inspiration of every word of the original Hebrew and Greek Scriptures. Let us believe that not only every book of the Bible, but every chapter—and not only every chapter, but every verse, and not only every verse, but every word, was originally given by inspiration of God. Inspiration, we must never shrink from asserting, extends not only to the thoughts and ideas of Scripture, but to the least words.

The principle before us, no doubt, is rudely assaulted in the present day. Let no Christian's heart fail because of these assaults. Let us stand our ground manfully, and defend the principle of plenary inspiration as we would the pupil of our eye. There are difficulties in Scripture, we need not shrink from conceding, things hard to explain, hard to reconcile, and hard to understand. But in almost all these difficulties, the fault, we may justly suspect, is not so much in Scripture as in our own weak minds. In all cases we may well be content to wait for more light, and to believe that all shall be made clear at last. One thing we may rest assured is very certain—if the difficulties of plenary inspiration are to be numbered by thousands, the difficulties of any other view of inspiration are to be numbered by tens of thousands. The wisest course is to walk in the old path—the path of faith and humility; and say, "I cannot give up a single word of my Bible. All Scripture is given by inspiration of God. The Scripture cannot be broken."

We should observe, lastly, in these verses, the importance which our Lord Jesus Christ attaches to His miracles. He appeals to them as the best evidence of His own Divine mission. He bids the Jews look at them, and deny them if they can. "If I do not the works of my Father, believe me not. But if I do, though you believe not Me, believe the works."

The mighty miracles which our Lord performed during the three years of His earthly ministry are probably not considered as much as they ought to be in the present day. These miracles were not few in number. Forty times and more we read in the Gospels of His doing things entirely out of the ordinary course of nature—healing sick people in a moment, raising the dead with a word, casting out devils, calming winds and waves in an instant, walking on the water as on solid ground. These miracles were not all done in private among friends. Many of them were wrought in the most public manner, under the eyes of unfriendly witnesses. We are so familiar with these things that we are apt to forget the mighty lesson they teach. They teach that He who worked these miracles must be nothing less than very God. They stamp His doctrines and precepts with the mark of Divine authority. He only who created all things at the beginning could suspend the laws of creation at His will. He who could suspend the laws of creation must be One who ought to be thoroughly believed and implicitly obeyed. To reject One who confirmed His mission by such mighty works is the height of madness and folly.

Hundreds of unbelieving men, no doubt, in every age, have tried to pour contempt on Christ's miracles, and to deny that they were ever worked at all. But they labor in vain. Proofs upon proofs exist that our Lord's ministry was accompanied by miracles; and that this was acknowledged by those who lived in our Lord's time. Objectors of this sort would do well to take up the one single miracle of our Lord's resurrection from the dead, and disprove it if they can. If they cannot disprove that, they ought, as honest men, to confess that miracles are possible. And then, if their hearts are truly humble, they ought to admit that He whose mission was confirmed by such evidence must have been the Son of God.

Let us thank God, as we turn from this passage, that Christianity has such abundant evidence that it is a religion from God. Whether we appeal to the internal evidence of the Bible, or to the lives of the first Christians, or to prophecy, or to miracles; or to history, we get one and the same answer. All say with one voice, "Jesus is the Son of God, and believers have life through His name."

Chapter 11

11:1-6

The Death of Lazarus

*N*ow a certain man named Lazarus was sick. He was from Bethany, the village
where Mary and her sister Martha lived. (Now it was Mary who anointed
the Lord with perfumed oil and wiped his feet dry with her hair, whose brother
Lazarus was sick.) So the sisters sent a message to Jesus, "Lord, look, the one you
love is sick." When Jesus heard this, he said, "This sickness will not lead to death,
but to God's glory, so that the Son of God may be glorified through it." (Now Jesus
loved Martha and her sister and Lazarus.) So when he heard that Lazarus was
sick, he remained in the place where he was for two more days.

The chapter we have now begun is one of the most remarkable in the New
Testament. For grandeur and simplicity, for pathos and solemnity, nothing
was ever written like it. It describes a miracle which is not recorded in the
other Gospels—the raising of Lazarus from the dead. Nowhere shall we find
such convincing proofs of our Lord's Divine power. As God, He makes the
grave itself yield up its tenants. Nowhere shall we find such striking illustrations of our Lord's ability to sympathize with His people. As man, He can
be touched with the feelings of our infirmities. Such a miracle well became
the end of such a ministry. It was fit and right that the victory of Bethany
should closely precede the crucifixion at Calvary.

These verses teach us that true Christians may be sick and ill as well as
others. We read that Lazarus of Bethany was one "whom Jesus loved," and
a brother of two well-known holy women. Yet Lazarus was sick, even unto

death! The Lord Jesus, who had power over all diseases, could no doubt have prevented this illness, if He had thought fit. But He did not do so. He allowed Lazarus to be sick, and in pain, and weary, and to languish and suffer like any other man.

The lesson is one which ought to be deeply engraved in our memories. Living in a world full of disease and death, we are sure to need it someday. Sickness, in the very nature of things, can never be anything but trying to flesh and blood. Our bodies and souls are strangely linked together, and that which vexes and weakens the body can hardly fail to vex the mind and soul. But sickness, we must always remember, is no sign that God is displeased with us; no, more, it is generally sent for the good of our souls. It tends to draw our affections away from this world, and to direct them to things above. It sends us to our Bibles, and teaches us to pray better. It helps to prove our faith and patience, and shows us the real value of our hope in Christ. It reminds us that we are not to live always, and tunes and trains our hearts for our great change. Then let us be patient and cheerful when we are laid aside by illness. Let us believe that the Lord Jesus loves us when we are sick no less than when we are well.

These verses teach us, secondly, that Jesus Christ is the Christian's best Friend in the time of need. We read that when Lazarus was sick, his sisters at once sent to Jesus, and laid the matter before Him. Beautiful, touching, and simple was the message they sent. They did not ask Him to come at once, or to work a miracle, and command the disease to depart. They only said, "Lord, he whom You love is sick," and left the matter there, in the full belief that He would do what was best. Here was the true faith and humility of saints! Here was gracious submission of will!

The servants of Christ, in every age and climate, will do well to follow this excellent example. No doubt when those whom we love are sick, we are to use diligently every reasonable means for their recovery. We must spare no pains to obtain the best medical advice. We must assist nature in every possible manner to fight a good fight against its enemy. But in all our doing, we must never forget that the best and ablest and wisest Helper is in heaven, at God's right hand. Like afflicted Job our first action must be to fall on our knees and worship. Like Hezekiah, we must spread our matters before the Lord. Like the holy sisters at Bethany, we must send up a prayer to Christ. Let us not forget, in the hurry and excitement of our feelings, that none can help like Him, and that He is merciful, loving, and gracious.

These verses teach us, thirdly, that Christ loves all who are true Christians. We read that "Jesus loved Martha, and her sister, and Lazarus." The characters of these three good people seem to have been somewhat different. Of Martha, we are told in a certain place, that she was "anxious and troubled about many things," while Mary "sat at Jesus' feet, and heard His word." Of Lazarus we are told nothing distinctive at all. Yet all these were loved by the Lord Jesus. They all belonged to His family, and He loved them all.

We must carefully bear this in mind in forming our estimate of Christians. We must never forget that there are varieties in character, and that the grace of God does not cast all believers into one and the same mold. Admitting fully that the foundations of Christian character are always the same, and that all God's children repent, believe, are holy, prayerful, and Scripture-loving, we must make allowances for wide varieties in their temperaments and habits of mind. We must not undervalue others because they are not exactly like ourselves. The flowers in a garden may differ widely, and yet the gardener feels interest in all. The children of a family may be curiously unlike one another, and yet the parents care for all. It is just so with the Church of Christ. There are degrees of grace, and varieties of grace; but the least, the weakest, the feeblest disciples are all loved by the Lord Jesus. Then let no believer's heart fail because of his infirmities; and, above all, let no believer dare to despise and undervalue a brother.

These verses teach us, lastly, that Christ knows best at what time to do anything for His people. We read that "when He had heard that Lazarus was sick, He abode two days still in the same place where He was." In fact, He purposely delayed His journey, and did not come to Bethany until Lazarus had been four days in the grave. No doubt He knew well what was going on; but He never moved until the time came which He saw was best. For the sake of the Church and the world, for the good of friends and enemies, He kept away.

The children of God must constantly school their minds to learn the great lesson now before us. Nothing so helps us to bear patiently the trials of life as an abiding conviction of the perfect wisdom by which everything around us is managed. Let us try to believe not only that all that happens to us is well done, but that it is done in the best manner, by the right instrument, and at the right time. We are all naturally impatient in the day of trial. We are apt to say, like Moses, when beloved ones are sick, "Heal her now, Lord, we beseech you." (Num. 12:13.) We forget that Christ is too wise a Physician to make any mistakes. It is the duty of faith to say, "My times are in Your hand. Do with me as You will, how You will, what You will, and when You will. Not my will, but Your be done." The highest degree of faith is to be able to wait, sit still, and not complain.

Let us turn from the passage with a settled determination to trust Christ entirely with all the concerns of this world, both public and private. Let us believe that He by whom all things were made at first is He who is managing all with perfect wisdom. The affairs of kingdoms, families, and private individuals are all alike overruled by Him. He chooses all the portions of His people. When we are sick, it is because He knows it to be for our good; when He delays coming to help us, it is for some wise reason. The hand that was nailed to the cross is too wise and loving to smite without a needs-be, or to keep us waiting for relief without a cause.

11:7-16

Then after this, he said to his disciples, "Let us go to Judea again." The disciples replied, "Rabbi, the Jewish authorities were just now trying to stone you to death! Are you going there again?" Jesus replied, "Are there not twelve hours in a day? If anyone walks about in the daytime, he does not stumble, because he sees the light of this world. But if anyone walks about in the night, he stumbles, because the light is not in him."

After he said this, he added, "Our friend Lazarus has fallen asleep. But I am going there to awaken him." Then the disciples replied, "Lord, if he has fallen asleep, he will recover." (Now Jesus had been talking about his death, but they thought he had been talking about real sleep.)

Then Jesus told them plainly, "Lazarus has died, and I am glad for your sake that I was not there, so that you may believe. But let us go to him." So Thomas (called Didymus) said to his fellow disciples, "Let us go too, so that we may die with him."

We should notice, in this passage, how mysterious are the ways in which Christ sometimes leads His people. We are told that when He talked of going back to Judea, His disciples were perplexed. It was the very place where the Jews had lately tried to stone their Master—to return there was to plunge into the midst of danger. These timid Galileans could not see the necessity or prudence of such a step. "Are You going there again?" they cried.

Things such as these are often going on around us. The servants of Christ are often placed in circumstances just as puzzling and perplexing as those of the disciples. They are led in ways of which they cannot see the purpose and object; they are called to fill positions from which they naturally shrink, and which they would never have chosen for themselves. Thousands in every age are continually learning this by their own experience. The path they are obliged to walk in is not the path of their own choice. At present they cannot see its usefulness or wisdom.

At times like these a Christian must call into exercise his faith and patience. He must believe that his Master knows best by what road His servant ought to travel, and that He is leading him, by the right way, to a city of habitation. He may rest assured that the circumstances in which be is placed are precisely those which are most likely to promote his graces and to check his besetting sins. He need not doubt that what he cannot see now, he will understand hereafter. He will find one day that there was wisdom in every step of his journey, though flesh and blood could not see it at the time. If the twelve disciples had not been taken back into Judea, they would not have seen the glorious miracle of Bethany. If Christians were allowed to choose their own course through life, they would never learn hundreds of lessons about Christ and His grace, which they are now taught in God's ways. Let us remember these things. The time may come when we shall be called to take some journey in life which we greatly dislike. When that time comes, let us set out cheerfully, and believe that all is right.

We should notice, secondly, in this passage, how tenderly Christ speaks of the death of believers. He announces the fact of Lazarus being dead in language of singular beauty and gentleness—"Our friend Lazarus sleeps." Every true Christian has a Friend in heaven, of almighty power and boundless love. He is thought of, cared for, provided for, defended by God's eternal Son. He has an unfailing Protector, who never slumbers or sleeps, and watches continually over his interests. The world may despise him, but he has no cause to be ashamed. Father and mother even may cast him out, but Christ having once taken him up will never let him go. He is the "friend of Christ" even after he is dead! The friendships of this world are often fair-weather friendships, and fail us like summer-dried fountains, when our need is the greatest; but the friendship of the Son of God is stronger than death, and goes beyond the grave. The Friend of sinners is a Friend that sticks closer than a brother.

The death of true Christians is "sleep," and not annihilation. It is a solemn and miraculous change, no doubt, but not a change to be regarded with alarm. They have nothing to fear for their souls in the change, for their sins are washed away in Christ's blood. The sharpest sting of death is the sense of unpardoned sin. Christians have nothing to fear for their bodies in the change; they will rise again by and by, refreshed and renewed, after the image of the Lord. The grave itself is a conquered enemy. It must render back its tenants safe and sound, the very moment that Christ calls for them at the last day.

Let us remember these things when those whom we love fall asleep in Christ, or when we ourselves receive our notice to depart this world. Let us call to mind, in such an hour, that our great Friend takes thought for our bodies as well as for our souls, and that He will not allow one hair of our heads to perish. Let us never forget that the grave is the place where the Lord Himself lay, and that as He rose again triumphant from that cold bed, so also shall all His people. To a mere worldly man death must needs be a terrible thing; but he that has Christian faith may boldly say, as he lays down life, "I will lay me down in peace, and take my rest—for it is You, Lord, that make me dwell in safety."

We should notice, lastly, in this passage, how much of natural temperament clings to a believer even after conversion. We read that when Thomas saw that Lazarus was dead, and that Jesus was determined, in spite of all danger, to return into Judea, he said, "Let us also go, that we may die with Him." There can only be one meaning in that expression—it was the language of a despairing and desponding mind, which could see nothing but dark clouds in the picture. The very man who afterwards could not believe that his Master had risen again, and thought the news too good to be true, is just the one of the twelve who thinks that if they go back to Judea they must all die!

Things such as these are deeply instructive, and are doubtless recorded for our learning. They show us that the grace of God in conversion does not so re-mold a man as to leave no trace of his natural bent of character. The sanguine do not altogether cease to be sanguine, nor the desponding to be desponding, when they pass from death to life, and become true Christians. They show us that we must make large allowances for natural temperament, in forming our estimate of individual Christians. We must not expect all God's children to be exactly one and the same. Each tree in a forest has its own peculiarities of shape and growth, and yet all at a distance look one mass of leaf and verdure. Each member of Christ's body has his own distinctive bias, and yet all in the main are led by one Spirit, and love one Lord. The two sisters Martha and Mary, the apostles Peter and John and Thomas, were certainly very unlike one another in many respects. But they had all one point in common—they loved Christ, and were His friends.

Let us take heed that we really belong to Christ. This is the one thing needful. If this is made sure, we shall be led by the right way, and end well at last. We may not have the cheerfulness of one brother, or the fiery zeal of another, or the gentleness of another. But if grace reigns within us, and we know what repentance and faith are by experience, we shall stand on the right hand in the great day. Happy is the man of whom, with all his defects, Christ says to saints and angels, "This is our friend."

11:17-29

When Jesus arrived, he found that Lazarus had been in the tomb four days already. (Now Bethany was less than two miles from Jerusalem, so many of the Jewish people who lived in Jerusalem had come to Martha and Mary to console them over the loss of their brother.) So when Martha heard that Jesus was coming, she went out to meet him, but Mary was sitting in the house. Martha said to Jesus, "Lord, if you had been here my brother would not have died. But even now I know that whatever you ask from God, God will grant you."

Jesus replied, "Your brother will come back to life again." Martha said, "I know that he will come back to life again in the resurrection at the last day." Jesus said to her, "I am the resurrection and the life. The one who believes in me will live even if he dies, and the one who lives and believes in me will never die. Do you believe this?" She replied, "Yes, Lord, I have believed that you are the Christ, the Son of God who comes into the world."

And when she had said this, Martha went and called her sister Mary, saying privately, "The Teacher is here and is asking for you." So when Mary heard this, she got up quickly and went to him.

There is a grand simplicity about this passage, which is almost spoiled by any human exposition. To comment on it seems like gilding gold or painting lilies. Yet it throws much light on a subject which we can never understand too well; that is, the true character of Christ's people. The portraits of Christians in the Bible are faithful likenesses. They show us saints just as they are.

We learn, firstly, what a strange mixture of grace and weakness is to be found even in the hearts of true believers.

We see this strikingly illustrated in the language used by Martha and Mary. Both these holy women had faith enough to say, "Lord, if You had been here, my brother would not have died." Yet neither of them seems to have remembered that the death of Lazarus did not depend on Christ's absence, and that our Lord, had He thought fit, could have prevented his death with a word, without coming to Bethany. Martha had knowledge enough to say, "I know, that even now, whatever You will ask of God, God will give it to You—I know that my brother shall rise again at the last day—I believe that You are the Christ, the Son of God." But even she could get no further. Her dim eyes and trembling hands could not grasp the grand truth that He who stood before her had the keys of life and death, and that in her Master dwelt "all the fullness of the Godhead bodily." (Colos. 2:9.) She saw indeed, but through a glass darkly. She knew, but only in part. She believed, but her faith was mingled with much unbelief. Yet both Martha and Mary were genuine children of God, and true Christians.

These things are graciously written for our learning. It is good to remember what true Christians really are. Many and great are the mistakes into which people fall, by forming a false estimate of the Christian's character. Many are the bitter things which people write against themselves, by expecting to find in their hearts what cannot be found on this side of heaven. Let us settle it in our minds that saints on earth are not perfect angels, but only converted sinners. They are sinners renewed, changed, sanctified, no doubt; but they are yet sinners, and will be until they die. Like Martha and Mary, their faith is often entangled with much unbelief, and their grace compassed round with much infirmity. Happy is that child of God who understands these things, and has learned to judge rightly both of himself and others. Rarely indeed shall we find the saint who does not often need that prayer, "Lord, I believe—help my unbelief."

We learn, secondly, what need many believers have of clear views of Christ's person, office, and power. This is a point which is forcibly brought out in the well-known sentence which our Lord addressed to Martha. In reply to her vague and faltering expression of belief in the resurrection at the last day, He proclaims the glorious truth, "I am the resurrection and the life;"—"I, even I, your Master, am He that has the keys of life and death in His hands." And then He presses on her once more that old lesson, which she had doubtless often heard, but never fully realized—"He who believes in me will live, even though he dies; and whoever lives and believes in me will never die."

There is matter here which deserves the close consideration of all true Christians. Many of them complain of lack of sensible comfort in their religion. They do not feel the inward peace which they desire. Let them know that vague and indefinite views of Christ are too often the cause of all their perplexities. They must try to see more clearly the great object on which their faith rests. They must grasp more firmly His love and power toward those who believe, and the riches He has laid up for them even now in this world. We are, many of us, sadly like Martha. A little general knowledge of Christ as the only Savior is often all that we possess. But of the fullness that dwells in Him, of His resurrection, His priesthood, His intercession, His unfailing compassion, we have tasted little or nothing at all. They are things of which our Lord might well say to many, as he did to Martha, "Do you believe this?"

Let us take shame to ourselves that we have named the name of Christ so long, and yet know so little about Him. What right have we to wonder that we feel so little sensible comfort in our Christianity? Our slight and imperfect knowledge of Christ is the true reason of our discomfort. Let the time past suffice us to have been lazy students in Christ's school; let the time to come find us more diligent in trying to "know Him and the power of His resurrection." (Philip. 3:10.) If true Christians would only strive, as Paul says, to "comprehend what is the breadth, and length, and depth, and height, and to know the love of Christ, which passes knowledge," they would be amazed at the discoveries they would make. They would soon find, like Hagar, that there are wells of water near them of which they had no knowledge. They would soon discover that there is more heaven to be enjoyed on earth than they had ever thought possible. The root of a happy religion is clear, distinct, well-defined knowledge of Jesus Christ. More knowledge would have saved Martha many sighs and tears. Knowledge alone no doubt, if unsanctified, only "puffs up." (1 Cor. 8:1.) Yet without clear knowledge of Christ in all His offices we cannot expect to be established in the faith, and steady in the time of need.

11:30-37

Now Jesus had not yet entered the village, but was still in the place where Martha had come out to meet him. Then the Jewish people from Jerusalem who were with Mary in the house consoling her saw her get up quickly and go out. They followed her, because they thought she was going to the tomb to weep there.

Now when Mary came to the place where Jesus was and saw him, she fell at his feet and said to him, "Lord, if you had been here my brother would not have died." When Jesus saw her weeping, and the Jewish people who had come with her weeping, he was intensely moved in spirit and greatly distressed. He asked, "Where

have you laid him?" They replied, "Lord, come and see." Jesus wept. Thus the Jewish
people who had come to mourn said, "Look how much he loved him!" But some
of them said, "This is the man who caused the blind man to see! Couldn't he have
done something to keep Lazarus from dying?"

Not many passages in the New Testament are more wonderful than the simple narrative contained in these eight verses. It brings out, in a most beautiful light, the sympathizing character of our Lord Jesus Christ. It shows us Him who is "able to save to the uttermost all who come to God by Him," as able to feel as He is to save. It shows us Him who is One with the Father, and the Maker of all things, entering into human sorrows, and shedding human tears.

We learn, for one thing, in these verses, how great a blessing God sometimes bestows on actions of kindness and sympathy.

It seems that the house of Martha and Mary at Bethany was filled with mourners when Jesus arrived. Many of these mourners, no doubt, knew nothing of the inner life of these holy women. Their faith, their hope, their love to Christ, their discipleship, were things of which they were wholly ignorant. But they felt for them in their heavy bereavement, and kindly came to offer what comfort they could. By so doing they reaped a rich and unexpected reward. They beheld the greatest miracle that Jesus ever wrought. They were eye-witnesses when Lazarus came forth from the tomb. To many of them, we may well believe, that day was a spiritual birth. The raising of Lazarus led to a resurrection in their souls. How small sometimes are the hinges on which eternal life appears to depend! If these people had not sympathized they might never have been saved.

We need not doubt that these things were written for our learning. To show sympathy and kindness to the sorrowful is good for our own souls, whether we know it or not. To visit the fatherless and widows in their affliction, to weep with those who weep, to try to bear one another's burdens, and lighten one another's cares—all this will make no atonement for sin, and will not take us to heaven. Yet it is healthy employment for our hearts, and employment which none ought to despise. Few perhaps are aware that one secret of being miserable is to live only for ourselves, and one secret of being happy is to try to make others happy, and to do a little good in the world. It is not for nothing that these words were written by Solomon, "It is better to go to the house of mourning than to the house of feasting." "The heart of the wise is in the house of mourning, but the heart of fools is in the house of mirth." (Eccl. 7:2, 4.) The saying of our Lord is too much overlooked—"Whoever shall give to drink to one of these little ones a cup of cold water only in the name of a disciple, verily I say unto you he shall in no wise lose his reward." (Matt. 10:42.) The friends of Martha and Mary found that promise wonderfully verified. In an age of inordinate selfishness and self-indulgence, it would be well if they had more imitators.

We learn, for another thing, what a depth of tender sympathy there is in Christ's heart towards His people. We read that when our Lord saw Mary weeping, and the Jews also weeping with her, "He groaned in the spirit and was troubled." We read even more than this. He gave outward expression to His feelings—He "wept." He knew perfectly well that the sorrow of the family of Bethany would soon be turned into joy, and that Lazarus in a few minutes would be restored to his sisters. But though he knew all this, he "wept."

This weeping of Christ is deeply instructive. It shows us that it is not sinful to sorrow. Weeping and mourning are sadly trying to flesh and blood, and make us feel the weakness of our mortal nature. But they are not in themselves wrong. Even the Son of God wept. It shows us that deep feeling is not a thing of which we need be ashamed. To be cold and stoical and unmoved in the sight of sorrow is no sign of grace. There is nothing unworthy of a child of God in tears. Even the Son of God could weep. It shows us, above all, that the Savior in whom believers trust is a most tender and feeling Savior. He is one who can be touched with sympathy for our infirmities. When we turn to Him in the hour of trouble, and pour out our hearts before Him, He knows what we go through and can pity. And He is One who never changes. Though He now sits at God's right hand in heaven, His heart is still the same that it was upon earth. We have an Advocate with the Father, who, when He was upon earth, could weep.

Let us remember these things in daily life, and never be ashamed of walking in our Master's footsteps. Let us strive to be men and women of a tender heart and a sympathizing spirit. Let us never be ashamed to weep with those who weep, and rejoice with those who rejoice. Well would it be for the Church and the world if there were more Christians of this stamp and character! The Church would be far more beautiful, and the world be far more happy.

11:38-46

Lazarus Raised from the Dead

Jesus, intensely moved again, came to the tomb. (Now it was a cave, and a stone was placed across it.) Jesus said, "Take away the stone." Martha, the sister of the deceased, replied, "Lord, by this time the body will have a bad smell, because he has been buried four days." Jesus responded, "Didn't I tell you that if you believe, you would see the glory of God?" So they took away the stone. Jesus looked upward and said, "Father, I thank you that you have listened to me. I knew that you always listen to me, but I said this for the sake of the crowd standing around here, that they may believe that you sent me." When he had said this, he shouted in a loud voice, "Lazarus, come out!" The one who had died came out, his feet and hands tied up with strips of cloth, and a cloth wrapped around his face. Jesus said to them, "Unwrap him and let him go."

Then many of the Jewish people from Jerusalem, who had come with Mary and had seen the things Jesus did, believed in him. But some of them went to the Pharisees and reported to them what Jesus had done.

These verses record one of the greatest miracles the Lord Jesus Christ ever worked, and supply an unanswerable proof of His divinity. He whose voice could bring back from the grave one that had been four days dead, must indeed have been very God! The miracle itself is described in such simple language that no human comment can throw light upon it. But the sayings of our Lord on this occasion are peculiarly interesting, and demand special notice.

We should mark, first, our Lord's words about the STONE which lay upon the grave of Lazarus. We read that He said to those around Him, when he came to the place of burial, "Take you away the stone."

Now why did our Lord say this? It was doubtless as easy for Him to command the stone to roll away untouched as to call a dead body from the tomb. But such was not His mode of proceeding. Here, as in other cases, He chose to give man something to do. Here, as elsewhere, He taught the great lesson that His almighty power was not meant to destroy man's responsibility. Even when He was ready and willing to raise the dead, He would not have man stand by altogether idle.

Let us treasure up this in our memories. It involves a point of great importance. In doing spiritual good to others—in training up our children for heaven—in following after holiness in our own daily walk—in all these things it is undoubtedly true that we are weak and helpless. "Without Christ we can do nothing." But still we must remember that Christ expects us to do what we can. "Take you away the stone" is the daily command which He gives us. Let us beware that we do not stand still in idleness, under the pretense of humility. Let us daily try to do what we can, and in the trying Christ will meet us and grant His blessing.

We should mark, secondly, the words which our Lord addressed to MARTHA, when she objected to the stone being removed from the grave. The faith of this holy woman completely broke down, when the cave where her beloved brother lay was about to be thrown open. She could not believe that it was of any use. "Lord," she cries, "by this time there is a bad smell." And then comes in the solemn reproof of our Lord—"Said I not unto you that if you would believe you should see the glory of God?"

That sentence is rich in meaning. It is far from unlikely that it contains a reference to the message which had been sent to Martha and Mary, when their brother first fell sick. It may be meant to remind Martha that her Master had sent her word, "This sickness is not unto death, but for the glory of God." But it is perhaps more likely that our Lord desired to recall to Martha's mind the old lesson He had taught her all through His ministry, the duty of always believing. It is as though He said, "Martha, Martha, you are forgetting the great doctrine of faith, which I have always taught you. Believe, and all will be well. Fear not—only believe."

The lesson is one which we can never know too well. How apt our faith is to break down in time of trial! How easy it is to talk of faith in the days of health and prosperity, and how hard to practice it in the days of darkness, when neither sun, moon, nor stars appear! Let us lay to heart what our Lord says in this place. Let us pray for such stores of inward faith, that when our turn comes to suffer, we may suffer patiently and believe all is well. The Christian who has ceased to say, "I must see, and then I will believe," and has learned to say, "I believe, and 'by and by' I shall see," has reached a high degree in the school of Christ.

We should mark, thirdly, the words which our Lord addressed to God the FATHER, when the stone was taken from the grave. We read that He said, "Father, I thank You that You have heard Me. And I knew that You hear Me always—but because of the people which stand by I said it, that they may believe that You have sent Me."

This wonderful language is totally unlike anything said by Prophets or Apostles, when they worked miracles. In fact, it is not prayer, but praise. It evidently implies a constant mysterious communion going on between Jesus and His Father in heaven, which it is past the power of man either to explain or conceive. We need not doubt that here, as elsewhere in John, our Lord meant to teach the Jews the entire and complete unity there was between Him and His Father, in all that He did, as well as in all that He taught. Once more He would remind those who he did not come among them as a mere Prophet, but as the Messiah who was sent by the Father, and who was one with the Father. Once more He would have them know that as the words which He spoke were the very words which the Father gave Him to speak, so the works which He wrought were the very works which the Father gave Him to do. In short, He was the promised Messiah, whom the Father always hears, because He and the Father are One.

Deep and high as this truth is, it is for the peace of our souls to believe it thoroughly, and to grasp it tightly. Let it be a settled principle of our religion, that the Savior in whom we trust is nothing less than eternal God, One whom the Father hears always, One who in very deed is God's Fellow. A clear view of the dignity of our Mediator's Person is one secret of inward comfort. Happy is he who can say, "I know whom I have believed, and that He is able to keep that which I have committed to Him." (2 Tim. 1:12.)

We should mark, lastly, the words which our Lord addressed to LAZARUS when he raised him from the grave. We read that "He cried with a loud voice, Lazarus, come forth!" At the sound of that voice, the king of terrors at once yielded up his lawful captive, and the insatiable grave gave up its prey. At once "He that was dead came forth, bound hand and foot with grave-clothes."

The greatness of this miracle cannot possibly be exaggerated. The mind of man can scarcely take in the vastness of the work that was done. Here, in open day, and before many hostile witnesses, a man, four days dead, was restored to life in a moment. Here was public proof that our Lord had absolute power over the material world! A corpse, already corrupt, was made alive!-Here was public proof that our Lord had absolute power over the world of spirits! A soul that had left its earthly tenement was called back from Paradise, and joined once more to its owner's body. Well may the Church of Christ maintain that He who could work such works was "God over all blessed forever." (Rom. 9:5.)

Let us turn from the whole passage with thoughts of comfort and consolation. Comfortable is the thought that the loving Savior of sinners, on whose mercy our souls entirely depend, is one who has all power in heaven, and earth, and is mighty to save. Comfortable is the thought that there is no sinner too far gone in sin for Christ to raise and convert. He that stood by the grave of Lazarus can say to the vilest of men, "Come forth loose him, and let him go." Comfortable, not least, is the thought that when we ourselves lie down in the grave, we may lie down in the full assurance that we shall rise again. The voice that called Lazarus forth will one day pierce our tombs, and bid soul and body come together. "The trumpets shall sound, and the dead shall be raised incorruptible, and we shall be changed." (1 Cor. 15:52.)

11:47-57

Then the chief priests and the Pharisees called the council together and said, "What are we doing? For this man is performing many miraculous signs. If we allow him to go on in this way, everyone will believe in him, and the Romans will come and take away our sanctuary and our nation."

Then one of them, Caiaphas, who was high priest that year, said, "You know nothing at all! You do not realize that it is more to your advantage to have one man die for the people than for the whole nation to perish." (Now he did not say this on his own, but because he was high priest that year, he prophesied that Jesus was going to die for the Jewish nation, and not for the Jewish nation only, but to gather together into one the children of God who are scattered.) So from that day they planned together to kill him.

Thus Jesus no longer walked about publicly among the Jewish people of Jerusalem, but went away from there to the region near the wilderness, to a town called Ephraim, and stayed there with his disciples. Now the Jewish feast of Passover was near, and many people went up to Jerusalem from the rural areas before the Passover to cleanse themselves ritually. Thus they were looking for Jesus, and saying to one another as they stood in the temple courts, "What do you think? That he won't come to the feast?" (Now the chief priests and the Pharisees had given orders that anyone who knew where Jesus was should report it, so that they could arrest him.)

These concluding verses of the eleventh chapter of John contain a melancholy picture of human nature. As we turn away from Jesus Christ and the grave at Bethany, and look at Jerusalem and the rulers of the Jews, we may well say, "Lord, what is man?"

We should observe, for one thing, in these verses, the desperate wickedness of man's natural heart. A mighty miracle was wrought within an easy walk of Jerusalem. A man four days dead was raised to life, in the sight of many witnesses. The fact was unmistakable, and could not be denied; and yet the chief priests and Pharisees would not believe that He who did this miracle ought to be received as the Messiah. In the face of overwhelming evidence they shut their eyes, and refused to be convinced. "This man," they admitted, "does many miracles." But so far from yielding to this testimony, they only plunged into further wickedness, and "took counsel to put Him to death." Great, indeed, is the power of unbelief!

Let us beware of supposing that miracles alone have any power to convert men's souls, and to make them Christians. The idea is a complete delusion. To fancy, as some do, that if they saw something wonderful done before their eyes in confirmation of the Gospel, they would at once cast off all indecision and serve Christ, is a mere idle dream. It is the grace of the Spirit in our hearts, and not miracles, that our souls require. The Jews of our Lord's day are a standing proof to mankind that men may see signs and wonders, and yet remain hard as stone. It is a deep and true saying, "If men believe not Moses and the Prophets, neither would they be persuaded though one rose from the dead." (Luke 16:31.)

We must never wonder if we see abounding unbelief in our own times, and around our own homes. It may seem at first unexplainable to us, how men cannot see the truth which seems so clear to ourselves, and do not receive the Gospel which appears so worthy of acceptance. But the plain truth is, that man's unbelief is a far more deeply seated disease than it is generally reckoned. It is proof against the logic of facts, against reasoning, against argument, against moral persuasion. Nothing can melt it down but the grace of God. If we ourselves believe, we can never be too thankful. But we must never count it a strange thing, if we see many of our fellows just as hardened and unbelieving as the Jews.

We should observe, for another thing, the blind ignorance with which God's enemies often act and reason. These rulers of the Jews said to one another, "If we let this Christ alone we shall be ruined. If we do not stop His course, and make an end of His miracles, the Romans will interfere, and make an end of our nation." Never, the event afterward proved, was there a more shortsighted and erring judgment than this. They rushed madly on the path they had chosen, and the very thing they feared came to pass. They did not leave our Lord alone, but crucified and slew Him. And what happened then? After a few years, the very calamity they had dreaded took place—the Roman armies did come, destroyed Jerusalem, burned the temple, and carried away the whole nation into captivity.

The well-read Christian need hardly be reminded of many such like things in the history of Christ's Church. The Roman emperors persecuted the Christians in the first three centuries, and thought it a positive duty not to let them alone. But the more they persecuted them, the more they increased. The blood of the martyrs became the seed of the Church. The English Papists, in the days of Queen Mary, persecuted the Protestants, and thought that truth was in danger if they were let alone. But the more they burned our forefathers, the more they confirmed men's minds in steadfast attachment to the doctrines of the Reformation. In short, the words of the second Psalm are continually verified in this world—"The kings of the earth set themselves, and the rulers take counsel together against the Lord." But "He who sits in the heavens shall laugh; the Lord shall have them in derision." God can make the designs of His enemies work together for the good of His people, and cause the wrath of man to praise Him. In days of trouble, and rebuke, and blasphemy, believers may rest patiently in the Lord. The very things that at one time seem likely to hurt them, shall prove in the end to be for their gain.

We should observe, lastly, what importance unsaved men sometimes attach to outward ceremonies, while their hearts are full of sin. We are told that many Jews "went up out of the country to Jerusalem, before the Passover, to purify themselves." The most of them, it may be feared, neither knew nor cared anything about inward purity of heart. They made much ado about the washings, and fastings, and ascetic observances, which formed the essence of popular Jewish religion in our Lord's time; and yet they were willing in a very few days to shed innocent blood. Strange as it may appear, these very sticklers for outward ceremonies were found ready to do the will of the Pharisees, and to put their own Messiah to a violent death.

Extremes like this meeting together in the same person are, unhappily, far from uncommon. Experience shows that a bad conscience will often try to satisfy itself, by a show of zeal for the cause of religion, while the "weightier matters" of the faith are entirely neglected. The very same man who is ready to compass sea and land to attain ceremonial purity is often the very man, who, if he had fit opportunity, would not shrink from helping to crucify Christ. Startling as these assertions may seem, they are abundantly borne out by plain facts. The cities where Lent is kept at this day with the most extravagant strictness are the very cities where the carnival after Lent is a season of glaring excess and immorality. The people in some parts of Christendom, who make much ado one week about fasting and priestly absolution, are the very people who another week will think nothing of murder! These things are simple realities. The hideous inconsistency of the Jewish formalists in our Lord's time has never been without a long succession of followers.

Let us settle it firmly in our minds that a religion which expends itself in zeal for outward formalities is utterly worthless in God's sight. The purity that God desires to see is not the purity of bodily washing and fasting, of holy water and self-imposed asceticism, but purity of heart. External worship and ceremonialism may "satisfy the flesh," but they do not tend to promote real godliness. The standard of Christ's kingdom must be sought in the sermon on the Mount—"Blessed are the pure in heart, for they shall see God." (Matt. 5:8; Col. 2:23.)

Chapter 12

*T*hen, six days before the Passover, Jesus came to Bethany, where Lazarus lived, whom he had raised from the dead. So they prepared a dinner for Jesus there. Martha was serving, and Lazarus was among those present at the table with him. Then Mary took three quarters of a pound of expensive aromatic oil from pure nard and anointed the feet of Jesus. She then wiped his feet dry with her hair. (Now the house was filled with the fragrance of the perfumed oil.) But Judas Iscariot, one of his disciples (the one who was going to betray him) said, "Why wasn't this oil sold for three hundred silver coins and the money given to the poor?" (Now Judas said this not because he was concerned about the poor, but because he was a thief. As keeper of the money box, he used to steal what was put into it.) So Jesus said, "Leave her alone. She has kept it for the day of my burial. For you always have the poor with you, but you don't always have me."

Now the large crowd of Jewish people from Jerusalem learned that Jesus was there, and so they came not only because of him but also to see Lazarus whom he had raised from the dead. So the chief priests planned to kill Lazarus too, for on account of him many of the Jewish people from Jerusalem were going away and believing in Jesus.

The chapter we have now begun finishes a most important division of John's Gospel. Our Lord's public addresses to the unbelieving Jews of Jerusalem are here brought to an end. After this chapter, John records nothing but what was said in private to the disciples.

We see, for one thing, in this passage, what abounding proofs exist of the truth of our Lord's greatest miracles.

We read of a supper at Bethany, where Lazarus "sat at the table" among the guests—Lazarus, who had been publicly raised from the dead, after lying four days in the grave. No one could pretend to say that his resurrection was a mere optical delusion, and that the eyes of the bystanders must have been deceived by a spirit or vision. Here was the very same Lazarus, after several weeks, sitting among his fellow-men with a real material body, and eating and drinking real material food. It is hard to understand what stronger evidence of a fact could be supplied. He that is not convinced by such evidence as this may as well say that he is determined to believe nothing at all.

It is a comfortable thought, that the very same proofs which exist about the resurrection of Lazarus are the proofs which surround that still mightier fact, the resurrection of Christ from the dead. Was Lazarus seen for several weeks by the people of Bethany, going in and coming out among them? So was the Lord Jesus seen by His disciples. Did Lazarus take material food before the eyes of his friends? So did the Lord Jesus eat and drink before His ascension. No one, in his sober senses, who saw Jesus take "broiled fish," and eat it before several witnesses, would doubt that He had a real body. (Luke 24:42.)

We shall do well to remember this. In an age of abounding unbelief and scepticism, we shall find that the resurrection of Christ will bear any weight that we can lay upon it. Just as He placed beyond reasonable doubt the rising again of a beloved disciple within two miles of Jerusalem, so in a very few weeks He placed beyond doubt His own victory over the grave. If we believe that Lazarus rose again, we need not doubt that Jesus rose again also. If we believe that Jesus rose again, we need not doubt the truth of His Messiahship, the reality of His acceptance as our Mediator, and the certainty of our own resurrection. Christ has risen indeed, and wicked men may well tremble. Christ has risen from the dead, and believers may well rejoice.

We see, for another thing, in this passage, what unkindness and discouragement Christ's friends sometimes meet with from man.

We read that, at the supper in Bethany, Mary, the sister of Lazarus, anointed the feet of Jesus with precious ointment, and wiped them with the hair of her head. Nor was this ointment poured on with a niggardly hand. She did it so liberally and profusely that "the house was filled with the odor of the ointment." She did it under the influence of a heart full of love and gratitude. She thought nothing too great and good to bestow on such a Savior. Sitting at His feet in days gone by, and hearing His words, she had found peace for her conscience, and pardon for her sins. At this very moment she saw Lazarus, alive and well, sitting by her Master's side—her own brother Lazarus, whom He had brought back to her from the grave. Greatly loved, she thought she could not show too much love in return. Having freely received, she freely gave.

But there were some present who found fault with Mary's conduct, and blamed her as guilty of wasteful extravagance. One especially, an apostle, a man of whom better things might have been expected, declared openly that the ointment would have been better employed if it had been sold, and the price "given to the poor." The heart which could conceive such thoughts must have had low views of the dignity of Christ's person, and still lower views of our obligations to Him. A cold heart and a stingy hand will generally go together.

There are only too many professing Christians of a like spirit in the present day. Myriads of baptized people cannot understand zeal of any sort, for the honor of Christ. Tell them of any vast outlay of money to push trade or to advance the cause of science, and they approve of it as right and wise. Tell them of any expense incurred for the preaching of the Gospel at home or abroad, for spreading God's Word, for extending the knowledge of Christ on earth, and they tell you plainly that they think it waste. They never give a farthing to such objects as these, and count those people fools who do. Worst of all, they often cover over their own backwardness to help purely Christian objects, by a pretended concern for the poor at home. Yet they find it convenient to forget the well-known fact that those who do most for the cause of Christ are precisely those who do most for the poor.

We must never allow ourselves to be moved from "patient continuance in well doing," by the unkind remarks of such people. It is vain to expect a man to do much for Christ, when he has no sense of debt to Christ. We must pity the blindness of our unkind critics, and work on. He who pleaded the cause of loving Mary, and said, "Let her alone," is sitting at the right hand of God, and keeps a book of remembrance. A day is soon coming when a wondering world will see that every cup of cold water given for Christ's sake, as well as every box of precious ointment, was recorded in heaven, and has its rewards. In that great day those who thought that anyone could give too much to Christ will find they had better never have been born.

We see, lastly, in this passage, what desperate hardness and unbelief there is in the heart of man.

Unbelief appears in the chief priests, who "consulted that they might put Lazarus to death." They could not deny the fact of his having been raised again. Living, and moving, and eating, and drinking within two miles of Jerusalem, after lying four days in the grave, Lazarus was a witness to the truth of Christ's Messiahship, whom they could not possibly answer or put to silence. Yet these proud men would not give way. They would rather commit a murder than throw down the arms of rebellion, and confess themselves in the wrong. No wonder that the Lord Jesus in a certain place "marveled" at unbelief. Well might He say, in a well-known parable, "If they believe not Moses and the Prophets, neither will they be persuaded though one rose from the dead." (Mark 6:6; Luke 16:31.)

Hardness appears in Judas Iscariot, who, after being a chosen Apostle, and a preacher of the kingdom of heaven, turns out at last a thief and a traitor. So long as the world stands this unhappy man will be a lasting proof of the depth of human corruption. That anyone could follow Christ as a disciple for three years, see all His miracles, hear all His teaching, receive at His hand repeated kindnesses, be counted an Apostle, and yet prove rotten at heart in the end, all this at first sight appears incredible and impossible! Yet the case of Judas shows plainly that the thing can be. Few things, perhaps, are so little realized as the extent of what desperate hardness and unbelief there is in the heart of man.

Let us thank God if we know anything of faith, and can say, with all our sense of weakness and infirmity, "I believe." Let us pray that our faith may be real, true, genuine, and sincere, and not a mere temporary impression, like the morning cloud and the early dew. Not least, let us watch and pray against the love of the world. It ruined one who basked in the full sunshine of privileges, and heard Christ Himself teaching every day. Then "let him that thinks he stands take heed lest he fall." (1 Cor. 10:12.)

12:12-19

The next day the large crowd that had come to the feast heard that Jesus was coming to Jerusalem. So they took branches of palm trees and went out to meet him. They began to shout, "Hosanna! Blessed is the one who comes in the name of the Lord! Blessed is the king of Israel!" Jesus found a young donkey and sat on it, just as it is written, "Do not be afraid, people of Zion; look, your king is coming, seated on a donkey's colt!" (His disciples did not understand these things when they first

184 | J.C. RYLE

happened, but when Jesus was glorified, then they remembered that these things were written about him and that these things had happened to him.)

So the crowd who had been with him when he called Lazarus out of the tomb and raised him from the dead were continuing to testify about it. Because they had heard that Jesus had performed this miraculous sign, the crowd went out to meet him. Thus the Pharisees said to one another, "You see that this is getting us nowhere. Look, the world has gone after him!"

A careful reader of the Gospels can hardly fail to observe that our Lord Jesus Christ's conduct, at this stage of His earthly ministry, is very peculiar. It is unlike anything else recorded of Him in the New Testament. Hitherto we have seen Him withdrawing as much as possible from public notice, retiring into the wilderness, and checking those who would have brought Him forward and made Him a king. As a rule He did not court popular attention. He did not "cry or strive, or cause His voice to be heard in the streets." (Matt. 12:19.) Here, on the contrary, we see Him making a public entry into Jerusalem, attended by an immense crowd of people, and causing even the Pharisees to say, "Behold, the world has gone after Him."

The explanation of this apparent inconsistency is not hard to find out. The time had come at last when Christ was to die for the sins of the world. The time had come when the true passover Lamb was to be slain, when the true blood of atonement was to be shed, when Messiah was to be "cut off" according to prophecy, (Dan. 9:26,) when the way into the holiest was to be opened by the true High Priest to all mankind. Knowing all this, our Lord purposely drew attention to Himself. Knowing this, He placed Himself prominently under the notice of the whole Jewish nation. It was only fit and right that this thing should not be "done in a corner." (Acts 26:26.) If ever there was a transaction in our Lord's earthly ministry which was public, it was the Sacrifice which He offered up on the cross of Calvary. He died at the time of year when all the tribes were assembled at Jerusalem for the passover feast. Nor was this all. He died in a week when, by His remarkable public entry into Jerusalem, He had caused the eyes of all Israel to be specially fixed upon Himself.

We learn, for one thing, in these verses, how entirely VOLUNTARY the sufferings of Christ were. It is impossible not to see in the history before us that our Lord had a mysterious influence over the minds and wills of all around Him, whenever He thought fit to use it. Nothing else can account for the effect which His approach to Jerusalem had on the multitudes which accompanied Him. They seem to have been carried forward by a secret constraining power, which they were obliged to obey, in spite of the disapproval of the leaders of the nation. In short, just as our Lord was able to make winds, and waves, and diseases, and devils obey Him, so was He able, when it pleased Him, to turn, the minds of men according to His will.

For the case before us does not stand alone. The men of Nazareth could not hold Him when He chose to "pass through the midst of them and go His way." (Luke 4:30.) The angry Jews of Jerusalem could not detain him when they would have laid violent hands on Him in the Temple; but, "going through the midst of them, He passed by." (John 8:59.) Above all, the very soldiers who apprehended Him in the garden, at first "went backward and fell to the ground." (John 18:6.) In each of these instances there is but one explanation. A Divine influence was put forth. There was about our Lord during His whole earthly ministry a mysterious "hiding of His power." (Hab. 3:4.) But He had almighty power when He was pleased to use it.

Why, then, did He not resist His enemies at last? Why did He not scatter the band of soldiers who came to seize Him, like chaff before the wind? There is but one answer. He was a willing Sufferer in order to procure redemption for a lost and ruined soul. He had undertaken to give His own life as a ransom, that we might live forever, and He laid it down on the cross with all the desire of His heart. He did not bleed and suffer and die because He was vanquished by superior force, and could not help Himself, but because He loved us, and rejoiced to give Himself for us as our Substitute. He did not die because He could not avoid death, but because He was willing with all His heart to make His soul an offering for sin.

Forever let us rest our hearts on this most comfortable thought. We have a most willing and loving Savior. It was His delight to do His Father's will, and to make a way for lost and guilty man to draw near to God in peace. He loved the work He had taken in hand, and the poor sinful world which He came to save. Never, then, let us give way to the unworthy thought that our Savior does not love to see sinners coming to Him, and does not rejoice to save them. He who was a most willing Sacrifice on the cross is also a most willing Savior at the right hand of God. He is just as willing to receive sinners who come to Him now for peace, as He was to die for sinners, when He held back His power and willingly suffered on Calvary.

We learn, for another thing, in these verses, how minutely the PROPH-ECIES concerning Christ's first coming were fulfilled. The riding into Jerusalem on a donkey, which is here recorded, might seem at first sight a simple action, and in no way remarkable. But when we turn to the Old

Testament, we find that this very thing had been predicted by the Prophet Zechariah five hundred years before. (Zech. 9:9.) We find that the coming of a Redeemer someday was not the only thing which the Holy Spirit had revealed to the Fathers, but that even the least particulars of His earthly career were predicted and written down with precise accuracy.

Such fulfillments of prophecy as this deserve the special attention of all who love the Bible and read it with reverence. They show us that every word of Holy Scripture was given by inspiration of God. They teach us to beware of the mischievous practice of spiritualizing and explaining away the language of Scripture. We must settle it in our minds that the plain, literal meaning of the Bible is generally the true and correct meaning. Here is a prediction of Zechariah literally and exactly fulfilled. Our Lord was not merely a very humble person as some spiritualizing interpreters would have explained Zechariah's words to mean, but He literally rode into Jerusalem on an donkey.

Above all, such fulfillments teach us what we may expect in looking forward to the second advent of Jesus Christ. They show us that we must look for a literal accomplishment of the prophecies concerning that second coming, and not for a figurative and a spiritual one. Forever let us hold fast this great principle. Happy is that Bible-reader who believes the words of the Bible to mean exactly what they seem to mean. Such a man has got the true key of knowledge in looking forward to things to come. To know that predictions about the second advent of Christ will be fulfilled literally, just as predictions about the first advent of Christ were fulfilled literally, is the first step towards a right understanding of unfulfilled prophecy.

12:20-26

Now some Greeks were among those who had gone up to worship at the feast. So these approached Philip, who was from Bethsaida in Galilee, and requested, "Sir, we would like to see Jesus." Philip went and told Andrew, and they both went and told Jesus. Jesus replied, "The time has come for the Son of Man to be glorified. I tell you the solemn truth, unless a kernel of wheat falls into the ground and dies, it remains by itself alone. But if it dies, it produces much grain. The one who loves his life destroys it, and the one who hates his life in this world guards it for eternal life. If anyone wants to serve me, he must follow me, and where I am, my servant will be too. If anyone serves me, the Father will honor him.

There is more going on in some people's minds than we are aware of. The case of the Greeks before us is a remarkable proof of this. Who would have thought when Christ was on earth, that foreigners from a distant land would have come forward in Jerusalem, and said, "Sir, we would like to see Jesus"? Who these Greeks were, what they meant, why they desired to see Jesus, what their inward motives were—all these are questions we cannot answer. Like Zaccheus, they may have been influenced by curiosity. Like the wise men from the East, they may have surmised that Jesus was the promised King of the Jews, whom all the eastern world was expecting. Enough for us to know that they showed more interest in Christ than Caiaphas and all his companions. Enough to know that they drew from our Lord's lips sayings which are still read in one hundred and fifty languages, from one end of the world to the other.

We learn, for one thing, from our Lord's words in this passage, that death is the way to spiritual life and glory. "Except a grain of wheat falls into the ground, it abides alone; but if it dies, it brings forth much fruit."

This sentence was primarily meant to teach the wondering Greeks the true nature of Messiah's kingdom. If they thought to see a King like the kings of this world, they were greatly mistaken. Our Lord would have them know that He came to carry a cross, and not to wear a crown. He came not to live a life of honor, ease, and magnificence, but to die a shameful and dishonored death. The kingdom He came to set up was to begin with a crucifixion, and not with a coronation. Its glory was to take its rise not from victories won by the sword, and from accumulated treasures of gold and silver, but from the death of its King.

But this sentence was also meant to teach a wider and broader lesson still. It revealed, under a striking figure, the mighty foundation truth, that Christ's death was to be the source of spiritual life to the world. From His cross and sufferings was to spring up a mighty harvest of benefit to all mankind. His death, like a grain of seed, was to be the root of blessings and mercies to countless millions of immortal souls. In short, the great principle of the Gospel was once more exhibited—that Christ's vicarious death (not His life, or miracles, or teaching, but His death) was to bring forth fruit to the praise of God, and to provide redemption for a lost world.

This deep and mighty sentence was followed by a practical application, which closely concerns ourselves. "He who hates his life shall keep it." He that would be saved must be ready to give up life itself, if necessary, in order to obtain salvation. He must bury his love of the world, with its riches, honors, pleasures, and rewards, with a full belief that in so doing he will reap a better harvest, both here and hereafter. He who loves the life that now is, so much that he cannot deny himself anything for the sake of his soul, will find at length that he has lost everything. He, on the contrary, who is ready to cast away everything most dear to him in this life, if it stands in the way of his soul, and to crucify the flesh with its affections and lusts, will find at length that he is no loser. In a word, his losses will prove nothing in comparison to his gains.

Truths such as these should sink deeply into our hearts, and stir up self-inquiry. It is as true of Christians as it is of Christ—there can be no life without death, there can be no sweet without bitter, there can be no crown without a cross. Without Christ's death there would have been no life for the world. Unless we are willing to die to sin, and crucify all that is most dear to flesh and blood, we cannot expect any benefit from Christ's death. Let us remember these things, and take up our cross daily, like men. Let us, for the joy set before us, endure the cross and despise the shame, and in the end we shall sit down with our Master at God's right hand. The way of self-crucifixion and sanctification may seem foolishness and wasteful to the world, just as burying good seed seems wasteful to the child and the fool. But there never lived the man who did not find that, by sowing to the Spirit, he reaped life everlasting.

We learn, for another thing, from our Lord's words, that if we profess to serve Christ, we must follow Him. "If any man serves Me," is the saying, "let him follow Me."

That expression, "following," is one of wide signification, and brings before our minds many familiar ideas. As the soldier follows his general, as the servant follows his master, as the scholar follows his teacher; as the sheep follows its shepherd, just so ought the professing Christian to follow Christ. Faith and obedience are the leading marks of real followers, and will always be seen in true believing Christians. Their knowledge may be very small, and their infirmities very great; their grace very weak, and their hope very dim. But they believe what Christ says, and strive to do what Christ commands. And of such Christ declares, "They serve Me, they are Mine."

Christianity like this receives little from man. It is too thorough, too decided, too strong, too real. To serve Christ in name and form is easy work, and satisfies most people, but to follow Him in faith and life demands more trouble than the generality of men will take about their souls. Laughter, ridicule, opposition, persecution, are often the only reward which Christ's followers get from the world. Their religion is one, "whose praise is not of men, but of God." (Rom. 2:29.)

Yet to him who follows, let us never forget, the Lord Jesus holds out abundant encouragement—"Where I am," He declares, "there also shall my servant be; if any man serves Me, him will my Father honor." Let us lay to heart these comfortable promises, and go forward in the narrow way without fear. The world may cast out our name as evil, and turn us out of its society; but when we dwell with Christ in glory, we shall have a home from which we can never be ejected. The world may pour contempt on our religion, and laugh us and our Christianity to scorn; but when the Father honors us at the last day, before the assembly of angels and men, we shall find that His praise makes amends for all.

12:27-33

"Now my soul is greatly distressed. And what should I say? 'Father, deliver me from this hour'? No, but for this very reason I have come to this hour. Father, glorify your name." Then a voice came from heaven, "I have glorified it, and I will glorify it again." The crowd that stood there and heard the voice said that it had thundered. Others said that an angel had spoken to him. Jesus said, "This voice has not come for my benefit but for yours. Now is the judgment of this world; now the ruler of this world will be driven out. And I, when I am lifted up from the earth, will draw all people to myself." (Now he said this to indicate clearly what kind of death he was going to die.)

These verses show us what Peter meant, when he said, "There are some things hard to be understood" in Scripture. (2 Pet. 3:16.) There are depths here which we have no line to fathom thoroughly. This need not surprise us, or shake our faith. The Bible would not be a book "given by inspiration of God," if it did not contain many things which pass man's finite understanding. With all its difficulties, it contains thousands of passages which the most unlearned may easily comprehend. Even here, if we look steadily at these verses, we may gather from them lessons of considerable importance.

We have, first, in these verses, a great DOCTRINE indirectly proved. That doctrine is the imputation of man's sin to Christ. We see the Savior of the world, the eternal Son of God troubled and disturbed in mind—"Now is my soul troubled." We see Him who could heal diseases with a touch, cast out devils with a word, and command the waves and winds to obey Him, in great agony and conflict of spirit. Now how can this be explained?

To say, as some do, that the only cause of our Lord's trouble was the prospect of His own painful death on the cross, is a very unsatisfactory explanation. At this rate it might justly be said that many a martyr has shown more calmness and courage than the Son of God. Such a conclusion is, to say the least, most revolting. Yet this is the conclusion to which men are driven if they adopt the modern notion, that Christ's death was only a great example of self-sacrifice.

Nothing can ever explain our Lord's trouble of soul, both here and in Gethsemane, except the old doctrine, that He felt the burden of man's sin pressing Him down. It was the mighty weight of a world's guilt imputed to Him and meeting on his head, which made Him groan and agonize, and cry, "Now is my soul troubled." Forever let us cling to that doctrine, not only as untying the knot of the passage before us, but as the only ground of solid comfort for the heart of a Christian. That our sins have been really laid on our Divine Substitute, and borne by Him, and that His righteousness is really imputed to us and accounted ours—this is the real warrant for Christian peace. And if any man asks how we know that our sins were laid on Christ, we bid him read such passages as that which is before us, and explain them on any other principle if he can. Christ has borne our sins, carried our sins, groaned under the burden of our sins, been "troubled" in soul by the weight of our sins, and really taken away our sins. This, we may rest assured, is sound doctrine this is Scriptural theology.

We have, secondly, in these verses, a great MYSTERY unfolded. That mystery is the possibility of much inward conflict of soul without sin.

We cannot fail to see in the passage before us a mighty mental struggle in our blessed Savior. Of its depth and intensity we can probably form very little conception. But the agonizing cry, "My soul is troubled,"—the solemn question, "What shall I say?"—the prayer of suffering flesh and blood, "Father, save Me from this hour,"—the meek confession, "For this cause came I unto this hour,"-the petition of a perfectly submissive will, "Father, glorify Your name,"—what does all this mean? Surely there can be only one answer. These sentences tell of a struggle within our Savior's breast, a struggle arising from the natural feelings of one who was perfect man, and as man could suffer all that man is capable of suffering. Yet He in whom this struggle took place was the Holy Son of God. "In Him is no sin." (1 John 3:5.)

There is a fountain of comfort here for all true servants of Christ, which ought never to be overlooked. Let them learn from their Lord's example that inward conflict of soul is not necessarily in itself a sinful thing. Too many, we believe, from not understanding this point, go heavily all their days on their way to heaven. They fancy they have no grace, because they find a fight in their own hearts. They refuse to take comfort in the Gospel, because they feel a battle between the flesh and the Spirit. Let them mark the experience of their Lord and Master, and lay aside their desponding fears. Let them study the experience of His saints in every age, from Paul downwards, and understand that as Christ had inward conflicts, so must Christians expect to have them also. To give way to doubts and unbelief, no doubt is wrong, and robs us of our peace. There is a faithless despondency, unquestionably, which is blameworthy, and must be resisted, repented of, and brought to the fountain for all sin, that it may be pardoned. But the mere presence of fight and strife and conflict in our hearts is in itself no sin. The believer may be known by his inward warfare as well as by his inward peace.

We have, thirdly, in these verses, a great MIRACLE exhibited. That miracle is the heavenly Voice described in this passage—a voice which was heard so plainly that people said it thundered—proclaiming, "I have glorified my name, and will glorify it again."

This wondrous Voice was heard three times during our Lord's earthly ministry. Once it was heard at His baptism, when the heavens were opened and the Holy Spirit descended on Him. Once it was heard at His transfiguration, when Moses and Elijah appeared for a season with Him, before Peter, James, and John. Once it was heard here at Jerusalem, in the midst of a mixed crowd of disciples and unbelieving Jews. On each occasion we know that it was the Voice of God the Father. But why this Voice was only heard on these occasions we are left to conjecture. The thing was a deep mystery, and we cannot now speak particularly of it.

Let it suffice us to believe that this miracle was meant to show the intimate relations and unbroken union of God the Father and God the Son, throughout the period of the Son's earthly ministry. At no period during His incarnation was there a time when the eternal Father was not close to Him, though unseen by man.

Let us also believe that this miracle was meant to signify to bystanders the entire approval of the Son by the Father, as the Messiah, the Redeemer, and the Savior of man. That approval the Father was pleased to signify by voice three times, as well as to declare by signs and mighty deeds, performed by the Son in His name. These things we may well believe. But when we have said all, we must confess that the Voice was a mystery. We may read of it with wonder and awe, but we cannot explain it.

We have, lastly, in these verses, a great PROPHECY delivered. The Lord Jesus declared, "I, if I be lifted up from the earth, will draw all men unto me." Concerning the true meaning of these words, there can be but one opinion in any honest mind. They do not mean, as is often supposed, that if the doctrine of Christ crucified is lifted up and exalted by ministers and teachers, it will have a drawing effect on hearers. This is undeniably a truth, but it is not the truth of the text. They simply mean that the death of Christ on the cross would have a drawing effect on all mankind. His death as our Substitute, and the Sacrifice for our sins, would draw multitudes out of every nation to believe on Him and receive Him as their Savior. By being crucified for us, and not by ascending a temporal throne, He would set up a kingdom in the world, and gather subjects to Himself.

How thoroughly this prophecy has been fulfilled for eighteen centuries, the history of the Church is an abundant proof. Whenever Christ crucified has been preached, and the story of the cross fully told, souls have been converted and drawn to Christ, in every part of the world, just as iron-filings are drawn to a magnet. No truth so exactly suits the needs of all children of Adam, of every color, climate, and language, as the truth about Christ crucified.

And the prophecy is not yet exhausted. It shall yet receive a more complete accomplishment. A day shall come when every knee shall bow before the Lamb that was slain, and every tongue confess that He is Lord to the glory of God the Father. He who was "lifted up" on the cross shall yet sit on the throne of glory, and before Him shall be gathered all nations. Friends and foes, each in their own order, shall be "drawn" from their graves, and appear before the judgment-seat of Christ. Let us take heed in that day that we are found on His right hand!

12:34-43

Then the crowd responded, "We have heard from the law that the Christ will remain forever. How can you say, 'The Son of Man must be lifted up'? Who is this Son of Man?" Jesus replied, "The light is with you for a little while longer. Walk while you have the light, so that the darkness may not overtake you. The one who walks in the darkness does not know where he is going. While you have the light,

*believe in the light, so that you may become sons of light." When Jesus had said
these things, he went away and hid himself from them.*

*Although Jesus had performed so many miraculous signs before them, they still
refused to believe in him, so that the word of Isaiah the prophet would be fulfilled.
He said, "Lord, who has believed our message, and to whom has the arm of the
Lord been revealed?" For this reason they could not believe, because again Isaiah
said, "He has blinded their eyes and hardened their heart, so that they would not
see with their eyes and understand with their heart, and turn to me, and I would
heal them."*

*Isaiah said these things because he saw Christ's glory, and spoke about him.
Nevertheless, even among the rulers many believed in him, but because of the
Pharisees they would not confess Jesus to be the Christ, so that they would not be put
out of the synagogue. For they loved praise from men more than praise from God.*

We may learn, from these verses, the duty of using present opportunities.
The Lord Jesus says to us all, "Yet a little while is the light with you. Walk
while you have the light, lest darkness come upon you. While you have light
believe in the light." Let us not think that these things were only spoken for
the sake of the Jews. They were written for us also, upon whom the ends of
the world are come.

The lesson of the words is generally applicable to the whole professing
Church of Christ. Its time for doing good in the world is short and limited.
The throne of grace will not always be standing—it will be removed one day,
and the throne of judgment will be set up in its place. The door of salvation
by faith in Christ will not always be open—it will be shut one day forever,
and the number of God's elect will be completed. The fountain for all sin
and uncleanness will not always be accessible; the way to it will one day be
barred, and there will remain nothing but the lake that burns with fire and
brimstone.

These are solemn thoughts; but they are true. They cry aloud to sleeping
Churchmen and drowsy congregations, and ought to arouse great searchings of heart. "Can nothing more be done to spread the Gospel at home and
abroad? Has every means been tried for extending the knowledge of Christ
crucified? Can we lay our hands on our hearts, and say that the Churches
have left nothing undone in the matter of missions? Can we look forward
to the Second Advent with no feelings of humiliation, and say that the
talents of wealth, and influence, and opportunities have not been buried in
the ground?" Such questions may well humble us, when we look, on one
side, at the state of professing Christendom, and, on the other, at the state

of the heathen world. We must confess with shame that the Church is not walking worthy of its light.

But the lesson of the words is specially applicable to ourselves as individuals. Our own time for getting good is short and limited; let us take heed that we make good use of it. Let us "walk while we have the light." Have we Bibles?

Let us not neglect to read them. Have we the preached Gospel? Let us not linger halting between two opinions, but believe to the saving of our souls. Have we Sabbaths? Let us not waste them in idleness, carelessness, and indifference, but throw our whole hearts into their sacred employments, and turn them to good account. Light is about us and around us and near us on every side. Let us each resolve to walk in the light while we have it, lest we find ourselves at length cast out into outer darkness forever. It is a true saying of an old divine, that the recollection of lost and misspent opportunities will be the very essence of hell.

We may learn, secondly, from these verses, the desperate hardness of the human heart. It is written of our Lord's hearers at Jerusalem, that, "though he had done so many miracles before them, yet they believed not on Him."

We err greatly if we suppose that seeing wonderful miraculous things will ever convert souls. Thousands live and die in this delusion. They fancy if they saw some miraculous sight, or witnessed some supernatural exercise of Divine grace, they would lay aside their doubts, and at once become decided Christians. It is a total mistake. Nothing short of a new heart and a new nature implanted in us by the Holy Spirit, will ever make us real disciples of Christ. Without this, a miracle might raise within us a little temporary excitement; but, the novelty once gone, we would find ourselves just as cold and unbelieving as the Jews.

The prevalence of unbelief and indifference in the present day ought not to surprise us. It is just one of the evidences of that mighty foundation-doctrine, the total corruption and fall of man. How feebly we grasp and realize that doctrine is proved by our surprise at human incredulity. We only half believe the heart's deceitfulness. Let us read our Bibles more attentively, and search their contents more carefully. Even when Christ wrought miracles and preached sermons, there were numbers of His hearers who remained utterly unmoved. What right have we to wonder if the hearers of modern sermons in countless instances remain unbelieving? "The disciple is not greater than his Master." If even the hearers of Christ did not believe, how much more should we expect to find unbelief among the hearers of His ministers! Let the truth be spoken and confessed. Man's obstinate unbelief is one among many indirect proofs that the Bible is true. The clearest prophecy in Isaiah begins with the solemn question, "Who has believed?" (Isaiah. 53:1.)

We may learn, thirdly, from these verses, the amazing power which the love of the world has over men. We read that "among the chief rulers many believed on Christ; but because of the Pharisees they did not confess Him, lest they should be put out of the synagogue. For they loved the praise of men more than the praise of God."

These unhappy men were evidently convinced that Jesus was the true Messiah. Reason, and intellect, and mind, and conscience, obliged them secretly to admit that no one could do the miracles which He did, unless God was with Him, and that the preacher of Nazareth really was the Christ of God. But they had not courage to confess it. They dared not face the storm of ridicule, if not of persecution, which confession would have entailed. And so, like cowards, they held their peace, and kept their convictions to themselves.

Their case, it may be feared, is a sadly common one. There are thousands of people who know far more in religion then they act up to. They know they ought to come forward as decided Christians. They know that they are not living up to their light. But the fear of man keeps them back. They are afraid of being laughed at, jeered at, and despised by the world. They dread losing the good opinion of society, and the favorable judgment of men and women like themselves. And so they go on from to year to year, secretly ill at ease and dissatisfied with themselves—knowing too much of religion to be happy in the world, and clinging too much to the world to enjoy any religion.

Faith is the only cure for soul ailments like this. A believing view of an unseen God, an unseen Christ, an unseen heaven, and an unseen judgment-day—this is the grand secret of overcoming the fear of man. The expulsive power of a new principle is required to heal the disease. "This is the victory that overcomes the world, even our faith." (1 John 5:4.) Let us pray for faith, if we would conquer that deadly enemy of souls, the fear of man and the love of man's praise. And if we have any faith, let us pray for more. Let our daily cry be, "Lord, increase our faith." We may easily have too much money, or too much worldly prosperity; but we can never have too much faith.

12:44-50

But Jesus shouted out, "The one who believes in me does not believe in me, but in the one who sent me, and the one who sees me sees the one who sent me. I have come as a light into the world, so that everyone who believes in me should not remain in darkness. If anyone hears my words and does not obey them, I do not judge him. For I have not come to judge the world, but to save the world. The one who rejects me and does not accept my words has a judge; the word I have spoken will judge him at the last day. For I have not spoken from my own authority, but the Father himself who sent me has commanded me what I should say and what I should speak. And I know that his commandment is eternal life. Thus the things I say, I say just as the Father has told me."

These verses throw light on two subjects which we can never understand too well. Our daily peace and our practice of daily watchfulness over ourselves are closely connected with a clear knowledge of these two subjects.

One thing shown in these verses is, the dignity of our Lord Jesus Christ. We find Him saying, "He that sees Me, sees Him that sent Me. I have come as a Light into the world, that whoever believes on Me should not abide in darkness." Christ's oneness with the Father, and Christ's office, are clearly exhibited in these words.

Concerning the unity of the Father and the Son, we must be content to believe reverently, what we cannot grasp mentally or explain distinctly. Let it suffice us to know that our Savior was not like the prophets and patriarchs, a man sent by God the Father, a friend of God, and a witness for God. He was something far higher and greater than this. He was in His Divine nature essentially one with the Father—and in seeing Him, men saw the Father who sent Him. This is a great mystery; but a truth of vast importance to our souls. He that casts His sins on Jesus Christ by faith is building on a rock. Believing on Christ, he believes not merely on Him, but on Him that sent Him.

Concerning the office of Christ, there can be little doubt that in this place He compares Himself to the sun. Like the sun, He has risen on this sin-darkened world with healing on His wings, and shines for the common benefit of all mankind. Like the sun, He is the great source and center of all spiritual life, comfort, and fertility. Like the sun, He illuminates the whole earth, and no one need miss the way to heaven, if he will only use the light offered for his acceptance.

Forever let us make much of Christ in all our religion. We can never trust Him too much, follow Him too closely, or commune with Him too unreservedly. He has all power in heaven and earth. He is able to save to the uttermost all who come to God by Him. None can pluck us out of the hand of Him who is one with the Father. He can make all our way to heaven bright and plain and cheerful; like the morning sun cheering the traveler.

Looking unto Him, we shall find light in our understandings, see light on the path of life we have to travel, feel light in our hearts, and find the days of darkness, which will come sometimes, stripped of half their gloom. Only let us abide in Him, and look to Him with a single eye. There is a mine of meaning in His words, "If your eye be single, your whole body shall be full of light." (Matt. 6:22.)

Another thing shown in these verses is, the certainty of a judgment to come. We find our Lord saying, "He that rejects Me, and receives not my words, has One that judges him—the word that I have spoken, the same shall judge him in the last day."

There is a last day! The world shall not always go on as it does now. Buying and selling, sowing and reaping, planting and building, marrying and giving in marriage—all this shall come to an end at last. There is a time appointed by the Father when the whole machinery of creation shall stop, and the present dispensation shall be changed for another. It had a beginning, and it shall also have an end. Banks shall at length close their doors forever. Stock exchanges shall be shut. Parliaments shall be dissolved. The very sun, which since Noah's flood has done his daily work so faithfully, shall rise and set no more. Well would it be if we thought more of this day! Pay-days, birth-days, wedding-days, are often regarded as days of absorbing interest; but they are nothing compared to the last day.

There is a judgment coming! Men have their reckoning days, and God will at last have His. The trumpet shall sound. The dead shall be raised incorruptible. The living shall be changed. All, of every name and nation, and people and tongue, shall stand before the judgment-seat of Christ. The books shall be opened, and the evidence brought forth. Our true character will come out before the world. There will be no concealment, no evasion, no false coloring. Every one shall give account of himself to God, and all shall be judged according to their works. The wicked shall go away into everlasting fire, and the righteous into life eternal.

These are dreadful truths! But they are truths, and ought to be told. No wonder that the Roman governor Felix trembled when Paul the prisoner discoursed about "righteousness, temperance, and judgment to come." (Acts 24:25.) Yet the believer in the Lord Jesus Christ has no cause to be afraid. For him, at any rate, there is no condemnation, and the last assize need have no terrors. The bias of his life shall witness for him; while the shortcomings of his life shall not condemn him. It is the man who rejects Christ, and will not hear His call to repentance—he is the man who in the judgment-day will have reason to be cast down and afraid.

Let the thought of judgment to come have a practical effect on our religion. Let us daily judge ourselves with righteous judgment, that we may not be judged and condemned of the Lord. Let us so speak and so act as men who will be judged by the law of liberty. Let us make conscience of all our hourly conduct, and never forget that for every idle word we must give account at the last day. In a word, let us live like those who believe in the truth of judgment, heaven, and hell. So living, we shall be Christians indeed and in truth, and have boldness in the day of Christ's appearing.

Let the judgment-day be the Christian's answer and apology when men ridicule him as too strict, too precise, and too particular in his religion. Irreligion may do tolerably well for a season, so long as a man is in health and prosperous, and looks at nothing but this world. But he who believes that he must give account to the Judge of quick and dead, at His appearing and kingdom, will never be content with an ungodly life. He will say, "There is a judgment. I can never serve God too much. Christ died for me. I can never do too much for Him."

Chapter 13

13:1-5

Washing the Disciples' Feet

Just before the Passover feast, Jesus knew that his time had come to depart from this world to the Father. Having loved his own who were in the world, he now loved them to the very end. The evening meal was in progress, and the devil had already put into the heart of Judas Iscariot, Simon's son, that he should betray Jesus. Because Jesus knew that the Father had handed all things over to him, and that he had come from God and was going back to God, he got up from the meal, removed his outer clothes, took a towel and tied it around himself. He poured water into the washbasin and began to wash the disciples' feet and to dry them with the towel he had wrapped around himself.

The passage we have now read begins one of the most interesting portions of John's Gospel. For five consecutive chapters we find the Evangelist recording matters which are not mentioned by Matthew, Mark, and Luke. We can never be thankful enough that the Holy Spirit has caused them to be written for our learning! In every age the contents of these chapters have been justly regarded as one of the most precious parts of the Bible. They have been the food and drink, the strength and comfort of all true-hearted Christians. Let us ever approach them with peculiar reverence. The place whereon we stand is holy ground.

We learn, for one thing, from these verses, what patient and continuing love there is in Christ's heart towards His people. It is written that "having loved His own which were in the world, He loved them unto the end."

Knowing perfectly well that they were about to forsake Him shamefully in a very few hours, in full view of their approaching display of weakness and infirmity, our blessed Master did not cease to have loving thoughts of His disciples. He was not weary of them—He loved them to the last.

The love of Christ to sinners is the very essence and marrow of the Gospel. That He should love us at all, and care for our souls—that He should love us before we love Him, or even know anything about Him, that He should love us so much as to come into the world to save us, take our nature on Him, bear our sins, and die for us on the cross—all this is wonderful indeed! It is a kind of love to which there is nothing like it, among men. The narrow selfishness of human nature cannot fully comprehend it. It is one of those things which even the angels of God "desire to look into." It is a truth which Christian preachers and teachers should proclaim incessantly, and never be weary of proclaiming.

But the love of Christ to saints is no less wonderful, in its way, than His love to sinners, though far less considered. That He should bear with all their countless infirmities from grace to glory—that He should never be tired of their endless inconsistencies and petty provocations—that He should go on forgiving and forgetting incessantly, and never be provoked to cast them off and give them up—all this is marvelous indeed! No mother watching over the waywardness of her feeble babe, in the days of its infancy, has her patience so thoroughly tried, as the patience of Christ is tried by Christians. Yet His patience is infinite. His compassions are a well that is never exhausted. His love is "a love that passes knowledge."

Let no man be afraid of beginning with Christ, if he desires to be saved. The chief of sinners may come to Him with boldness, and trust Him for pardon with confidence. This loving Savior is One who delights to "receive sinners." (Luke 15:2.) Let no man be afraid of going on with Christ after he has once come to Him and believed. Let him not fancy that Christ will cast him off because of failures, and dismiss him into his former hopelessness on account of infirmities. Such thoughts are entirely unwarranted by anything in the Scriptures. Jesus will never reject any servant because of feeble service and weak performance. Those whom He receives He always keeps. Those whom He loves at first He loves at last. His promise shall never be broken, and it is for saints as well as sinners—"Him that comes unto Me I will in no wise cast out." (John 6:37.)

We learn, for another thing, from these verses, what deep corruption may sometimes be found in the heart of a great professor of religion. It is written that "the devil put into the heart of Judas Iscariot, Simon's son, to betray Christ."

This Judas, we must always remember, was one of the twelve Apostles. He had been chosen by Christ Himself, at the same time with Peter, James, John, and their companions. For three years he had walked in Christ's society, had seen His miracles, had heard His preaching, had experienced many proofs of His loving-kindness. He had even preached himself and wrought miracles in Christ's name; and when our Lord sent out His disciples two and two, Judas Iscariot no doubt must have been one of some couple that was sent. Yet here we see this very man possessed by the devil, and rushing headlong to destruction.

On all the coasts of England there is not such a beacon to warn sailors of danger as Judas Iscariot is to warn Christians. He shows us what length a man may go in religious profession, and yet turn out a rotten hypocrite at last, and prove never to have been converted. He shows us the uselessness of the highest privileges, unless we have a heart to value them and turn them to good account. Privileges alone without grace save nobody, and will only make hell deeper. He shows us the uselessness of mere head-knowledge. To know things with our brains, and be able to talk and preach and speak to others, is no proof that our own feet are in the way of peace. These are terrible lessons-but they are true.

Let us never be surprised if we see hypocrisy and false profession among Christians in modern days. There is nothing new in it, nothing peculiar, nothing that did not happen even among Christ's own immediate followers, and under Christ's own eyes. Counterfeit money is a strong proof that there is good coin somewhere. Hypocrisy is a strong indirect evidence that there is such a thing as true religion.

Above all, let us pray daily that our own Christianity may at any rate be genuine, sincere, real and true. Our faith may be feeble, our hope dim, our knowledge small, our failures frequent, our faults many. But at all events let us be real and true. Let us be able to say with poor, weak, erring Peter, "You, Lord, who know all things, know that I love You." (John 21:17.)

13:6-15

Then he came to Simon Peter. Peter said to him, "Lord, are you going to wash my feet?" Jesus replied, "You do not understand what I am doing now, but you will

*understand after these things." Peter said to him, "You will never wash my feet!"
Jesus replied, "If I do not wash you, you have no share with me." Simon Peter said to
him, "Lord, wash not only my feet, but also my hands and my head!" Jesus replied,
"The one who has bathed needs only to wash his feet, but is completely clean. And
you disciples are clean, but not every one of you." (For Jesus knew the one who
was going to betray him. For this reason he said, "Not every one of you is clean.")*

*So when Jesus had washed their feet and put his outer clothing back on, he
took his place at the table again and said to them, "Do you understand what I
have done for you? You call me 'Teacher' and 'Lord,' and do so correctly, for that
is what I am. If I then, your Lord and Teacher, have washed your feet, you too
ought to wash one another's feet. For I have given you an example-you should do
just as I have done for you.*

The verses we have now read conclude the story of our Lord's washing
the feet of His disciples, the night before He was crucified. It is a story full
of touching interest, which for some wise reason no Evangelist records except John. The wonderful condescension of Christ, in doing such a menial
action, can hardly fail to strike any reader. The mere fact that the Master
should wash the feet of the servants might well fill us with surprise. But the
circumstances and sayings which arose out of the action are just as interesting as the action itself. Let us see what they were.

We should notice, firstly, the hasty ignorance of the Apostle Peter. One
moment we find him refusing to allow his Master to do such a servile work
as He is about to do—"Do you wash my feet?" "You shall never wash my
feet." Another moment we find him rushing with characteristic impetuosity
into the other extreme—"Lord, wash not my feet only, but my hands and
my head." But throughout the transaction we find him unable to take in the
real meaning of what his eyes behold. He sees, but he does not understand.

Let us learn from Peter's conduct that a man may have plenty of faith and
love, and yet be sadly destitute of clear knowledge. We must not set down
men as graceless and godless because they are dull, and stupid, and blundering
in their religion. The heart may often be quite right when the head is quite
wrong. We must make allowances for the corruption of the understanding,
as well as of the will. We must not be surprised to find that the brains as
well as the affections of Adam's children have been hurt by the fall. It is a
humbling lesson, and one seldom fully learned except by long experience.
But the longer we live the more true shall we find it, that a believer, like
Peter, may make many mistakes and lack understanding, and yet, like Peter,
have a heart right before God, and get to heaven at last.

Even at our best estate we shall find that many of Christ's dealings with us are hard to understand in this life. The "why" and "wherefore" of many a providence will often puzzle and perplex us quite as much as the washing puzzled Peter. The wisdom, and fitness, and necessity of many a thing will often be hidden from our eyes. But at times like these we must remember the Master's words, and fall back upon them—"What I do you know not now, but you shall know hereafter." There came days, long after Christ had left the world, when Peter saw the full meaning of all that happened on the memorable night before the crucifixion. Even so there will be a day when every dark page in our life's history will be explained, and when, as we stand with Christ in glory, we shall know all.

We should notice, secondly, in this passage, the plain practical lesson which lies upon its surface. That lesson is read out to us by our Lord. He says, "I have given you an example, that you should do as I have done to you."

HUMILITY is evidently one part of the lesson. If the only-begotten Son of God, the King of kings, did not think it beneath Him to do the humblest work of a servant, there is nothing which His disciples should think themselves too great or too good to do. No sin is so offensive to God, and so injurious to the soul as pride. No grace is so commended, both by precept and example, as humility. "Be clothed with humility." "He who humbles himself shall be exalted." "Let this mind be in you, which was also in Christ Jesus; who, being in the form of God, thought it not robbery to be equal with God—but made Himself of no reputation, and took upon Him the form of a servant, and was made in the likeness of men—and being found in fashion as a man, He humbled Himself." (1 Pet. 5:5; Luke 18:14; Phil. 2:5-8.) Well would it be for the Church if this very simple truth was more remembered, and real humility was not so sadly rare. Perhaps there is no sight so displeasing in God's eyes as a self-conceited, self-satisfied, self-contented, stuck-up professor of religion. Alas, it is a sight only too common! Yet the words which John here records have never been repealed. They will be a swift witness against many at the last day, except they repent.

LOVE is manifestly the other part of the great practical lesson. Our Lord would have us love others so much that we should delight to do anything which can promote their happiness. We ought to rejoice in doing kindnesses, even in little things. We ought to count it a pleasure to lessen sorrow and multiply joy, even when it costs us some self-sacrifice and self-denial. We ought to love every child of Adam so well, that if in the least trifle we can do anything to make him more happy and comfortable, we should be glad to do it. This was the mind of the Master, and this the ruling principle of His conduct upon earth. There are but few who walk in His steps, it may be feared; but these few are men and women after His own heart.

The lesson before us may seem a very simple one; but its importance can never be overrated. Humility and love are precisely the graces which the men of the world can understand, if they do not comprehend doctrines. They are graces about which there is no mystery, and they are within reach of all Christians. The poorest and most ignorant Christian can every day find occasion for practicing love and humility. Then if we would do good to the world, and make our calling and election sure, let no man forget our Lord's example in this passage. Like Him, let us be humble and loving towards all.

We should notice, lastly, in this passage, the deep spiritual lessons which lie beneath its surface. They are three in number, and lie at the very root of religion, though we can only touch them briefly.

For one thing, we learn that all need to be washed by Christ. "If I wash you not, then have no part in Me." No man or woman can be saved unless his sins are washed away in Christ's precious blood. Nothing else can make us clean or acceptable before God. We must be "washed, sanctified, and justified, in the name of the Lord Jesus, and by the Spirit of our God." (1 Cor. 6:11.) Christ must wash us, if we are ever to sit down with saints in glory. Then let us take heed that we apply to Him by faith, wash and become clean. They only are washed who believe.

For another thing, we learn that even those who are cleansed and forgiven need a daily application to the blood of Christ for daily pardon. We cannot pass through this evil world without defilement. There is not a day in our lives but we fail and come short in many things, and need fresh supplies of mercy. Even "he that is washed needs to wash his feet," and to wash them in the same fountain where he found peace of conscience when he first believed. Then let us daily use that fountain without fear. With the blood of Christ we must begin, and with the blood of Christ we must go on.

Finally, we learn that even those who kept company with Christ, and were baptized with water as His disciples, were "not all" washed from their sin. These words are very solemn—"You are clean—but not all." Then let us take heed to ourselves, and beware of false profession. If even Christ's own disciples are not all cleansed and justified, we have reason to be on our guard. Baptism and Churchmanship are no proof that we are right in the sight of God.

13:16-20

"I tell you the solemn truth, the slave is not greater than his master, nor is the one who is sent as a messenger greater than the one who sent him. If you understand these things, you will be blessed if you do them.

"What I am saying does not refer to all of you. I know the ones I have chosen. But this is to fulfill the scripture, 'The one who eats my bread has turned against me.' I am telling you this now, before it happens, so that when it happens you may believe that I am he. I tell you the solemn truth, whoever accepts the one I send accepts me, and whoever accepts me accepts the one who sent me."

If we would understand the full meaning of these verses, we must mark carefully where they stand in the chapter. They follow right after the remarkable passage in which we read of Christ washing His disciples' feet. They stand in close connection with His solemn command, that the disciples should do as they had seen Him do. Then come the five verses which we have now to consider.

We are taught, for one thing, in these verses, that Christians must never be ashamed of doing anything that Christ has done. We read, "Verily, I say unto you, The servant is not greater than his Lord; neither he that is sent greater than he that sent him."

There seems little doubt that our Lord's all-seeing eye saw a rising unwillingness in the minds of the Apostles to do such menial things as they had just seen Him do. Puffed up with their old Jewish expectation of thrones and kingdoms in this world, secretly self-satisfied with their own position as our Lord's friends, these poor Galileans were startled at the idea of washing people's feet! They could not bring themselves to believe that Messiah's service entailed work like this. They could not yet take in the grand truth, that true Christian greatness consisted in doing good to others. And hence they needed our Lord's word of warning. If He had humbled Himself to do humbling work, His disciples must not hesitate to do the same.

The lesson is one of which we all need to be reminded. We are all too apt to dislike any work which seems to entail trouble, self-denial, and going down to our inferiors. We are only too ready to relegate such work to others, and to excuse ourselves by saying, "It is not in our way." When feelings of this kind arise within us we shall find it good to remember our Lord's words in this passage, no less than our Lord's example. We ought never to think it beneath us to show kindness to the lowest of men. We ought never to hold our hand because the objects of our kindness are ungrateful or unworthy.

Such was not the mind of Him who washed the feet of Judas Iscariot as well as Peter. He who in these matters cannot stoop to follow Christ's example, gives little evidence of possessing true love or true humility.

We are taught, for another thing, in these verses, the uselessness of religious knowledge if not accompanied by practice. We read, "If you know these things, happy are you if you do them." It sounds as if our Lord would warn His disciples that they would never be really happy in His service if they were content with a barren head-knowledge of duty, and did not live according to their knowledge.

The lesson is one which deserves the continual remembrance of all professing Christians. Nothing is more common than to hear people saying of doctrine or duty—"We know it, we know it;" while they sit still in unbelief or disobedience. They actually seem to flatter themselves that there is something creditable and redeeming in knowledge, even when it bears no fruit in heart, character, or life. Yet the truth is precisely the other way. To know what we ought to be, believe, and do, and yet to be unaffected by our knowledge, only adds to our guilt in the sight of God. To know that Christians should be humble and loving, while we continue proud and selfish, will only sink us deeper in the pit, unless we awake and repent. Practice, in short, is the very life of religion. "To him that knows to do good, and does it not, to him it is sin." (James 4:17.)

Of course we must never despise knowledge. It is in one sense the beginning of Christianity in the soul. So long as we know nothing of sin, or God, or Christ, or grace, or repentance, or faith, or conscience, we are of course nothing better than heathens. But we must not overrate knowledge. It is altogether valueless unless it produces results in our conduct, and influences our lives, and moves our wills. In fact knowledge without practice does not raise us above the level of the devil. He could say to Jesus, "I know You who You are, the Holy One of God." The devils, says James, "believe and tremble." (James 2:19.) Satan knows truth, but has no will to obey it, and is miserable. He that would be happy in Christ's service must not only know, but do.

We are taught, for another thing, in these verses, the perfect knowledge which Christ has of all His people. He can distinguish between false profession and true grace. The Church may be deceived, and rank men as Apostles, who are nothing better than brethren of Judas Iscariot. But Jesus is never deceived, for He can read hearts. And here He declares with peculiar emphasis, "I know whom I have chosen."

This perfect knowledge of our Lord Jesus Christ is a very solemn thought, and one which cuts two ways. It ought to fill the hypocrite with alarm, and drive him to repentance. Let him remember that the eyes of the all-seeing Judge already see him through and through, and detect the absence of a wedding garment. If he would not be put to shame before assembled worlds, let him cast aside his false profession, and confess his sin before it is too late. Believers, on the other hand, may think of an all-knowing Savior with comfort. They may remember, when misunderstood and slandered by an evil world, that their Master knows all. He knows that they are true and sincere, however weak and failing. A time is coming when He will confess them before His Father, and bring forth their characters clear and bright as the summer sun at noon-day.

We are taught, finally, in these verses, the true dignity of Christ's disciples. The world may despise and ridicule the Apostles because they care more for works of love and humility than the pursuits of the world. But the Master bids them remember their commission, and not be ashamed. They are God's ambassadors, and have no cause to be cast down. "Verily, verily," He declares, "He that receives whomsoever I send receives Me; and he that receives Me receives Him that sent Me."

The doctrine here laid down is full of encouragement. It ought to cheer and hearten all who lay themselves out to do good, and specially to do good to the fallen and the poor. Work of this kind gets little praise from men, and they who give themselves up to it are often regarded as miserable enthusiasts, and meet with much opposition. Let them however work on, and take comfort in the words of Christ which we are now considering. To spend and be spent in trying to do good, makes a man far more honorable in the eyes of Jesus than to command armies or amass a fortune. The few who work for God in Christ's way have no cause to be ashamed. Let them not be cast down if the children of the world laugh and sneer and despise them. A day comes when they will hear the words, "Come you blessed children of my Father, inherit the kingdom prepared for you." (Matt. 25:34.)

13:21-30

When he had said these things, Jesus was greatly distressed in spirit, and testi-fied, "I tell you the solemn truth, one of you will betray me." The disciples began to look at one another, worried and perplexed to know which of them he was talking about. One of his disciples, the one Jesus loved, was at the table at Jesus' right in the place of honor. So Simon Peter gestured to this disciple to ask Jesus who it was he was referring to. Then the disciple whom Jesus loved leaned back against Jesus' chest and asked him, "Lord, who is it?" Jesus replied, "It is the one to whom I will give this piece of bread after I have dipped it in the dish." Then he dipped the piece of bread in the dish and gave it to Judas Iscariot, Simon's son. And after Judas took the piece of bread, Satan entered into him. Jesus said to him, "What you are about to do, do quickly." (Now none of those present at the table understood why Jesus said this to Judas. Some thought that, because Judas had the money box, Jesus was telling him to buy whatever they needed for the feast, or to give something to the poor.) Judas took the piece of bread and went out immediately. Now it was night.

The subject of the verses before us is a very painful one. They describe the last scene between our Lord Jesus Christ and the false Apostle Judas Iscariot. They contain the last words which passed between them before they parted forever in this world. They never seem to have met again on earth, excepting in the garden when our Lord was taken prisoner. Within a short time both the holy Master and the treacherous servant were dead. They will never meet again in the body until the trumpet sounds, and the dead are raised, and the judgment is set, and the books are opened. What an dreadful meeting will that be!

Let us mark, firstly, in this passage, what trouble our Lord Jesus went through for the sake of our souls. We are told that shortly after washing the disciples' feet, He "was troubled in spirit, and said, One of you shall betray Me."

The whole length and breadth and depth of our Master's troubles during His earthly ministry are far beyond the conception of most people. His death and suffering on the cross were only the heading up and completion of His sorrows. But all throughout His life—partly from the general unbelief of the Jews—partly from the special hatred of the Pharisees and Sadducees—partly from the weakness and infirmity of His few followers—He must have been in a peculiar degree "a Man of sorrows and acquainted with grief." (Isa. 53:3.)

But the trouble before us was a singular and exceptional one. It was the bitter sorrow of seeing a chosen Apostle deliberately becoming an apostate, a backslider, and an ungrateful traitor. That it was a foreseen sorrow from the beginning we need not doubt; but sorrow is not less acute because long foreseen. That it was a peculiarly cutting sorrow is very evident. Nothing is found so hard for flesh and blood to bear as ingratitude. Even a poet of our own has said that it is "sharper than a serpent's tooth to have a thankless child." Absalom's rebellion seems to have been David's heaviest trouble, and

Judas Iscariot's treachery seems to have been one of the heaviest trials of the Son of David. When He saw it drawing near He was "troubled in spirit."

Passages like these should make us see the amazing love of Christ to sinners. How many cups of sorrow He drained to the dregs in working out our salvation, beside the mighty cup of bearing our sins. They show us how little reason we have for complaining when friends fail us, and men disappoint us. If we share our Master's lot we have no cause to be surprised. Above all, they show us the perfect suitableness of Christ to be our Savior. He can sympathize with us. He has suffered Himself, and can feel for those who are ill-used and forsaken.

Let us mark, secondly, in these verses, the power and malignity of our great enemy the devil. We are told in the beginning of the chapter that he "put it into the heart" of Judas to betray our Lord. We are told here that he "entered into" him. First he suggests—then he commands. First he knocks at the door and asks permission to come in—then, once admitted, he takes complete possession, and rules the whole inward man like a tyrant.

Let us take heed that we are not "ignorant of Satan's devices." He is still going to and fro in the earth, seeking whom he may devour. He is about our path, and about our bed, and spies out all our ways. Our only safety lies in resisting him at the first, and not listening to his first advances. For this we are all responsible. Strong as he is, he has no power to do us harm, if we cry to the stronger One in heaven, and use the means which He has appointed. It is a standing principle of Christianity, and will ever be found true. "Resist the devil, and he will flee from you." (James 4:7.)

Once let a man begin tampering with the devil, and he never knows how far he may fall. Trifling with the first thoughts of sin—making light of evil ideas when first offered to our hearts—allowing Satan to talk to us, and flatter us, and put bad notions into our hearts—all this may seem a small matter to many. It is precisely at this point that the road to ruin often begins. He that allows Satan to sow wicked thoughts will soon find within his heart a crop of wicked habits. Happy is he who really believes that there is a devil, and believing, watches and prays daily that he may be kept from his temptations.

Let us mark, lastly, in these verses, the extreme hardness which comes over the heart of a backsliding professor of religion. This is a thing which is most painfully brought out in the case of Judas Iscariot. One might have thought that the sight of our Lord's trouble, and the solemn warning, "One of you shall betray Me," would have stirred the conscience of this unhappy man. But it did not do so. One might have thought that the solemn words, "what you do, do quickly," would have arrested him, and made him ashamed of his intended sin. But nothing seems to have moved him. Like one whose conscience was dead, buried, and gone, he rises and goes out to do his wicked work, and parts with his Lord forever.

The extent to which we may harden ourselves by resisting light and knowledge is one of the most fearful facts in our nature. We may become past feeling, like those whose limbs are mortified before they die. We may lose entirely all sense of fear, or shame, or remorse, and have a heart as hard as the nether millstone, blind to every warning, and deaf to every appeal. It is a painful disease, but one which unhappily is not uncommon among professing Christians. None seem so liable to it as those who, having great light and privilege, deliberately turn their backs on Christ, and return to the world. Nothing seems likely to touch such people, but the voice of the archangel and the trumpet of God. Let us watch jealously over our hearts, and beware of giving way to the beginnings of sin. Happy is he who fears always, and walks humbly with his God. The strongest Christian is the one who feels his weakness most, and cries most frequently, "Hold me up, and I shall be safe." (Psalm 119:117; Prov. 28:14.)

13:31-38

When Judas had gone out, Jesus said, "Now the Son of Man is glorified, and God is glorified in him. If God is glorified in him, God will also glorify him in himself, and he will glorify him right away. Children, I am still with you for a little while. You will look for me, and just as I said to the Jewish authorities, 'Where I am going you cannot come,' now I tell you the same.

"I give you a new commandment—to love one another. Just as I have loved you, you also are to love one another. Everyone will know by this that you are my disciples—if you have love for one another."

Simon Peter said to him, "Lord, where are you going?" Jesus replied, "Where I am going, you cannot follow me now, but you will follow later." Peter said to him, "Lord, why can't I follow you now? I will lay down my life for you!" Jesus answered, "Will you lay down your life for me? I tell you the solemn truth, the rooster will not crow until you have denied me three times!

In this passage we find the Lord Jesus at last alone with His eleven faithful disciples. The traitor, Judas Iscariot, had left the room, and gone out to do his wicked deed of darkness. Freed from his painful company, our Lord opens His heart to His little flock more fully than He had ever done before. Speaking to them for the last time before His passion, He begins a discourse which for touching interest surpasses any portion of Scripture.

These verses show us what glory the crucifixion brought both to God the Father and to God the Son. It seems impossible to avoid the conclusion that this was what our Lord had in His mind when He said, "Now is the Son of man glorified, and God is glorified in Him." It is as though He said, "The time of my crucifixion is at hand. My work on earth is finished. An event is about to take place tomorrow, which, however painful to you who love Me, is in reality most glorifying both to Me and My Father."

This was a dark and mysterious saying, and we may well believe that the eleven did not understand it. And no wonder! In all the agony of the death on the cross, in all the ignominy and humiliation which they saw afar off, or heard of next day, in hanging naked for six hours between two thieves—in all this there was no appearance of glory!—On the contrary, it was an event calculated to fill the minds of the Apostles with shame, disappointment, and dismay. And yet our Lord's saying was true.

The crucifixion brought glory to the FATHER. It glorified His wisdom, faithfulness, holiness, and love. It showed Him wise, in providing a plan whereby He could be just, and yet the Justifier of the ungodly. It showed Him faithful, in keeping His promise, that the seed of the woman should bruise the serpent's head. It showed Him holy, in requiring His law's demands to be satisfied by our great Substitute. It showed Him loving, in providing such a Mediator, such a Redeemer, and such a Friend for sinful man as His coeternal Son.

The crucifixion brought glory to the SON. It glorified His compassion, His patience, and His power. It showed Him most compassionate, in dying for us, suffering in our stead, allowing Himself to be counted sin and a curse for us, and buying our redemption with the price of His own blood. It showed Him most patient, in not dying the common death of most men, but in willingly submitting to such horrors and unknown agonies as no mind can conceive, when with a word he could have summoned His Father's angels, and been set free. It showed Him most powerful, in bearing the weight of all a world's transgressions, and vanquishing Satan and despoiling him of his prey.

Forever let us cling to these thoughts about the crucifixion. Let us remember that painting and sculpture can never tell a tenth part of what took place on the cross. Crucifixes and pictures at best can only show us a human being agonizing in a painful death. But of the length and breadth and depth and height of the work transacted on the cross—of God's law honored, man's sins borne, sin punished in a Substitute, free salvation bought for man—of all this they can tell nothing. Yet all this lies hid under the crucifixion. No wonder Paul cries, "God forbid that I should glory, save in the cross of our Lord Jesus Christ." (Gal. 6:14.)

These verses show us, secondly, what great importance our Lord Jesus attaches to the grace of brotherly love. Almost as soon as the false Apostle had left the faithful eleven, comes the injunction, "Love one another." Immediately after the sad announcement that He would leave them soon, the commandment is given, "Love one another." It is called a "new" commandment, not because it had never been given before, but because it was to be more honored, to occupy a higher position, to be backed by a higher example than it ever had been before. Above all, it was to be the test of Christianity before the world. "By this shall all men know that you are my disciples, if you have love one to another."

Let us take heed that this well-known Christian grace is not merely a notion in our heads, but a practice in our lives. Of all the commands of our Master there is none which is so much talked about and so little obeyed as this. Yet, if we mean anything when we profess to have charity and love toward all men, it ought to be seen in our tempers and our words, our bearing and our doing, our behavior at home and abroad, our conduct in every relation of life. Specially it ought to show itself forth in all our dealing with other Christians. We should regard them as brethren and sisters, and delight to do anything to promote their happiness. We should abhor the idea of envy, malice, and jealousy towards a member of Christ, and regard it as a downright sin. This is what our Lord meant when He told us to love one another.

Christ's cause in the earth would prosper far more than it does if this simple law was more honored. There is nothing that the world understands and values more than true charity. The very men who cannot comprehend doctrine, and know nothing of theology, can appreciate charity. It arrests their attention, and makes them think. For the world's sake, if for no other cause, let us follow after charity more and more.

These verses show us, lastly, how much self-ignorance there may be in the heart of a true believer. We see Simon Peter declaring that he was ready to lay down his life for his Master. We see his Master telling him that in that very night he would "deny Him three times." And we all know how the matter ended. The Master was right, and Peter was wrong.

Let it be a settled principle in our religion, that there is an amount of weakness in all our hearts, of which we have no adequate conception, and that we never know how far we might fall if we were tempted. We fancy sometimes, like Peter, that there are some things we could not possibly do. We look pitifully upon others who fall, and please ourselves in the thought that at any rate we would not have done so. We know nothing at all. The seeds of every sin are latent in our hearts, even when renewed, and they only need occasion, or carelessness and the withdrawal of God's grace for a season, to put forth an abundant crop. Like Peter, we may think we can do wonders for Christ, and like Peter, we may learn by bitter experience that we have no power and might at all.

The servant of Christ will do wisely to remember these things. "Let him that thinks he stands, take heed lest he fall." (1 Cor. 10:12.) A humble sense of our own innate weakness, a constant dependence on the Strong for strength, a daily prayer to be held up, because we cannot hold up ourselves—these are the true secrets of safety. The great Apostle of the Gentiles said, "When I am weak, then I am strong." (2 Cor. 12:10.)

Chapter 14

14:1-3

Jesus' Parting Words to His Disciples

"*Do not let your hearts be distressed. You believe in God; believe also in me. There are many dwelling places in my Father's house. Otherwise, I would have told you. I am going away to make ready a place for you. And if I go and make ready a place for you, I will come again and take you to be with me, so that where I am you may be too.*

The three verses we have now read are rich in precious truth. For eighteen centuries they have been peculiarly dear to Christ's believing servants in every part of the world. Many are the sick rooms which they have lightened! Many are the dying hearts which they have cheered! Let us see what they contain.

We have, first, in this passage a precious remedy against an old disease. That disease is trouble of heart. That remedy is faith.

Heart-trouble is the commonest thing in the world. No rank, or class, or condition is exempt from it. No bars, or bolts, or locks can keep it out. Partly from inward causes and partly from outward causes—partly from the body and partly from the mind—partly from what we love and partly from what we fear, the journey of life is full of trouble. Even the best of Christians have many bitter cups to drink between grace and glory. Even the holiest saints find the world a valley of tears.

Faith in the Lord Jesus is the only sure medicine for troubled hearts. To believe more thoroughly, trust more entirely, rest more unreservedly, lay hold more firmly, lean back more completely—this is the prescription which our Master urges on the attention of all His disciples. No doubt the members of that little band which sat round the table at the last supper, had believed already. They had proved the reality of their faith by giving up everything for Christ's sake. Yet what does their Lord say to them here? Once more He presses on them the old lesson, the lesson with which they first began-"Believe! Believe more! Believe on Me!" (Isaiah. 26:3.)

Never let us forget that there are degrees in faith, and that there is a wide difference between weak and strong believers. The weakest faith is enough to give a man a saving interest in Christ, and ought not to be despised, but it will not give a man such inward comfort as a strong faith. Vagueness and dimness of perception are the defect of weak believers. They do not see clearly what they believe and why they believe. In such cases more faith is the one thing needed. Like Peter on the water, they need to look more steadily at Jesus, and less at the waves and wind. Is it not written, "You will keep him in perfect peace whose mind is stayed on You"? (Isaiah. 26:3.)

We have, secondly, in this passage a very comfortable account of heaven, or the future abode of saints. It is but little that we understand about heaven while we are here in the body, and that little is generally taught us in the Bible by negatives much more than positives. But here, at any rate, there are some plain things.

Heaven is "a Father's house,"—the house of that God of whom Jesus says, "I go to my Father, and your Father." It is, in a word, HOME—the home of Christ and Christians. This is a sweet and touching expression. Home, as we all know, is the place where we are generally loved for our own sakes, and not for our gifts or possessions; the place where we are loved to the end, never forgotten, and always welcome. This is one idea of heaven. Believers are in a strange land, and at school, in this life. In the life to come they will be at home.

Heaven is a place of "MANSIONS"—of lasting, permanent, and eternal dwellings. Here in the body we are in temporary lodgings, tents, and tabernacles, and must submit to many changes. In heaven we shall be settled at last, and go out no more. "Here we have no continuing city." (Heb. 13:14.) Our house not made with hands shall never be taken down.

Heaven is a place of "MANY mansions." There will be room for all believers and room for all sorts, for little saints as well as great ones, for the weakest believer as well as for the strongest. The feeblest child of God need not fear there will be no place for him. None will be shut out but impenitent sinners and obstinate unbelievers.

Heaven is a place where CHRIST HIMSELF SHALL BE PRESENT. He will not be content to dwell without His people—"Where I am, there you shall be also." We need not think that we shall be alone and neglected. Our Savior-our elder Brother—our Redeemer, who loved us and gave Himself for us, shall be in the midst of us forever. What we shall see, and whom we shall see in heaven, we cannot fully conceive yet, while we are in the body. But one thing is certain—we shall see Christ.

Let these things sink down into our minds. To the worldly and careless they may seem nothing at all. To all who feel in themselves the working of the Spirit of God they are full of unspeakable comfort. If we hope to be in heaven it is pleasant to know what heaven is like.

We have, lastly, in this passage a solid ground for expecting good things to come. The evil heart of unbelief within us is apt to rob us of our comfort about heaven. "We wish we could think it was all true." "We fear we shall never be admitted into heaven." Let us hear what Jesus says to encourage us.

One cheering word is this—"I go to PREPARE a place for you." Heaven is a prepared place for a prepared people—a place which we shall find Christ Himself has made ready for true Christians. He has prepared it by procuring a right for every sinner who believes to enter in. None can stop us, and say we have no business there. He has prepared it by going before us as our Head and Representative, and taking possession of it for all the members of His mystical body. As our Forerunner He has marched in, leading captivity captive, and has planted His banner in the land of glory. He has prepared it by carrying our names with Him as our High Priest into the holy of holies, and making angels ready to receive us. Those who enter heaven will find they are neither unknown nor unexpected.

Another cheering word is this—"I will come again and receive you unto myself." Christ will not wait for believers to come up to Him, but will come down to them, to raise them from their graves and escort them to their heavenly home. As Joseph came to meet Jacob, so will Jesus come to call His people together and guide them to their inheritance. The second advent ought never to be forgotten. Great is the blessedness of looking back to Christ coming the first time to suffer for us, but no less great is the comfort of looking forward to Christ coming the second time, to raise and reward His saints.

Let us leave the whole passage with solemnized feelings and serious self-examination. How much they miss who live in a dying world and yet know nothing of God as their Father and Christ as their Savior! How much they possess who live the life of faith in the Son of God, and believe in Jesus! With all their weaknesses and crosses they have that which the world can neither give nor take away. They have a true Friend while they live, and a true home when they die.

14:4-11

"And you know the way where I am going." Thomas said, "Lord, we don't know where you are going. How can we know the way?" Jesus replied, "I am the way, and the truth, and the life. No one comes to the Father except through me. If you have known me, you will know my Father too. And from now on you do know him and have seen him."

Philip said, "Lord, show us the Father, and we will be content." Jesus replied, "Have I been with you for so long, and you have not known me, Philip? The person who has seen me has seen the Father! How can you say, 'Show us the Father'? Do you not believe that I am in the Father, and the Father is in me? The words that I say to you, I do not speak on my own initiative, but the Father residing in me performs his miraculous deeds. Believe me that I am in the Father, and the Father is in me, but if you do not believe me, believe because of the miraculous deeds themselves.

We should mark in these verses how much better Jesus speaks of believers than they speak of themselves. He says to His disciples, "You know where I go, and you know the way." And yet Thomas at once breaks in with the remark, "We know neither the where nor the way." The apparent contradiction demands explanation. It is more seeming than real.

Certainly, in one point of view, the knowledge of the disciples was very small. They knew little before the crucifixion and resurrection compared to what they might have known, and little compared to what they afterwards knew after the day of Pentecost. About our Lord's purpose in coming into the world, about His sacrificial death and substitution for us on the cross, their ignorance was glaring and great. It might well be said, that they "knew in part" only, and were children in understanding.

And yet, in another point of view, the knowledge of the disciples was very great. They knew far more than the great majority of the Jewish nation, and received truths which the Scribes and Pharisees entirely rejected. Compared to the world around them, they were in the highest sense enlightened. They knew and believed that their Master was the promised Messiah, the Son of the living God; and to know Him was the first step towards heaven. All things go by comparison. Before we lightly esteem the disciples because of their ignorance, let us take care that we do not underrate their knowledge. They knew more precious truth than they were aware of themselves. Their hearts were better than their heads.

The plain truth is, that all believers are apt to undervalue the work of the Spirit in their own souls, and to fancy they know nothing because they do not know everything. Many true Christians are thought more of in heaven while they live, than they think of themselves, and will find it out to their surprise at the last day. There is One above who takes far more account of heart knowledge than head-knowledge. Many go mourning all the way to heaven because they know so little, and fancy they will miss the way altogether, and yet have hearts with which God is well pleased.

We should mark, secondly, in these verses, what glorious names the Lord Jesus gives Himself. He says, "I am the way, the truth, and the life." The fullness of these precious words can probably never be taken in by man. He that attempts to unfold them does little more than scratch the surface of a rich soil.

Christ is "the WAY,"—the way to heaven and peace with God. He is not only the guide, and teacher, and lawgiver, like Moses; He is Himself the door, the ladder, and the road, through whom we must draw near to God. He has opened the way to the tree of life, which was closed when Adam and Eve fell, by the satisfaction He made for us on the cross. Through His blood we may draw near with boldness, and have access with confidence into God's presence.

Christ is "the TRUTH,"—the whole substance of true religion which the mind of man requires. Without Him the wisest heathen groped in gross darkness and knew nothing about God. Before He came even the Jews saw "through a glass darkly," and discerned nothing distinctly under the types, figures, and ceremonies of the Mosaic law. Christ is the whole truth, and meets and satisfies every desire of the human mind.

Christ is "the LIFE,"—the sinner's title to eternal life and pardon, the believer's root of spiritual life and holiness, the surety of the Christian's resurrection life. He that believes on Christ has everlasting life. He that abides in Him, as the branch abides in the vine, shall bring forth much fruit. He that believes on Him, though he were dead, yet shall he live. The root of all life, for soul and for body, is Christ.

Forever let us grasp and hold fast these truths. To use Christ daily as the way, to believe Christ daily as the truth—to live on Christ daily as the life, this is to be a well-informed, a thoroughly furnished and an established Christian.

We should mark, thirdly, in these verses, how expressly the Lord Jesus shuts out all ways of salvation but Himself. "No man," He declares, "No man comes unto the Father but by Me."

It avails nothing that a man is clever, learned, highly gifted, amiable, charitable, kind-hearted, and zealous about some sort of religion. All this will not save his soul if he does not draw near to God by Christ's atonement, and make use of God's own Son as his Mediator and Savior. God is so holy that all men are guilty and debtors in His sight. Sin is so sinful that no mortal man can make satisfaction for it. There must be a mediator, a ransom-payer, a redeemer, between ourselves and God, or else we can never be saved. There is only one door, one bridge, one ladder, between earth and heaven—the crucified Son of God. Whoever will enter in by that door may be saved; but to him who refuses to use that door the Bible holds out, no hope at all. Without shedding of blood there is no remission.

Let us beware, if we love life, of supposing that mere earnestness will take a man to heaven, though he knows nothing of Christ. The idea is a deadly and ruinous error. Sincerity will never wipe away our sins. It is not true that every man will be saved by his own religion, no matter what he believes, so long as he is diligent and sincere. We must not pretend to be wiser than God. Christ has said, and Christ will stand to it, "No man comes unto the Father but by Me."

We should mark, lastly, in these verses, how close and mysterious is the union of God the Father and God the Son. Four times over this mighty truth is put before us in words that cannot be mistaken. "If you had known Me, you would have known my Father." "He that has seen Me has seen the Father." "I am in the Father, and the Father in Me." "The Father that dwells in Me, He does the works."

Sayings like these are full of deep mystery. We have no eyes to see their meaning fully—no line to fathom it—no language to express it—no mind to take it in. We must be content to believe when we cannot explain, and to admire and revere when we cannot interpret. Let it suffice us to know and hold that the Father is God and the Son is God, and yet that they are one in essence though two distinct Persons—ineffably one, and yet ineffably distinct. These are high things, and we cannot attain to a full comprehension of them.

Let us however take comfort in the simple truth, that Christ is very God of very God; equal with the Father in all things, and One with Him. He who loved us, and shed His blood for us on the cross, and bids us trust Him for pardon, is no mere man like ourselves. He is "God over all, blessed forever," and able to save to the uttermost the chief of sinners. Though our sins be as scarlet, He can make them white as snow. He that casts his soul on Christ has an Almighty Friend—a Friend who is One with the Father, and very God.

14:12-17

I tell you the solemn truth, the person who believes in me will perform the miraculous deeds that I am doing, and will perform greater deeds than these, because I am going to the Father. And I will do whatever you ask in my name, so that the Father may be glorified in the Son. If you ask me anything in my name, I will do it.

"If you love me, you will obey my commandments. Then I will ask the Father, and he will give you another Advocate to be with you forever—the Spirit of truth, whom the world cannot accept, because it does not see him or know him. But you know him, because he resides with you and will be in you.

These verses are an example of our Lord's tender consideration for the weakness of His disciples. He saw them troubled and faint-hearted at the prospect of being left alone in the world. He cheers them by THREE PROMISES, peculiarly suited to their circumstances. "A word spoken in season, how good is it!"

We have first in this passage, a striking promise about the works that Christians may do. Our Lord says, "He that believes on Me, the works that I do shall he do also; and greater works than these shall he do; because I go unto my Father."

The full meaning of this promise is not to be sought in the miracles which the Apostles wrought after Christ left the world. Such a notion seems hardly borne out by facts. We read of no Apostle walking on the water, or raising a person four days dead, like Lazarus. What our Lord has in view seems to be the far greater number of conversions, the far wider spread of the Gospel, which would take place under the ministry of the Apostles, than under his own teaching. This was the case, we know from the Acts of the Apostles. We read of no sermon preached by Christ, under which three thousand were converted in one day, as they were on the day of Pentecost. In short, "greater works" mean more conversions. There is no greater work possible than the conversion of a soul.

Let us admire the condescension of our Master in allowing to the ministry of His weak servants more success than to His own. Let us learn that His visible presence is not absolutely necessary to the progress of His kingdom.

He can help forward His cause on earth quite as much by sitting at the right hand of the Father, and sending forth the Holy Spirit, as by walking to and fro in the world. Let us believe that there is nothing too hard or too great for believers to do, so long as their Lord intercedes for them in heaven. Let us work on in faith, and expect great things, though we feel weak and lonely, like the disciples. Our Lord is working with us and for us, though we cannot see Him. It was not so much the sword of Joshua that defeated Amalek, as the intercession of Moses on the hill. (Ex. 17:11.)

We have, secondly, in this passage, a striking promise about things that Christians may get by prayer. Our Lord says, "Whatever you shall ask in my name, that will I do . . . If you shall ask anything in my name, I will do it."

These words are a direct encouragement to the simple, yet great duty of praying. Everyone who kneels daily before God, and from his heart "says his prayers," has a right to take comfort in these words. Weak and imperfect as his supplications may be, so long as they are put in Christ's hands, and offered in Christ's name, they shall not be in vain. We have a Friend at Court, an Advocate with the Father; and if we honor Him by sending all our petitions through Him, He pledges His word that they shall succeed. Of course it is taken for granted that the things we ask are for our souls' good, and not mere temporal benefits. "Anything" and "whatever" do not include wealth, and money, and worldly prosperity. These things are not always good for us, and our Lord loves us too well to let us have them. But whatever is really good for our souls, we need not doubt we shall have, if we ask in Christ's name.

How is it that many true Christians have so little? How is it that they go halting and mourning on the way to heaven, and enjoy so little peace, and show so little strength in Christ's service? The answer is simple and plain. "They have not, because they ask not." They have little because they ask little. They are no better than they are, because they do not ask their Lord to make them better. Our languid desires are the reason of our languid performances. We are not straitened in our Lord, but in ourselves. Happy are they who never forget the words, "Open your mouth wide, and I will fill it." (Ps. 81:10.) He that does much for Christ, and leaves his mark in the world, will always prove to be one who prays much.

We have, lastly, in this passage, a striking promise about the Holy Spirit. Our Lord says, "I will ask the Father, and He shall give you another Comforter, even the Spirit of truth."

This is the first time that the Holy Spirit is mentioned as Christ's special gift to His people. Of course we are not to suppose that He did not dwell in the hearts of all the Old Testament saints. But He was given with peculiar influence and power to believers when the New Testament dispensation came in, and this is the special promise of the passage before us. We shall find it useful, therefore, to observe closely the things that are here said about Him.

The Holy Spirit is spoken of as "a Person." To apply the language before us to a mere influence or inward feeling, is an unreasonable strain of words.

The Holy Spirit is called "the Spirit of truth." It is His special office to apply truth to the hearts of Christians, to guide them into all truth, and to sanctify them by the truth.

The Holy Spirit is said to be one whom "the world cannot receive and does not know." His operations are in the strongest sense foolishness to the natural man. The inward feelings of conviction, repentance, faith, hope, fear, and love, which He always produces, are precisely that part of religion which the world cannot understand.

The Holy Spirit is said to "dwell in" believers, and to be known by them. They know the feelings that He creates, and the fruits that He produces, though they may not be able to explain them, or see at first whence they come. But they all are what they are—new men, new creatures, light and salt in the earth, compared to the worldly, by the indwelling of the Holy Spirit.

The Holy Spirit is given to the Church of the elect, "to abide with them" until Christ comes the second time. He is meant to supply all the needs of believers, and to fill up all that is lacking while Christ's visible presence is removed. He is sent to abide with and help them until Christ returns.

These are truths of vast importance. Let us take care that we grasp them firmly, and never let them go. Next to the whole truth about Christ, it concerns our safety and peace to see the whole truth about the Holy Spirit. Any doctrine about the Church, the ministry, or the Sacraments, which obscures the Spirit's inward work, or turns it into mere form, is to be avoided as deadly error. Let us never rest until we feel and know that He dwells in us. "If any man has not the Spirit of Christ, he is none of His." (Rom. 8:9.)

14:18-20

"I will not abandon you as orphans, I will come to you. In a little while the world will not see me any longer, but you will see me; because I live, you will live too. You will know at that time that I am in my Father and you are in me and I am in you.

The short passage before us is singularly rich in "precious promises." Twice our Lord Jesus Christ says, "I will." Twice He says to believers, "You shall."

We learn from this passage, that Christ's second coming is meant to be the special comfort of believers. He says to His disciples, "I will not leave you comfortless—I will come to you."

Now what is the "coming" here spoken of? It is only fair to say that this is a disputed point among Christians. Many refer it to our Lord's coming to His disciples after His resurrection. Many refer it to His invisible coming into the hearts of His people by the grace of the Holy Spirit. Many refer it to His coming by the outpouring of the Holy Spirit on the day of Pentecost. It may well be doubted, however, whether any one of these three views conveys the full meaning of our Lord's words, "I will come."

The true sense of the expression appears to be the second personal coming of Christ at the end of the world. It is a wide, broad, sweeping promise, intended for all believers, in every age, and not for the Apostles alone—"I will not stay always in heaven—I will one day come back to you." It is like the message which the angels brought to the disciples after the ascension—"This same Jesus shall come in like manner as you have seen Him go." (Acts. 1:11.) It is like the last promise which winds up the Book of Revelation-"Surely I come quickly." (Rev. 22:20.) Just in the same way the parting consolation held out to believers, the night before the crucifixion, is a personal return—"I will come."

Let us settle it in our minds that all believers are comparatively "orphans," and children in their minority, until the second advent. Our best things are yet to come. Faith has yet to be exchanged for sight, and hope for certainty. Our peace and joy are at present very imperfect. They are as nothing to what we shall have when Christ returns. For the return let us look and long and pray. Let us place it in the forefront of all our doctrinal system, next to the atoning death and the interceding life of our Lord. The highest style of Christians are the men who look for and love the Lord's appearing. (2 Tim. 4:8.)

We learn for another thing, that Christ's life secures the life of His believing people. He says, "Because I live you shall live also."

There is a mysterious and indissoluble union between Christ and every true Christian. The man that is once joined to Him by faith, is as closely united as a member of the body is united to the head. So long as Christ, his Head, lives, so long he will live. He cannot die unless Christ can be plucked from heaven, and Christ's life destroyed. But this, since Christ is very God, is totally impossible! "Christ being raised from the dead, dies no more—death has no more dominion over Him." (Rom. 6:9.) That which is divine, in the very nature of things, cannot die.

Christ's life secures the continuance of spiritual life to His people. They shall not fall away. They shall persevere unto the end. The divine nature of which they are partakers, shall not perish. The incorruptible seed within them shall not be destroyed by the devil and the world. Weak as they are in themselves, they are closely knit to an immortal Head, and not one member of His mystical body shall ever perish.

Christ's life secures the resurrection life of His people. Just as He rose again from the grave, because death could not hold Him one moment beyond the appointed time, so shall all His believing members rise again in the day when He calls them from the tomb. The victory that Jesus won when He rolled the stone away, and came forth from the tomb, was a victory not only for Himself, but for His people. If the Head rose, much more shall the members.

Truths like these ought to be often pondered by true Christians. The careless world knows little of a believer's privileges. It sees little but the outside of him. It does not understand the secret of his present strength, and of his strong hope of good things to come. And what is that secret? Invisible union with an invisible Savior in heaven! Each child of God is invisibly linked to the throne of the Rock of Ages. When that throne can be shaken, and not until then, we may despair. But Christ lives, and we shall live also.

We learn, finally, from this passage, that full and perfect knowledge of divine things will never be attained by believers until the second advent. Our Lord says, "At that day," the day of my coming, "you shall know that I am in my Father, and you in Me, and I in you."

The best of saints knows but little so long as he is in the body. The fall of our father Adam has corrupted our understandings, as well as our consciences, hearts, and wills. Even after conversion we see through a glass darkly, and on no point do we see so dimly as on the nature of our own union with Christ, and of the union of Christ and the Father. These are matters in which we must be content to believe humbly, and, like little children, to receive on trust the things which we cannot explain.

But it is a blessed and cheering thought that when Christ comes again, the remains of ignorance shall be rolled away. Raised from the dead, freed from the darkness of this world, no longer tempted by the devil and tried by the flesh, believers shall see as they have been seen, and know as they have been known. We shall have light enough one day. What we know not now, we shall know hereafter.

Let us rest our souls on this comfortable thought, when we see the mournful divisions which rend the Church of Christ. Let us remember that a large portion of them arise from ignorance. We know in part, and therefore misunderstand one another. A day comes when Lutherans shall no longer wrangle with Zwinglians, nor Calvinist with Arminian, nor Churchman with Dissenter. That day is the day of Christ's second coming. Then and then only will the promise receive its complete fulfillment—"At that day you shall know."

14:21-26

The person who has my commandments and obeys them is the one who loves me. The one who loves me will be loved by my Father, and I will love him and will reveal myself to him."

"Lord," Judas (not Judas Iscariot) said, "what has happened that you are going to reveal yourself to us and not to the world?" Jesus replied, "If anyone loves me, he will obey my word, and my Father will love him, and we will come to him and take up residence with him. The person who does not love me does not obey my words. And the word you hear is not mine, but the Father's who sent me.

"I have spoken these things while staying with you. But the Advocate, the Holy Spirit, whom the Father will send in my name, will teach you everything, and will cause you to remember everything I said to you.

We learn from these verses that keeping Christ's commandments is the best test of love to Christ. This is a lesson of vast importance and one that needs continually pressing on the attention of Christians. It is not talking about religion, and talking fluently and well too, but steadily doing Christ's will and walking in Christ's ways, that is the proof of our being true believers. Good feelings and desires are useless if they are not accompanied by action. They may even become mischievous to the soul, induce hardness of conscience, and do certain harm. Passive impressions which do not lead to action, gradually deaden and paralyze the heart. Living and doing are the only real evidence of grace. Where the Holy Spirit is, there will always be a holy life. A jealous watchfulness over tempers, words, and deeds, a constant endeavor to live by the rule of the Sermon on the Mount, this is the best proof that we love Christ.

Of course such maxims as these must not be wrested and misunderstood. We are not to suppose for a moment that "keeping Christ's commandments" can save us. Our best works are full of imperfection. When we have done all we can, we are feeble and unprofitable servants. "By grace are you saved through faith—not of works." (Ep. 2:8.) But while we hold one class of truths, we must not forget another. Faith in the blood of Christ must always be attended by loving obedience to the will of Christ. What the Master has joined together, the disciple must not put asunder. Do we profess to love Christ? Then let us show it by our lives. The Apostle who said, "You know that I love You!" received the charge, "Feed my lambs." That meant, "Do something. Be useful—follow my example." (John 21:17.)

We learn, secondly, from these verses, that there are special comforts laid up for those who love Christ, and prove it by keeping His words. This, at any rate, seems the general sense of our Lord's language—"My Father will love him, and we will come unto him, and make our abode with him."

The full meaning of this promise, no doubt, is a deep thing. We have no line to fathom it. It is a thing which no man can understand except he that receives and experiences it. But we need not shrink from believing that eminent holiness brings eminent comfort with it, and that no man has such sensible enjoyment of his religion as the man who, like Enoch and Abraham, walks closely with God. There is more of heaven on earth to be obtained than most Christians are aware of. "The secret of the Lord is with those who fear Him, and He will show them His covenant." "If any man hear my voice and open the door, I will come in to him, and dine with him, and he with Me." (Ps. 25:14; Rev. 3:20.) Promises like these, we may be sure, mean something, and were not written in vain.

How is it, people often ask, that so many professing believers have so little happiness in their religion? How is it that so many know little of "joy and peace in believing," and go mourning and heavy-hearted towards heaven? The answer to these questions is a sorrowful one, but it must be given. Few believers attend as strictly as they should to Christ's practical sayings and words. There is far too much loose and careless obedience to Christ's commandments. There is far too much forgetfulness, that while good works cannot justify us they are not to be despised. Let these things sink down into our hearts. If we want to be eminently happy, we must strive to be eminently holy.

We learn, lastly, from these verses, that one part of the Holy Spirit's work is to teach, and to bring things to remembrance. It is written, "The Comforter shall teach you all things, and bring all things to your remembrance."

To confine this promise to the eleven Apostles, as some do, seems a narrow and unsatisfactory mode of interpreting Scripture. It appears to reach far beyond the day of Pentecost, and the gift of writing inspired books of God's Holy Word. It is safer, wiser, and more consistent with the whole tone of our Lord's last discourse, to regard the promise as the common property of all believers, in every age of the world. Our Lord knows the ignorance and forgetfulness of our nature in spiritual things. He graciously declares that when He leaves the world, His people shall have a teacher and remembrancer.

Are we sensible of spiritual ignorance? Do we feel that at best we know in part and see in part? Do we desire to understand more clearly the doctrines of the Gospel? Let us pray daily for the help of the "teaching" Spirit. It is His office to illuminate the soul, to open the eyes of the understanding, and to guide us into all truth. He can make dark places light, and rough places smooth.

Do we find our memory of spiritual things defective? Do we complain that though we read and hear, we seem to lose as fast as we gain? Let us pray daily for the help of the Holy Spirit. He can bring things to our remembrance. He can make us remember "old things and new." He can keep in our minds the whole system of truth and duty, and make us ready for every good word and work.

14:27-31

"Peace I leave with you; my peace I give to you; I do not give it to you as the world does. Do not let your hearts be distressed or lacking in courage. You heard me say to you, 'I am going away and I am coming back to you.' If you loved me, you would be glad that I am going to the Father, because the Father is greater than I am. I have told you now before it happens, so that when it happens you may believe. I will not speak with you much longer, for the ruler of this world is coming. He has no power over me, but I am doing just what the Father commanded me, so that the world may know that I love the Father. Get up, let us go from here."

We ought not to leave the closing portion of this wonderful chapter without noticing one striking feature in it. That feature is the singular frequency with which our Lord uses the expression, "My Father," and "the Father." In the last five verses we find it four times. In the whole chapter it occurs no less than twenty-two times. In this respect the chapter stands alone in the Bible.

The reason of this frequent use of the expression, is a deep subject. Perhaps the less we speculate and dogmatize about it the better. Our Lord was one who never spoke a word without a meaning, and we need not doubt there was a meaning here. Yet may we not reverently suppose that He desired to leave on the minds of His disciples a strong impression of his entire unity with the Father? Seldom does our Lord lay claim to such high dignity, and such power of giving and supplying comfort to His Church, as in this discourse. Was there not, then, a fitness in His continually reminding His disciples that in all His giving He was one with the Father, and did nothing without the Father? This, at any rate, seems a fair conjecture. Let it be taken for what it is worth.

We should observe, for one thing, in this passage, Christ's last legacy to His people. We find Him saying, "Peace I leave with you, my peace I give unto you; not as the world gives, give I unto you."

Peace is Christ's distinctive gift—not money, not worldly ease, not temporal prosperity. These are at best very questionable possessions. They often do more harm than good to the soul. They act as clogs and weights to our spiritual life. Inward peace of conscience, arising from a sense of pardoned sin and reconciliation with God, is a far greater blessing. This peace is the property of all believers, whether high or low, rich or poor.

The peace which Christ gives He calls "my peace." It is specially His own to give, because He bought it by His own blood, purchased it by His own substitution, and is appointed by the Father to dispense it to a perishing world. Just as Joseph was sealed and commissioned to give grain to the starving Egyptians, so is Christ specially commissioned, in the counsels of the Eternal Trinity, to give peace to mankind.

The peace that Christ gives is not given as the world gives. What He gives the world cannot give at all, and what He gives is given neither unwillingly, nor sparingly, nor for a little time. Christ is far more willing to give than the world is to receive. What He gives He gives to all eternity, and never takes away. He is ready to give abundantly above all that we can ask or think. "Open your mouth wide," He says, "and I will fill it." (Psalm 81:10.)

Who can wonder that a legacy like this should be backed by the renewed emphatic charge, "Let not your heart be troubled, neither let it be afraid?" There is nothing lacking on Christ's part for our comfort, if we will only come to Him, believe, and receive. The chief of sinners has no cause to be afraid. If we will only look to the one true Savior, there is medicine for every trouble of heart. Half our doubts and fears arise from dim perceptions of the real nature of Christ's Gospel.

We should observe, for another thing, in this passage, Christ's perfect holiness. We find Him saying, "The prince of this world comes, and has no power over Me."

The meaning of these remarkable words admits of only one interpretation. Our Lord would have his disciples know that Satan, "the prince of this world," was about to make his last and most violent attack on Him. He was mustering all his strength for one more tremendous onset. He was coming up with his utmost malice to try the second Adam in the garden of Gethsemane, and on the cross of Calvary. But our blessed Master declares, "He has no power over Me." "There is nothing he can lay hold on. There is no weak and defective point in Me. I have kept my Father's commandment, and finished the work He gave me to do. Satan, therefore, cannot overthrow Me. He can lay nothing to my charge. He cannot condemn Me. I shall come forth from the trial more than conqueror."

Let us mark the difference between Christ and all others who have been born of woman. He is the only one in whom Satan has no power over. He came to Adam and Eve, and found weakness. He came to Noah, Abraham, Moses, David, and all the saints, and found imperfection. He came to Christ, and found "nothing" at all. He was a Lamb "without blemish and without spot," a suitable Sacrifice for a world of sinners, a suitable Head for a redeemed race.

Let us thank God that we have such a perfect, sinless Savior; that His righteousness is a perfect righteousness, and His life a blameless life. In ourselves and our doings we shall find everything imperfect; and if we had no other hope than our own goodness, we might well despair. But in Christ we have a perfect, sinless, Representative and Substitute. Well may we say, with the triumphant Apostle, "Who shall lay anything to our charge?" (Rom. 8:33.) Christ has died for us, and suffered in our stead. In Him Satan can find nothing. We are hidden in Him. The Father sees us in Him, unworthy as we are, and for His sake is well pleased.

Chapter 15

15:1-6

The Vine and the Branches

"*I am the true vine and my Father is the gardener. He takes away every branch that does not bear fruit in me. He prunes every branch that bears fruit so that it will bear more fruit. You are clean already because of the word that I have spoken to you. Remain in me, and I will remain in you. Just as the branch cannot bear fruit by itself, unless it remains in the vine, so neither can you unless you remain in me.*

"*I am the vine; you are the branches. The one who remains in me—and I in him—bears much fruit, because apart from me you can accomplish nothing. If anyone does not remain in me, he is thrown out like a branch, and dries up; and such branches are gathered up and thrown into the fire, and are burned up.*

These verses, we must carefully remember, contain a parable. In interpreting it we must not forget the great rule which applies to all Christ's parables. The general lesson of each parable is the main thing to be noticed. The minor details must not be tortured and pressed to an excess, in order to extract a meaning from them. The mistakes into which Christians have fallen by neglecting this rule, are neither few nor small.

We are meant to learn first, from these verses, that the union between Christ and believers is very close. He is "the Vine," and they are "the branches."

The union between the branch of a vine and the main stem, is the closest that can be conceived. It is the whole secret of the branch's life, strength, vigor, beauty, and fertility. Separate from the parent stem, it has no life of its own. The sap and juice that flow from the stem are the origin and maintaining power of all its leaves, buds, blossoms, and fruit. Cut off from the stem, it must soon wither and die.

The union between Christ and believers is just as close, and just as real. In themselves believers have no life, or strength, or spiritual power. All that they have of vital religion comes from Christ. They are what they are, and feel what they feel, and do what they do, because they draw out of Jesus a continual supply of grace, help, and ability. Joined to the Lord by faith, and united in mysterious union with Him by the Spirit, they stand, and walk, and continue, and run the Christian race. But every jot of good about them is drawn from their spiritual Head, Jesus Christ.

The thought before us is both comfortable and instructive. Believers have no cause to despair of their own salvation, and to think they will never reach heaven. Let them consider that they are not left to themselves and their own strength. Their root is Christ, and all that there is in the root is for the benefit of the branches. Because He lives, they shall live also. Worldly people have no cause to wonder at the continuance and perseverance of believers. Weak as they are in themselves, their Root is in heaven, and never dies. "When I am weak," said Paul, "then am I strong." (2 Cor. 12:10.)

We are meant to learn, secondly, from these verses, that there are false Christians as well as true ones. There are "branches in the vine" which appear to be joined to the parent stem, and yet bear no fruit. There are men and women who appear to be members of Christ, and yet will prove finally to have had no vital union with Him.

There are myriads of professing Christians in every Church whose union with Christ is only outward and formal. Some of them are joined to Christ by baptism and Church-membership. Some of them go even further than this, and are regular communicants and loud talkers about religion. But they all lack the one thing needful. Notwithstanding services, and sermons, and sacrament, they have no grace in their hearts, no faith, no inward work of the Holy Spirit. They are not one with Christ, and Christ in them. Their union with Him is only nominal, and not real. They have "a name to live," but in the sight of God they are dead.

Christians of this stamp are aptly represented by branches in a vine which bear no fruit. Useless and unsightly, such branches are only fit to be cut off and burned. They draw nothing out of the parent stem, and make no return for the place they occupy. Just so will it be at the last day with false professors and nominal Christians. Their end, except they repent, will be destruction. They will be separated from the company of true believers, and cast out, as withered, useless branches, into everlasting fire. They will find at last, whatever they thought in this world, that there is a worm that never dies, and a fire that is not quenched.

We are meant to learn, thirdly, from these verses, that the fruits of the Spirit are the only satisfactory evidence of a man being a true Christian. The disciple that "abides in Christ," like a branch abiding in the vine, will always bear fruit.

He that would know what the word "fruit" means, need not wait long for an answer. Repentance toward God, faith toward our Lord Jesus Christ, holiness of life and conduct, these are what the New Testament calls "fruit." These are the distinguishing marks of the man who is a living branch of the true Vine. Where these things are lacking, it is vain to talk of possessing dormant grace and spiritual life. Where there is no fruit there is no life. He that lacks these things is "dead while he lives."

True grace, we must not forget, is never idle. It never slumbers and never sleeps. It is a vain notion to suppose that we are living members of Christ, if the example of Christ is the only satisfactory evidence of saving union between Christ and our souls. Where there is no fruit of the Spirit to be seen, there is no vital religion in the heart. The Spirit of Life in Christ Jesus will always make Himself known in the daily conduct of those in whom He dwells. The Master Himself declares, "Every tree is known by his own fruit." (Luke 6:44.)

We are meant, lastly, to learn from these verses, that God will often increase the holiness of true Christians by His providential dealings with them. "Every branch," it is written, "that bears fruit, He prunes, that it may bear more fruit."

The meaning of this language is clear and plain. Just as the gardener prunes and cuts back the branches of a fruitful vine, in order to make them more fruitful, so does God purify and sanctify believers by the circumstances of life in which He places them.

Trial, to speak plainly, is the instrument by which our Father in heaven makes Christians more holy. By trial He calls out their passive graces, and proves whether they can suffer His will as well as do it. By trial He weans them from the world, draws them to Christ, drives them to the Bible and prayer, shows them their own hearts, and makes them humble. This is the process by which He "prunes" them, and makes them more fruitful. The lives of the saints in every age, are the best and truest comment on the text. Never, hardly, do we find an eminent saint, either in the Old Testament or the New, who was not purified by suffering, and, like His Master, a "man of sorrows."

Let us learn to be patient in the days of darkness, if we know anything of vital union with Christ. Let us remember the doctrine of the passage before us, and not murmur and complain because of trials. Our trials are not meant to do us harm, but good. God chastens us "for our profit, that we may be partakers of His holiness." (Heb. 12:10.) Fruit is the thing that our Master desires to see in us, and He will not spare the pruning knife if He sees we need it. In the last day we shall see that all was well done.

15:7-11

"If you remain in me and my words remain in you, ask whatever you want, and it will be done for you. My Father is honored by this, that you bear much fruit and show that you are my disciples.

"Just as the Father has loved me, I have also loved you; remain in my love. If you obey my commandments, you will remain in my love, just as I have obeyed my Father's commandments and remain in his love. I have told you these things so that my joy may be in you, and your joy may be complete."

There is a wide difference between believers and believers. In some things they are all alike. All feel their sins; all trust in Christ; all repent and strive to be holy. All have grace, and faith, and new hearts. But they differ widely in the degree of their attainments. Some are far happier and holier Christians than others, and have far more influence on the world.

Now what are the inducements which the Lord Jesus holds out to His people, to make them aim at eminent holiness? This is a question which ought to be deeply interesting to every pious mind. Who would not like to be a singularly useful and happy servant of Christ? The passage before us throws light on the subject in three ways.

In the first place, our Lord declares, "If you abide in Me, and my words abide in you, you shall ask what you will, and it shall be done unto you." This is a distinct promise of power and success in prayer. And what does it turn upon?

We must "abide in Christ," and Christ's "words must abide in us."

To abide in Christ means to keep up a habit of constant close communion with Him—to be always leaning on Him, resting on Him, pouring out our hearts to Him, and using Him as our Fountain of life and strength, as our chief Companion and best Friend. To have His words abiding in us, is to keep His sayings and precepts continually before our memories and minds, and to make them the guide of our actions and the rule of our daily conduct and behavior.

Christians of this stamp, we are told, shall not pray in vain. Whatever they ask they shall obtain, so long as they ask things according to God's mind. No work shall be found too hard, and no difficulty insurmountable. Asking they shall receive, and seeking they shall find. Such men were Martin Luther, the German Reformer, and our own martyr, Bishop Latimer. Such a man was John Knox, of whom Queen Mary said, that she feared his prayers more than an army of twenty thousand men. It is written in a certain place, "The effectual fervent prayer of a righteous man avails much." (James 5:16.)

Now, why is there so little power of prayer like this in our own time? Simply because there is so little close communion with Christ, and so little strict conformity to His will. Men do not "abide in Christ," and therefore pray in vain. Christ's words do not abide in them, as their standard of practice, and therefore their prayers seem not to be heard. They ask and receive not, because they ask amiss. Let this lesson sink down into our hearts. He that would have answers to his prayers, must carefully remember Christ's directions. We must keep up intimate friendship with the great Advocate in heaven, if our petitions are to prosper.

In the second place, our Lord declares, "Herein is my Father glorified, that you bear much fruit; showing yourselves to be my disciples." The meaning of this promise seems to be, that fruitfulness in Christian practice will not only bring glory to God, but will supply the best evidence to our own hearts that we are real disciples of Christ.

Assurance of our own interest in Christ, and our consequent eternal safety, is one of the highest privileges in religion. To be always doubting and fearing is miserable work. Nothing is worse than suspense in any matter of importance, and above all in the matter of our souls. He that would know one of the best receipts for obtaining assurance, should diligently study Christ's words now before us. Let him strive to bear much fruit in his life, his habits, his temper, his words, and his works. So doing he shall feel the "witness of the Spirit" in his heart, and give abundant proof that he is a living branch of the true Vine. He shall find inward evidence in his own soul that he is a child of God, and shall supply the world with outward evidence that cannot be disputed. He shall leave no room for doubt that he is a disciple.

Would we know why so many professing Christians have little comfort in their religion, and go fearing and doubting along the road to heaven? The question receives a solution in the saying of our Lord we are now considering. Men are content with a little Christianity, and a little fruit of the Spirit, and do not labor to be holy in all of life. They must not wonder if they enjoy little peace, feel little hope, and leave behind them little evidence. The fault lies with themselves. God has linked together holiness and happiness; and what God has joined together we must not think to put asunder.

In the third place, our Lord declares, "If you keep my commandments, you shall abide in my love." The meaning of this promise is near akin to that of the preceding one. The man who makes conscience of diligently observing Christ's precepts, is the man who shall continually enjoy a sense of Christ's love in his soul.

Of course we must not misunderstand our Lord's words when He speaks of "keeping His commandments." There is a sense in which no one can keep them. Our best works are imperfect and defective, and when we have done our best we may well cry, "God be merciful to me a sinner." Yet we must not run into the other extreme, and give way to the lazy idea that we can do nothing at all. By the grace of God we may make Christ's laws our rule of life, and show daily that we desire to please Him. So doing, our gracious Master will give us a constant sense of His favor, and make us feel His face smiling on us, like the sun shining on a fine day. "The secret of the Lord is with those who fear Him, and He will show them His covenant." (Ps. 25:14.)

Lessons like these may be legal to some, and bring down much blame on those who advocate them. Such is the narrow-mindedness of human nature, that few can look on more than one side of truth! Let the servant of Christ call no man his master. Let him hold on his way, and never be ashamed of diligence, fruitfulness, and jealous watchfulness, in his obedience to Christ's commands. These things are perfectly consistent with salvation by grace and justification by faith, whatever any one may say to the contrary.

Let us hear the conclusion of the whole matter. The Christian who is careful over his words and tempers and works, will generally be the most happy Christian. "Joy and peace in believing" will never accompany an inconsistent life. It is not for nothing that our Lord concludes the passage—"These things have I spoken unto you, that your joy might be full."

15:12-16

My commandment is this—to love one another just as I have loved you. No one has greater love than this—that one lays down his life for his friends. You are my friends if you do what I command you. I no longer call you slaves, because the slave does not understand what his master is doing. But I have called you friends, because I have revealed to you everything I heard from my Father. You did not choose me, but I chose you and appointed you to go and bear fruit, fruit that remains, so that whatever you ask the Father in my name he will give you.

Three weighty points demand our attention in this passage. On each of these the language of our Lord Jesus Christ is full of striking instruction.

We should observe first, how our Lord speaks of the grace of brotherly love.

He returns to it a second time, though He has already spoken of it in the former part of His discourse. He would have us know that we can never think too highly of love, attach too much weight to it, labor too much to practice it. Truths which our Master thinks it needful to enforce on us by repetition, must needs be of first-class importance.

He commands us to love one another. "This is my commandment." It is a positive duty laid on our consciences to practice this grace. We have no more right to neglect it than any of the ten precepts given on Mount Sinai.

He supplies the highest standard of love—"Love one another as I have loved you." No lower measure must content us. The weakest, the lowest, the most ignorant, the most defective disciple, is not to be despised. All are to be loved with an active, self-denying, self-sacrificing love. He that cannot do this, or will not try to do it, is disobeying the command of his Master.

A precept like this should stir up in us great searchings of heart. It condemns the selfish, ill-natured, jealous, ill-tempered spirit of many professing Christians, with a sweeping condemnation. Sound views of doctrine, and knowledge of controversy, will avail us nothing at last, if we have known nothing of love. Without charity we may pass muster very well as Churchmen. But without charity we are no better, says Paul, than "sounding brass and tinkling cymbal." (1 Cor. 13:1.) Where there is no Christ-like love, there is no grace, no work of the Spirit, and no reality in our religion. Blessed are those who do not forget Christ's commandment! They are those who shall have right to the tree of life, and enter the celestial city. The unloving professor is unfit for heaven.

We should observe, secondly, how our Lord speaks of the relation between Himself and true believers. He says, "Henceforth I call you not servants . . . but I have called you friends."

This is indeed a glorious privilege. To know Christ, serve Christ, follow Christ, obey Christ, work in Christ's vineyard, fight Christ's battles, all this is no small matter. But for sinful men and women like ourselves to be called "friends of Christ," is something that our weak minds can hardly grasp and take in. The King of kings and Lord of lords not only pities and saves all those who believe in Him, but actually calls them His "friends." We need not wonder, in the face of such language as this, that Paul should say, the "love of Christ passes knowledge." (Ephes. 3:19.)

Let the expression before us encourage Christians to deal familiarly with Christ in prayer. Why should we be afraid to pour out all our hearts, and unbosom all our secrets, in speaking to one who calls us His "friends"? Let it cheer us in all the troubles and sorrows of life, and increase our confidence in our Lord. "He that has friends," says Solomon, "will show himself friendly." (Prov. 18:24.) Certainly our great Master in heaven will never forsake His "friends." Poor and unworthy as we are, He will not cast us off, but will stand by us and keep us to the end. David never forgot Jonathan, and the Son of David will never forget His people. None so rich, so strong, so well off, so thoroughly provided for, as the man of whom Christ says, "This is my friend!"

We should observe, lastly, how our Lord speaks of the doctrine of election. He says, "You have not chosen Me, but I have chosen you, that you should go and bring forth fruit." The choosing here mentioned is evidently twofold. It includes not only the election to the Apostolic office, which was peculiar to the eleven, but the election to eternal life, which is the privilege of all believers. To this last "choosing," as it specially concerns ourselves, we may profitably direct our attention.

Election to eternal life, is a truth of Scripture which we must receive humbly, and believe implicitly. Why the Lord Jesus calls some and does not call others, quickens whom He will, and leaves others alone in their sins, these are deep things which we cannot explain. Let it suffice us to know that it is a fact. God must begin the work of grace in a man's heart, or else a man will never be saved. Christ must first choose us and call us by His Spirit, or else we shall never choose Christ. Beyond doubt, if not saved, we shall have none to blame but ourselves. But if saved, we shall certainly trace up the beginning of our salvation, to the choosing grace of Christ. Our song to all eternity will be that which fell from the lips of Jonah—"Salvation is of the Lord." (Jonah 2:9.)

Election is always to sanctification. Those whom Christ chooses out of mankind, He chooses not only that they may be saved, but that they may bear fruit, and fruit that can be seen. All other election beside this is a mere vain delusion, and a miserable invention of man. It was the faith and hope and love of the Thessalonians, which made Paul say, "I know your election of God." (1 Thess. 1:4.) Where there is no visible fruit of sanctification, we may be sure there is no election.

Armed with such principles as these, we have no cause to be afraid of the doctrine of election. Like any other truth of the Gospel, it is liable to be abused and perverted. But to a pious mind, as the seventeenth Article of the Church of England truly says, it is a doctrine "full of sweet, pleasant, and unspeakable comfort."

15:17-21

"This I command you—to love one another."

"If the world hates you, be aware that it hated me first. If you belonged to the world, the world would love you as its own. However, because you do not belong to the world, but I chose you out of the world, for this reason the world hates you. Remember what I told you, 'A slave is not greater than his master.'

If they persecuted me, they will also persecute you. If they obeyed my word, they will obey yours too. But they will do all these things to you on account of my name, because they do not know the one who sent me.

The passage before us opens with a renewed exhortation to brotherly love. For the third time in this discourse our Lord thinks it needful to press this precious grace on the attention of His disciples. Rare, indeed, must genuine charity be, when such repeated mention of it is made! In the present instance the connection in which it stands should be carefully observed. Christian love is placed in contrast to the hatred of the world.

We are shown first, in this passage, what true Christians must expect to meet in this world—hatred and persecution. If the disciples looked for kindness and gratitude from man they would be painfully disappointed. They must lay their account to be ill-treated like their Master. "The world hates you. Be not moved or surprised. If they have persecuted Me, they will also persecute you; if they have kept my word, they will keep yours also."

Facts, painful facts in every age, supply abundant proof that our Lord's warning was not without cause. Persecution was the lot of the Apostles and their companions wherever they went. Not more than one or two of them died quietly in his bed. Persecution has been the lot of true believers throughout the eighteen Christian centuries of history. The doings of Roman Emperors and Roman Popes, the Spanish inquisition, the martyrdoms of Queen Mary's reign, all tell the same story. Persecution is the lot of all really godly people at this very day. Ridicule, mockery, slander, misrepresentations still show the feeling of unconverted people against the true Christian. As it was in Paul's day, so it is now. In public and in private, at school and at college, at home and abroad, "all that will live godly in Christ Jesus shall suffer persecution." (2 Tim. 3:12.) Mere churchmanship and outward profession are a cheap religion, of course, and cost a man nothing. But real vital Christianity will always bring with it a cross.

To know and understand these things is of the utmost importance to our comfort. Nothing is so mischievous as the habit of indulging false expectations. Let us realize that human nature never changes, that "the carnal mind is enmity against God," and against God's image in His people. Let us settle it in our minds that no holiness of life or consistency of conduct will ever prevent wicked people hating the servants of Christ, just as they hated their blameless Master. Let us remember these things, and then we shall not be disappointed.

We are shown secondly, in this passage, two reasons for patience under the persecution of this world. Each is weighty, and supplies matter for much thought.

For one thing, persecution is the cup of which Christ Himself drank. Faultless as He was in everything, in temper, word, and deed—unwearied as He was in works of kindness, always going about doing good—never was any one so hated as Jesus was to the last day of His earthly ministry. Scribes and High Priests, Pharisees and Sadducees, Jews and Gentiles, united in pouring contempt on Him, and opposing Him, and never rested until He was put to death.

Surely this simple fact alone should sustain our spirits and prevent our being cast down by the hatred of man. Let us consider that we are only walking in our Master's footsteps, and sharing our Master's portion. Do we deserve to be better treated? Are we better than He? Let us fight against these murmuring thoughts. Let us drink quietly the cup which our Father gives us. Above all, let us often call to mind the saying, "Remember the word that I spoke unto you, The servant is not greater than his Master."

For another thing, persecution helps to prove that we are children of God, and have treasure in heaven. It supplies evidence that we are really born again, that we have grace in our hearts, and are heirs of glory—"If you were of the world, the world would love his own—but because you are not of the world, but I have chosen you out of the world, therefore the world hates you." Persecution, in short, is like the goldsmith's stamp on real silver and gold—it is one of the marks of a converted man.

Let us nerve our minds with this cheering thought, when we feel ready to faint and give way under the world's hatred. No doubt it is hard to bear, and the more hard when our conscience tells us we are innocent. But after all let us never forget that it is a token for good. It is a symptom of a work begun within us by the Holy Spirit, which can never be overthrown. We may fall back on that wonderful promise, "Blessed are you when men shall revile you, and persecute you, and shall say all manner of evil against you falsely, for my sake. Rejoice, and be exceeding glad—for great is your reward in heaven." (Matt. 5:11, 12.) When the world has said and done its worst, it cannot rob believers of that promise.

Let us leave the whole subject with a feeling of deep pity for those who persecute others on account of their religion. Often, very often, as our Lord says, they do it because they know no better. "They know not Him that sent Me." Like our Divine Master and His servant Stephen, let us pray for those who despitefully use us and persecute us. Their persecution rarely does us harm, and often drives us nearer to Christ, the Bible, and the throne of grace. Our intercession, if heard on high, may bring down blessings on their souls.

15:22-27

"If I had not come and spoken to them, they would not be guilty of sin. But they no longer have any excuse for their sin. The one who hates me hates my Father too. If I had not performed among them the miraculous deeds that no one else did, they would not be guilty of sin. But now they have seen the deeds and have hated both me and my Father. Now this happened to fulfill the word that is written in their law, 'They hated me without reason.' When the Advocate comes, whom I will send you from the Father—the Spirit of truth who goes out from the

Father—he will testify about me, and you also will testify, because you have been with me from the beginning."

In these verses our Lord Jesus Christ handles three subjects of great importance. They are difficult subjects, no doubt, subjects on which we may easily fall into error. But the words before us throw much light upon them.

We should observe, for one thing, how our Lord speaks of the misuse of religious privileges. It intensifies man's guilt, and will increase his condemnation. He tells His disciples that if He had not "spoken" and "done" among the Jews things which none ever spoke or did before, "they would not be guilty of sin." By this, we must remember, He means, "they had not been so sinful and so guilty as they are now. But now they were utterly without excuse." They had seen Christ's works, and heard Christ's teaching, and yet remained unbelieving. What more could be done for them? Nothing. absolutely nothing! They wilfully sinned against the clearest possible light, and were of all men most guilty.

Let us settle it down as a first principle in our religion, that religious privileges are in a certain sense very dangerous things. If they do not help us toward heaven, they will only sink us deeper into hell. They add to our responsibility.

"To whomsoever much is given, of him shall much be required." (Luke 12:48.) He that dwells in a land of open Bibles and preached Gospel, and yet dreams that he will stand in the judgment day on the same level with an untaught Chinese, is fearfully deceived. He will find to his own cost, except he repents, that his judgment will be according to his light. The mere fact that he had knowledge and did not improve it, will of itself prove one of his greatest sins.

"He that knew His Master's will and did it not, shall be beaten with many stripes." (Luke 12:47.)

Well would it be for all professing Christians in England, if this point was more thoroughly considered! Nothing is more common than to hear men taking comfort in the thought that they "know what" is right, while at the same time they are evidently unconverted, and unfit to die. They rest in that unhappy phrase, "We know it, we know it," as if knowledge could wash away all their sins—forgetting that the devil has more knowledge than any of us, and yet is no better for it. Let the burning words of our Lord in the passage now before us, sink down into our hearts, and never be forgotten—"If I had not come and spoken unto them, they would not be guilty of sin—but now they have no cloak for their sin." To see light and not use it, to possess knowledge and yet not turn it to account, to he able to say "I know," and yet not to say "I believe," will place us at the lowest place on Christ's left hand, in the great day of judgment.

We should observe, for another thing, in these verses, how our Lord speaks of the Holy Spirit. He speaks of Him as a Person. He is "the Comforter" who is to come; He is One sent and "proceeding;" He is One whose office it is to "testify." These are not words that can be used of a mere influence or inward feeling. So to interpret them is to contradict common sense, and to strain the meaning of plain language. Reason and fairness require us to understand that it is a personal Being who is here mentioned, even He whom we are justly taught to adore as the third Person in the blessed Trinity.

Again, our Lord speaks of the Holy Spirit as One whom He "will send from the Father," and One "who proceeds from the Father." These are deep sayings, no doubt, so deep that we have no line to fathom them. The mere fact that for centuries the Eastern and Western Churches of Christendom have been divided about their meaning, should teach us to handle them with modesty and reverence. One thing, at all events, is very clear and plain. There is a close and intimate connection between the Spirit, the Father, and the Son. Why the Holy Spirit should be said to be sent by the Son, and to proceed from the Father, in this verse, we cannot tell. But we may quietly repose our minds in the thought expressed in an ancient creed, that "In this Trinity none is afore or after other—none is greater or less than another." "Such as the Father is such is the Son, and such is the Holy Spirit." Above all, we may rest in the comfortable truth that in the salvation of our souls all three Persons in the Trinity equally co-operate. It was God in Trinity who said, "Let us create," and it is God in Trinity who says, "Let us save."

Forever let us take heed to our doctrine about the Holy Spirit. Let us make sure that we hold sound and Scriptural views of His nature, His Person, and His operations. A religion which entirely leaves Him out, and gives Him no place, is far from uncommon. Let us beware that such a religion is not ours.

"Where is the Lamb, the Lord Jesus Christ?" should be the first testing question about our Christianity. "Where is the Holy Spirit?" should be the second question. Let us take good heed that the work of the Spirit is not so buried under extravagant views of the Church, the ministry, and the Sacraments, that the real Holy Spirit of Scripture is completely put out of sight.

"If any man has not the Spirit of Christ, he is none of His." (Rom. 8:9.) No religion deserves to be called Scriptural and apostolic, in which the work of the Spirit does not stand forth prominently, and occupy a principal place.

We should observe lastly, in these verses, how our Lord speaks of the special office of the Apostles. They were to be His witnesses in the world. "You also shall bear witness."

The expression is singularly instructive and full of meaning. It taught the eleven what they must expect their portion to be, so long as they lived. They would have to bear testimony to facts which many would not believe, and to truths which the natural heart would dislike. They would often have to stand alone, a few against many, a little flock against a great multitude. None of these things must move them. They must count it no strange thing to be persecuted, hated, opposed, and discredited. They must not mind it. To witness of Christ was their grand duty, whether men believed them or not. So witnessing, their record would be on high, in God's book of remembrance; and so witnessing, sooner or later, the Judge of all would give them a crown of glory that fades not away.

Let us never forget, as we leave this passage, that the position of the Apostles is that which, in a certain sense, every true Christian must fill, as long as the world stands. We must all be witnesses for Christ. We must not be ashamed to stand up for Christ's cause, to speak out for Christ, and to persist in maintaining the truth of Christ's Gospel. Wherever we live, in town or in country, in public or in private, abroad or at home, we must boldly confess our Master on every opportunity. So doing, we shall walk in the steps of the Apostles, though at a long interval. So doing, we shall please our Master, and may hope at last that we shall receive the Apostles' reward.

Chapter 16

16:1-7

"*I have told you all these things so that you will not fall away. They will put you out of the synagogue, yet a time is coming when the one who kills you will think he is offering service to God. They will do these things because they have not known the Father or me. But I have told you these things so that when their time comes you will remember that I told you about them.*

"*I did not tell you these things from the beginning because I was with you. But now I am going to the one who sent me, and not one of you is asking me, 'Where are you going?' Instead your hearts are filled with sadness because I have said these things to you. But I tell you the truth, it is to your advantage that I am going away. For if I do not go away, the Advocate will not come to you, but if I go, I will send him to you.*

The opening verses of this chapter contain three important utterances of Christ, which deserve our special attention.

For one thing, we find our Lord delivering a remarkable prophecy. He tells His disciples that they will be cast out of the Jewish Church, and persecuted even to the death—"They shall put you out of the synagogues—yes, the time comes, that whoever kills you will think that he does God service."

How strange that seems at first sight! Excommunication, suffering, and death, are the portion that the Prince of Peace predicts to His disciples. So far from receiving them and their message with gratitude, the world would hate them, despitefully use them, and put them to death. And, worst of all, their persecutors would actually persuade themselves that it was right to persecute, and would inflict the cruelest injuries in the sacred name of religion.

How true the prediction has turned out! Like every other prophecy of Scripture, it has been fulfilled to the very letter. The Acts of the Apostles show us how the unbelieving Jews persecuted the early Christians. The pages of history tell us what horrible crimes have been committed by the Popish Inquisition. The annals of our own country inform us how our holy Reformers were burned at the stake for their religion, by men who professed to do all they did from zeal for pure Christianity. Unlikely and incredible as it might seem at the time, the great Prophet of the Church has been found in this, as in everything else, to have predicted nothing but literal truth.

Let it never surprise us to hear of true Christians being persecuted, in one way or another, even in our own day. Human nature never changes. Grace is never really popular. The quantity of persecution which God's children have to suffer in every rank of life, even now, if they confess their Master, is far greater than the thoughtless world supposes. They only know it who go through it, at school, at college, in the counting-house, in the barracks-room, on board the ship. Those words shall always be found true—"All who will live godly in Christ Jesus, shall suffer persecution." (2 Tim. 3:12.)

Let us never forget that religious earnestness alone is no proof that a man is a sound Christian. Not all zeal is right—it may be a zeal without knowledge. No one is so mischievous as a blundering, ignorant zealot. Not all earnestness is trustworthy—without the leading of God's Spirit, it may lead a man so far astray, that, like Saul, he will persecute Christ himself. Some bigots imagine they are doing God service, when they are actually fighting against His truth, and trampling on His people. Let us pray that we may have light as well as zeal.

For another thing, we find our Lord explaining His special reason for delivering the prophecy just referred to, as well as all His discourse. "These things," He says, "I have spoken unto you, that you should not be offended."

Well did our Lord know that nothing is so dangerous to our comfort as to indulge false expectations. He therefore prepared His disciples for what they must expect to meet with in His service. Forewarned, forearmed! They must not look for a smooth course and a peaceful journey. They must make up their minds to battles, conflicts, wounds, opposition, persecution, and perhaps even death. Like a wise general, He did not conceal from His soldiers the nature of the campaign they were beginning. He told them all that was before them, in faithfulness and love, that when the time of trial came, they might remember His words, and not be disappointed and offended. He wisely forewarned them that the cross was the way to the crown.

To count the cost is one of the first duties that ought to be pressed on Christians in every age. It is no kindness to young beginners to paint the service of Christ in false colors, and to keep back from them the old truth, "Through much tribulation we must enter the kingdom of God." By prophesying smooth things, and crying "Peace," we may easily fill the ranks of Christ's army with professing soldiers. But they are just the soldiers, who, like the stony-ground hearers, in time of tribulation will fall away, and turn back in the day of battle.

No Christian is in a healthy state of mind who is not prepared for trouble and persecution. He that expects to cross the troubled waters of this world, and to reach heaven with wind and tide always in his favor, knows nothing yet as he ought to know. We never can tell what is before us in life. But of one thing we may be very sure—we must carry the cross if we would wear the crown. Let us grasp this principle firmly, and never forget it. Then, when the hour of trial comes, we shall "not be offended."

In the last place, we find our Lord giving a special reason why it was expedient for Him to go away from His disciples. "If I do not go away," He says, "the Comforter will not come unto you."

We can well suppose that our gracious Lord saw the minds of His disciples crushed at the idea of His leaving them. Little as they realized His full meaning, on this, as well as on other occasions, they evidently had a vague notion that they were about to be left, like orphans, in a cold and unkind world, by their Almighty Friend. Their hearts quailed and shrunk back at the thought. Most graciously does our Lord cheer them by words of deep and mysterious meaning. He tells those who His departure, however painful it might seem, was not an evil, but a good. They would actually find it was not a loss, but a gain. His bodily absence would be more useful than His presence.

It is vain to deny that this is a somewhat mysterious saying. It seems at first sight hard to understand how in any sense it could be good that Christ should go away from His disciples. Yet a little reflection may show us that, like our Lord's sayings, this remarkable utterance was wise, and right, and true. The following points, at any rate, deserve attentive consideration.

If Christ had not died, risen again, and ascended up into heaven, it is plain that the Holy Spirit could not have come down with special power on the day of Pentecost, and bestowed His manifold gifts on the Church. Mysterious as it may be, there was a connection in the eternal counsels of God, between the ascension of Christ and the outpouring of the Spirit.

If Christ had remained bodily with the disciples, He could not have been in more places than one at the same time. The presence of the Spirit whom He sent down, would fill every place where believers were assembled in His name, in every part of the world.

If Christ had remained upon earth, and not gone up into heaven, He could not have become a High Priest for His people in the same full and perfect manner that He became after His ascension. He went away to sit down at the right hand of God, and to appear for us, in our human nature glorified, as our Advocate with the Father.

Finally, if Christ had always remained bodily with His disciples, there would have been far less room for the exercise of their faith and hope and trust, than there was when He went away. Their graces would not have been called into such active exercise, and they would have had less opportunity of glorifying God, and exhibiting His power in the world.

After all, there remains the broad fact that after the Lord Jesus went away, and the Comforter came down on the day of Pentecost, the religion of the disciples became a new thing altogether. The growth of their knowledge, and faith, and hope, and zeal, and courage, was so remarkable, that they were twice the men they were before. They did far more for Christ when He was absent, than they had ever done when He was present. What stronger proof can we require that it was expedient for those who their Master should go away!

Let us leave the whole subject with a deep conviction that it is not the bodily presence of Christ in the midst of us, so much as the presence of the Holy Spirit in our hearts, that is essential to a high standard of Christianity. What we should all desire and long for is not Christ's body literally touched with our hands and received into our mouths, but Christ dwelling spiritually in our hearts by the grace of the Holy Spirit.

16:8-15

"And when he comes, he will prove the world wrong concerning sin and righteousness and judgment—concerning sin, because they do not believe in me; concerning righteousness, because I am going to the Father and you will see me no longer; and concerning judgment, because the ruler of this world has been condemned.

"I have many more things to say to you, but you cannot bear them now. But when he, the Spirit of truth, comes, he will guide you into all truth. For he will not speak on his own authority, but will speak whatever he hears, and will tell you what is to come. He will glorify me, because he will receive from me what is mine and will tell it to you. Everything that the Father has is mine; that is why I said the Spirit will receive from me what is mine and will tell it to you."

When our Lord in this passage speaks of the Holy Spirit "coming," we must take care that we do not misunderstand His meaning. On the one hand, we must remember that the Holy Spirit was in all believers in the Old Testament days, from the very beginning. No man was ever saved from the power of sin, and made a saint, except by the renewing of the Holy Spirit. Abraham, and Isaac, and Samuel, and David, and the Prophets, were made what they were by the operation of the Holy Spirit.

On the other hand, we must never forget that after Christ's ascension the Holy Spirit was poured down on men with far greater energy as individuals, and with far wider influence on the nations of the world at large, than He has ever poured out before. It is this increased energy and influence that our Lord has in view in the verses before us. He meant that after His own ascension the Holy Spirit would "come" down into the world with such a vastly increased power, that it would seem as if He had "come" for the first time, and had never been in the world before.

The difficulty of rightly explaining the wondrous sayings of our Lord in this place is undeniably very great. It may well be doubted whether the full meaning of His words has ever been entirely grasped by man, and whether there is not something at the bottom which has not been completely unfolded. The common, superficial explanation, that our Lord only meant that the work of the Spirit in saving individual believers is to convince them of their own sins, of Christ's righteousness, and of the certainty of judgment at last, will hardly satisfy thinking minds. It is a short-cut and superficial way of getting over Scripture difficulties. It contains excellent and sound doctrine, no doubt, but it does not meet the full meaning of our Lord's words. It is truth, but not the truth of the text. It is not individuals here and there whom He says the Spirit is to convince, but the world. Let us see whether we cannot find a fuller and more satisfactory interpretation.

For one thing, our Lord probably meant to show us what the Holy Spirit would do to the world of unbelieving JEWS. He would convince them "of sin, and righteousness, and judgment."

He would convince the Jews "of sin." He would compel them to feel and acknowledge in their own minds, that in rejecting Jesus of Nazareth they had committed a great sin, and were guilty of gross unbelief.

He would convince the Jews of "righteousness." He would press home on their consciences that Jesus of Nazareth was not an impostor and a deceiver, as they had said, but a holy, just, and blameless Person, whom God had owned by receiving up into heaven.

He would convince the Jews of "judgment." He would oblige them to see that Jesus of Nazareth had conquered, overcome, and judged the devil and all his host, and was exalted to be a Prince and a Savior at the right hand of God.

That the Holy Spirit did actually so convince the Jewish nation after the day of Pentecost, is clearly shown by the Acts of the Apostles. It was He who gave the humble fishermen of Galilee such grace and might in testifying of Christ, that their adversaries were put to silence. It was His reproving and convincing power which enabled them to "fill Jerusalem with their doctrine." Not a few of the nation, we know, were savingly convinced, like Paul, and "a great company of priests" became obedient to the faith. Myriads more, we have every reason to believe, were mentally convinced, if they had not courage to come out and take up the cross. The whole tone of the Jewish people towards the end of the Acts of the Apostles is unlike what it is at the beginning. A vast reproving and convincing influence even where not saving, seems to have gone over their minds. Surely this was partly what our Lord had in view in these verses when He said, "The Holy Spirit shall reprove and convince."

For another thing, our Lord probably meant to foretell what the Holy Spirit would do for the whole of MANKIND, both Gentiles as well as Jews.

He would reprove in every part of the earth the current ideas of men about sin, righteousness, judgment, and convince people of some far higher ideas on these points than they had before acknowledged. He would make men see more clearly the nature of sin, the need of righteousness, the certainty of judgment. In a word, He would insensibly be an Advocate and convincing Pleader for God throughout the whole world, and raise up a standard of morality, purity and knowledge, of which formerly men had no conception.

That the Holy Spirit actually did so in every part of the earth, after the day of Pentecost, is a simple matter of fact. The unlearned and lowly Jews, whom He sent forth and strengthened to preach the Gospel after our Lord's ascension, "turned the world upside down," and in two or three centuries altered the habits, tastes, and practices of the whole civilized world. The power of the devil received a decided check. Even infidels dare not deny that the doctrines of Christianity had an enormous effect on men's ways, lives, and opinions, when they were first preached, and that there were no special graces or eloquence in the preachers that can account for it. In truth, the world was "reproved and convinced," in spite of itself; and even those who did not become believers became better men. Surely this also was partly what our Lord had in view when He said to His disciples, "When the Holy Spirit comes, He shall convince the world of sin, and righteousness, and judgment."

Let us leave the whole passage, deep and difficult as it is, with a thankful remembrance of one comfortable promise which it contains. "The Spirit of truth," says our Lord to His weak and half-informed followers, "shall guide you into all truth." That promise was for our sakes, no doubt, as well as for theirs. Whatever we need to know for our present peace and sanctification, the Holy Spirit is ready to teach us. All truth in science, nature, and philosophy of course is not included in this promise. But into all spiritual truth that is really profitable, and that our minds can comprehend and bear, the Holy Spirit is ready and willing to guide us. Then let us never forget, in reading the Bible, to pray for the teaching of the Holy Spirit. We must not wonder if we find the Bible a dark and difficult book, if we do not regularly seek light from Him by whom it was first inspired. In this, as in many other things, "we have not because we ask not."

16:16-24

"In a little while you will see me no longer; again after a little while, you will see me." Then some of his disciples said to one another, "What is the meaning of what he is saying, 'In a little while you will not see me; again after a little while, you will see me,' and, 'because I am going to the Father'?" So they kept on repeating, "What is the meaning of what he says, 'In a little while'? We do not understand what he is talking about."

Jesus could see that they wanted to ask him about these things, so he said to them, "Are you asking each other about this—that I said, 'In a little while you will not see me; again after a little while, you will see me'? I tell you the solemn truth, you will weep and wail, but the world will rejoice; you will be sad, but your sadness will turn into joy. When a woman gives birth, she has distress because her time has come, but when her child is born, she no longer remembers the suffering because of her joy that a human being has been born into the world. So also you have sorrow now, but I will see you again, and your hearts will rejoice, and no one will take your joy away from you. At that time you will ask me nothing. I tell you the solemn truth, whatever you ask the Father in my name he will give you. Until now you have not asked for anything in my name. Ask and you will receive it, so that your joy may be complete."

Not all Christ's sayings were understood by His disciples. We are told this distinctly in the passage we have now read. "What is this that he says? We cannot tell what he says." None ever spoke so plainly as Jesus. None were so thoroughly accustomed to His style of teaching as the Apostles. Yet even the Apostles did not always take in their Master's meaning. Surely we have no right to be surprised if we cannot interpret Christ's words. There are many depths in those who we have no line to fathom. But let us thank God that there are many sayings of our Lord recorded which no honest mind can fail to understand. Let us use diligently the light that we have, and not doubt that "to him that has, more shall be given."

We learn, for one thing, in these verses, that Christ's absence from the earth will be a time of sorrow to believers, but of joy to the world. It is written, "You shall weep and lament, but the world shall rejoice." To confine these words to the single point of Christ's approaching death and burial, appears a narrow view of their meaning. Like many of our Lord's sayings on the last evening of His earthly ministry, they seem to extend over the whole period of time between His first and second advents.

Christ's personal absence must needs be a sorrow to all true-hearted believers. "The children of the bride-chamber cannot but fast when the bridegroom is taken from them." Faith is not sight. Hope is not certainty. Reading and hearing are not the same as beholding. Praying is not the same as speaking face to face. There is something, even in the hearts of the most eminent saints, that will never be fully satisfied as long as they are on earth and Christ is in heaven. So long as they dwell in a body of corruption, and see through a glass darkly—so long as they behold creation groaning under the power of sin, and all things not put under Christ—so long their happiness and peace must needs be incomplete. This is what Paul meant when he said, "We ourselves, which have the first fruits of the Spirit, groan within ourselves, waiting for the adoption, to wit, the redemption of our body." (Rom. 8:23.)

Yet this same personal absence of Christ is no cause of sorrow to the children of this world. It was not sorrow to the unbelieving Jews, we may be sure. When Christ was condemned and crucified, they rejoiced and were glad. They thought that the hated reprover of their sins and false teaching was silenced forever. It is not sorrow to the careless and the wicked of our day, we may be sure. The longer Christ keeps away from this earth, and lets them alone, the better will they be pleased. "We do not want this Christ to reign over us," is the feeling of the world. His absence causes them no pain. Their so-called happiness is complete without Him. All this may sound very painful and startling. But where is the thinking reader of the Bible who can deny that it is true? The world does not want Christ back again, and thinks that it does very well without Him. What a fearful waking up there will be by-and-by!

We learn, for another thing in this verse, that Christ's personal return shall be a source of boundless joy to His believing people. It is written, "I will see you again, and your heart shall rejoice, and your joy no man takes from you." Once more we must take care that we do not narrow the meaning of these words by tying them down to our Lord's resurrection. They surely reach much further than this. The joy of the disciples when they saw Christ risen from the dead, was a joy soon obscured by His ascension and withdrawal into heaven. The true joy, the perfect joy, the joy that can never be taken away, will be the joy which Christ's people will feel when Christ returns the second time, at the end of this world.

The second personal advent of Christ, to speak plainly, is the one grand object on which our Lord, both here and elsewhere, teaches all believers to fix their eyes. We ought to be always looking for and "loving His appearing," as the perfection of our happiness, and the consummation of all our hopes. (2 Peter 3:12; 2 Tim. 4:8.) That same Jesus who was taken up visibly into heaven, shall also come again visibly, even as He went. Let the eyes of our faith be always fixed on this coming. It is not enough that we look backward to the cross, and rejoice in Christ dying for our sins; and upwards to the right hand of God, and rejoice in Christ's interceding for every believer. We must do more than this. We must look forward to Christ's return from heaven to bless His people, and to wind up the work of redemption. Then, and then only, will the prayer of eighteen centuries receive its complete answer—"Your kingdom come, Your will be done on earth as it is in heaven." Well may our Lord say that in that day of resurrection and reunion our "hearts shall rejoice." "When we awake up after His likeness we shall be satisfied." (Psalm 17:15.)

We learn, lastly, in these verses, that while Christ is absent believers must ask much in prayer. It is written, "Hitherto have you asked nothing in My name—ask and you shall receive, that your joy may be full."

We may well believe that up to this time the disciples had never realized their Master's full dignity. They had certainly never understood that He was the one Mediator between God and man, in whose name and for whose sake they were to put up their prayers. Here they are distinctly told that henceforward they are to "ask in His name." Nor can we doubt that our Lord would have all His people, in every age, understand that the secret of comfort during His absence is to be instant in prayer. He would have us know that if we cannot see Him with our bodily eyes any longer, we can talk with Him, and through Him have special access to God. "Ask and you shall receive," He proclaims to all His people in every age; "and your joy shall be full."

Let the lesson sink down deeply into our hearts. Of all the list of Christian duties there is none to which there is such abounding encouragement, as prayer. It is a duty which concerns all. High and low, rich and poor, learned and unlearned—all must pray. It is a duty for which all are accountable. All cannot read, or hear, or sing; but all who have the spirit of adoption can pray. Above all, it is a duty in which everything depends on the heart and motive within. Our words may be feeble and ill-chosen, and our language broken and ungrammatical, and unworthy to be written down. But if the heart be right, it matters not. He that sits in heaven can spell out the meaning of every petition sent up in the name of Jesus, and can make the asker know and feel that he receives.

"If we know these things, happy are we if we do them." Let prayer in the name of Jesus be a daily habit with us every morning and evening of our lives. Keeping up that habit, we shall find strength for duty, comfort in trouble, guidance in perplexity, hope in sickness, and support in death. Faithful is He that promised, "Your joy shall be full;" and He will keep His word, if we ask in prayer.

16:25-33

"I have told you these things in obscure figures of speech; a time is coming when I will no longer speak to you in obscure figures, but will tell you plainly about the Father. At that time you will ask in my name, and I do not say that I will ask the Father on your behalf. For the Father himself loves you, because you have loved me and have believed that I came from God. I came from the Father and entered into the world, but in turn, I am leaving the world and going back to the Father."

His disciples said, "Look, now you are speaking plainly and not in obscure figures of speech! Now we know that you know everything and do not need anyone to ask you anything. Because of this we believe that you have come from God."

Jesus replied, "Do you now believe? Look, a time is coming—and has come—when you will be scattered, each one to his own home, and I will be left alone. Yet I am not alone, because my Father is with me. I have told you these things so that in me you may have peace. In the world you have trouble and suffering, but have courage—I have conquered the world."

The passage we have now read is a very remarkable portion of Scripture, for two reasons. On the one hand, it forms a suitable conclusion to our Lord's long parting address to His disciples. It was fit and right that such a solemn sermon should have a solemn ending. On the other hand it contains the most general and unanimous profession of belief that we ever find the Apostles making—"Now are we sure that You know all things . . . by this we believe that you came forth from God."

That there are things hard to be understood in the passage it would be useless to deny. But there lie on its surface three plain and profitable lessons, to which we may usefully confine our attention.

We learn, for one thing, that clear knowledge of God the Father is one of the foundations of the Christian religion. Our Lord says to His disciples, "The time comes when I shall show you plainly of the Father." He does not say, we should mark, "I will show you plainly about myself." It is the Father whom He promises to show.

The wisdom of this remarkable saying is very deep. There are few subjects of which men know so little in reality as the character and attributes of God the Father. It is not for nothing that it is written, "No man knows the Father save the Son, and he to whomsoever the Son shall reveal Him." (Matt. 11:27.) "The only begotten Son, who is in the bosom of the Father, He has declared Him." (John 1:18.) Thousands imagine that they know the Father because they think of Him as great, and almighty, and all-hearing, and wise, and eternal, but they think no further. To think of Him as just and yet the justifier of the sinner who believes in Jesus—as the God who sent His Son to suffer and die—as God in Christ reconciling the world unto Himself—as God specially well-pleased with the atoning sacrifice of His Son, whereby His law is honored; to think of God the Father in this way is not given to most men. No wonder that our Master says, "I will show you plainly of the Father."

Let it be part of our daily prayers, that we may know more of "the only true God," as well as of Jesus Christ whom He has sent. Let us beware alike of the mistakes which some make, who speak of God as if there was no Christ; and of the mistakes which others make, who speak of Christ as if there was no God. Let us seek to know all three Persons in the blessed Trinity, and give to each One the honor due to him. Let us lay hold firmly of the great truth, that the Gospel of our salvation is the result of the eternal counsels of Father, Son, and Holy Spirit; and that we are as thoroughly debtors to the love of the Father, as to the love of the Spirit, or the love of the Son. No one has learned of Christ so deeply as the man who is ever drawing nearer to the Father through the Son—ever feeling more childlike confidence in Him—and ever understanding more thoroughly that in Christ, God is not an angry judge, but a loving Father and Friend.

We learn, for another thing, in this passage, that our Lord Jesus Christ makes much of a little grace, and speaks kindly of those who have it. We see Him saying to the disciples—"The Father Himself loves you, because you have loved Me, and have believed that I came out from God."

How weak was the faith and love of the Apostles! How soon, in a very few hours, they were buried under a cloud of unbelief and cowardice! These very men whom Jesus commends for loving and believing, before the morning sun arose, forsook Him and fled. Yet, weak as their graces were, they were real and true and genuine. They were graces which hundreds of learned priests and scribes and Pharisees never attained, and, not attaining, died miserably in their sins.

Let us take great comfort in this blessed truth. The Savior of sinners will not cast off those who believe in Him, because they are babes in faith and knowledge. He will not break the bruised reed or quench the smoking flax. He can see reality under much infirmity, and where He sees it, He is graciously pleased. The followers of such a Savior may well be bold and confident. They have a Friend who despises not the least member of His flock, and casts out none who come to Him, however weak and feeble, if they are only true.

We learn, for another thing, in this passage, that the best Christians know but little of their own hearts. We see the disciples professing loudly, "Now You speak plainly—now we are sure—now we believe." Brave words these! And yet the very men that spoke them, in a very short time were scattered like timid sheep, and left their Master alone.

We need not doubt that the profession of the eleven was real and sincere. They honestly meant what they said. But they did not know themselves. They did not know what they were capable of doing under the pressure of the fear of men and of strong temptation. They had not rightly estimated the weakness of the flesh, the power of the devil, the feebleness of their own resolutions, the shallowness of their own faith. All this they had yet to learn by painful experience. Like young recruits, they had yet to learn that it is one thing to know the soldier's drill and wear the uniform, and quite another thing to be steadfast in the day of battle.

Let us mark these things, and learn wisdom. The true secret of spiritual strength is self-distrust and deep humility. "When I am weak," said a great Christian, "then am I strong." (2 Cor. 12:10.) None of us, perhaps, have the least idea how much we might fall if placed suddenly under the influence of strong temptation. Happy is he who never forgets the words, "Let him that thinks he stands take heed lest he fall;" and, remembering our Lord's disciples, prays daily "Hold me up and then I shall be safe."

We learn, lastly, from this passage, that Christ is the true source of peace. We read that our Lord winds up all His discourse with these soothing words- "These things have I spoken unto you, that you might have peace." The end and scope of His parting address, He would have us know, is to draw us nearer to Himself as the only fountain of comfort. He does not tell us that we shall have no trouble in the world. He holds out no promise of freedom from tribulation, while we are in the body. But He bids us rest in the thought that He has fought our battle and won a victory for us. Though tried, and troubled, and vexed with things here below, we shall not be destroyed. "Be of good cheer," is His parting charge—"Be of good cheer; I have overcome the world."

Let us lean back our souls on these comfortable words, and take courage. The storms of trial and persecution may sometimes beat heavily on us; but let them only drive us closer to Christ. The sorrows, and losses, and crosses, and disappointments of our life may often make us feel sorely cast down; but let them only make us tighten our hold on Christ. Armed with this very promise let us, under every cross, come boldly to the throne of grace, that we may obtain mercy, and find grace to help in time of need. Let us often say to our souls, "Why are you cast down, and why are you disturbed?" And let us often say to our gracious Master—"Lord, did not You say, Be of good cheer? Lord, do as You have said, and cheer us to the end."

Chapter 17

17:1-8

When Jesus had finished saying these things, he looked upward to heaven and said, "Father, the time has come. Glorify your Son, so that your Son may glorify you—just as you have given him authority over all humanity, so that he may give eternal life to everyone you have given him. Now this is eternal life-that they know you, the only true God, and Jesus Christ, whom you sent. I glorified you on earth by completing the work you gave me to do. And now, Father, glorify me at your side with the glory I had with you before the world was created.

"I have revealed your name to the men you gave me out of the world. They belonged to you, and you gave them to me, and they have obeyed your word. Now they understand that everything you have given me comes from you, because I have given them the words you have given me. They accepted them and really understand that I came from you, and they believed that you sent me.

These verses begin one of the most wonderful chapters in the Bible. It is a chapter in which we see our Lord Jesus Christ addressing a long prayer to God the Father. It is wonderful as a specimen of the communion that was ever kept up between the Father and the Son, during the period of the Son's ministry on earth. It is wonderful as a pattern of the intercession which the Son, as an High Priest, is ever carrying on for us in heaven. Not least it is wonderful as an example of the sort of things that believers should mention in prayer. What Christ asks for His people, His people should ask for themselves. It has been well and truly said by an old divine, that "the best and fullest sermon ever preached was followed by the best of prayers."

It is needless to say that the chapter before us contains many deep things. It could hardly be otherwise. He that reads the words spoken by one Person of the blessed Trinity to another Person, by the Son to the Father, must surely be prepared to find much that he cannot fully understand, much that he has no line to fathom. There are sentences, words, and expressions, in the twenty-six verses of this chapter, which no one probably has ever unfolded completely. We have not minds to do it, or to understand the matters it contains, if we could. But there are great truths in the chapter which stand out clearly and plainly on its face, and to these truths we shall do well to direct our best attention.

We should notice, firstly, in these verses, what a glorious account they contain of our Lord Jesus Christ's office and dignity. We read that the Father has "given Him power over all flesh, that He should give eternal life." The keys of heaven are in Christ's hands. The salvation of every soul of mankind is at His disposal. We read, furthermore, that "it is life eternal to know the only true God, and Jesus Christ whom He has sent." The mere knowledge of God is not sufficient, and saves none. We must know the Son as well as the Father. God known without Christ, is a Being whom we can only fear, and dare not approach. It is "God in Christ, reconciling the world unto Himself," who alone can give to the soul life and peace. We read, furthermore, that Christ "has finished the work which the Father gave Him to do." He has finished the work of redemption, and wrought out a perfect righteousness for His people. Unlike the first Adam, who failed to do God's will and brought sin into the world, the second Adam has done all, and left nothing undone that He came to do. Finally, we read that Christ "had glory with the Father before the world was." Unlike Moses and David, He existed from all eternity, long before He came into the world; and He shared glory with the Father, before He was made flesh and born of the Virgin Mary.

Each of these marvelous sayings contains matter which our weak minds have not power fully to comprehend. We must be content to admire and reverence what we cannot thoroughly grasp and explain. But one thing is abundantly clear—sayings like these can only be used of one who is very God. To no patriarch, or prophet, or king, or apostle, is any such language ever applied in the Bible. It belongs to none but God.

Forever let us thank God that the hope of a Christian rests on such a solid foundation as a Divine Savior. He to whom we are commanded to flee for pardon, and in whom we are bid to rest for peace, is God as well as man. To all who really think about their souls, and are not careless and worldly, the thought is full of comfort. Such people know and feel that great sinners need a great Savior, and that no mere human redeemer would meet their needs. Then let them rejoice in Christ, and lean back confidently on Him. Christ has all power, and is able to save to the uttermost, because Christ is divine. Office, power, and pre-existence, all combine to prove that He is God.

We should notice, secondly, in these verses, what a gracious account they contain of our Lord Jesus Christ's disciples. We find our Lord Himself saying of them, "They have kept Your Word—they have known that all things You have given Me are of You—they have received Your words—they have known surely that I came out from You—they have believed that You did send Me."

These are wonderful words when we consider the character of the eleven men to whom they were applied. How weak was their faith! How slender their knowledge! How shallow their spiritual attainments! How faint their hearts in the hour of danger! Yet a very little time after Jesus spoke these words they all forsook Him and fled, and one of them denied Him three times with an oath. No one, in short, can read the four Gospels with attention, and fail to see that never had a great master such weak servants as Jesus had in the eleven apostles. Yet these very weak servants were the men of whom the gracious Head of the Church speaks here in high and honorable terms.

The lesson before us is full of comfort and instruction. It is evident that Jesus sees far more in His believing people than they see in themselves, or than others see in them. The least degree of faith is very precious in His sight. Though it be no bigger than a grain of mustard seed, it is a plant of heavenly growth, and makes a boundless difference between the possessor of it and the man of the world. Wherever the gracious Savior of sinners sees true faith in Himself, however feeble, He looks with compassion on many infirmities, and passes by many defects. It was even so with the eleven apostles. They were weak and unstable as water; but they believed and loved their Master when millions refused to own Him. And the language of Him who declared that a cup of cold water given in the name of a disciple should not lose its reward, shows clearly that their loyalty was not forgotten.

The true servant of God should mark well the feature in Christ's character which is here brought out, and rest his soul upon it. The best among us must often see in himself a vast amount of defects and infirmities, and must feel ashamed of his poor attainments in religion. But do we simply believe in Jesus? Do we cling to Him, and roll all our burdens on Him? Can we say with sincerity and truth, as Peter said afterwards, "Lord, You know all things—You know that I love You"? Then let us take comfort in the words of Christ before us, and not give way to despondency. The Lord Jesus did not despise the eleven because of their feebleness, but bore with them and saved them to the end, because they believed. And He never changes. What He did for them, He will do for us.

17:9-16

"I am praying on behalf of them. I am not praying on behalf of the world, but on behalf of those you have given me, because they belong to you. Everything I have belongs to you, and everything you have belongs to me, and I have been glorified by them. I am no longer in the world, but they are in the world, and I am coming to you. Holy Father, keep them safe in your name that you have given me, so that they may be one just as we are one. When I was with them I kept them safe and watched over them in your name that you have given me. Not one of them was lost except the one destined for destruction, so that the scripture could be fulfilled. But now I am coming to you, and I am saying these things in the world, so they may experience my joy completed in themselves. I have given them your word, and the world has hated them, because they do not belong to the world just as I do not belong to the world. I am not asking you to take them out of the world, but that you keep them safe from the evil one. They do not belong to the world just as I do not belong to the world.

These verses, like every part of this wonderful chapter, contain some deep things which are "hard to be understood." But there are two plain points standing out on the face of the passage which deserve the special attention of all true Christians. Passing by all other points, let us fix our attention on these two.

We learn, for one thing, that the Lord Jesus does things for His believing people which He does not do for the wicked and unbelieving. He helps their souls by special intercession. He says, "I pray for them—I pray not for the world, but for those who You have given Me."

The doctrine before us is one which is specially hated by the world. Nothing gives such offence, and stirs up such bitter feeling among the wicked, as the idea of God making any distinction between man and man, and loving one person more than another. Yet the world's objections to the doctrine are, as usual, weak and unreasonable. Surely a little reflection might show us that a God who regarded good and bad, holy and unholy, righteous and unrighteous, with equal complacency and favor, would be a very strange kind of God! The special intercession of Christ for His saints is agreeable to reason and to common sense.

Of course, like every other Gospel truth, the doctrine before us needs careful statement and Scriptural guarding. On the one hand, we must not narrow the love of Christ to sinners; and on the other we must not make it too broad. It is true that Christ loves all sinners, and invites all to be saved; but it is also true that He specially loves the "blessed company of all faithful people," whom He sanctifies and glorifies. It is true that He has wrought out a redemption sufficient for all mankind, and offers it freely to all; but it is also true that His redemption is effectual only to those who believe. Just so it is true that He is the Mediator between God and man; but it is also true that He intercedes actively for none but those who come unto God by Him. Hence it is written, "I pray for them—I pray not for the world."

This special intercession of the Lord Jesus is one grand secret of the believer's safety. He is daily watched, and thought for, and provided for with unfailing care, by One whose eye never slumbers and never sleeps. Jesus is "able to save them to the uttermost who come unto God by Him, because He ever lives to make intercession for them." (Heb. 7:25.) They never perish, because He never ceases to pray for them, and His prayer must prevail. They stand and persevere to the end, not because of their own strength and goodness, but because Jesus intercedes for them. Judas fell never to rise again; while Peter fell, but repented, and was restored. The reason of the difference lay under those words of Christ to Peter, "I have prayed for you, that your faith fail not." (Luke 22:32.)

The true servant of Christ ought to lean back his soul on the truth before us, and take comfort in it. It is one of the peculiar privileges and treasures of a believer, and ought to be well known. However much it may be wrested and abused by false professors and hypocrites, it is one which those who really feel in themselves the workings of the Spirit should hold firmly and never let go. Well says the judicious Hooker—"No man's condition so safe as ours—the prayer of Christ is more than sufficient both to strengthen us, be we ever so weak; and to overthrow all adversary power, be it ever so strong and potent."

We learn, for another thing, in these verses, that Christ does not wish His believing people to be taken out of the world, but to be kept from the evil of it.

We need not doubt that our Lord's all-seeing eye detected in the hearts of His disciples an impatient desire to get away from this troubled world. Few in number and weak in strength, surrounded on every side by enemies and persecutors, they might well long to be released from the scene of conflict, and to go home. Even David had said in a certain place, "Oh, that I had wings like a dove, then would I flee away and be at rest!" (Psalm 55:6.) Seeing all this, our Lord has wisely placed on record this part of His prayer for the perpetual benefit of His Church. He has taught us the great lesson that He thinks it better for His people to remain in the world and be kept from its evil, than to be taken out of the world and removed from the presence of evil altogether.

Nor is it difficult on reflection to see the wisdom of our Lord's mind about His people, in this as in everything else. Pleasant as it might be to flesh and blood to be snatched away from conflict and temptation, we may easily see that it would not be profitable. How could Christ's people do any good in the world, if taken away from it immediately after conversion? How could they exhibit the power of grace, and make proof of faith, and courage, and patience, as good soldiers of a crucified Lord? How could they be duly trained for heaven, and taught to value the blood and intercession and patience of their Redeemer, unless they purchased their experience by suffering? Questions like these admit of only one kind of answer. To abide here in this valley of tears, tried, tempted, assaulted, and yet kept from falling into sin, is the surest plan to promote the sanctification of Christians, and to glorify Christ. To go to heaven at once, in the day of conversion, would doubtless be an easy course, and would save us much trouble. But the easiest course is not always the path of duty. He that would win the crown must carry the cross, and show himself light in the midst of darkness, and salt in the midst of corruption. "If we suffer, we shall also reign with Him." (2 Tim. 2:12.)

If we have any hope that we are Christ's true disciples, let us be satisfied that Christ knows better than we do what is for our good. Let us leave "our times in His hand," and be content to abide here patiently as long as He pleases, however hard our position, so long as He keeps us from evil. That He will so keep us we need not doubt, if we ask Him, because He prays that we may be "kept." Nothing, we may be sure, glorifies grace so much as to live like Daniel in Babylon, and the saints in Nero's household—in the world and yet not of the world—tempted on every side and yet conquerors of temptation, not taken out of the reach of evil and yet kept and preserved from its power.

17:17-26

"Set them apart in the truth; your word is truth. Just as you sent me into the world, so I sent them into the world. And I set myself apart on their behalf, so that they too may be truly set apart.

"I am not praying only on their behalf, but also on behalf of those who believe in me through their testimony, that they may all be one, just as you, Father, are in me and I am in you. I pray that they may be in us, so that the world may believe that you sent me. The glory you gave to me I have given to them, that they may be one just as we are one—I in them and you in me—that they may be completely one, so that the world may know that you sent me, and you have loved them just as you have loved me.

"Father, I want those you have given me to be with me where I am, so that they may see my glory that you gave me because you loved me before the creation of the world. Righteous Father, even if the world does not know you, I know you, and these men know that you sent me. I made known your name to them, and I will continue to make it known, so that the love you have loved me with may be in them, and I may be in them."

These wonderful verses form a fitting conclusion of the most wonderful prayer that was ever prayed on earth—the last Lord's prayer after the first Lord's Supper. They contain three most important petitions which our Lord offered up in behalf of His disciples. On these three petitions let us fix our attention. Passing by all other things in the passage, let us look steadily at these three points.

We should mark, first, how Jesus prays that His people may be sanctified. "Sanctify them," He says, "through your truth—Your word is truth."

We need not doubt that, in this place at any rate, the word "sanctify" means "make holy." It is a prayer that the Father would make His people more holy, more spiritual, more pure, more saintly in thought and word and deed, in life and character. Grace had done something for the disciples already—called, converted, renewed, and changed them. The great Head of the Church prays that the work of grace may be carried higher and further, and that His people may be more thoroughly sanctified and made holy in body, soul, and spirit—in fact more like Himself.

Surely we need not say much to show the matchless wisdom of this prayer. More holiness is the very thing to be desired for all servants of Christ. Holy living is the great proof of the reality of Christianity. Men may refuse to see the truth of our arguments, but they cannot evade the evidence of a godly life. Such a life adorns religion and makes it beautiful, and sometimes wins those who are not "won by the Word." Holy living trains Christians for heaven. The nearer we live to God while we live, the more ready shall we be to dwell forever in His presence when we die. Our entrance into heaven will be entirely by grace, and not of works; but heaven itself would be no heaven to us if we entered it with an unsanctified character. Our hearts must be in tune for heaven if we are to enjoy it. There must be a moral "fitness for the inheritance of the saints in light," as well as a title. Christ's blood alone can give us a title to enter the inheritance. Sanctification must give us a capacity to enjoy it.

Who, in the face of such facts as these, need wonder that increased sanctification should be the first thing that Jesus asks for His people? Who that is really taught of God can fail to know that holiness is happiness, and that those who walk with God most closely, are always those who walk with Him most comfortably? Let no man deceive us with vain words in this matter. He who despises holiness and neglects good works, under the vain pretense of giving honor to justification by faith, shows plainly that he has not the mind of Christ.

We should mark, secondly, in these verses, how Jesus prays for the unity and oneness of His people. "That they all may be one—that they may be one in Us—that they may be one even as We are one"—and "that so the world may believe and know that You have sent Me,"—this is a leading petition in our Lord's prayer to His Father.

We can ask no stronger proof of the value of unity among Christians, and the sinfulness of division, than the great prominence which our Master assigns to the subject in this passage. How painfully true it is that in every age divisions have been the scandal of religion, and the weakness of the Church of Christ!

How often Christians have wasted their strength in contending against their brethren, instead of contending against sin and the devil! How repeatedly they have given occasion to the world to say, "When you have settled your own internal differences we will believe!" All this, we need not doubt, the Lord Jesus foresaw with prophetic eye. It was the foresight of it which made Him pray so earnestly that believers might be "one."

Let the recollection of this part of Christ's prayer abide in our minds, and exercise a constant influence on our behavior as Christians. Let no man think lightly, as some men seem to do, of schism, or count it a small thing to multiply sects, parties, and denominations. These very things, we may depend, only help the devil and damage the cause of Christ. "If it be possible, as much as lies in us, let us live peaceably with all men." (Rom. 12:18.) Let us bear much, concede much, and put up with much, before we plunge into secessions and separations. They are movements in which there is often much false fire. Let rabid zealots who delight in sect-making and partyforming, rail at us and denounce us if they please. We need not mind them. So long as we have Christ and a good conscience, let us patiently hold on our way, follow the things that make for peace, and strive to promote unity. It was not for nothing that our Lord prayed so fervently that His people might be "one."

We should mark, finally, in these verses, how Jesus prays that His people may at last be with Him and behold His glory. "I will," He says, "that those whom You have given Me, be with Me where I am—that they may behold my glory."

This is a singularly beautiful and touching conclusion to our Lord's remarkable prayer. We may well believe that it was meant to cheer and comfort those who heard it, and to strengthen them for the parting scene which was fast drawing near. But for all who read it even now, this part of his prayer is full of sweet and unspeakable comfort.

We do not see Christ now. We read of Him, hear of Him, believe in Him, and rest our souls in His finished work. But even the best of us, at our best, walk by faith and not by sight, and our poor halting faith often makes us walk very feebly in the way to heaven. There shall be an end of all this state of things one day. We shall at length see Christ as He is, and know as we have been known. We shall behold Him face to face, and not through a glass darkly. We shall actually be in His presence and company, and go out no more. If faith has been pleasant, much more will sight be; and if hope has been sweet, much more will certainty be. No wonder that when Paul has written, "We shall ever be with the Lord," he adds, "Comfort one another with these words." (1 Thess. 4:17, 18.)

We know little of heaven now. Our thoughts are all confounded, when we try to form an idea of a future state in which pardoned sinners shall be perfectly happy. "It does not yet appear what we shall be." (I John 3:2.) But we may rest ourselves on the blessed thought, that after death we shall be "with Christ." Whether before the resurrection in paradise, or after the resurrection in final glory, the prospect is still the same. True Christians shall be "with Christ." We need no more information. Where that blessed Person is who was born for us, died for us, and rose again, there can be no lack of

266 | J.C. RYLE

anything. David might well say, "In Your presence is fullness of joy, and at Your right hand are pleasures forevermore." (Psalm 16:11.)

Let us leave this wonderful prayer with a solemn recollection of the three great petitions which it contains. Let holiness and unity by the way, and Christ's company in the end, be subjects never long out of our thoughts or distant from our minds. Happy is that Christian who cares for nothing so much as to be holy and loving like his Master, while he lives, and a companion of his Master when he dies.

Chapter 18

18:1-11

Betrayal and Arrest

When he had said these things, Jesus went out with his disciples across the Kidron Valley. There was an orchard there, and he and his disciples went into it. (Now Judas, the one who betrayed him, knew the place too, because Jesus had met there many times with his disciples.) So Judas obtained a squad of soldiers and some officers of the chief priests and Pharisees. They came to the orchard with lanterns and torches and weapons.

Then Jesus, because he knew everything that was going to happen to him, came and asked them, "Who are you looking for?" They replied, "Jesus the Nazarene." He told them, "I am he." (Now Judas, the one who betrayed him, was standing there with them.) So when Jesus said to them, "I am he," they retreated and fell to the ground. Then Jesus asked them again, "Who are you looking for?" And they said, "Jesus the Nazarene." Jesus replied, "I told you that I am he. If you are looking for me, let these men go." He said this to fulfill the word he had spoken, "I have not lost a single one of those whom you gave me."

Then Simon Peter, who had a sword, pulled it out and struck the high priest's slave, cutting off his right ear. (Now the slave's name was Malchus.) But Jesus said to Peter, "Put your sword back into its sheath! Am I not to drink the cup that the Father has given me?"

These verses begin John's account of Christ's sufferings and crucifixion. We now enter on the closing scene of our Lord's ministry, and pass at once from His intercession to His sacrifice. We shall find that, like the other Gospel writers, the beloved disciple enters fully into the story of the cross. But we shall also find, if we read carefully, that he mentions several interesting points in the story, which Matthew, Mark, and Luke, for some wise reasons, have passed over.

We should notice, first, in these verses, the exceeding hardness of heart to which a backsliding professor may attain. We are told that Judas, one of the twelve Apostles, became guide to those who captured Jesus. We are told that he used his knowledge of the place of our Lord's retirement, in order to bring His deadly enemies upon Him; and we are told that when the band of men and officers approached his Master, in order to take Him prisoner, Judas "stood with them." Yet this was a man who for three years had been a constant companion of Christ, had seen His miracles, had heard His sermons, had enjoyed the benefit of His private instruction, had professed himself a believer, had even worked and preached in Christ's name! "Lord," we may well say, "what is man?" From the highest degree of privilege down to the lowest depth of sin, there is but a succession of steps. Privileges misused seem to paralyze the conscience. The same fire that melts wax, will harden clay.

Let us beware of resting our hopes of salvation on religious knowledge, however great; or religious advantages, however many. We may know all doctrinal truth and be able to teach others, and yet prove rotten at heart, and go down to the pit with Judas. We may bask in the full sunshine of spiritual privileges, and hear the best of Christian teaching, and yet bear no fruit to God's glory, and be found withered branches of the vine, only fit to be burned.

"Let him that thinks he stands, take heed lest he fall." (1 Cor. 10:12.) Above all, let us beware of cherishing within our hearts any secret besetting sin, such as love of money or love of the world. One faulty link in a chain-cable may cause a shipwreck. One little leak may sink a ship. One allowed and unmortified sin may ruin a professing Christian. Let him that is tempted to be a careless man in his religious life, consider these things, and take care. Let him remember Judas Iscariot. His history is meant to be a lesson.

We should notice, secondly, in these verses, the entire voluntariness of Christ's sufferings. We are told that the first time that our Lord said to the soldiers, "I am He, they went backward, and fell to the ground." A secret invisible power, no doubt, accompanied the words. In no other way can we account for a band of hardy Roman soldiers falling prostrate before a single unarmed man. The same miraculous influence which tied the priests and Pharisees powerless at the triumphant entry into Jerusalem—which stopped all opposition when the temple was purged of buyers and sellers—that same mysterious influence was present now. A real miracle was wrought, though few had eyes to see it. At the moment when our Lord seemed weak, He showed that He was strong.

Let us carefully remember that our blessed Lord suffered and died of His own free will. He did not die because He could not help it; He did not suffer because He could not escape. All the soldiers of Pilate's army could not have taken Him, if He had not been willing to be taken. They could not have hurt a hair of His head, if He had not given them permission. But here, as in all His earthly ministry, Jesus was a willing sufferer. He had set His heart on accomplishing our redemption. He loved us, and gave Himself for us, cheerfully, willingly, gladly, in order to make atonement for our sins. It was "the joy set before Him" which made Him endure the cross, and despise the shame, and yield Himself up without reluctance into the bands of His enemies. Let this thought abide in our hearts, and refresh our souls. We have a Savior who was far more willing to save us than we are willing to be saved. If we are not saved, the fault is all our own. Christ is just as willing to receive and pardon, as He was willing to be taken prisoner, to bleed, and to die.

We should notice, thirdly, in these verses, our Lord's tender care for His disciples' safety. Even at this critical moment, when His own unspeakable sufferings were about to begin, He did not forget the little band of believers who stood around Him. He remembered their weakness. He knew how little fit they were to go into the fiery furnace of the High Priest's Palace, and Pilate's judgment-hall. He mercifully makes for them a way of escape. "If you seek Me, let these go their way." It seems most probable that here also a miraculous influence accompanied his words. At any rate, not a hair of the disciples' heads was touched. While the Shepherd was taken, the sheep were allowed to flee away unharmed.

We need not hesitate to see in this incident an instructive type of all our Savior's dealings with His people even at this day. He will not allow them "to be tempted above that which they are able to bear." He will hold the winds and storms in His hands, and not allow believers, however sifted and buffeted, to be utterly destroyed. He watches tenderly over every one of His children, and, like a wise physician, measures out the right quantity of their trials with unerring skill. "They shall never perish, neither shall any one pluck them out of His hand." (John 10:28.) Forever let us lean our souls on this precious truth. In the darkest hour the eye of the Lord Jesus is upon us, and our final safety is sure.

We should notice, lastly, in these verses, our Lord's perfect submission to his Father's will. Once, in another place, we find Him saying, "If it be possible, let this cup pass from Me—nevertheless, not as I will, but as You will." Again, in another place, we find Him saying, "If this cup may not pass away from Me except I drink it, Your will be done." Here, however, we find even a higher pitch of cheerful acquiescence—"The cup that my Father has given Me, shall I not drink it?" (Matt. 26:39-42; John 18:11.)

Let us see in this blessed frame of mind, a pattern for all who profess and call themselves Christians. Far as we may come short of the Master's standard, let this be the mark at which we continually aim. Determination to have our own way, and do only what we like, is one great source of unhappiness in the world. The habit of laying all our matters before God in prayer, and asking Him to choose our portion, is one chief secret of peace. He is the truly wise man who has learned to say at every stage of his journey, "Give me what you will, place me where You will, do with me as You will; but not my will, but Yours be done." This is the man who has the mind of Christ. By self-will Adam and Eve fell, and brought sin and misery into the world. Entire submission of will to the will of God is the best preparation for that heaven where God will be all.

18:12-27

Then the squad of soldiers with their commanding officer and the officers of the Jewish religious leaders arrested Jesus and tied him up. They brought him first to Annas, for he was the father-in-law of Caiaphas, who was high priest that year. (Now it was Caiaphas who had advised the Jewish leaders that it was to their advantage that one man die for the people.)

Simon Peter and another disciple followed them as they brought Jesus to Annas. (Now the other disciple was acquainted with the high priest, and he went with Jesus into the high priest's courtyard.) But Simon Peter was left standing outside by the door. So the other disciple who was acquainted with the high priest came out and spoke to the slave girl who watched the door, and brought Peter inside. The girl who was the doorkeeper said to Peter, "You're not one of this man's disciples too, are you?" He replied, "I am not." (Now the slaves and the guards were standing around a charcoal fire they had made, warming themselves because it was cold. Peter also was standing with them, warming himself.)

While this was happening, the high priest questioned Jesus about his disciples and about his teaching. Jesus replied, "I have spoken publicly to the world. I always taught in the synagogues and in the temple courts, where all the Jewish people assemble together. I have said nothing in secret. Why do you ask me? Ask those who heard what I said. They know what I said." When Jesus had said this, one of the high priest's officers who stood nearby struck him on the face and said, "Is that the way you answer the high priest?" Jesus replied, "If I have said something wrong, confirm what is wrong. But if I spoke correctly, why strike me?" Then Annas sent him, still tied up, to Caiaphas the high priest.

Meanwhile Simon Peter was standing in the courtyard warming himself. They said to him, "You aren't one of his disciples too, are you?" Peter denied it "I am not!" One of the high priest's slaves, a relative of the man whose ear Peter had cut off, said, "Did I not see you in the orchard with him?" Then Peter denied it again, and immediately a rooster crowed.

In this part of John's history of Christ's sufferings, three wonderful things stand out upon the surface of the narrative. To these three let us confine our attention.

We should mark, for one thing, the amazing hardness of unconverted men. We see this in the conduct of the men by whom our Lord was taken prisoner. Some of them most probably were Roman soldiers, and some of them were Jewish servants of the priests and Pharisees. But in one respect they were all alike. Both parties saw our Lord's divine power exhibited, when they "went backward, and fell to the ground." Both saw a miracle, according to Luke's Gospel, when Jesus touched the ear of Malchus and healed him. Yet both remained unmoved, cold, indifferent and insensible, as if they had seen nothing out of the common way. They went on coolly with their odious business; "They took Jesus, bound Him, and led Him away."

The degree of hardness and insensibility of conscience to which men may attain, when they live twenty or thirty years without the slightest contact with religion, is something dreadful and appalling. God and the things of God seem to sink out of sight and disappear from the mind's eye. The world and the things of the world seem to absorb the whole attention. In such cases we may well believe miracles would produce little or no effect, as in the case before us. The eye would gaze on them, like the eye of a beast looking at a romantic landscape, without any impression being made on the heart. He who thinks that seeing a miracle would convert him into a thorough Christian has got much to learn.

Let us not wonder if we see cases of hardness and unbelief in our own day and generation. Such cases will continually be found among those classes of mankind, who from their profession or position are completely cut off from means of grace. Twenty or thirty years of total irreligion, without the influence of Sunday, Bible, or Christian teaching, will make a man's heart hard as the nether mill-stone. His conscience at last will seem dead, buried, and gone. He will appear past feeling. Painful as these cases are, we must not think them peculiar to our own times. They existed under Christ's own eyes, and they will exist until Christ returns. The Church which allows any portion of a population to grow up in practical heathenism, must never be surprised to see a rank crop of practical infidelity.

We should mark, for another thing, the amazing condescension of our Lord Jesus Christ. We see the Son of God taken prisoner and led away bound like a malefactor—arraigned before wicked and unjust judges—insulted and treated with contempt. And yet this unresisting prisoner had only to will His deliverance, and He would at once have been free. He had only to command the confusion of His enemies, and they would at once have been confounded. Above all He was One who knew full well that Annas and Caiaphas, and all their companions, would one day stand before His judgment seat and receive an eternal sentence. He knew all these things, and yet condescended to be treated as a malefactor without resisting.

One thing at any rate is very clear. The love of Christ to sinners is "a love that passes knowledge." To suffer for those whom we love, and who are in some sense worthy of our affections, is suffering that we can understand. To submit to ill-treatment quietly, when we have no power to resist, is submission that is both graceful and wise. But to suffer voluntarily, when we a have the power to prevent it, and to suffer for a world of unbelieving and ungodly sinners, unasked and unthanked—this is a line of conduct which passes man's understanding. Never let us forget that this is the peculiar beauty of Christ's sufferings, when we read the wondrous story of His cross and passion.

He was led away captive, and dragged before the High Priest's bar, not because He could not help Himself, but because He had set His whole heart on saving sinners, by bearing their sins, by being treated as a sinner, and by being punished in their stead. He was a willing prisoner, that we might be set free. He was willingly arraigned and condemned, that we might be absolved and declared innocent. "He suffered for sins, the just for the unjust, that He might bring us unto God." "Though He was rich, yet for our sakes He became poor, that we through His poverty might be rich." "He was made sin for us who knew no sin, that we might be made the righteousness of God in Him." (1 Peter 3:18; 2 Cor. 8:9; 5:21.) Surely if there is any doctrine of the Gospel which needs to be clearly known, it is the doctrine of Christ's voluntary substitution. He suffered and died willingly and unresistingly, because He knew that He had come to be our substitute, and by substitution to purchase our salvation.

We should mark, lastly, the amazing degree of weakness that may be found in a real Christian. We see this exemplified in a most striking manner, in the conduct of the Apostle Peter. We see that famous disciple forsaking his Master, and acting like a coward—running away when he ought to have stood by His side—ashamed to own Him when he ought to have confessed Him—and finally denying three times that He knew Him. And this takes place immediately after receiving the Lord's' Supper—after hearing the most touching address and prayer that mortal ear ever heard. after the plainest possible warnings—under the pressure of no very serious temptation. "Lord," we may well say, "what is man that You are mindful of him?" "Let him that thinks he stands, take heed lest he fall." (1 Cor. 10:12.)

This fall of Peter is doubtless intended to be a lesson to the whole Church of Christ. It is recorded for our learning, that we be kept from like sorrowful overthrow. It is a beacon mercifully set up in Scripture, to prevent others making shipwreck. It shows us the danger of pride and self-confidence. If Peter had not been so sure that although all denied Christ, he never would, he would probably never have fallen. It shows us the danger of laziness. If Peter had watched and prayed, when our Lord advised him to do so, he would have found grace to help him in the time of need. It shows us, not least, the painful influence of the fear of man. Few are aware, perhaps, how much more they fear the face of man whom they can see, than the eye of God whom they cannot see. These things are written for our admonition. Let us remember Peter and be wise.

After all let us leave the passage with the comfortable reflection that we have a merciful and pitiful High Priest, who can be touched with the feeling of our infirmities, and will not break the bruised reed. Peter no doubt fell shamefully, and only rose again after heartfelt repentance and bitter tears. But he did rise again. He was not left to reap the consequence of his sin, and cast off for evermore. The same pitying hand that saved him from drowning, when his faith failed him on the waters, was once more stretched out to raise him when he fell in the High Priest's hall. Can we doubt that he rose a wiser and better man? If Peter's fall has made Christians see more clearly their own great weakness and Christ's great compassion, then Peter's fall has not been recorded in vain.

18:28-40

Then they brought Jesus from Caiaphas to the Roman governor's residence. (Now it was very early morning.) They did not go into the governor's residence so they would not be ceremonially defiled, but could eat the Passover meal. So Pilate came outside to them and said, "What accusation do you bring against this man?" They replied, "If this man were not a criminal, we would not have handed him over to you."

Pilate told them, "Take him yourselves and pass judgment on him according to your own law!" The Jewish religious leaders replied, "We cannot legally put anyone to death." (This happened to fulfill the word Jesus had spoken when he indicated what kind of death he was going to die.)

So Pilate went back into the governor's residence, summoned Jesus, and asked him, "Are you the king of the Jews?" Jesus replied, "Are you saying this on your own initiative, or have others told you about me?" Pilate answered, "I am not a Jew, am I? Your own people and your chief priests handed you over to me. What have you done?"

Jesus replied, "My kingdom is not from this world. If my kingdom were from this world, my servants would be fighting to keep me from being handed over to the Jewish authorities. But as it is, my kingdom is not from here." Then Pilate said, "So you are a king!" Jesus replied, "You say that I am a king. For this reason I was born, and for this reason I came into the world—to testify to the truth. Everyone who belongs to the truth listens to my voice." Pilate asked, "What is truth?"

When he had said this he went back outside to the Jewish religious leaders and announced, "I find no basis for an accusation against him. But it is your custom that I release one prisoner for you at the Passover. So do you want me to release for you the king of the Jews?" Then they shouted back, "Not this man, but Barabbas!" (Now Barabbas was a revolutionary.)

The verses we have now read contain four striking points, which are only found in John's narrative of Christ's passion. We need not doubt that there were good reasons why Matthew, Mark, and Luke were not inspired to record them. But they are points of such deep interest, that we should feel thankful that they have been brought forward by John.

The first point that we should notice is the false conscientiousness of our Lord's wicked enemies. We are told that the Jews who brought Christ before Pilate would not go into "the judgment hall, lest they should be defiled; but that they might eat the passover." That was scrupulosity indeed! These hardened men were actually engaged in doing the wickedest act that mortal man ever did. They wanted to kill their own Messiah. And yet at this very time they talked of being "defiled," and were very fastidious about the passover!

The conscience of unconverted men is a very curious part of their moral nature. While in some cases it becomes hardened, seared, and dead, until it feels nothing; in others it becomes morbidly scrupulous about the lesser matters of religion. It is no uncommon thing to find people excessively meticulous about the observance of trifling forms and outward ceremonies, while they are the slaves of degrading sins and detestable immoralities. Robbers and murderers in some countries are extremely strict about confession, and absolution, and prayers to saints. Fastings and self-imposed austerities in Lent, are often followed by excess of worldliness when Lent is over. There is but a step from Lent to Carnival. The attendants at daily services in the morning are not infrequently the patrons of balls and theaters at night. All these are symptoms of spiritual disease, and a heart secretly dissatisfied. Men who know they are wrong in one direction, often struggle to make things right by excess of zeal in another direction. That very zeal is their condemnation.

Let us pray that our consciences may always be enlightened by the Holy Spirit, and that we may be kept from a one-sided and deformed Christianity. A religion that makes a man neglect the weightier matters of daily holiness and separation from the world, and concentrate his whole attention on forms, sacraments, ceremonies, and public services, is to say the least, very suspicious. It may be accompanied by immense zeal and show of earnestness, but it is not sound in the sight of God. The Pharisees paid tithe of mint, anise, and cummin, and compassed sea and land to make proselytes, while they neglected "judgment, mercy, and faith." (Matt. 23:23.) The very Jews who thirsted for Christ's blood were the Jews who feared the defilement of a Roman judgment hall, and made much ado about keeping the passover!

Let their conduct be a beacon to Christians, as long as the world stands. That religion is worth little which does not make us say, "I esteem all Your commandments concerning all things to be right, and I hate every false way." (Ps. 119:128.) That Christianity is worthless which makes us make up for the neglect of heart religion and practical holiness, by an extravagant zeal for man-made ceremonies or outward forms.

276 | J.C. RYLE

The second point that we should notice in these verses, is the account that our Lord Jesus Christ gives of His kingdom. He says, "My kingdom is not of this world." These famous words have been so often perverted and wrested out of their real sense, that their true meaning has been almost buried under a heap of false interpretations. Let us make sure that we know what they mean.

Our Lord's main object in saying "My kingdom is not of this world," was to inform Pilate's mind concerning the true nature of His kingdom, and to correct any false impression he might have received from the Jews. He tells him that He did not come to set up a kingdom which would interfere with the Roman Government. He did not aim at establishing a temporal power, to be supported by armies and maintained by taxes. The only dominion He exercised was over men's hearts, and the only weapons that His subjects employed were spiritual weapons. A kingdom which required neither money nor servants for its support, was one of which the Roman Emperors need not be afraid. In the highest sense it was a kingdom "not of this world."

But our Lord did not intend to teach that the kings of this world have nothing to do with religion, and ought to ignore God altogether in the government of their subjects. No such idea, we may be sure, was in His mind. He knew perfectly well that it was written, "By Me kings reign" (Prov. 8:15), and that kings are as much required to use their influence for God, as the lowest of their subjects. He knew that the prosperity of kingdoms is wholly dependent on the blessing of God, and that kings are as much bound to encourage righteousness and godliness, as to punish unrighteousness and immorality. To suppose that He meant to teach Pilate that, in His judgment, an infidel might be as good a king as a Christian, and a man like Gallio as good a ruler as David or Solomon, is simply absurd.

Let us carefully hold fast the true meaning of our Lord's words in these latter days. Let us never be ashamed to maintain that no Government can expect to prosper which refuses to recognize religion, which deals with its subjects as if they had no souls, and cares not whether they serve God, or Baal, or no God at all. Such a Government will find, sooner or later, that its line of policy is suicidal, and damaging to its best interests. No doubt the kings of this world cannot make men Christians by laws and statutes. But they can encourage and support Christianity, and they will do so if they are wise. The kingdom where there is the most industry, temperance, truthfulness, and honesty, will always be the most prosperous of kingdoms. The king who wants to see these things abound among his subjects, should do all that lies in his power to help Christianity and to discourage irreligion.

The third point that we should notice in these verses is the account that our Lord gives of His own mission. He says, "To this end was I born, and for this cause came I into the world, that I should bear witness unto the truth."

Of course we are not to suppose our Lord meant that this was the only end of His mission. No doubt He spoke with special reference to what He knew was passing through Pilate's mind. He did not come to win a kingdom with the sword, and to gather adherents and followers by force. He came armed with no other weapon but "truth." To testify to fallen man the truth about God, about sin, about the need of a Redeemer, about the nature of holiness—to declare and lift up before man's eyes this long lost and buried "truth,"—was one great purpose of His ministry. He came to be God's witness to a lost and corrupt world. That the world needed such a testimony, He does not shrink from telling the proud Roman Governor. And this is what Paul had in view, when he tells Timothy, that "before Pontius Pilate Christ witnessed a good confession." (1 Tim. 6:13.)

The servants of Christ in every age must remember that our Lord's conduct in this place is meant to be their example. Like Him we are to be witnesses to God's truth, salt in the midst of corruption, light in the midst of darkness, men and women not afraid to stand alone, and to testify for God against the ways of sin and the world. To do so may entail on us much trouble, and even persecution. But the duty is clear and plain. If we love life, if we would keep a good conscience, and be owned by Christ at the last day, we must be "witnesses." It is written, "Whoever shall be ashamed of Me and of my words in this adulterous and sinful generation, of him also shall the Son of man be ashamed, when He comes in the glory of His Father with the holy angels." (Mark 8:38.)

The last point that we should notice in these verses is the question that Pontius Pilate addressed to our Lord. We are told that when our Lord spoke of the truth, the Roman Governor replied, "What is truth?" We are not told with what motive this question was asked, nor does it appear on the face of the narrative that he who asked it waited for an answer. It seems far more likely that the saying was the sarcastic, sneering exclamation of one who did not believe that there was any such thing as "truth." It sounds like the language of one who had heard, from his earliest youth, so many barren speculations about "truth" among Roman and Greek philosophers, that he doubted its very existence. "Truth indeed! What is truth?"

Melancholy as it may appear, there are multitudes in every Christian land whose state of mind is just like that of Pilate. Hundreds, it may be feared among the upper classes, are continually excusing their own irreligion by the specious plea that, like the Roman Governor, they cannot find out "what is truth." They point to the endless controversies of Romanists and Protestants, of High Churchmen and Low Churchmen, of Churchmen and Dissenters, and pretend to say that they do not understand who is right and who is wrong. Sheltered under this favorite excuse, they pass through life without any decided religion, and in this wretched, comfortless state, too often die.

But is it really true that truth cannot be discovered? Nothing of the kind! God never left any honest, diligent inquirer without light and guidance. Pride is one reason why many cannot discover truth. They do not humbly go down on their knees and earnestly ask God to teach them. Laziness is another reason. They do not honestly take pains, and search the Scriptures. The followers of unhappy Pilate, as a rule, do not deal fairly and honestly with their consciences. Their favorite question—What is truth? is nothing better than a pretense and an excuse. The words of Solomon will be found true as long as the world stands—"If you cry after knowledge, and lift up your voice for understanding; if you do you seek her as silver, and search for her as for hid treasures; then shall you understand the fear of the Lord, and find the knowledge of God." (Prov. 2:4, 5.) No man ever followed that advice and missed the way to heaven.

Chapter 19

19:1-16

*T*hen Pilate took Jesus and had him flogged severely. The soldiers braided a crown of thorns and put it on his head, and they clothed him in a purple robe. They came up to him again and again and said, "Hail, king of the Jews!" And they struck him repeatedly in the face.

Again Pilate went out and said to the Jewish religious leaders, "Look, I am bringing him out to you, so that you may know that I find no reason for an accusation against him." So Jesus came outside, wearing the crown of thorns and the purple robe. Pilate said to them, "Look, here is the man!" When the chief priests and their officers saw him, they shouted out, "Crucify him! Crucify him!" Pilate said, "You take him and crucify him! For I find no reason for an accusation against him!" The Jewish religious leaders replied, "We have a law, and according to our law he ought to die, because he claimed to be the Son of God!"

When Pilate heard what they said, he was more afraid than ever, and he went back into the governor's residence and said to Jesus, "Where do you come from?" But Jesus gave him no answer. So Pilate said, "Do you refuse to speak to me? Don't you know I have the authority to release you, and to crucify you?" Jesus replied, "You would have no authority over me at all, unless it was given to you from above. Therefore the one who handed me over to you is guilty of greater sin."

From this point on Pilate tried to release him. But the Jewish religious leaders shouted out, "If you release this man, you are no friend of Caesar! Everyone who claims to be a king opposes Caesar!" When Pilate heard these words he brought Jesus outside and sat down on the judgment seat in the place called "The Stone Pave-

ment" (Gabbatha in Aramaic). (Now it was the day of preparation for the Passover, about noon.) Pilate said to the Jewish religious leaders, "Look, here is your king!"

Then they shouted out, "Away with him! Away with him! Crucify him!" Pilate asked, "Shall I crucify your king?" The high priests replied, "We have no king except Caesar!" Then Pilate handed him over to them to be crucified.

These verses exhibit to our eyes a wonderful picture, a picture which ought to be deeply interesting to all who profess and call themselves Christians. Like every great historical picture, it contains special points on which we should fix our special attention. Above all, it contains three life-like portraits, which we shall find it useful to examine in order.

The first portrait in the picture is that of our Lord JESUS CHRIST himself. We see the Savior of mankind scourged, crowned with thorns, mocked, smitten, rejected by His own people, unjustly condemned by a judge who saw no fault in Him, and finally delivered up to a most painful death. Yet this was He who was the eternal Son of God, whom the Father's countless angels delighted to honor. This was He who came into the world to save sinners, and after living a blameless life for thirty years, spent the last three years of His time on earth in going about doing good, and preaching the Gospel. Surely the sun never shone on a more wondrous sight since the day of its creation!

Let us admire that love of Christ which Paul declares, "passes knowledge," and let us see an endless depth of meaning in the expression. There is no earthly love with which it can be compared, and no standard by which to measure it. It is a love that stands alone. Never let us forget when we ponder this tale of suffering, that Jesus suffered for our sins, the Just for the unjust, that He was wounded for our transgressions and bruised for our iniquities, and that with His stripes we are healed.

Let us diligently follow the example of His patience in all the trials and afflictions of life, and specially in those which may be brought upon us by religion. When He was reviled, He reviled not again; when He suffered, He threatened not, but committed Himself to Him that judges righteously. Let us arm ourselves with the same mind. Let us consider Him who endured such contradiction of sinners without a murmur, and strive to glorify Him by suffering well, no less than by doing well.

The second portrait in the picture before us, is that of the UNBELIEVING JEWS who favored our Lord's death. We see them for three or four long hours obstinately rejecting Pilate's offer to release our Lord—fiercely demanding His crucifixion, savagely claiming His condemnation to death as a right-persistently refusing to acknowledge Him as their King—declaring that they had no King but Caesar—and finally accumulating on their own heads the greater part of the guilt of His murder. Yet, these were the children of Israel and the seed of Abraham, to whom pertained the promises and the Mosaic ceremonial, the temple sacrifices and the temple priesthood. These were men who professed to look for a Prophet like unto Moses, and a son of David who was to set up a kingdom as Messiah. Never, surely, was there such an exhibition of the depth of human wickedness since the day when Adam fell.

Let us mark with fear and trembling the enormous danger of long-continued rejection of light and knowledge. There is such a thing as judicial blindness; and it is the last and sorest judgment which God can send upon men. He who, like Pharaoh and Ahab, is often reproved but refuses to receive reproof, will finally have a heart harder than the nether mill-stone, and a conscience past feeling, and seared as with a hot iron. This was the state of the Jewish nation during the time of our Lord's ministry; and the heading up of their sin was their deliberate rejection of Him, when Pilate desired to let Him go. From such judicial blindness may we all pray to be delivered! There is no worse judgment from God than to be left to ourselves, and given over to our own wicked hearts and the devil. There is no surer way to bring that judgment upon us than to persist in refusing warnings and sinning against light. These words of Solomon are very dreadful—"But since you rejected me when I called and no one gave heed when I stretched out my hand, since you ignored all my advice and would not accept my rebuke, I in turn will laugh at your disaster; I will mock when calamity overtakes you." (Prov. 1:24-26.) Never let it be forgotten, that, like the Jews, we may at length be given up to strong delusion, so that we believe lies, and think that we are doing God service while we are committing sin. (2 Thess. 2:11.)

The third, and last portrait in the picture before us, is that of PONTIUS PILATE. We see a Roman Governor—a man of rank and high position—an imperial representative of the most powerful nation on earth—a man who ought to have been the fountain of justice and equity—halting between two opinions in a case as clear as the sun at noonday. We see him knowing what was right, and yet afraid to act up to his knowledge—convinced in his own conscience that he ought to acquit the prisoner before him, and yet afraid to do it lest he should displease His accusers—sacrificing the claims of justice to the base fear of man—sanctioning from sheer cowardice, an enormous crime-and finally countenancing, from love of man's good opinion, the murder of an innocent person. Never perhaps did human nature make such a contemptible exhibition. Never was there a name so justly handed down to a world's scorn as the name which is embalmed in all our creeds—the name of Pontius Pilate.

Let us learn what miserable creatures great men are, when they have no high principles within them, and no faith in the reality of a God above them. The lowest laborer who has grace and fears God, is a nobler being in the eyes of his Creator than the King, ruler, or statesman, whose first aim it is to please the people. To have one conscience in private and another in public—one rule of duty for our own souls, and another for our public actions—to see clearly what is right before God, and yet for the sake of popularity to do wrong—this may seem to some both right, and politic, and statesmanlike, and wise. But it is a character which no Christian man can ever regard with respect.

Let us pray that our own country may never be without men in high places who have grace to think right, and courage to act up to their knowledge, without truckling to the opinion of men. Those who fear God more than man, and care for pleasing God more than man, are the best rulers of a nation, and in the long run of years are always most respected. Men like Pontius Pilate, who are always trimming and compromising, led by popular opinion instead of leading popular opinion, afraid of doing right if it gives offence, ready to do wrong if it makes them personally popular, such men are the worst governors that a country can have. They are often God's heavy judgment on a nation because of a nation's sins.

19:17-27

So they took Jesus, and carrying his own cross he went out to the place called "The Place of the Skull" (called in Aramaic Golgotha). There they crucified him along with two other men, one on each side, with Jesus in the middle. Pilate also had a notice written and fastened to the cross, which read "Jesus the Nazarene, the king of the Jews." Thus many of the Jewish residents of Jerusalem read this notice, because the place where Jesus was crucified was near the city, and the notice was written in Aramaic, Latin, and Greek. Then the chief priests of the Jews said to Pilate, "Do not write, 'The king of the Jews,' but rather, 'This man said, I am king of the Jews.'" Pilate answered, "What I have written, I have written."

Now when the soldiers crucified Jesus, they took his clothes and made four shares, one for each soldier, and the tunic remained. (Now the tunic was seamless, woven from top to bottom as a single piece.) So the soldiers said to one another, "Let us not tear it, but throw dice to see who will get it." This took place to fulfill the scripture that says, "They divided my garments among them, and for my clothing they threw dice." So the soldiers did these things.

Now standing beside Jesus' cross were his mother, his mother's sister, Mary the wife of Clopas, and Mary Magdalene. So when Jesus saw his mother and the disciple whom he loved standing there, he said to his mother, "Woman, look, here is your son!" He then said to his disciple, "Look, here is your mother!" From that very time the disciple took her into his own home.

He that can read a passage like this without a deep sense of man's debt to Christ, must have a very cold, or a very thoughtless heart. Great must be the love of the Lord Jesus to sinners, when He could voluntarily endure such sufferings for their salvation. Great must be the sinfulness of sin, when such an amount of vicarious suffering was needed in order to provide redemption.

We should observe, first, in this passage, how our Lord had to bear His CROSS when He went forth from the city to Golgotha.

We need not doubt that there was a deep meaning in all this circumstance. For one thing, it was part of that depth of humiliation to which our Lord submitted as our substitute. One portion of the punishment imposed on the vilest criminals, was that they should carry their own cross when they went to execution; and this portion was laid upon our Lord. In the fullest sense He was reckoned a sinner, and counted a curse for our sakes. For another thing, it was a fulfillment of the great type of the sin-offering of the Mosaic law. It is written, that "The bull and goat given as sin offerings, whose blood Aaron brought into the Most Holy Place to make atonement for Israel, will be carried outside the camp to be burned." (Lev. 16:27.) Little did the blinded Jews imagine, when they madly hounded on the Romans to crucify Jesus outside the gates, that they were unconsciously perfecting the mightiest sin-offering that was ever seen. It is written, "So also Jesus suffered and died outside the city gates in order to make his people holy by shedding his own blood." (Heb. 13:12.)

The practical lesson which all true Christians should gather from the fact before us, is one that should be kept in continual remembrance. Like our Master, we must be content to go forth "outside the camp," bearing His reproach. We must come out from the world and be separate, and be willing, if need be, to stand alone. Like our Master, we must be willing to take up our cross daily, and to be persecuted both for our doctrine and our practice. Well would it be for the Church if there was more of the true cross to be seen among Christians! To wear material crosses as an ornament, to place material crosses on churches and tombs, all this is cheap and easy work, and entails no trouble. But to have Christ's cross in our hearts, to carry Christ's cross in our daily walk, to know the fellowship of His sufferings, to be made conformable to His death, to have crucified affections, and live crucified lives-all this needs self-denial; and Christians of this stamp are few and far between. Yet, this, we may be sure, is the only cross-bearing and cross-carrying that does good in the world. The times require less of the cross outwardly and more of the cross within.

We should observe, secondly, in this passage, how our Lord was crucified as a KING. The title placed over our Lord's head made this plain and unmistakable. The reader of Greek, or Latin, or Hebrew, could not fail to see that He who hung on the central cross of the three on Golgotha, had a royal title over His head. The overruling hand of God so ordered matters, that the strong will of Pilate overrode for once the wishes of the malicious Jews. In spite of the chief priests, our Lord was crucified as "the King of the Jews."

It was fit and right that so it should be. Even before our Lord was born, the angel Gabriel declared to the Virgin Mary, "The Lord God shall give unto Him the throne of His father David—and He shall reign over the house of Jacob forever; and of His kingdom there shall be no end." (Luke 1:32, 33.) Almost as soon as He was born, there came wise men from the East, saying, "Where is He that is born King of the Jews?" (Matt. 2:2.) The very week before the crucifixion, the multitude who accompanied our Lord at His triumphal entry into Jerusalem, had cried, "Blessed is the King of Israel who comes in the name of the Lord." (John 12:13.) The current belief of all godly Jews was, that when Messiah, the Son of David came, He would come as a King. A kingdom of heaven and a kingdom of God was continually proclaimed by our Lord throughout His ministry. A King indeed He was, as He told Pilate, of a kingdom utterly unlike the kingdoms of this world, but for all that a true King of a true kingdom, and a Ruler of true subjects. As such He was born. As such He lived. As such He was crucified. And as such He will come again, and reign over the whole earth, King of kings and Lord of lords.

Let us take care that we ourselves know Christ as our King, and that His kingdom is set up within our hearts. They only will find Him their Savior at the last day, who have obeyed Him as King in this world. Let us cheerfully pay Him that tribute of faith, and love, and obedience, which He prizes far above gold. Above all, let us never be afraid to own ourselves His faithful subjects, soldiers, servants and followers, however much He may be despised by the world. A day will soon come when the despised Nazarene who hung on the cross, shall take to Himself His great power and reign, and put down every enemy under His feet. The kingdoms of this world, as Daniel foretold, shall be swept aside, and become the kingdom of our God and of His Christ. And at last every knee shall bow to Him, and every tongue confess that Jesus Christ is Lord.

We should observe, lastly, in these verses, how tenderly our Lord took thought for Mary, His mother. We are told that even in the dreadful agonies of body and mind which our Lord endured, He did not forget her of whom He was born. He mercifully remembered her desolate condition, and the crushing effect of the sorrowful sight before her. He knew that, holy as she was, she was only a woman, and that, as a woman, she must deeply feel the death of such a Son. He therefore commended her to the protection of His best-loved and best-loving disciple, in brief and touching words—"Woman," He said, "behold your son! Then He said to the disciple, Behold your mother! And from that hour that disciple took her unto his own home."

We surely need no stronger proof than we have here, that Mary, the mother of Jesus, was never meant to be honored as divine, or to be prayed to, worshiped, and trusted in, as the friend and patroness of sinners. Common sense points out that she who needed the care and protection of another, was never likely to help men and women to heaven, or to be in any sense a mediator between God and man! It is not too much to say, however painful the assertion, that of all the inventions of the Church of Rome, there never was one more utterly devoid of foundation, both in Scripture and reason, than the doctrine of Mary-worship.

Let us turn from points of controversy to a subject of far more practical importance. Let us take comfort in the thought that we have in Jesus a Savior of matchless tenderness, matchless sympathy, matchless concern for the condition of His believing people. Let us never forget His words, "Whoever shall do the will of God, the same is my brother, and my sister, and mother." (Mark 3:35.) The heart that even on the cross felt for Mary, is a heart that never changes. Jesus never forgets any who love Him, and even in their worst estate remembers their need. No wonder that Peter says, "Casting all your care upon Him; for He cares for you." (1 Pet. 5:7.)

19:28-37

After this Jesus, realizing that by this time everything was completed, said (in order to fulfill the scripture), "I am thirsty!" A jar full of sour wine was there, so they put a sponge soaked in sour wine on a branch of hyssop and lifted it to his mouth. So when he had received the sour wine, Jesus said, "It is completed!" Then he bowed his head and gave up his spirit.

Then, because it was the day of preparation, so that the bodies should not stay on the crosses on the Sabbath (for that Sabbath was an especially important one), the Jewish religious authorities asked Pilate to have the legs of the crucified men broken and the bodies taken down. So the soldiers came and broke the legs of the two men who had been crucified with Jesus, first the one and then the other. But when they came to Jesus and saw that he was already dead, they did not break his legs. But one of the soldiers pierced his side with a spear, and blood and water flowed out immediately. And the person who saw it has testified (and his testimony is true, and he knows that he is telling the truth), so that you also may believe. For these things happened so that the scripture would be fulfilled, "Not a bone of his will be broken." And again another scripture says, "They will look on the one whom they have pierced."

This part of John's narrative of Christ's passion, contains points of deep interest, which are silently passed over by Matthew, Mark, and Luke. The reason of this silence we are not told. Suffice it for us to remember that, both in what they recorded and in what they did not record, all four Evangelists wrote by inspiration of God.

Let us mark, for one thing, in these verses, the frequent fulfillments of prophetic Scripture throughout every part of Christ's crucifixion. Three different predictions are specially mentioned, in Exodus, Psalms, and Zechariah, which received their accomplishment at the cross. Others, as every well-informed Bible-reader knows, might easily be added. All combine to prove one and the same thing. They prove that the death of our Lord Jesus Christ at Golgotha was a thing foreseen and predetermined by God. Hundreds of years before the crucifixion, every part of the solemn transaction was arranged in the Divine counsels, and the minutest particulars were revealed to the Prophets. From first to last it was a thing foreknown, and every portion of it was in accordance with a settled plan and design. In the highest, fullest sense, when Christ died, He "died according to the Scriptures." (1 Cor. 15:3.)

We need not hesitate to regard such fulfillments of prophecy as strong evidence of the Divine authority of God's Word. The Prophets foretell not only Christ's death, but the particulars of His death. It is impossible to explain so many accomplishments of predicted circumstances upon any other theory. To talk of luck, chance, and accidental coincidence, as sufficient explanation, is preposterous and absurd. The only rational account is the inspiration of God. The Prophets who foretold the particulars of the crucifixion, were inspired by Him who foresees the end from the beginning; and the books they wrote under His inspiration ought not to be read as human compositions, but Divine. Great indeed are the difficulties of all who pretend to deny the inspiration of the Bible. It really requires more unreasoning faith to be an infidel than to be a Christian. The man who regards the repeated fulfillments of minute prophecies about Christ's death, such as the prophecies about His dress, His thirst, His pierced side, and His bones, as the result of chance, and not of design, must indeed be a credulous man.

We should mark, secondly, in these verses, the peculiarly solemn saying which came from our Lord's lips just before He died. John relates that "when He had received the vinegar, He said, it is finished; and He bowed His head and gave up the spirit." It is surely not too much to say, that of all the seven famous sayings of Christ on the cross, none is more remarkable than this, which John alone has recorded.

The precise meaning of this wondrous expression, "It is finished," is a point which the Holy Spirit has not thought good to reveal to us. There is a depth about it, we must all instinctively feel, which man has probably no line to fathom. Yet there is perhaps no irreverence in conjecturing the thoughts that were in our Lord's mind, when the word was spoken. The finishing of all the known and unknown sufferings which He came to endure, as our Substitute-the finishing of the ceremonial law, which He came to wind up and fulfill, as the true Sacrifice for sin—the finishing of the many prophecies, which He came to accomplish—the finishing of the great work of man's redemption, which was now close at hand—all this, we need not doubt, our Lord had in view when He said, "It is finished." There may have been more behind, for anything we know. But in handling the language of such a Being as our Savior, on such an occasion, and at so mysterious a crisis of His history, it is well to be cautious.

"The place whereon we stand is holy ground."

One comfortable thought, at all events, stands out most clearly on the face of this famous expression. We rest our souls on a "finished work," if we rest them on the work of Jesus Christ the Lord. We need not fear that either sin, or Satan, or law shall condemn us at the last day. We may lean back on the thought, that we have a Savior who has done all, paid all, accomplished all, performed all that is necessary for our salvation. We may take up the challenge of the Apostle, "Who is he that condemns? It is Christ who died-yes, rather that is risen again; who is even at the right hand of God; who also makes intercession for us." (Rom. 8:34.) When we look at our own works, we may well be ashamed of their imperfections. But when we look at the finished work of Christ, we may feel peace. We "are complete in Him," if we believe. (Colos. 2:10.)

We should mark, lastly, in these verses, the reality and truth of Christ's death. We are told that "one of the soldiers with a spear pierced His side, and blood and water flowed out." This incident, small as it may seem at first sight, supplies probable proof that the heart of our blessed Lord was pierced, and that life was consequently extinct. He did not merely faint, or swoon away, or become insensible, as some have dared to insinuate. His heart actually ceased to beat, and He actually died. Great, indeed, was the importance of this fact. We must all see, on a moment's reflection, that without a real death there could be no real sacrifice; that without a real death there could be no real resurrection; and that without a real death and real resurrection, the whole of Christianity is a house built on sand, and has no foundation at all. Little indeed did that reckless Roman soldier dream that he was a mighty helper of our holy religion, when he thrust his spear into our Lord's side.

That the "blood and water" mentioned in this place had a deep spiritual meaning, we can hardly doubt. John himself seems to refer to them in his first Epistle, as highly significant. "This is He that came by water and blood." (1 John 5:6.) The Church in every age has been of one mind in holding that they are emblems of spiritual things. Yet the precise meaning of the blood and water is a subject about which Christians have never agreed, and perhaps will never agree until the Lord returns.

The favorite theory that the blood and water mean the two Sacraments, however plausible and popular, may be reasonably regarded as somewhat destitute of solid foundation. Baptism and the Lord's Supper were ordinances already in existence when our Lord died, and they needed no reappointing. It is surely not necessary to drag in these two blessed Sacraments on every occasion, and to insist on thrusting them forward, as the hidden sense of every disputed text where the number "two" is mentioned. Such pertinacious application of hard places in Scripture to Baptism and the Lord's Supper does no real good, and brings no real honor to the Sacraments. It is questionable whether it does not tend to vulgarize them, and bring them into contempt.

The true meaning of the blood and water is probably to be sought in the famous prophecy of Zechariah, where he says, "In that day there shall be a fountain opened to the house of David, and to the inhabitants of Jerusalem, for sin and uncleanness." (Zech. 13:1.) When was that fountain so truly and really opened as in the hour when Christ died? What emblem of atonement and purification was so well known to the Jews as blood and water? Why then should we hesitate to believe that the flow of "blood and water" from our Lord's side was a significant declaration to the Jewish nation, that the true fountain for sin was at length thrown open, and that henceforth sinners might come boldly to Christ for pardon, and wash and be clean? This interpretation, at any rate, deserves serious thought and consideration.

Whatever view we take of the blood and water, let us make sure that we ourselves are "washed and made white in the blood of the Lamb." (Rev. 7:14.) It will matter nothing at the last day, that we held during life the most exalted view of the sacraments, if we never came to Christ by faith, and never had personal dealings with Him. Faith in Christ is the one thing needful. "He that has the Son has life, and he that has not the Son of God has not life." (1 John 5:12.)

19:38-42

After this Joseph of Arimathea, a disciple of Jesus (but secretly, because he feared the Jewish authorities), asked Pilate if he could remove the body of Jesus. Pilate gave him permission, so he went and took the body away. Nicodemus, the man who had previously come to Jesus at night, accompanied Joseph, carrying a mixture of myrrh and aloes weighing about seventy-five pounds. Then they took Jesus' body and wrapped it, with the aromatic spices, in strips of linen cloth according to Jewish burial customs. Now at the place where Jesus was crucified there was a garden, and in the garden was a new tomb where no one had yet been buried. So because it was the Jewish day of preparation and the tomb was nearby, they placed Jesus' body there.

There is a peculiar interest attached to these five verses of Scripture. They introduce us to a stranger, of whom we never heard before. They bring in an old friend, whose name is known wherever the Bible is read. They describe the most important funeral that ever took place in this world. From each of these three points of interest we may learn a very profitable lesson.

We learn, for one thing, from these verses, that there are some true Christians in the world of whom very little is known. The case of Joseph of Arimathea teaches this very plainly. Here is a man named among the friends of Christ, whose very name we never find elsewhere in the New Testament, and whose history, both before and after this crisis, is completely withheld from the Church. He comes forward to do honor to Christ, when the Apostles had forsaken Him and fled. He cares for Him and delights to do Him service, even when dead—not because of any miracle which he saw Him do, but out of free and gratuitous love. He does not hesitate to confess himself one of Christ's friends, at a time when Jews and Romans alike had condemned Him as a malefactor, and put Him to death. Surely the man who could do such things must have had strong faith! Can we wonder that, wherever the Gospel is preached, throughout the whole world, this pious action of Joseph is told of as a memorial of him?

Let us hope and believe that there are many Christians in every age, who, like Joseph, are the Lord's hidden servants, unknown to the Church and the world, but well known to God. Even in Elijah's time there were seven thousand in Israel who had never bowed the knee to Baal, although the desponding prophet knew nothing of it. Perhaps, at this very day, there are saints in the back streets of some of our great towns, or in the lanes of some of our country parishes, who make no noise in the world, and yet love Christ and are loved by Him. Ill-health, or poverty, or the daily cares of some laborious calling, render it impossible for them to come forward in public; and so they live and die comparatively unknown. Yet the last day may show an astonished world that some of these very people, like Joseph, honored Christ as much as any on earth, and that their names were written in heaven. After all, it is special circumstances that bring to the surface special Christians. It is not those who make the greatest show in the Church, who are always found the closest friends of Christ.

We learn, for another thing, from these verses, that there are some servants of Christ whose latter end is better than their beginning. The case of Nicodemus teaches that lesson very plainly. The only man who dared to help Joseph in his holy work of burying our Lord, was one who at first "came to Jesus by night," and was nothing better than an ignorant inquirer after truth. At a later period in our Lord's ministry we find this same Nicodemus coming forward with somewhat more boldness, and raising in the Council of the Pharisees the question, "Does our law judge any man, before it hear him, and know what he does?" (John 7:51.) Finally, we see him in the passage before us, ministering to our Lord's dead body, and not ashamed to take an active part in giving to the despised Nazarene an honorable burial. How great the contrast between the man who timidly crept into the Lord's lodging to ask a question, and the man who brought a hundred pounds weight of myrrh and aloes to anoint His dead body! Yet it was the same Nicodemus. How great may be a man's growth in grace, and faith, and knowledge, and courage, in the short space of three years.

We shall do well to store up these things in our minds, and to remember the case of Nicodemus, in forming our estimate of other people's religion. We must not condemn others as graceless and godless, because they do not see the whole truth at once, and only reach decided Christianity by slow degrees. The Holy Spirit always leads believers to the same foundation truths, and into the same highway to heaven. In these there is invariable uniformity. But the Holy Spirit does not always lead believers through the same experience, or at the same rate of speed. In this there is much diversity in His operations.

He that says conversion is a needless thing, and that an unconverted man may be saved, is undoubtedly under a strange delusion. But he that says that no one is converted except he becomes a full-blown and established Christian in a single day, is no less under a delusion. Let us not judge others rashly and hastily. Let us believe that a man's beginnings in religion may be very small, and yet his latter end may greatly increase. Has a man real grace? Has he within him the genuine work of the Spirit? This is the grand question. If he has, we may safely hope that his grace will grow, and we should deal with him gently, and bear with him charitably, though at present he may be a mere babe in spiritual attainments. The life in a helpless infant is as real and true a thing as the life in a full-grown man—the difference is only one of degree.

"Who has despised the day of small things?" (Zech. 4:10.) The very Christian who begins his religion with a timid night-visit, and an ignorant inquiry, may stand forward alone one day, and confess Christ boldly in the full light of the sun.

We learn, lastly, from these verses, that the burial of the dead is an act which God sanctions and approves. We need not doubt that this is part of the lesson which the passage before us was meant to convey to our minds. Of course, it supplies unanswerable evidence that our Lord really died, and afterwards really rose again; but it also teaches that, when the body of a Christian is dead, there is fitness in burying it with decent honor. It is not for nothing that the burials of Abraham, and Isaac, and Jacob, and Joseph, and Moses are carefully recorded in holy writ. It is not for nothing that we are told that John the Baptist was laid in a tomb; and that "devout men carried Stephen to his burial, and made great lamentation over him." (Acts 8:2.) It is not for nothing that we are told so particularly about the burial of Christ.

The true Christian need never be ashamed of regarding a funeral with peculiar reverence and solemnity. It is the body, which may be the instrument of committing the greatest sins, or of bringing the greatest glory to God. It is the body, which the eternal Son of God honored by dwelling in it for thirty and three years, and finally dying in our stead. It is the body, with which He rose again and ascended up into heaven. It is the body, in which He sits at the right hand of God, and represents us before the Father, as our Advocate and Priest. It is the body, which is now the temple of the Holy Spirit, while the believer lives. It is the body, which will rise again, when the last trumpet sounds, and, reunited to the soul, will live in heaven to all eternity. Surely, in the face of such facts as these, we never need suppose that reverence bestowed on the burial of the body is reverence thrown away.

Let us leave the subject with one word of caution. Let us take care that we do not regard a sumptuous funeral as an atonement for a life wasted in carelessness and sin. We may bury a man in the most expensive style, and spend thousands of dollars in mourning. We may place over his grave a costly marble stone, and inscribe on it a flattering epitaph. But all this will not save our souls or his. The turning point at the last day will not be how we are buried, but whether we were "buried with Christ," and repented and believed. (Rom. 6:4.) Better a thousand times to die the death of the righteous, have a lowly grave and a pauper's funeral, than to die graceless, and lie under a marble tomb!

Chapter 20

20:1-10

Now very early on the first day of the week, while it was still dark, Mary Magdalene came to the tomb and saw that the stone had been moved away from the entrance. So she went running to Simon Peter and the other disciple whom Jesus loved and told them, "They have taken the Lord from the tomb, and we don't know where they have put him!" Then Peter and the other disciple set out to go to the tomb. The two were running together, but the other disciple ran faster than Peter and reached the tomb first. He bent down and saw the strips of linen cloth lying there, but he did not go in. Then Simon Peter, who had been following him, arrived and went right into the tomb. He saw the strips of linen cloth lying there, and the face cloth, which had been around Jesus' head, not lying with the strips of linen cloth but rolled up in a place by itself. Then the other disciple who had reached the tomb first came in, and he saw and believed. (For they did not yet understand the scripture that Jesus must rise from the dead.) So the disciples went back to their homes.

The chapter we have now begun takes us from Christ's death to Christ's resurrection. Like Matthew, Mark, and Luke, John dwells on these two great events with peculiar fullness and particularity. And we need not wonder. The whole of saving Christianity hinges on the two facts, that Christ died for our sins, and rose again for our justification. The chapter before our eyes deserves special attention. Of all the four evangelists, none supplies such deeply interesting evidence of the resurrection, as the disciple whom Jesus loved.

We are taught in the passage before us, that those who love Christ most are those who have received most benefit from him.

The first whom John names among those who came to Christ's sepulcher, is Mary Magdalene. The history of this faithful woman, no doubt, is hidden in much obscurity. A vast amount of needless ridicule has been heaped upon her memory, as if she was once an habitual sinner against the seventh commandment. Yet there is literally no evidence whatever that she was anything of the kind! But we are distinctly told that she was one out of whom the Lord had cast "seven devils" (Mark 16:9; Luke 8:2)—one who had been subjected in a peculiar way to Satan's possession—and one whose gratitude to our Lord for deliverance was a gratitude that knew no bounds. In short, of all our Lord's followers on earth, none seem to have loved Him so much as Mary Magdalene. None felt that they owed so much to Christ. None felt so strongly that there was nothing too great to do for Christ. Hence, as Andrews beautifully puts it—"She was last at His cross, and first at His grave. She stayed longest there, and was soonest here. She could not rest until she was up to seek Him. She sought Him while it was yet dark, even before she had light to seek Him by." In a word, having received much, she loved much; and loving much, she did much, in order to prove the reality of her love.

The case before us throws broad and clear light on a question, which ought to be deeply interesting to every true-hearted servant of Christ. How is it that many who profess and call themselves Christians, do so little for the Savior whose name they bear? How is it that many, whose faith and grace it would be uncharitable to deny, work so little, give so little, say so little, take so little pains, to promote Christ's cause, and bring glory to Christ in the world? These questions admit of only one answer. It is a low sense of debt and obligation to Christ, which is the account of the whole matter. Where sin is not felt at all, nothing is done; and where sin is little felt, little is done. The man who is deeply conscious of his own guilt and corruption, and deeply convinced that without the death and intercession of Christ he would sink deservedly into the lowest hell, this is the man who will spend and be spent for Jesus, and think that he can never do enough to show forth His praise. Let us daily pray that we may see the sinfulness of sin, and the amazing grace of Christ, more clearly and distinctly. Then, and then only, shall we cease to be cool, and lukewarm, and slovenly in our work for Jesus. Then, and then only, shall we understand such burning zeal as that of Mary; and comprehend what Paul meant when he said, "The love of Christ constrains us; because we thus judge that if One died for all, then were all dead—and that He died for all, that they which live should not henceforth live unto themselves, but unto Him which died for them, and rose again." (2 Cor. 5:14, 15.)

We are taught, secondly, in these verses, that there are widely different temperaments in different believers.

This is a point which is curiously brought out in the conduct of Peter and John, when Mary Magdalene told them that the Lord's body was gone. We are told that they both ran to the sepulcher; but John, the disciple whom Jesus loved, outran Peter, and reached the empty grave first. Then comes out the difference between the two men. John, of the two more gentle, quiet, tender, reserved, retiring, deep-feeling, stooped down and looked in, but went no further. Peter, more hot, and zealous, and impulsive, and fervent, and forward, cannot be content without going down into the sepulcher, and actually seeing with his own eyes. Both, we may be sure, were deeply attached to our Lord. The hearts of both, at this critical juncture, were full of hopes, and fears, and anxieties, and expectations, all tangled together. Yet each behaves in his own characteristic fashion. We need not doubt that these things were intentionally written for our learning.

Let us learn, from the case before us, to make allowances for wide varieties in the inward character of believers. To do so will save us much trouble in the journey of life, and prevent many an uncharitable thought. Let us not judge brethren harshly, and set them down in a low place, because they do not see or feel things exactly as we see and feel, and because things do not affect or strike them just as they affect and strike us. The flowers in the Lord's garden are not all of one color and one scent, though they are all planted by one Spirit. The subjects of His kingdom are not all exactly of one tone and temperament, though they all love the same Savior, and are written in the same book of life. The Church of Christ has some in its ranks who are like Peter, and some who are like John; and a place for all, and a work for all to do. Let us love all who love Christ in sincerity, and thank God that they love Him at all. The great thing is to love Jesus.

We are taught, finally, in these verses, that there may be much ignorance even in true believers.

This is a point which is brought out here with singular force and distinctness. John himself, the writer of this Gospel, records of himself and his companion Peter, "As yet they knew not the Scripture, that He must rise again from the dead." How truly incredible this seems! For three long years these two leading Apostles had heard our Lord speak of His own resurrection as a fact, and yet they had not understood Him. Again and again He had staked the truth of His Messiahship on His rising from the dead, and yet they had never taken in His meaning. We little realize the power over the mind which is exercised by wrong teaching in childhood, and by early prejudices imbibed in our youth. Surely the Christian minister has little right to complain of ignorance among his hearers, when he marks the ignorance of Peter and John, under the teaching of Christ Himself.

After all we must remember that true grace, and not head knowledge, is the one thing needful. We are in the hands of a merciful and compassionate Savior, who passes by and pardons much ignorance, when He sees "a heart right in the sight of God." Some things indeed we must know, and without knowing them we cannot be saved. Our own sinfulness and guilt, the office of Christ as a Savior, the necessity of repentance and faith—such things as these are essential to salvation. But he that knows these things may, in other respects, be a very ignorant man. In fact, the extent to which one man may have grace together with much ignorance, and another may have much knowledge and yet no grace, is one of the greatest mysteries in religion, and one which the last day alone will unfold. Let us then seek knowledge, and be ashamed of ignorance. But above all let us make sure that, like Peter and John, we have grace and right hearts.

20:11-18

But Mary stood outside the tomb weeping. As she wept, she bent down and looked into the tomb. And she saw two angels in white sitting where Jesus' body had been lying, one at the head and one at the feet. They said to her,

"Woman, why are you weeping?" Mary replied, "They have taken my Lord away, and I do not know where they have put him!" When she had said this, she turned around and saw Jesus standing there, but she did not know that it was Jesus.

Jesus said to her, "Woman, why are you weeping? Who are you looking for?" Because she thought he was the gardener, she said to him, "Sir, if you have carried him away, tell me where you have put him, and I will take him." Jesus said to her, "Mary." She turned and said to him in Aramaic, "Rabboni" (which means Teacher). Jesus replied, "Do not touch me, for I have not yet ascended to my Father. Go to my brothers and tell them, 'I am ascending to my Father and your Father, to my

God and your God.'" Mary Magdalene came and informed the disciples, "I have seen the Lord!" And she told them what Jesus had said to her.

The interview between the Lord Jesus and Mary Magdalene immediately after His resurrection, described in these verses, is a narrative peculiar to John. No other Evangelist has been inspired to record it. Of all the accounts of the appearances of our Lord, after He rose from the dead, none perhaps is so affecting and touching as this. He that can read this simple story without a deep interest, must have a very cold and unfeeling heart.

We see, first, in these verses, that those who love Christ most diligently and perseveringly, are those who receive most privileges from Christ's hand. It is a touching fact, and one to be carefully noted, that Mary Magdalene would not leave the sepulcher, when Peter and John went away to their own home. Love to her gracious Master would not let her leave the place where He had been lain. Where He was now she could not tell. What had become of Him she did not know. But love made her linger about the empty tomb, where Joseph and Nicodemus had recently laid Him. Love made her honor the last place where His precious body had been seen by mortal eyes. And her love reaped a rich reward. She saw the angels whom Peter and John had never observed. She actually heard them speak, and had soothing words addressed to her. She was the first to see our Lord after He rose from the dead, the first to hear His voice, the first to hold conversation with Him. Can anyone doubt that this was written for our learning? Wherever the Gospel is preached throughout the world, this little incident testifies that those who honor Christ will be honored by Christ.

As it was in the morning of the first Resurrection day, so will it be as long as the Church stands. The great principle contained in the passage before us, will hold good until the Lord comes again. All believers have not the same degree of faith, or hope, or knowledge, or courage, or wisdom; and it is vain to expect it. But it is a certain fact that those who love Christ most fervently, and cleave to Him most closely, will always enjoy most communion with Him, and feel most of the witness of the Spirit in their hearts. It is precisely those who wait on the Lord, in the temper of Mary Magdalene, to whom the Lord will reveal Himself most fully, and make them know and feel more than others. To know Christ is good; but to "know that we know Him" is far better.

We see, secondly, in these verses, that the fears and sorrows of believers are often quite needless. We are told that Mary stood at the sepulcher weeping, and wept as if nothing could comfort her. She wept when the angels spoke to her; "Woman," they said, "why are you weeping?" She was weeping still when our Lord spoke to her—"Woman," He also said,"why are you weeping?" And the burden of her complaint was always the same—"They have taken away my Lord, and I know not where they have laid Him." Yet all this time her risen Master was close to her, with "body, flesh, and bones, and all things pertaining to the perfection of man's nature." Her tears were needless. Her anxiety was unnecessary. Like Hagar in the wilderness, she had a well of water by her side, but she had not eyes to see it.

What thoughtful Christian can fail to see, that we have here a faithful picture of many a believer's experience? How often we are anxious when there is no just cause for anxiety! How often we mourn over the absence of things which in reality are within our grasp, and even at our right hand! Two-thirds of the things we fear in life never happen at all, and two-thirds of the tears we shed are thrown away, and shed in vain. Let us pray for more faith and patience, and allow more time for the full development of God's purposes. Let us believe that things are often working together for our peace and joy, which seem at one time to contain nothing but bitterness and sorrow. Old Jacob said at one time of his life, "all these things are against me" (Gen. 42:36); yet he lived to see Joseph again, rich and prosperous, and to thank God for all that had happened. If Mary had found the seal of the tomb unbroken, and her Master's body lying cold within, she might well have wept! The very absence of the body which made her weep, was a token for good, and a cause of joy for herself and all mankind.

We see, thirdly, in these verses, what low and earthly thoughts of Christ may creep into the mind of a true believer. It seems impossible to gather any other lesson from the solemn words which our Lord addressed to Mary Magdalene, when He said, "Touch Me not; for I am not yet ascended to my Father." No doubt the language is somewhat mysterious, and ought to be delicately and reverently handled. Yet it is only reasonable to suppose that the first surprise, and the reaction from great sorrow to great joy, was more than the mind of Mary could bear. She was only a woman, though a holy and faithful woman. It is highly probable that, in the first excess of her joy, she threw herself at our Lord's feet, and made greater demonstrations of feeling than were seemly or becoming. Very likely she behaved too much like one who thought all must be right if she had her Lord's bodily presence, and all must be wrong in His bodily absence. This was not the highest style of faith. She acted, in short, like one who forgot that her Master was God as well as man. She made too little of His divinity, and too much of His humanity. And hence she called forth our Lord's gentle rebuke, "Touch Me not! There is no need of this excessive demonstration of feeling. I am not yet ascending to my Father for forty days-your present duty is not to linger at my feet, but to go and tell my brethren that I have risen. Think of the feelings of others as well as of your own."

After all, we must confess that the fault of this holy woman was one into which Christians have always been too ready to fall. In every age there has been a tendency in the minds of many, to make too much of Christ's bodily presence, and to forget that He is not a mere earthly friend, but one who is "God over all, blessed forever," as well as man. The pertinacity with which Romanists and their allies cling to the doctrine of Christ's real corporal presence in the Lord's Supper, is only another exhibition of Mary's feeling when she wanted Christ's body, or no Christ at all. Let us pray for a right judgment in this matter, as in all other things concerning our Lord's person. Let us be content to have Christ dwelling in our hearts by faith, and present when two or three are met in His name, and to wait for the real presence of Christ's body until He comes again. What we really need is not His literal flesh, but His Spirit. It is not for nothing that it is written, "It is the Spirit that quickens—the flesh profits nothing." "If we have known Christ after the flesh, yet henceforth know we Him no more." (John 6:63; 2 Cor. 5:16.)

We see, lastly, in these verses, how kindly and graciously our Lord speaks of His disciples. He bids Mary Magdalene carry a message to them as "His brethren." He bids her tell those who His Father was their Father, and His God their God. It was but three days before that they had all forsaken Him shamefully, and fled. Yet this merciful Master speaks as if all was forgiven and forgotten. His first thought is to bring back the wanderers, to bind up the wounds of their consciences, to reanimate their courage, to restore them to their former place. This was indeed a love that passes knowledge. To trust deserters, and to show confidence in backsliders, was a compassion which man can hardly understand. So true is that word of David—"Like as a Father pities his children, so the Lord pities those who fear Him. For He knows our frame; He remembers that we are dust." (Psalm 103:13, 14.)

Let us leave the passage with the comfortable reflection that Jesus Christ never changes. He is the same yesterday, today, and forever. As He dealt with His erring disciples in the morning of His resurrection, so will He deal with all who believe and love Him, until He comes again. When we wander out of the way He will bring us back. When we fall He will raise us again. But he will never break His royal word—"Him that comes to Me I will in no wise cast out." (John 6:37.) The saints in glory will have one anthem in which every voice and heart will join—"He has not dealt with us after our sins, nor rewarded us according to our iniquities." (Psalm 103:10.)

20:19-23

On the evening of that day, the first day of the week, the disciples had gathered together and locked the doors of the place for fear of the Jewish authorities. Jesus came and stood among them and said to them, "Peace be with you." When he had said this, he showed them his hands and his side. Then the disciples rejoiced when they saw the Lord. So Jesus said to them again, "Peace be with you. Just as the Father has sent me, I also send you." And after he said this, he breathed on them and said, "Receive the Holy Spirit. If you forgive anyone's sins, they are forgiven; if you retain anyone's sins, they are retained."

The verses we have now read contain things hard to be understood. Like all the events which followed our Lord's resurrection, there is much in the facts before us which is mysterious, and requires reverent handling. Our Lord's actions, in suddenly appearing among the disciples when the doors were closed, and in breathing upon them, might soon draw us into unprofitable speculation. It is easy, in such cases, to darken counsel by words without knowledge. We shall find it safer and wiser to confine our attention to points which are plain and instructive.

We should observe, for one thing, the remarkable language with which our Lord greeted the apostles, when He first met them after His resurrection. Twice over he addressed them with the kindly words, "Peace be unto you." We may dismiss as untenable, in all probability, the cold and cautious suggestion, that this was nothing better than an unmeaning phrase of courtesy. He who "spoke as never man spoke," said nothing without meaning. He spoke, we may be sure, with special reference to the state of mind of the eleven apostles, with special reference to the events of the last few days, and with special reference to their future ministry. "Peace" and not blame—"peace" and not fault-finding—"peace" and not rebuke—was the first word which this little company heard from their Master's lips, after He left the tomb.

It was right and fitting, that it should be so, and in full harmony with things that had gone before. "Peace on earth" was the song of the heavenly host, when Christ was born. Peace and rest of soul, was the general subject that Christ continually preached for three years. Peace, and not riches, had been the great legacy which He had left with the eleven the night before His crucifixion. Surely it was in full keeping with all the tenor of our Lord's dealings, that, when He revisited His little company of disciples after His resurrection, His first word should be "Peace." It was a word that would soothe and calm their minds.

Peace, we may safely conclude, was intended by our Lord to be the keynote to the Christian ministry. That same peace which was so continually on the lips of the Master, was to be the grand subject of the teaching of His disciples. Peace between God and man through the precious blood of atonement-peace between man and man through the infusion of grace and charity—to spread such peace as this was to be the work of the Church. Any religion, like that of Mahomet, who made converts with the sword, is not from above, but from beneath. Any form of Christianity which burns men at the stake, in order to promote its own success, carries about with it the stamp of an apostasy. That is the truest and best religion which does most to spread real, true peace.

We should observe, for another thing, in these verses, the remarkable evidence which our Lord supplied of His own resurrection. He graciously appealed to the senses of His trembling disciples. He showed them "His hands and His side." He bade them see with their own eyes, that He had a real material body, and that He was not a spirit or a spirit. "Handle Me and see," were His words, according to Luke—"a spirit has not flesh and bone, as you see Me have." Great indeed was the condescension of our blessed Master, in thus coming down to the feeble faith of the eleven Apostles! But great also was the principle which He established for the use of His Church in every age, until He returns. That principle is, that our Master requires us to believe nothing is contrary to our senses. Things above our reason we must expect to find in a religion that comes from God, but not things contrary to reason.

Let us lay firm hold on this great principle, and never forget to use it. Specially let us take care that we use it, in estimating the effect of the sacraments and the work of the Holy Spirit. To require people to believe that men have the quickening power of the Holy Spirit, when our eyes tell us they are living in habitual carelessness and sin, or that the bread and wine in the Lord's Supper are Christ's real body and blood, when our senses tell us they are still bread and wine—this is to require more belief than Christ ever required of His disciples. It is to require that which is flatly contradictory to reason and common sense. Such requisitions Christ never made. Let us not try to be wiser than our Lord.

We should observe, lastly, in these verses, the remarkable commission which our Lord conferred upon His eleven Apostles. We are told that He said, "Just as the Father has sent me, I also send you. And after he said this, he breathed on them and said, Receive the Holy Spirit. If you forgive anyone's sins, they are forgiven; if you retain anyone's sins, they are retained." It is vain to deny that the true sense of these solemn words has been for centuries a subject of controversy and dispute. It is useless perhaps to expect that the controversy will ever be closed. The utmost that we can hope to do with the passage is to supply a probable exposition.

It seems then highly probable that our Lord in this place solemnly commissioned His Apostles to go into all the world, and preach the Gospel as He had preached it. He also conferred on them the power of declaring with peculiar authority whose sins were forgiven, and whose sins were not forgiven. That this is precisely what the Apostles did is a simple matter of fact, which any one may verify for himself by reading the book of the Acts. When Peter proclaimed to the Jews, "Repent, and be converted,"—and when Paul declared at Antioch of Iconium—"to you is the word of this salvation sent"-"Through this man is preached the forgiveness of sins, and by Him all that believe are justified"—they were doing what this passage commissioned the Apostles to do. They were opening with authority the door of salvation, and inviting with authority all sinners to enter in by it and be saved. (Acts 3:19; 13:26-38.) It seems, on the other hand, most improbable that our Lord intended in this verse to sanction the practice of private absolution, after private confession of sins.

Whatever some may please to say, there is not a single instance to be found in the Acts of any Apostle using such absolution after confession. Above all, there is not a trace in the two pastoral Epistles to Timothy and Titus, of such confession and absolution being recommended, or thought desirable. In short, whatever men may say about private priestly absolution, there is not a single precedent for it in God's Word.

Let us leave the whole passage with a deep sense of the importance of the minister's office, when that office is duly exercised according to the mind of Christ. No higher honor can be imagined than that of being Christ's ambassadors, and proclaiming in Christ's name the forgiveness of sins to a lost world. But let us ever beware of investing the ministerial office with one jot more of power and authority than Christ conferred upon it. To treat ministers as being in any sense mediators between God and man, is to rob

Christ of His prerogative, to hide saving truth from sinners, and to exalt ordained men to a position which they are totally unqualified to fill.

20:24-31

Now Thomas (called Didymus), one of the twelve, was not with them when Jesus came. The other disciples told him, "We have seen the Lord!" But he replied, "Unless I see the wounds from the nails in his hands, and put my finger into the wounds from the nails, and put my hand into his side, I will never believe it!"

Eight days later the disciples were again together in the house, and Thomas was with them. Although the doors were locked, Jesus came and stood among them and said, "Peace be with you!" Then he said to Thomas, "Put your finger here, and examine my hands. Extend your hand and put it into my side. Do not continue in your unbelief, but believe." Thomas replied to him, "My Lord and my God!" Jesus said to him, "Have you believed because you have seen me? Blessed are the people who have not seen and yet have believed."

Now Jesus performed many other miraculous signs in the presence of his disciples that are not recorded in this book. But these are recorded so that you may believe that Jesus is the Christ, the Son of God, and that by believing you may have life in his name.

The story of the unbelief of Thomas, related in these verses, is a narrative peculiar to the Gospel of John. For wise and good reasons it is passed over in silence by Matthew, Mark, and Luke, and was probably not given to the world until Thomas was dead. It is precisely one of those passages of Scripture which supply strong internal evidence of the honesty of the inspired writers. If impostors and deceivers had compiled the Bible for their own private advantage, they would never have told mankind that one of the first founders of a new religion behaved as Thomas here did.

We should mark, for one thing, in these verses, how much Christians may lose by not regularly attending the assemblies of God's people. Thomas was absent the first time that Jesus appeared to the disciples after His resurrection, and consequently Thomas missed a blessing. Of course we have no certain proof that the absence of the Apostle could not admit of explanation. Yet, at such a crisis in the lives of the eleven, it seems highly improbable that he had any good reason for not being with his brethren, and it is far more likely that in some way he was to blame. One thing, at any rate, is clear and plain. By being absent he was kept in suspense and unbelief a whole week, while all around him were rejoicing in the thought of a risen Lord. It is difficult to suppose that this would have been the case, if there had not been a fault somewhere. It is hard to avoid the suspicion that Thomas was absent when he might have been present.

We shall all do well to remember the charge of the Apostle Paul—"Forsake not the assembling of yourselves together, as the manner of some is." (Heb. 10:25.) Never to be absent from God's house on Sundays, without good reason—never to miss the Lord's Supper when administered in our own congregation—never to let our place be empty when means of grace are going on, this is one way to be a growing and prosperous Christian. The very sermon that we needlessly miss, may contain a precious word in season for our souls. The very assembly for prayer and praise from which we stay away, may be the very gathering that would have cheered, and established, and quickened our hearts. We little know how dependent our spiritual health is on little, regular, habitual helps, and how much we suffer if we miss our medicine. The wretched argument that many attend means of grace and are no better for them, should be no argument to a Christian. It may satisfy those who are blind to their own state, and destitute of grace, but it should never satisfy a real servant of Christ. Such an one should remember the words of Solomon—"Blessed is the man that hears me, watching daily at my gates, waiting at the posts of my doors." (Prov. 8:34.) Above all he should bind around his heart the Master's promise—"Wheresoever two or three are gathered together in my name, there am I in the midst of them." (Matt. 18:20.) Such a man will rarely be left like Thomas, shut out in the cold chill of unbelief, while others are warmed and filled.

We should mark for another thing in this verse, how kind and merciful Christ is to dull and slow believers. Nowhere, perhaps, in all the four Gospels, do we find this part of our Lord's character so beautifully illustrated as in the story before our eyes. It is hard to imagine anything more tiresome and provoking than the conduct of Thomas, when even the testimony of ten faithful brethren had no effect on him, and he doggedly declared, "Except I see with my own eyes and touch with my own hands, I will not believe." But it is impossible to imagine anything more patient and compassionate, than our Lord's treatment of this weak disciple. He does not reject him, or dismiss him, or excommunicate him. He comes again at the end of a week, and apparently for the special benefit of Thomas. He deals with him according to his weakness, like a gentle nurse dealing with a froward child—"Reach here your finger, and behold my hands; reach here your hand, and thrust it into my side." If nothing but the grossest, coarsest, most material evidence could satisfy him, even that evidence was supplied. Surely this was a love that passes knowledge, and a patience that passes understanding.

A passage of Scripture like this, we need not doubt, was written for the special comfort of all true believers. The Holy Spirit knew well that the dull, and the slow, and the stupid, and the doubting, are by far the commonest type of disciples in this evil world. The Holy Spirit has taken care to supply abundant evidence that Jesus is rich in patience as well as compassion, and that He bears with the infirmities of all His people. Let us take care that we drink into our Lord's spirit, and copy His example. Let us never set down men in a low place, as gracious and godless, because their faith is feeble and their love is cold. Let us remember the case of Thomas, and be very compassionate and of tender mercy. Our Lord has many weak children in His family, many dull pupils in His school, many raw soldiers in His army, many lame sheep in His flock. Yet He bears with them all, and casts none away. Happy is that Christian who has learned to deal likewise with his brethren. There are many in the Church, who, like Thomas, are dull and slow, but for all that, like Thomas, are real and true believers.

We should mark, lastly, in these verses, how Christ was addressed by a disciple as "God," without prohibition or rebuke on His part. The noble exclamation which burst from the lips of Thomas, when convinced that his Lord had risen indeed; the noble exclamation, "My Lord and my God"—admits of only one meaning. It was a distinct testimony to our blessed Lord's divinity. It was a clear, unmistakable declaration that Thomas believed Him, whom he saw and touched that day, to be not only man, but God. Above all, it was a testimony which our Lord received and did not prohibit, and a declaration which He did not say one word to rebuke. When Cornelius fell down at the feet of Peter and would have worshiped him, the Apostle refused such honor at once—"Stand up; I myself also am a man." (Acts 10:26.) When the people of Lystra would have done sacrifice to Paul and Barnabas, "they tore their clothes, and ran in among the people, saying, Sirs, why do you these things? We also are men of like passions with you." (Acts 14:14.) But when Thomas says to Jesus, "My Lord and my God," the words do not elicit a syllable of reproof from our holy and truth-loving Master. Can we doubt that these things were written for our learning?

Let us settle it firmly in our minds that the divinity of Christ is one of the grand foundation truths of Christianity, and let us be willing to go to the stake rather than let it go. Unless our Lord Jesus is very God of very

God, there is an end of His mediation, His atonement, His advocacy, His priesthood, His whole work of redemption. These glorious doctrines are useless blasphemies, unless Christ is divine. Forever let us bless God that the divinity of our Lord is taught everywhere in the Scriptures, and stands on evidence that can never be overthrown. Above all, let us daily repose our sinful souls on Christ with undoubting confidence, as one who is perfect God as well as perfect man. He is man, and therefore can be touched with the feeling of our infirmities. He is God, and therefore is "able to save to the uttermost all who come unto God by Him." That Christian has no cause to fear, who can look to Jesus by faith, and say with Thomas, "My Lord and my God." With such a Savior we need not be afraid to begin the life of real religion, and with such a Savior we may boldly go on.

Chapter 21

21:1-14

*A*fter this Jesus revealed himself again to the disciples by the Sea of Tiberias. Now this is how he did so. Simon Peter, Thomas (called Didymus), Nathanael (who was from Cana in Galilee), the sons of Zebedee, and two other disciples of his were together. Simon Peter told them, "I am going fishing." "We will go with you," they replied. They went out and got into the boat, but that night they caught nothing.

When it was already very early morning, Jesus stood on the beach, but the disciples did not know that it was Jesus. So Jesus said to them, "Children, you don't have any fish, do you?" They replied, "No." He told them, "Throw your net on the right side of the boat, and you will find some." So they threw the net, and were not able to pull it in because of the large number of fish.

Then the disciple whom Jesus loved said to Peter, "It is the Lord!" So Simon Peter, when he heard that it was the Lord, tucked in his outer garment (for he had nothing on underneath it), and plunged into the sea. Meanwhile the other disciples came with the boat, dragging the net full of fish, for they were not far from land, only about a hundred yards.

When they got out on the beach, they saw a charcoal fire ready with a fish placed on it, and bread. Jesus said, "Bring some of the fish you have just now caught." So Simon Peter went aboard and pulled the net to shore. It was full of large fish, one hundred fifty-three, but although there were so many, the net was not torn. "Come, have breakfast," Jesus said. But none of the disciples dared to ask him, "Who are you?" because they knew it was the Lord. Jesus came and took the bread and gave *it to them, and did the same with the fish. This was now the third time Jesus was revealed to the disciples after he was raised from the dead.*

The appearance of our Lord Jesus Christ after His resurrection, described in these verses, is a deeply interesting portion of the Gospel history. The circumstances attending it have always been regarded as highly allegorical and figurative, in every age of the Church. It may, however, be justly doubted whether commentators and interpreters have not gone too far in this direction. It is quite possible to spiritualize and filter away the narratives of the Gospels, until we completely lose sight of the plain meaning of words. In the present case we shall find it wise to confine ourselves to the great, simple lessons, which the passage undoubtedly contains.

We should observe, for one thing, in these verses, the poverty of the first disciples of Christ. We find them working with their own hands, in order to supply their temporal needs, and working at one of the humblest of callings-the calling of a fisherman. Silver and gold they had none, lands and revenues they had none, and therefore they were not ashamed to return to the business to which they had, most of them, been trained. Striking is the fact, that some of the seven here named were fishing, when our Lord first called them to be Apostles, and again fishing, when He appeared to them almost the last time. We need not doubt that to the minds of Peter, James, and John, the coincidence would come home with peculiar power.

The poverty of the Apostles goes far to prove the divine origin of Christianity. These very men who toiled all night in a boat, dragging about a cold wet net, and taking nothing—these very men who found it necessary to work hard in order that they might eat—these very men were some of the first founders of the mighty Church of Christ, which has now overspread one-third of the globe. These were they who went forth from an obscure corner of the earth, and turned the world upside down. These were the unlearned and ignorant men, who boldly confronted the subtle systems of ancient philosophy, and silenced its advocates by the preaching of the cross. These were the men who at Ephesus, and Athens, and Rome, emptied the heathen temples of their worshipers, and turned away multitudes to a new and better faith. He that can explain these facts, except by admitting that Christianity came down from God, must be a strangely incredulous man. Reason and common sense lead us to only one conclusion in the matter. Nothing can account for the rise and progress of Christianity but the direct interposition of God.

We should observe, for another thing, in these verses, the different characters of different disciples of Christ. Once more, on this deeply interesting occasion, we see Peter and John side by side in the same boat, and once more, as at the sepulcher, we see these two good men behaving in different ways. When Jesus stood on the shore, in the dim twilight of the morning, John was the first to perceive who it was, and to say, "It is the Lord;" but Peter was the first to spring into the water, and to struggle to get close to his Master. In a word, John was the first to see; but Peter was the first to act. John's gentle loving spirit was quickest to discern; but Peter's fiery, impulsive nature was quickest to stir and move. And yet both were believers, both were true-hearted disciples, both loved the Lord in life, and were faithful to Him unto death. But their natural temperaments were not the same.

Let us never forget the practical lesson before us. As long as we live, let us diligently use it in forming our estimate of believers. Let us not condemn others as graceless and unconverted, because they do not see the path of duty from our stand-point, or feel things exactly as we feel them. "There are diversities of gifts, but the same Spirit." (1 Cor. 12:4.) The gifts of God's children are not bestowed precisely in the same measure and degree. Some have more of one gift, and some have more of another. Some have gifts which shine more in public, and some which shine more in private. Some are more bright in a passive life, and some are more bright in an active one. Yet each and all the members of God's family, in their own way and in their own season, bring glory to God. Martha was "careful and troubled about much serving," when Mary "sat at the feet of Jesus and heard His word." Yet there came a day at Bethany, when Mary was crushed and prostrated by overmuch sorrow, and Martha's faith shone more brightly than her sister's. (Luke 10:39, 40; John 11:20-28.) Nevertheless both were loved by our Lord. The one thing needful is to have the grace of the Spirit, and to love Christ. Let us love all of whom this can be said, though they may not see with our eyes in everything. The Church of Christ needs servants of all kinds, and instruments of every sort; pen-knives as well as swords, axes as well as hammers, chisels as well as saws, Marthas as well as Marys, Peters as well as Johns. Let our ruling maxim be this, "Grace be with all those who love our Lord Jesus Christ in sincerity." (Ephes. 6:24.)

We should observe, lastly, in these verses, the abundant evidence which Scripture supplies of our Lord Jesus Christ's resurrection. Here, as in other places, we find an unanswerable proof that our Lord rose again with a real material body, and a proof seen by seven grown-up men with their own eyes, at one and the same time. We see Him sitting, talking, eating, drinking, on the shore of the lake of Galilee, and to all appearance for a considerable time. The morning sun of spring shines down on the little party. They are alone by the well-known Galilean lake, far away from the crowd and noise of Jerusalem. In the midst sits the Master, with the nail-prints in His hands—the very Master whom they had all followed for three years, and one of them, at least, had seen hanging on the cross. They could not be deceived. Will anyone pretend to say that stronger proof could be given that Jesus rose from the dead? Can any one imagine better evidence of a fact? That Peter was convinced and satisfied we know. He says himself to Cornelius, We "ate and drink with Him after He rose from the dead." (Acts 10:41.) Those who in modern times say they are not convinced, may as well say that they are determined not to believe any evidence at all.

Let us all thank God that we have such a cloud of witnesses to prove that our Lord rose again. The resurrection of Christ is the grand proof of Christ's divine mission. He told the Jews they need not believe He was the Messiah, if He did not rise again the third day. The resurrection of Christ is the top-stone of the work of redemption. It proved that He finished the work He came to do, and, as our Substitute, had overcome the grave. The resurrection of Christ is a miracle that no infidel can explain away. Men may carp and cavil at Balaam's donkey, and Jonah in the whale's belly, if they please, but until they can prove that Christ did not rise again we need not be moved. Above all, the resurrection of Christ is the pledge of our own. As the grave could not detain the Head, so it shall not detain the members. Well may we say with Peter, "Blessed be the God and Father of our Lord Jesus Christ, who has begotten us again unto a living hope by the resurrection of Jesus Christ from the dead." (1 Peter 1:3.)

21:15-17

Then when they had finished breakfast, Jesus said to Simon Peter, "Simon, son of John, do you love me more than these do?" He replied, "Yes, Lord, you know I love you." Jesus told him, "Feed my lambs." Jesus said a second time, "Simon, son of John, do you love me?" He replied, "Yes, Lord, you know I love you." Jesus told him, "Shepherd my sheep." Jesus said a third time, "Simon, son of John, do you love me?" Peter was distressed that Jesus asked him a third time, "Do you love me?"

and said, "Lord, you know everything. You know that I love you." Jesus replied,
"Feed my sheep.

These verses describe a remarkable conversation between our Lord Jesus
Christ and the Apostle Peter. To the careful Bible reader, who remembers
the Apostle's thrice-repeated denial of Christ, the passage cannot fail to be
a deeply interesting portion of Scripture. Well would it be for the Church,
if all "after-meal" conversations among Christians were as useful and edify-
ing as this.

We should notice first, in these verses, Christ's question to Peter—"Simon,
son of John, do you love Me?" Three times we find the same inquiry made.
It seems most probable that this three-fold repetition was meant to remind
the Apostle of his own thrice-repeated denial. Once we find a remarkable
addition to the inquiry—"do you love Me more than these?" It is a reasonable
supposition that those three words "more than these," were meant to remind
Peter of his over-confident assertion—"Though all men deny You, yet I will
not." It is just as if our Lord would say, "Will you now exalt yourself above
others? Have you yet learned your own weakness?"

"Do you love Me" may seem at first sight a simple question. In one sense
it is so. Even a child can understand love, and can say whether he loves another or not. Yet "Do you love Me" is, in reality, a very searching question.
We may know much, and do much, and profess much, and talk much, and
work much, and give much, and go through much, and make much show
in our religion, and yet be dead before God, from lack of love, and at last
go down to the pit. Do we love Christ? That is the great question. Without
this there is no vitality about our Christianity. We are no better than painted
wax figures, lifeless stuffed beasts in a museum, sounding brass and tinkling
cymbals. There is no life where there is no love.

Let us take heed that there is some feeling in our religion. Knowledge,
orthodoxy, correct views, regular use of forms, a respectable moral life—all
these do not make up a true Christian. There must be some personal feeling
towards Christ. Feeling alone, no doubt, is a poor useless thing, and may be
here today and gone tomorrow. But the entire absence of feeling is a very bad
symptom, and speaks ill for the state of a man's soul. The men and women
to whom Paul wrote his Epistles had feelings, and were not ashamed of
them. There was One in heaven whom they loved, and that One was Jesus
the Son of God. Let us strive to be like them, and to have some real feeling
in our Christianity, if we hope to share their reward.

We should notice, secondly, in these verses, Peter's answer to Christ's question. Three times we find the Apostle saying, "You know that I love You." Once we are told that he said, "You know all things." Once we have the touching remark made, that he was "grieved to be asked the third time." We need not doubt that our Lord, like a skillful physician, stirred up this grief intentionally. He intended to pierce the Apostle's conscience, and to teach him a solemn lesson. If it was grievous to the disciple to be questioned, how much more grievous must it have been to the Master to be denied!

The answer that the humbled Apostle gave, is the one account that the true servant of Christ in every age can give of his religion. Such an one may be weak, and fearful, and ignorant, and unstable, and failing in many things, but at any rate he is real and sincere. Ask him whether he is converted, whether he is a believer, whether he has grace, whether he is justified, whether he is sanctified, whether he is elect, whether he is a child of God—ask him any one of these questions and he may perhaps reply that he really does not know! But ask him whether he loves Christ, and he will reply, "I do!" He may add that he does not love Him as much as he ought to do; but he will not say that he does not love Him at all. The rule will be found true with very few exceptions. Wherever there is true grace, there will be a consciousness of love towards Christ.

What, after all, is the great secret of loving Christ? It is an inward sense of having received from Him pardon and forgiveness of sins. Those love much who feel much forgiven. He who has come to Christ with his sins, and tasted the blessedness of free and full absolution, he is the man whose heart will be full of love towards his Savior. The more we realize that Christ has suffered for us, and paid our debt to God, and that we are washed and justified through His blood, the more we shall love Him for having loved us, and given Himself for us. Our knowledge of doctrines may be defective. Our ability to defend our views in argument may be small. But we cannot be prevented feeling. And our feeling will be like that of the Apostle Peter—"You, Lord, who know all things, You know my heart; and You know that I love You."

We should notice, lastly, in these verses, Christ's command to Peter. Three times we find Him saying, "Feed my flock." Once, "Feed my lambs;" and twice, "Feed my sheep." Can we doubt for a moment that this thrice-repeated charge was full of deep meaning? It was meant to commission Peter once more to do the work of an Apostle, notwithstanding his recent fall. But this was only a small part of the meaning. It was meant to teach Peter and the whole Church the mighty lesson, that usefulness to others is the grand test of love, and working for Christ the great proof of really loving Christ. It is not loud talk and high profession; it is not even impetuous, spasmodic zeal, and readiness to draw the sword and fight—it is steady, patient, laborious effort to do good to Christ's sheep scattered throughout this sinful world, which is the best evidence of being a true-hearted disciple. This is the real secret of Christian greatness. It is written in another place, "Whoever wants to be a leader among you must be your servant, and whoever wants to be first must become your slave." (Matt. 20:26-28.)

Forever let the parting charge of our blessed Master abide in our consciences, and come up in the practice of our daily lives. It is not for nothing we may be sure, that we find these things recorded for our learning, just before He left the world. Let us aim at a loving, doing, useful, hard-working, unselfish, kind, unpretentious religion. Let it be our daily desire to think of others, care for others, do good to others, and to lessen the sorrow, and increase the joy of this sinful world. This is to realize the great principle which our Lord's command to Peter was intended to teach. So living, and so laboring to order our ways, we shall find it abundantly true, that "it is more blessed to give than to receive." (Acts 20:35.)

21:18-25

"I tell you the solemn truth, when you were young, you tied your clothes around you and went wherever you wanted, but when you are old, you will stretch out your hands, and others will tie you up and bring you where you do not want to go." (Now Jesus said this to indicate clearly by what kind of death Peter was going to glorify God.) After he said this, Jesus told Peter, "Follow me."

Peter turned around and saw the disciple whom Jesus loved following them. (This was the disciple who had leaned back against Jesus' chest at the meal and asked, "Lord, who is the one who is going to betray you?") So when Peter saw him, he asked Jesus, "Lord, what about him?" Jesus replied, "If I want him to live until I come back, what concern is that of yours? You follow me!" So the saying circulated among the brothers and sisters that this disciple was not going to die. But Jesus did not say to him that he was not going to die, but rather, "If I want him to live until I come back, what concern is that of yours?"

This is the disciple who testifies about these things and has written these things, and we know that his testimony is true.

There are many other things that Jesus did. If every one of them were written down, I suppose the whole world would not have room for the books that would be written.

These verses form the conclusion of John's Gospel, and bring to an end the most precious book in the Bible. The man is much to be pitied who can read the passage without serious and solemn feelings. It is like listening to the parting words of a friend, whom we may possibly not see again. Let us reverently consider the lessons which this Scripture contains.

We learn, for one thing, from these verses, that the future history of Christians, both in life and death, is foreknown by Christ. The Lord tells Simon Peter, "When you are old, you shall stretch forth your hands, and another shall gird you, and carry you where you would not." These words, without controversy, were a prediction of the manner of the Apostle's death. They were fulfilled in after days, it is commonly supposed, when Peter was crucified as a martyr for Christ's sake. The time, the place, the manner, the painfulness to flesh and blood of the disciple's death, were all matters foreseen by the Master.

The truth before us is eminently full of comfort to a true believer. To obtain foreknowledge of things to come would, in most cases, be a sorrowful possession. To know what was going to befall us, and yet not to be able to prevent it, would make us simply miserable. But it is an unspeakable consolation to remember, that our whole future is known and fore-arranged by Christ. There is no such thing as luck, chance, or accident, in the journey of our life. Everything from beginning to end is foreseen—arranged by One who is too wise to err, and too loving to do us harm.

Let us store up this truth in our minds, and use it diligently in all the days of darkness through which we may yet have to pass. In such days we should lean back on the thought, "Christ knows this, and knew it when He called me to be His disciple." It is foolish to repine and murmur over the troubles of those whom we love. We should rather fall back on the thought that all is well done. It is useless to fret and be rebellious, when we ourselves have bitter cups to drink. We should rather say, "This also is from the Lord—He foresaw it, and would have prevented it, if it had not been for my good." Happy are those who can enter into the spirit of that old saint, who said, "I have made a covenant with my Lord, that I will never take amiss anything that He does to me." We may have to walk sometimes through rough places, on our way to heaven. But surely it is a comforting, soothing reflection, "Every step of my journey was foreknown by Christ."

We learn, secondly, in these verses, that a believer's death is intended to glorify God. The Holy Spirit tells us this truth in plain language. He graciously interprets the dark saying, which fell from our Lord's lips about Peter's end. He tells us that Jesus spoke this, "signifying by what death he should glorify God."

The thing before us is probably not considered as much as it ought to be. We are so apt to regard life as the only season for honoring Christ, and action as the only mode of showing our religion, that we overlook death, except as a painful termination of usefulness. Yet surely this ought not so to be. We may die to the Lord; as well as live to the Lord; we may be patient sufferers as well as active workers. Like Samson, we may do more for God in our death, than we ever did in our lives. It is probable that the patient deaths of our martyred Reformers had more effect on the minds of English-men, than all the sermons they preached, and all the books they wrote. One thing, at all events, is certain—the blood of the English martyrs was the seed of the English Church.

We may glorify God in death, by being ready for it whenever it comes. The Christian who is found like a sentinel at his post, like a servant with his loins girded and his lamp burning, with a heart packed up and ready to go, the man to whom sudden death, by the common consent of all who knew him, is sudden glory—this, this is a man whose end brings glory to God. We may glorify God in death, by patiently enduring its pains. The Christian whose spirit has complete victory over the flesh, who quietly feels the pins of his earthly tabernacle plucked up with great bodily agonies, and yet never murmurs or complains, but silently enjoys inward peace—this, this again, is a man whose end brings glory to God. We may glorify God in death, by testifying to others the comfort and support that we find in the grace of Christ. It is a great thing, when a mortal man can say with David, "Though I walk through the valley of the shadow of death, I will fear no evil." (Psalm 23:4.) The Christian who, like Standfast in "Pilgrim's Progress," can stand for a while in the river, and talk calmly to his companions, saying, "My foot is fixed sure—my toilsome days are ended,"—this, this is a man whose end brings glory to God. Deaths like these leave a mark on the living, and are not soon forgotten.

Let us pray, while we live in health, that we may glorify God in our end. Let us leave it to God to choose the where, and when, and how, and all the manner of our departing. Let us only ask that it may "glorify God." He is a wise man who takes John Bunyan's advice, and keeps his last hour continually in mind, and makes it his company-keeper. It was a weighty saying of John Wesley, when one found fault with the doctrines and practices of the Methodists—"At any rate our people die well."

We learn, thirdly, in these verses, that whatever we may think about the condition of other people, we should think first about our own. When Peter inquired curiously and anxiously about the future of the Apostle John, he received from our Lord an answer of deep meaning—"If I will that he tarry until I come, what is that to you? Follow Me." Hard to understand as some part of that sentence may be, it contains a practical lesson which cannot be mistaken. It commands every Christian to remember his own heart first, and to look at home.

Of course our blessed Lord does not wish us to neglect the souls of others, or to take no interest in their condition. Such a state of mind would be nothing less than uncharitable selfishness, and would prove plainly that we had not the grace of God. The servant of Christ will have a wide, broad heart, like his Master, and will desire the present and eternal happiness of all around him. He will long and labor to lessen the sorrows, and to increase the joys, of everyone within his reach, and, as he has opportunity, to do good to all men. But, in all his doing, the servant of Christ must never forget his own soul. Charity, and true religion, must both begin at home.

It is vain to deny that our Lord's solemn caution to His impetuous disciple is greatly needed in the present day. Such is the weakness of human nature, that even true Christians are continually liable to run into extremes. Some are so entirely absorbed in their own inward experience, and their own heart's conflict, that they forget the world outside. Others are so busy about doing good to the world, that they neglect to cultivate their own souls. Both are wrong, and both need to see a more excellent way; but none perhaps do so much harm to religion as those who are busy-bodies about others' salvation, and at the same time neglecters of their own. From such a snare as this may the ringing words of our Lord deliver us! Whatever we do for others (and we never can do enough), let us not forget our own inner man. Unhappily, the Bride, in Canticles, is not the only person who has cause to complain—"They made me keeper of the vineyards; but my own vineyard I have not kept." (Cant. 1:6.)

We learn, lastly, from these verses, the number and greatness of Christ's works during His earthly ministry. John concludes his Gospel with these remarkable words, "There are many other things which Jesus did, the which, if they should be written every one, I suppose the world itself could not contain the books that should be written."—Of course we must not torture these words, by pressing them to an excessively literal interpretation. To suppose that the Evangelist meant the world could not hold the material volumes which would be written, is evidently unreasonable and absurd. The only sensible interpretation must be a spiritual and figurative one.

As much of Christ's sayings and doings is recorded as the mind of man can take in. It would not be good for the world to have more. The human mind, like the body, can only digest a certain quantity. The world could not contain more, because it would not. As many miracles, as many parables, as many sermons, as many conversions, as many words of kindness, as many deeds of mercy, as many journeys, as many prayers, as many warnings, as many promises, are recorded, as the world can possibly require. If more had been recorded they would have been only thrown away. There is enough to make every unbeliever without excuse, enough to show every inquirer the way to heaven, enough to satisfy the heart of every honest believer, enough to condemn man if he does not repent and believe, enough to glorify God. The largest vessel can only contain a certain quantity of liquid. The mind of all mankind would not appreciate more about Christ, if more had been written. There is enough and to spare. This witness is true. Let us deny it if we can.

And now let us close the Gospel of John with mingled feelings of deep humility and deep thankfulness. We may well be humble when we think how ignorant we are, and how little we comprehend of the treasures which this Gospel contains. But we may well be thankful, when we reflect how clear and plain is the instruction which it gives us about the way of salvation. The man who reads this Gospel profitably, is he who "believes that Jesus is the Christ, and, believing, has life through His Name." Do we so believe? Let us never rest till we can give a satisfactory answer to that question!

Made in the USA
Lexington, KY
05 September 2019